TUTORSHIP COURSE BOOKS

PREFACE

Gain a professional qualification and the knowledge to develop your career in the shipping industry by embarking on a TutorShip course of the Institute of Chartered Shipbrokers (ICS).

The Institute of Chartered Shipbrokers (ICS) is the professional body to commercial shipping worldwide. The ICS syllabus reflects the breadth and complexity of all the shipping sectors. The syllabus aims to be Relevant to and Respected by the shipping industry whilst being a Robust challenge to those candidates embarking on a career in shipping.

The TutorShip series of course books are aimed at preparing students for ICS examinations through a distance learning programme. Each course has a combination of self assessment questions and a tutor marked assignment at the end of each chapter. Additionally students are encouraged to submit a mock examination for marking. On enrolment of a TutorShip programme a student is allocated a tutor – an experienced practitioner in their sector – who will guide a student through the course by marking and providing feedback on the assignments submitted.

Although the TutorShip course books are an invaluable reference to any shipping company library their true value can only be realised by enrolling on a TutorShip distance learning programme supported by the expert knowledge of the approved tutors.

For further details on TutorShip courses please contact **tutorship@ics.org.uk** or visit **www.ics.org.uk**

THE INTRODUCTION TO SHIPPING SYLLABUS

COMMERCIAL GEOGRAPHY

Continents: Geographical regions for example Far East, Mediterranean, S.E. Asia. Location of major countries and ports. All the continents, the major centres of which they are comprised and the manner in which they are grouped in geographical regions.

The location of major ports, canals and waterways.

Oceans of the world and the seas of which they are comprised. The effects of tides, currents, climate and weather.

An awareness of different map projections; latitude and longitude.

INTERNATIONAL TRADE

Understand the role of different markets that comprise the global market. Be aware of the difference between absolute and comparative advantage. Understand the role of shipping arising from derived demand.

CARGOES AND TRADE ROUTES

Thoroughly understand the different roles of liners and tramps. In liners understand the main unitised systems and break bulk operations. Be aware of major liner routes.

Understand the major dry bulk trades and the origins and distribution of principle cargoes.

The oil and other liquid trades.

Understand the origin and distribution of principle cargoes distinguishing between crude oil and products.

Be aware of the categorisation of cargoes into clean, dirty, chemicals, gas, vegetable oils and juices.

SHIP TYPES

Thoroughly understand the basic characteristics of bulk carriers etc and the types of trades in which they are used.

Understand the main sizes of vessel in each class.

Expect to illustrate any answers with simple sketches.

CONTRACTS OF CARRIAGE

Thoroughly understand the basic contracts:

Charter Parties for tramp and tankers.

Bills of Lading for liners.

Be aware of the role of the Bill of Lading under a Charter Party.

Understand the difference between Voyage and Time Charter Parties and the basic elements of each.

Understand the three functions of the Bill of Lading and its role in international trade.

Understand the main specialist abbreviations, terms and expressions used in Charter Parties and Bills of Lading.

LAW OF CARRIAGE

Understand the duty of care and the nature of tortious acts outside of contracts.

Be aware of the way in which international conventions are established and the major conventions relative to shipping.

Understand the basic application of Hague/Hague-Visby/Hamburg rules, their requirement for seaworthiness and the limitation of carrier liability. Be aware of the differences between these rules.

Understand the legal effect of the Bill of Lading as a document of title and the implication of its role in the delivery of goods.

Be aware of the role of marine insurance and P & I Associations.

SHIP REGISTRATION AND CLASSIFICATION

Thoroughly understand the concept of ship registration and its flag state.

Understand the differences between registering in the country of beneficial ownership, offshore registry and flag of convenience.

Be aware of Port State Control.

Understand the need for classification and the role of classification societies.

THE PRACTIONERS IN SHIPPING BUSINESS

Thoroughly understand the difference between principals and intermediaries.

Understand the role and function of:

Principals –   shipowners, charterers, shippers and
                     NVOCs (non vessel operating carriers)

Intermediaries –   Brokers in dry cargo chartering, tanker chartering, ship sale and
                     purchase

                     Port agents and liner agents and the differences between them

                     Ship managers and freight forwarders.

Be aware that all classes of intermediaries may be independent businesses or in-house departments of the principal.

BASIC ACCOUNTING

Understand the fundamentals of bookkeeping & corporate accounts.

Thoroughly understand the definitions and functions of Revenue, Cost, Profit, Capital, Cash-flow, Interest.

Thoroughly understand the importance of maintaining positive cash flow.

Be aware of the structure of various different types of business entity and understand the concept of limited liability.

CONTENTS

3 THE SHIP (continued)

4 THE DRY-CARGO CHARTERING MARKET 35

5 THE TANKER CHARTERING MARKET 43

5   THE TANKER CHARTERING MARKET (continued)

6   LINERS   53

7   THE PRACTITIONERS IN SHIPPING BUSINESS   63

7   THE PRACTITIONERS IN SHIPPING BUSINESS (continued)

8   MARITIME GEOGRAPHY   75

9   ACCOUNTS   85

Chapter 1

THE REASONS FOR SEA TRANSPORT

1.1 INTRODUCTION

Shipbroker is a time-honoured title of a profession which can trace its roots back to the 17th Century but to a few people the name conjures up a somewhat narrow concept of its meaning instead of the many and varied specialised tasks which today's shipbroker may undertake. So while the members of the Institute are proud to call themselves Shipbrokers you will often find reference to shipping business as your reading proceeds. There is more about the different specialities that are encompassed by the term shipbroking in Chapter 7 of this book and it will be seen that they all concern themselves with the business of shipping.

The Chapters in this publication will not explore the great depths and intricacies of the different aspects but will endeavour to touch upon many of the topics that provide the background knowledge necessary for anyone seeking to embark upon a career in this profession.

As well as dealing with ships themselves, and the markets in which their business is arranged, it will explore the geography of the maritime and commercial world, consider some of the legal aspects of working in the business of shipping and, as all commerce must eventually concern itself with money, look at basic accounting matters and corporate structures.

Unlike bulk commodities, consumer goods are needed relatively quickly in these days of 'just in time' logistics. For this reason ocean going container ships are usually capable of speeds 50-80% higher than bulk carriers or oil tankers. Even so, in times of high oil prices, a strategy of 'slow steaming' may be adopted by the operator to save fuel.

1.2 WHY SHIPS?

More than two thirds of the world's surface is covered in water but, with the exception of passengers who go on cruises, nobody wants merchant shipping for its own sake. Some passengers certainly need ships to take them from one place to another but the matter that this book is mostly about, is the need for ships to carry **cargo**.

The demand for ships is derived from the demand for the goods that they carry; that is why economists refer to merchant shipping as a **derived demand**. The customer, who is usually but not always, in a different country from the producer of the goods, wants those goods to be delivered to him safely and at minimum cost. Note that the word 'quickly' was not included with the other two requirements. Speed is certainly important for some commodities and for these there are other forms of transport such as air freight which is ideal for small but highly valuable items of cargo. But air freight is very costly so that it would be ridiculously expensive to transport, say, coal or iron ore by air even if it were possible.

Sea transport may be considered a relatively slow but inexpensive form of transport and because modern ships are capable of carrying hundreds of thousands of tonnes, the cost per tonne/kilometre adds only a small amount to the cost of the commodity being carried. As will be explained later in this text, this enables bulk materials to be moved half way around the world and still arrive at an economic price. That is why by far the greatest volume of goods involved in international trade is carried by sea.

Earlier, the statement was made that the customer for the goods being carried is usually but not always, in another country from the seller of those goods. One must not overlook the fact that, as shipping is the way to move large quantities of goods cheaply, it is equally suitable for transporting commodities from one place to another in the same country. This is, of course, especially important if the country concerned is made up of a series of islands. Coastal shipping, as it is often called, is vital to several countries and you may encounter it under its more technical name of **cabotage,** although this term tends to be used in reference to countries seeking to restrict such trade solely to ships owned in that country.

Inland shipping between countries across lakes and on rivers is a common form of transport in many parts of the world but, although related to ocean transport, unless the vessels involved venture out to sea there is very little common ground between the two industries.

It was also suggested that speed of transport was not important when considering shipping. If you are comparing the equivalent of 20 kilometres per hour with 800 kilometres per hour, achieving the higher speed will be far too expensive for relatively low valued goods. However, you will see that when comparing the equivalent of 20 kph with 40 kph, many factors may favour the higher speed so at these levels of comparison speed can be important, you will also learn that speeds at sea are referred to in **knots** which is the word for nautical miles per hour. A nautical mile is 1852 metres (approx 6080 feet) and how it is derived will be explained in the Chapter on geography.

1.3   AN INTRODUCTION TO THE THEORY OF TRADE

The movement of cargo by sea comes about as a result of one party, the **exporter,** selling a commodity to another party, the **importer**, this sale from one to another is, of course, referred to as **trade.** You will often hear the exporter referred to as the **consignor** or **shipper** and any subtle differences between these terms will be explained later in this text. Similarly you may see the importer referred to as the **consignee** or as the **receiver**.

The first obvious question is why should "A" buy goods from "B"? The immediate and equally obvious answer is that "A" needs or wants what "B" produces. This comes about due to the uneven distribution of resources throughout the world. Note that the reference was to distribution of **resources** not simply the distribution of commodities. For example, Great Britain, once a major exporter of coal still has substantial reserves but only a very small annual production because extraction is uneconomic. Australia also has coal and although the two countries are more than 10,000 nautical miles apart, Australia is able to sell coal to Britain.

Before dealing with this apparent paradox, let us concentrate first upon the implications of 'resources', there are two more expressions commonly used by economists that need to be mastered when considering the theory of trade. The first is **absolute advantage,** which refers to a commodity that one country has in exportable quantities but which another country has none. Examples could be bananas or coffee, these cannot be produced in Northern Europe whilst they are in abundance in the West Indies and Brazil. Such an absolute advantage is the result of **climate.** Absolute advantage may also come about through **geology** and a good example is copper that is mined in several parts of Southern Africa whereas many countries that need it to produce goods have no such mineral deposits of their own.

Therefore, in the case of absolute advantage, the resource is simply the physical availability of the commodity. Other factors are, however, involved which lead to **comparative advantage**. In simplistic terms this means where one country produces a commodity more cheaply or in a more desirable form than another.

In addition to climate and geology there are other **factors of production** that create a comparative advantage. These factors tend to fall into four categories namely Land, Labour, Capital and Enterprise. No two countries have exactly the same resources and few, if any, countries can be considered as being self-sufficient. For example, even with the wide-ranging natural resources that are present in a country like South Africa, the lack of appreciable quantities of oil prevents the country being self-sufficient.

Land incorporates climate and geology in terms of absolute advantage but it can have a profound effect also in the case of comparative advantage. Reference was made to the fact that Australia can sell coal to Britain, which actually still has vast reserves of coal. Where geology plays its part is in the way that coal in Australia is much easier and therefore cheaper, to extract from the earth.

Labour takes cognisance of the fact that the cost of living in some countries is considerably lower than in others and so they can produce certain items at a much lower cost. This has been particularly demonstrated in the case of shipbuilding which was at one time almost exclusively carried out in northern Europe and the USA but is now much reduced in those places but has developed enormously in countries like Japan, South Korea and, more recently, China.

Capital does not simply mean money, but just as much the things which money has provided, such as manufacturing equipment, roads, ports and all the other items which permit goods to be produced and brought to a place from which they can conveniently be exported.

Both Labour and Capital may be involved in **enterprise.** Countries with high labour costs have used their skill and knowledge to develop a high degree of automation in production enabling the same amount of work to be carried out by far fewer people (labour) but automation demands a huge amount of money (capital) to be invested.

Land (geology and climate) may be considered static as most mineral deposits have been located, even if not yet being worked, and despite the effects of global-warming the changes in weather patterns are not hugely affecting global production. Short term changes though can be brought about by natural phenomena such as drought or flooding.

Labour and Enterprise, however, can change radically in a relatively short time. Mention was made earlier how shipbuilding moved from Europe to South Korea but before South Korea attained its present capacity, Japan was the leader in this activity. Japanese workers, however, began to seek higher wages so that, despite more and more automation, their country's competitive edge was eroded. Today a similar situation has occurred in South Korea with the result that China, where workers are paid much less, is experiencing a boom in shipbuilding for export. The world leader position is still a struggle between Japan and South Korea although both countries have admitted that within 10 years China may have surpassed them both.

Enterprise tends to change by evolutionary processes through populations becoming more technologically advanced but more drastic changes may be brought about by **politics**. A narrow comparative advantage favouring imports can easily be reversed by the imposition of **customs duty** which would make the imported goods more expensive thus favouring a boost to domestic production in order to reduce unemployment. The converse may be where a government gives money to manufacturers in its own country in the form known as a **subsidy**. The object here being to enable the goods so produced to be competitive in the export market. This device was practised for several years in UK and other European countries in a vain attempt to retain their position as major shipbuilders. The theory of subsidies is that it is better to use tax-payers money to maintain competitiveness in manufacture and earn foreign currency rather than use possibly more money paying benefits to large numbers of unhappy unemployed workers.

Another example of politics bringing about rapid changes is in the former Soviet Union. Throughout the 1980s and 1990s vast amounts of grain were imported to supplement the inefficient collective farming system, but at the end of 2002 Russia and the Ukraine are both net exporters of grain having altered farming practices after the collapse of the state run economy.

Patterns of Trade influence imports and exports where politics as well as enterprise can have their effect. Until the middle of the twentieth century, several European countries, especially Great Britain, had direct interests in territories overseas; countries which were at one time parts of their empires. Traditional trading patterns were, therefore, between the mother countries and these overseas nations many of which deliberately developed items which were required in Europe. Typical of these were the farming and dairy products (meat, butter sugar etc.) that are so important to such areas as Australia and New Zealand.

Latterly the economic and political links forged in **Europe** have brought about a reduction in the amount of trade with former colonies. This in turn has had the effect of countries like Australia creating new trading patterns with the Far East and in so doing finding it logical to boost its extraction of coal, iron ore and other minerals.

Politics can also have a direct influence on trading patterns in other ways. Warlike operations in the Middle-East have caused the Suez Canal to be closed for long periods on more than one occasion. This produced the incentive to design and build the 'Capesize' tankers needed to transport crude oil round Africa instead of via the Suez Canal and still deliver it in Europe at the same price.

The dominance of Arab countries in oil production and complicated Middle Eastern politics surrounding attitudes of the Western world to Israel and its neighbours have led on several occasions to oil prices rising so steeply that world-wide trade recession have resulted. The political events in North Africa and other parts of the Arab world in early 2011 are too recent to predict what effect they may have on world trade and oil prices.

An important influence upon trade and trading patterns that has little or nothing to do with the actual factors of production has been the technological advances in ship design and production. Until the 1950s, 10,000 tonnes was large for a dry-cargo ship and a so-called "super-tanker" carried 42,000 tonnes.

Today ships more than ten times these sizes are commonplace. Such increases in size brought about what economists call **economies of scale.** Very simply this means that you do not need a crew ten times the size for such bigger ships. Indeed, other technological advances have had the reverse effect and crew numbers on a modern 100,000 tonner are often less than a third of those of a 1950s 10,000 tonner. Similarly you do not need an engine burning ten times the amount of fuel to propel the larger ships.

The effect of these economies of scale has been to enable quite inexpensive raw materials to move half way round the world and still arrive at a competitive price. Mention was made earlier of the way Australian coal can be marketed in Europe. Not only raw materials move long distances cheaply, one can move goods in freight containers vast distances and only add a few dollars to their unit price; a small amount in the overall price of, for example, washing machines or television sets.

All these practical and political influences on trade and trading patterns are not the end of the story. Simple preference, encouraged by clever advertising, can take advantage of the cheapness of modern sea carriage. The USA has the biggest car producing companies in the world and yet you can encounter German, British and many types of Japanese cars in American streets. Walk along the aisles of a supermarket in any European country and food items from all over the world can be found on the shelves. These countries are able to produce almost all the food that is essential for life but here again, personal fancy is now an important part of comparative advantage. This has led to the term '**globalisation**' being applied to the worldwide distribution of, especially, consumer goods.

1.4   THE DIFFERENT SHIPPING MARKETS

It is important, from the outset, to grasp that shipping is divided clearly into two types, one of which divides into two again. The two divisions are the **liner trades** and the **tramp trades.** The tramp trades then divide again into **dry cargo** and bulk liquids known as the **tanker trade.**

1.4.1   Liners

Liners are so-called because they trade according to a schedule of ports of loading and discharge, usually adhering to a published time table on set conditions of carriage and often charged at a published rate of freight. Their cargoes are made up of a large number of different **consignments** from a number of different shippers. Each consignment has to be separately documented and could be as small as one carton or as large as several tonnes. Documentation is a subject that will be dealt with in a later Chapter.

Liner cargo is *almost always* made up of manufactured or partly-manufactured goods; the italics are used because there are occasional exceptions. The vast majority, perhaps as much as 90%, of liner cargo is now carried in **containers**. The standard cargo **container** was introduced in the early 1960s and since the 1970s each new generation of liner ships have been specially designed to accommodate them. Full details of containerisation will be dealt with in later lessons but the containers themselves are so familiar, being seen on roads and railways throughout the world. In the ports, ships are rapidly loaded with hundreds or thousands of these containers that are emptied of their cargo at their destination after the ship has discharged them and has sailed away.

Prior to the introduction of containers liner cargo, usually referred to as **general cargo,** was loaded piece by piece needing expert knowledge to decide how and where it should be stowed in order to ensure its undamaged arrival; it was a very slow, labour-intensive process. Not every exporter has enough cargo to fill a container so that the expression 'generals' is still used to these small LCL (less than container load) consignments that have to be **consolidated** into containers in order to be loaded.

There are still a very few routes which are not containerised and one still sometimes hears their cargo referred to as **conventional** cargo which is a throw-back to the days when containerisation was still an innovation. More usually non-containerised cargo is now referred to as **break-bulk** cargo and comprises those items that are genuinely impossible to containerise.

1.4.2   Bulk Dry-cargo

Bulk dry-cargo is carried in ships that, even today, are referred to as tramps. Not because they are dirty and disreputable like a tramp (hobo or vagrant) but because like a tramp, they go from place to place depending upon where they can find cargoes. They do not follow a schedule but go where the market draws them so that they may load a cargo at place A discharge it at B and if they cannot actually load another cargo at B they will sail empty (in ballast) to C and load for D and so on.

The expression "even today are referred to as tramps" was used at the beginning of this section because in recent years, some dry bulk cargo ships have become highly specialised and whilst they do not follow an advertised schedule like liners they do tend to stay in one trade which often involves returning from the discharging port back to the loading port empty. Details of the different types of bulk dry cargo ships will be dealt with in a later lesson; it is sufficient here to visualise a market in which many of the ships are extremely large, built with certain bulk cargoes in mind together with a many more general-purpose ships that continue to fulfil the role of typical tramps.

Unlike liners, tramps are *almost always* carrying raw materials or semi-raw material, *almost always* carrying only one commodity at a time and *almost always* carrying a cargo from only one shipper on behalf of a charterer.

Typical cargoes in the tramp market are coal, iron ore and other minerals, grains, fertilizers, steel and timber. Again, unlike liners tramp cargoes are carried at rates and upon conditions individually negotiated in each case.

1.4.3   Bulk Liquids

Bulk liquids are carried in ships called tankers that may be looked upon as highly specialised tramps. The main cargo carried in tankers is, of course, oil and some of the world's largest ships have been built for this trade. The oil these monsters carry is crude oil, that is in the state that it comes out of the ground. This material is then transported to oil refineries which tend to be situated close to the main area of the consumption of the finished product. Some of these products may be transported overland by pipeline, railway or road vehicle but much of it is carried by smaller ships. These ships will be just as specialised, some designed to carry the simpler products, referred to as refined petroleum products which include such things as petrol (gasoline), kerosene (paraffin), diesel oil, fuel oil, lubricants etc.

Some by-products of oil refining are chemicals for various purposes that require smaller tankers many of which have to be very carefully constructed so that they are not harmed by the chemicals they carry or do not contaminate the chemicals they are carrying. Included under the tanker heading are some of the world's most sophisticated ships, the gas carriers. Designed to carry liquefied petroleum gasses such as butane and propane or liquefied natural gas (Methane) the ships are referred to as LPGs and LNGs respectively. Whilst most of the world's tankers are employed in carrying oil or gas, there are other liquid trades including chemicals, acids, vegetable oils, wine, molasses and even orange juice.

Freight rates for the carriage of liquid cargoes are also freely negotiated and fluctuate according to the market's demands but as will be learnt in a later Chapter the tanker chartering market is separate from and rather different from the dry cargo market.

1.5   WHO TRADES?

Mention has already been made of the principal characters in the trading world – exporters and importers, shippers and receivers, consignors and consignees but as this text proceeds, more detail will be given about the many other parties involved in international trade. Meantime, set out below are some preliminary definitions within the scope of this Chapter.

This being seaborne trade, the **shipowner** plays a very important part. Most, but by no means all, ships are owned by companies. Some may own just a few ships whilst others may have very large fleets. Some shipowners, especially those with small fleets or institutions who have bought ships as a speculative investment, employ **ship managers** to manage their ships for them.

Where bulk cargoes are concerned, the entity employing the ship, if not the owner carrying his own cargoes, is referred to as the **charterer**. A charterer may be the actual exporter or importer but might also be a **trader** who acts between them. With bulk cargoes it is most usual for the entire ship to be chartered although part-charters occasionally occur. The charterer may take the ship for a **single voyage** when it is customary for the owner to charge a rate per tonne or a lumpsum to carry the goods from A to B. The charterer may, however, need to have more flexibility than a voyage charter permits and will then take the ship on time charter in which case it is customary to pay a rate per day for the time agreed. Sometimes a charterer may have large volumes of cargo to move and rather than negotiating many individual voyage charters he will enter into a **Contract of Affreightment (COA)** with a single ship owner. The owner must then provide ships as they are needed according to the pre-arranged agreement.

The shipowners and charterers involved in arranging the fixture are referred to as the **principals** but is quite usual for the actual chartering deal – called a **fixture** – to be negotiated on behalf of the charterer and the shipowner by **shipbrokers**.

For greater clarity it is common for the shipbroker representing the owner to be referred to as the **owner's broker** and the one acting for the charterer to be called the **charterer's agent** or **charterer's broker**. The term charterer's agent is also (loosely) used in another context when referring to port representation, this is discussed in a later Chapter. Such shipbrokers may be, and often are, independent firms or companies but among the larger shipowners and charterers it is quite common for the shipbrokers involved to be members of departments within the principal's own company. Some individuals also make a living in this field.

Mention has already been made of the way in which liners carry goods for many different exporters in which case the person, firm or company contracting with the owner will be the **shipper** who may be the actual manufacturer or may be a trader.

Again, the contract for the carriage of those goods may be arranged by the shipping department of the actual exporter, or alternatively an independent firm or company known as a **freight forwarder** (sometimes referred to as a **forwarding agent** or even a **shipping and forwarding agent**) may make the arrangements for them. Such a forwarder or agent will perform whatever duties the exporter requires in order to arrange for the goods to move from the premises to where the shipowner takes over responsibility.

With the majority of general cargo now moving in containers there has been a development of the function of freight forwarders in which a firm or company takes on the role of carrier instead of acting as an intermediary. These are known as **NVOCs (Non Vessel-Operating Carrier)**. As the name implies, they do not own ships, they may or may not even own road transport. They do, however, take on the full responsibility for moving the goods from the exporter's factory right the way through to the importer's premises which they achieve by contracting with hauliers and shipowners in their own name. For once the lawyer's definition is a simple rather than complex way to understand what an NVOC does as they are described as "deemed to be the carrier but not actually the carrier". You will often see the initials as **NVOCC**, the additional "C" refers to the word "common" because in some countries such as the USA, the law insists that such people refer to themselves in this way. Very briefly a common carrier is one who offers its services to the public at large. The alternative (a private carrier) would be a ship under contract to a charterer.

One further definition is **ship operator**. It is quite common for companies, even major companies, to operate ships as if they own them either on a line or in the tramp trades without actually owning them. This is done by taking the ships they require on time charter or another form of long term lease known as a bareboat charter, in which event they may be referred to as the **disponent owner**. The definition of a disponent owner is "deemed to be the owner but not actually the owner". The reason for acting in this way is that the operator has much greater flexibility to react to market changes and of course, does not have to find the large amounts of money that would be necessary in they were to buy all the ships they need. The term ship operator is also used in a more general sense to cover ship owners, ship managers and ship operators collectively.

1.6 CONCLUSION

Earlier in this Chapter the point was made that the demand for shipping is derived from the demand for the commodities they carry. It was also stressed that, especially in the 'tramp' trades, the cost of carrying those commodities, rates of freight, are freely negotiated and you may hear economist stating that the international chartering market is the nearest one can get to perfect competition.

Some of the competition and the rate fluctuations that flow from it, directly spring from the supply of ships. In its simplest terms, two ships and only one cargo makes a weak market, two cargoes and only one available ship makes a firm market.

The major fluctuations in demand for ships follow the fluctuation in the demand for commodities.

These can be long or short term and can arise from a wide variety of reasons. For example, a poor grain harvest in one part of the world may increase the demand for imports whilst, conversely, a bumper crop could have the opposite effect. Even something as short-term as a serious strike could create a sudden demand for a particular type of ship that might have repercussions in other markets.

Trade recessions, which could originate from a variety of reasons, can have a profound effect of the demand for ships. Political decisions such as the OPEC countries raising the price of crude oil can cause worldwide changes in the demand for all types of ships. Conversely, the outbreak of war can create a sudden and enormous increase in demand for shipping space with a commensurate soaring of freight rates.

1.7   SELF-ASSESSMENT AND TEST QUESTIONS

Attempt the following and check your answers from the text.

1.   Why is shipping referred to as a "derived demand"?

2.   How is the speed of a ship referred to?

3.   What does "cabotage" mean?

4.   What is the definition of a disponent owner?

5.   What is the definition of an NVOCC?

6.   What is the term used to describe the agreement between a charterer and an owner?

7.   Why were "Capesize" tankers designed and built?

Having completed Chapter One, attempt the following and submit your essay to your Tutor:

1.   Give details of two trades of your choice (not oil) which are driven by:
    a)   Comparative advantage
    b)   Absolute advantage

    One of the chosen trades should be most suited to carriage in a tramp ship, the other most suited for liner transport.

    In your essay indicate factors that might cause the demand of the commodity to fluctuate also what might cause the demand for sea transport to change while the demand for the commodity remains constant.

2.   Identify and discuss a major change in an international trading pattern **different from** those mentioned in this Chapters text.

Chapter 2

THE SUPPLY OF SHIPS

To understand the shipping industry the environment in which it operates must be appreciated. The aim of this Chapter is to give an insight into some important aspects and constraints that have created, and are continuing to shape, the shipping world of today.

2.1   A BRIEF HISTORY

Ships have been used for **trade** for thousands of years but shipping business today is really the result of technology and practices established over the last 150 years.

Today's ships owe much to the inventors of the 19th Century and two developments in particular that caused the eventual demise of wooden sailing ships.

Firstly came the use of **iron** for ship construction. It took quite a long while for people to have confidence in iron instead of wood with many claiming that it would be impossible for a heavy material like iron to float. However, common sense prevailed and it was discovered that larger ships than had been possible with wood could now be built. It was at this time that the magnificent 'tea clippers' reached the height of their splendour. However, even the stoutest sailing ships were still at the mercy of the weather and knowing when (or even if) a ship would complete its voyage was not possible with any accuracy. Note the reference to 'iron' as the material because the general use of steel came much later; the first **steel** ship was launched in 1877.

Then came the development of the **steam** engine first as a supplement to sails and finally to replace wind power altogether. Steam engines had been around for many years and had been doing useful work on land from the end of the 17th century. It was not until 1830, however, that steam engines were considered reliable enough to propel ships. Although early attempts would probably not be considered a roaring success, the first – *s.s. "Hindostan"* only carried 200 tons of cargo but needed 500 tons of coal for fuel.

Steamship development was relatively slow at first because the high cost of operating machinery had to compete with the continued development of sailing ships which were still being built for the carriage of low value cargoes well into the 20th century. The main advantage of steam-propelled ships was, however, their ability to adhere to a timetable in all but really extreme weather, something sailing ships still could not do. In addition, steam ships could take more direct routes as they were not obliged to follow the prevailing winds.

In the early days of steam it was, of course, the requirements of passenger traffic rather than cargoes that encouraged owners and builders to develop ocean shipping. By the turn of the century the White Star Line had built the first of the 'luxury' liners the *s.s. "Oceanic"* 17,274 tons and capable of 21 knots.

There was a third 'milestone' in the development of merchant shipping which was **wireless telegraphy**. In these days of electronic and satellite communications it may be difficult to imagine the enormous step forward which was achieved when it became possible not only to communicate instantly with customers overseas but also to make contact with the ships themselves. In the late 1990s all seagoing ships were obliged to update their radio and communications equipment when the Global Maritime Distress and Safety System (GMDSS) convention came into full effect. A consequence of this is that all ships must now carry Inmarsat C equipment which, providing the appropriate contracts with airtime suppliers is in force, also allows ships to send and receive e-mails.

The spur to international trade provided by these technological advances was matched by advances in port development and the constructing of canals for ocean going ships – The Suez Canal in 1869, Kiel Canal in 1895, and the Panama Canal in 1915.

The Suez Canal was so effective in shortening the voyage time to the Indian sub-continent that the world suddenly experienced an effective over-supply of ships that was responsible for the formation of the first Liner Conference in 1875.

Development of passenger ships continued, including the class that included the ill-fated *"Titantic"* (1912) and the magnificent *"Queen Mary"* (1936), advances in machinery included oil-burning steam turbines for the best of the luxury liners. **Oil** also started to became the fuel of choice for reciprocating steam engines and the first **diesel** engines began to appear in the 1930s although coal-fired tramp ships were still very much in service well into the 1950s.

The second World-War had a profound effect on merchant shipping. First, of course, because a major element in the initial years of the war was submarine warfare that resulted in thousands of merchant ships being sunk. To counteract these losses a type of ship was designed which could be mass-produced by semi-skilled labour. The vast majority of these ships were built in North America, they were all of a similar pattern being about 10,000 tons deadweight, oil-burning reciprocating engines and capable of about 10 knots on 24 tons of fuel oil per day.

The most famous of these was the "Liberty" class and although they were looked upon as being 'expendable' they continued in service for many years after the war was over. Furthermore, towards the later months of the war the counter-measures against submarines had become so effective that merchant ship losses were minimal but the production lines were going full pelt. The result was that despite a massive upsurge in world trade in the late 1940s early 1950s, there was an ample supply of ships to fulfil requirements. For this reason there was no strong incentive to develop merchant shipping for several years after the war and even passenger liners were feeling the effect of improved air transport.

Eventually the end of the "Libertys" was predictable and so far as bulk cargoes were concerned, the demand for economies of scale became pressing. Provided the loading and discharging terminals could be developed in step with ship sizes there was no apparent limit to the increase. This meant that, as oil companies had little difficulty in extending refinery jetties, progressively larger tankers could be accommodated. Sizes quickly rose from the wartime 15,000 tons to 50,000 tons (which were called "super tankers" at that time). It was then only a matter of evolution for ships in the 100,000 to 200,000 ton sizes to be developed under the name of Very Large Crude Carriers (VLCCs) and then eventually even larger which earned the name of Ultra Large Crude Carriers (ULCCs), the largest of which is around half a million tons cargo carrying capacity.

Cargoes such a iron ore, coal, grain etc although experiencing rather more modest growth also sought to achieve economies of scale as new loading and discharging terminals were built with new ore and coal deposits being developed.

There is, however, no economy with size if the **time in port** is prolonged and the improvement in port time for ships handling **manufactured goods** showed little if any improvement. Time is clearly more money to a ship than to many other business activities. While a ship is at sea, on passage, money is being earned. Remaining still in port for anything other than the minimum of time is not earning money. Quick port turn-round allows more voyages per year to be undertaken. It was not, therefore, until the advent of **containerisation** that commenced in the 1960s, that significant developments took place with ships intended for the **liner** trades. Once the switch to freight containers was firmly established and, aided by a massive investment in new port infrastructure and equipment, it took less than three decades for container ship sizes to increase from barely 2000 container capacity to more than 6000, with ships able to carry over 8000 containers now being delivered on a regular basis from the shipyards in Asia.

2.2   THE SUPPLY OF SHIPPING

The effective supply of shipping world-wide is influenced by four main factors:

1.   The number of ships.

2.   The size of ships.

3.   Ship speed.

4.   Time spent in port.

It will be seen that these four factors are interdependent. If there are two ships of 10,000 tons, they provide the same carrying capacity as one ship of 20,000 tons. Similarly if a ship steams at 20 nautical miles per hour (20 knots) it will spend only half the time and therefore provide twice the carrying capacity as a ship capable of steaming at only 10 knots. And the effective increase in tonnage capacity as a result of rapid port turn-round of ships is just as easy to envisage.

Numbers of ships this century have increased three-fold and when it is remembered that ship sizes have, in many cases, increased more than ten-fold, the increase in world trade can be seen to be of very substantial proportions.

The chronology of increases in ship **size** is most easily seen in tankers and is shown in the following table:

By 1914	a large tanker was				8,000dwt
" 1945	"	"	"	"	15,000dwt
" 1952	"	"	"	"	50,000dwt
" 1959	"	"	"	"	100,000dwt
" 1967	"	"	"	"	200,000dwt (VLCC)
" 1972	"	"	"	"	300,000dwt (ULCC)
" 1974	"	"	"	"	555,000dwt

(world's largest tanker)

It is worth noting that tanker sizes have not increased since 1974 and you may pause to consider that as well as economies there can be **diseconomies** of scale. Whilst it is true that a ship of twice the size of another will not need twice as big a crew or need twice the fuel consumption to drive it, there comes a time when big is no longer beautiful. Larger ships need larger ports but a stage is eventually reached when a port cannot be deepened further or can only be deepened at prohibitive expense. Refineries or other industrial processes only need to be big enough to meet the demands of the markets they supply so that facilities to take in far more raw material than they can handle is counter-productive. Thus the oil companies appear to have decided that VLCCs providing a steady supply, make more economic sense than over-large sporadic consignments even though, in theory, the cost per ton-mile of oil in a bigger ship is lower. Nevertheless ULCCs are still being produced, the latest being Stena's innovative and sophisticated VMax class which, unusually for large tankers, have twin engines and propellers making them more manoeuvrable and safer than many smaller ships.

Perhaps the best example of economies of scale in the shipping business has been in container ships. Ships of 2000 and 3000 twenty-foot equivalent units (TEUs) were once considered "large" (containership-capacity is generally measured in TEUs because containers are standard size 'boxes' of 8 feet wide, 8'6" high and either 20 feet or 40 feet long thus one 20 foot container is one TEU and a forty foot is two TEU's). Throughout the 1970s world trade increased so rapidly that naval architects were pressed to design the largest container ship that could transit the Panama Canal, the so-called "Panamax" size. This took container

11

capacities up to nearly 4000 TEUs and by stretching design skills to the limit the "Panamax" dimensions can be made to carry 5,000 TEUs. The tremendous economies that ever-larger container ships provide has had the effect of world trade virtually 'feeding on itself'. The cost of carrying manufactured goods in containers from one side of the world to the other now adds so little to the final cost that goods can compete one with another with very little concern as to distance travelled.

This **"global economy"** has encouraged even bigger container ships. Liner companies calculated that with substantially larger ships they could trade economically *other* than via the Panama Canal and sizes quickly rose from the 4,000 TEU level to 6,000 TEUs which many thought was the limit. In fact it was being said towards the middle of the 1990s the "the idea of an 8,000 TEU container ship was just as idiotic as the one million ton tanker". Whilst no tankers larger than the "*Seawise Giant*" 555,000 dwt (now renamed "Jahre Viking" and with a 564,763 dwt after re-building) were ever seriously contemplated, 12-15,000 TEU container ships are now reality. In February 2011 A P Moller Maersk announced it had commissioned a series of ships of a new type of vessel called the 'Triple E' type. This type would be able to carry 18,000 TEUs but would likely have a top speed of around 18.5 knots instead of the 24-25 knots typical of modern large container ships.

Container traffic has an advantage over some other transport methods due to its **intermodalism** which is the word used to describe the way, because of their standard design, containers can easily be transferred from one transport medium to another. This allows for trucks or trains to be involved in pre- or post-shipment movement and also allows for ports too small to be called at by giant container carriers to be served by **"feeder"** ships. Thus the port with greatest capacity becomes the "hub" port in a container service. Unfortunately for ship designers, intermodalism is also a double edged sword. Because of inland trade, more containers travel by road and rail than by sea and in recent years larger lorries have been introduced in Europe and the US. This means that even when carrying a 40 foot box, there is unused space on the lorry trailer. As a result boxes of 45 feet length are growing in popularity. Many of the latest container ships being built have holds designed to take a mix of 40 feet and 45 feet boxes. Each new design seems to have more space allocated to the larger containers indicating that at some point 45 foot containers will be the most popular.

The **speed** of merchant ships has improved considerably since the 10 knots or less of the WW2 period. There is always a balancing act with the speed of merchant ships in that whilst the faster a ship travels the more voyages (and so more income) it can achieve in a year, more speed has always meant more fuel being burnt. After a certain rate of speed, any increase will require a disproportionately greater increase in fuel consumption and there is usually an ideal speed range for every size of ship and above *or below* this speed is uneconomical running.

Engine designers have made considerable advances in machinery since **diesel** engines became the standard power plant for ships. Marine diesel engines use more or less the same grades of oil as used to be burnt in the boilers of reciprocating steam engines and not the lighter fuels used by road vehicles. Two targets have been aimed at by designers, the first is obviously that of high speed with maximum fuel economy and the second is the widest possible range of economical speeds so that a ship is able to maintain a **lower speed** to save money when markets are poor. In more prosperous times a wide margin of economical speeds enables a ship to increase or decrease its speed in order to comply with a schedule; a most important factor for container ships. Currently the large container ships have the capability of cruising at 24 – 27 knots although bulk carriers and tankers tend to be content with speeds around 15 knots. Containership speed has become a major talking point following the economic downturn of 2008. A large number of ships included some very large vessels capable of carrying around 12-13,000 TEU ordered in anticipation of ever increasing world trade have begun to be delivered and the presence of so many new vessels during a depression has pushed freight rates to very low levels. As a result many liner operators have been forced to lay-up (keep idle) vessels and to operate their remaining ships at reduced speed.

This situation was anticipated even earlier by some in the industry notably the German classification society Germanischer Lloyd which has been questioning the need for such fast container vessels for several years. Presently, a speed of 20 knots is considered as being the most economic with many believing that this may even reduce to 18 knots in the not too distant future.

In 2003, the maximum size of container ships was around 8,000 TEU. At that point in time, world trade was accelerating upwards from the downturn that occurred following the terrorist attacks in New York in September 2001. Owners who had been forced to lay-up ships during that recession suddenly felt much more optimistic and initiated a rapid ordering programme for bigger vessels. Over the next four years the size of the largest vessels would increase from 8,000 to 13,500TEU and even bigger vessels were being talked about with innovations such as twin engine rooms and diesel electric drive until the crash of 2008. At the time of writing, one leading owner had already commissioned a series of 18,000 TEU vessels but construction had not commenced. The initial announcement indicated that a twin-engined, twin propeller propulsion system was being considered as a possible option for the vessels.

Events like this highlight one of the biggest problems that ship operators face when trying to gauge future demand. Ships can be as long as two years in the design and build stages before they are ready to carry cargo and in that time the perceived demand that decided the owner to opt for a new ship may have evaporated. Fortunately for those owners affected by the events of 2001, world trade proved more resilient than many had thought and by the middle of 2003 freight rates had not only regained their previous levels but had moved to highs never before experienced. This was mostly due to China gaining membership of the World Trade Organisation and the opening up of its massive markets – both import and export.

While most engine manufacturers and naval architects are looking at ways to increase the size of container ships there are others preparing to take advantage of promising new technologies in ship propulsion. The ship of the future could well be electric powered using multiple podded propulsion units such as are now being installed on large passenger ships, and water jets that are already used for fast ferries that can achieve speeds of close to 40 knots. The ships would generate their own electricity using a combination of diesel generators, gas turbines burning ìcleanî LNG and Hydrogen fuel cells. The ships envisaged for a trans Atlantic service would be around 1,500 TEU but would travel at 40 – 50 knots.

When trade grows it can do so in a variety of ways. More or bigger vessels are a good way to cope with increased trade between existing ports of loading and discharging but coping with most modern trade growth is not so simple.

As demand for commodities and products grows, existing sources cannot always cope with demand. This has meant finding new sources and very often these are at greater distances from the end market than was previously the case. In some instances, sources once considered uneconomic suddenly become attractive as demand soars. The impact on shipping is such that, for example a 10% increase in total tonnage traded of a particular product requires a much greater, as much as 30-50%, increase in tonne miles. So many more new ships are required to carry the extra cargo.

Bulk carriers are another type that appears already to have found its optimum sizes which are a complex combination of maximum economies of scale coupled with the demands of the consumers plus certain limitations imposed by the physical problems of exceeding certain dimensions. The sea is capable of being savage and there have been too many casualties to bulk carriers that experts say have been due to structural failure caused by a combination of design faults and poor maintenance. The matter has become so urgent that in 2002 the leading classification societies introduced much stricter building standard requirements for new bulk carriers and compulsory structural changes to existing vessels at certain stages of their working lives.

Improvements in ship design would have been of little use without a corresponding improvement in port facilities so **Port authorities** have tended to keep pace with advances in the ships themselves. In the case of bulk cargoes, the terminals are often owned or operated by the organisations that are extracting or utilising the minerals concerned. In other cases the pressure imposed by commercial competition has been sufficient to ensure that the size of the port or terminal is appropriate to the ships that wish to use it.

The effect of competition between ports is particularly noticeable in the container industry. The key is, of course, intermodalism which is such an important aspect of container traffic. A container moves smoothly from the ship to a road or rail vehicle and then remains on wheels until it reaches its final destination. For this reason it is no longer vital for the ship to call at a port as near as possible to where the importer or exporter is based. Shipowners can, instead, choose their ports on the basis of what provides the most beneficial result to the voyage.

The first consideration would be the port's geographical position because it is in the owner's interest to ensure that the voyage is kept as short as possible. After location would come accommodation so that even the largest of the owner's ships can approach the berth with little or no delay. The port authority can often influence this by employing dredgers to deepen the approaches to, and areas alongside, the berths. The port of **Rotterdam** for example increased its depth of water by 15 metres (50 feet) over the course of the 20th Century.

The next selling point that the port would have to offer is its **equipment** and **infrastructure**. Loading and discharging ships today, especially container ships, is considered in terms of minutes and hours, not days and weeks as was the case thirty or forty years ago. The accommodation and equipment available will determine the time a ship takes in port and time is money. Money also is directly involved in the decision-making because of course, what the port charges per ton of cargo or per container moved will influence a shipowner.

2.3   WHY OPERATE SHIPS?

The most obvious reason for owning and operating ships is to make a profit. There are, however, other reasons that might apply particularly to governments and these can result in a state-owned merchant fleet or a government policy which encourages the owning of ships under the national flag. The main reasons for a government encouraging the development of a shipping industry are:

2.3.1   Conserving Foreign Exchange

Nations with a limited ability to earn foreign currency through exports may seek to ensure that all, or most, of the goods they export or import are carried in their own ships. This means that the freight charges are paid to themselves rather than to foreign vessels. As the major costs of operating their own ships are paid for in their own currency there is no drain on foreign reserves. This limiting of use of foreign ships has been implemented in some cases by directing cargo to state-owned ships and in others by arranging preference to be given to ships flying the national flag.

2.3.2   Control of Trade and 'Prestige'

There was a tendency, when many of the former colonies of European countries were first becoming independent, for the governments of these new countries to seek to break away from the influence of the maritime 'establishment'. Thus, in some cases, the desire to have a national line and to control all the country's trade went beyond merely wishing to conserve foreign exchange. It seemed essential first for an airline to be established and then a shipping line. Those countries have become more sophisticated and more financially viable so that whilst national airlines still seem indispensable the desire for national shipping fleets is far less apparent. Often this is because their original plans were based around fleets of second hand 'tween deckers' that were once widely used in liner trades. Containerships are more costly to build and require additional expenditure on the containers themselves so, as lines switched to containers, the older ships became obsolete and too expensive to replace.

2.3.3 Earning Foreign Exchange

Some countries have seen that operating ships, especially passenger cruise ships, can be profitable in foreign currency terms and often in real terms as well. The former Soviet Union, with its major construction and operating costs all being in roubles, was able to provide reasonable quality, low-cost cruising with a substantial profit left over for the state operators. Attempting to achieve similar profits with merchant ships is more difficult because of the high cost of competing in the open market against the major maritime nations unless the country concerned has sufficient natural resources that are in demand. Then of course the state can restrict shipment to its own flag ships ensuring a good basic income for local shipping companies.

2.3.4 Strategic Needs

During the time that the 'cold war' was a major world problem, many countries felt that they had to have a minimum level of merchant tonnage under their own national flag to be used for moving strategic supplies should actual fighting break out. With less of a threat of a major war this attitude is less apparent but has not disappeared entirely.

2.4 PROTECTIONISM

The foregoing are typical methods of protecting a nation's shipping industry either state or privately owned; few of them have proved entirely successful. The main problem has been that many of the cargo preference schemes or state-owned lines were established initially when the countries concerned were far from prosperous so that the ships had to be acquired as cheaply as possible and thus had a very limited life. When the time came to replace them the problem of raising enough finance meant seeking funds from the world markets. Having to expend vast sums of interest and loan repayments in foreign currency tended to undermine the whole purpose of cargo preference. This became steadily more apparent as both bulk carriers and tankers (and more especially container ships) became larger, more sophisticated and therefore much more costly. Thus, only countries with a substantial shipbuilding industry of its own (such as South Korea) have been really able to maintain a viable cargo preference scheme.

There are, however, other forms of protection that a state may afford to its shipping industry. It must be remembered that shipping is a truly international market, which means that the same rates of freight are payable, the same income is achieved, regardless of the ship's nationality. But different countries have different economies and different costs of living so that the wage levels in, say, the USA or Germany are vastly different from the wage levels in, say, the Philippines or Sri Lanka. Crewing costs are a major cost item for ship owners, consequently if one is able to employ a crew from the Philippines, at wages appropriate to their local level, such ships will be far cheaper to operate than a similar ship employing a European crew.

The most obvious way for a government to assist its shipping industry is by granting a direct cash subsidy for the purchase of ships which is, for example, how the USA has maintained a sufficient fleet of ships to satisfy what it perceives as its strategic merchant fleet requirement. Direct subsidies to the ship builders are almost as effective and have been practised by many countries as a means of maintaining a viable shipbuilding industry against otherwise unbeatable competition.

Several countries prefer to operate a form of indirect subsidy which may be in the form of special income tax concessions. Others operate a scheme of providing capital finance at rates of interest far below the market level.

2.5   SHIP REGISTRATION

All seagoing ships have to have a nationality. Just as a person needs a passport when travelling to other countries, so a ship must have a register showing which country is its 'home'; in fact a ship's register gives the actual **port of registry**. That same port is printed beneath the ship's name across the stern and the vessel flies the national flag of its country of registry on the short mast at the stern; you will often hear the expression that a ship is **flagged** in a certain country which is the same as saying she is registered there.

Incidentally you will see another national flag flying from the ship's mainmast whenever she is in port, this has nothing to do with its place of registry but is the flag of the country the ship is visiting at the time and is called the **courtesy flag.**

Originally flagging was simple. A ship was registered where the owner had his office and although this is always called the 'port' of registry it is sometimes not actually a port. Countries like Switzerland and Zambia own ships from time to time but theirs are never able to reach their home 'port'.

However, as mentioned earlier in this lesson, ship owners began to find that registering ships in their own country was no longer financially comfortable. Taxation might be far too severe, or local wage levels far too high to be competitive. Over-enthusiastic governments or over-zealous trades unions might impose minimum numbers of crew members, manning levels, higher than those of other countries.

Shipowners were faced with giving up ship-owning or seeking a remedy and this caused them to seek countries with no taxation, little or no imposition of control upon ships under their flag and a simple scheme to enable shipowners to establish a 'shell' company – often a brass plate 10cm × 5cm outside a lawyer's office – for a nominal fee and to register ships for a similarly modest charge. Countries such as Panama and Liberia were in the forefront of this movement, in fact the Liberian flag was actively encouraged by American shipowners who found they had no chance of surviving under their own flag unless they were among those fortunate enough to get government assistance.

Many other countries have followed the pattern of Panama and Liberia; they are now known collectively at **flags of convenience.** In latter years the traditional maritime nations have made attempts to meet the problem half way by creating **'open registries'** which retain the national flag and the national compliance with international safety conventions but relax many of the financial and crewing strictures.

The major problem with some Flags of Convenience (**FOCs**) is that their lack of imposed control carries with it a lack of care about the observance of safety measures. The sea can be a very dangerous place and there are several international safety conventions that have been agreed within the **International Maritime Organization (IMO),** a part of the United Nations based in London. The most famous are the **SOLAS (Safety of Life at Sea)** and the **MARPOL (Marine Pollution)** conventions, all traditional maritime nations *as well as many flag of convenience countries* have ratified these agreements. Several, sadly, have not done so and such flags tend to attract some shipowners who have scant regard for the safety of their personnel or for the cargoes they carry. This is a great pity because "there are no bad flags, only bad shipowners" but the fact remains that even the good owners and the more responsible FOCs tend to find themselves undeservedly sharing the same reputation as the owners of the "rustbuckets".

It is worth noting that most IMO conventions require ratification by a certain number of states controlling a certain percentage of the world fleet before they are effective. Without the support of FOC countries like Panama and Liberia none of the conventions would have attained the levels required to make them effective. In some instances FOC countries are much more supportive of the conventions than traditional maritime states. Liberia for example was the first nation to ratify the section of MARPOL that controls polluting emissions from ships' engines. Despite being home to a major share of the world's shipowners and managers, Western

European countries are particularly slow at ratifying IMO conventions. So much so that the EU Commission often found itself promoting regulations more severe than those formulated by the IMO in an attempt to persuade member states that some action is necessary.

Criticism about their lack of control of ships flying their flags has lead to many FOC countries taking a greater interest in control and enforcement of standards on board, some have begun the process of removing the worst ships, while others have closed the doors to newcomers. It should be understood that many of the FOC registers, particularly those with the worst standards, are not run by the governments of the countries concerned but are commercial enterprises who pay part of their income to the government. The countries are usually very small with very low GDPs and so allowing a FOC to operate is seen as a way of generating income for the government. There are also many states around the world with national-flag ships that compare unfavourably with the average FOC ship and yet they do not seem to attract the same attention that the FOC states do.

Attempts are made to counteract the problem of **sub-standard** ships. An international affiliation of transport trades unions known as the **International Transport Workers Federation (ITF)** from time to time arranges a 'swoop' on a ship employing what the ITF considers an underpaid and/or badly accommodated crew and tries to ensure that all the unions in the port where the ship is lying 'black-list' the ship until the owners agree to sign a contract with its crew on terms laid down by the ITF. Unfortunately, as with many militant organisations, there are occasions when principles become confused and the blacklisting is more aimed at trying to force the shipowner to employ European crews rather than seeking to improve the lot of Asian crews.

The ITF campaign against FOC vessels is not new having begun more than 50 years ago, shortly after the end of WW2. It was then that a great many shipowners were exploring the use of FOCs, not just for financial reasons but more to avoid the situation that had occurred just a few years earlier with ships being requisitioned by governments whose countries were at war.

The ITF was at that time still mostly a European organisation and was concerned with ensuring employment for merchant seaman being released from military service. Since then it has expanded globally and does seek to look after all its members. Perhaps the most justified criticism of the way the ITF works is that a uniform wage for seamen pitched near the salary levels of developed countries, will actually encourage more workers from poorer states to seek employment as seafarers.

The differences in wage levels is well illustrated by a survey carried out by the International Shipping Federation who found that, for example, the cost of employing a UK seaman is almost two and a half times that of one from the Phillipines. The cost of employing a Norwegian Chief Officer is nearly four times that of one from the Phillipines.

There is, however, another side to the equation. Countries like the Philippines are unlikely ever to be significant ship-operating nations and yet one of the major sources of foreign exchange, that they depend upon, comes from the wages earned by their seafarers serving on ships flying free flags.

2.6 PORT STATE CONTROL

Throughout most of history governments of nations with ports and access to the sea have taken little interest in the condition and operating standards of ships belonging to other states. Providing they paid their dues, such ships were free to trade without any controls or sanctions from the states of the ports they visited.

In the last two decades of the 20th century a growing emphasis on safety and environmental issues was clearly in evidence. Public pressure was forcing authorities to take measures that would be seen as protecting the environment around their coasts, and it was in this atmosphere that the idea of port state control was developed.

At first, individual states gave themselves the power to intervene and impose restrictions on any ships that were in such a condition as to pose a threat to the interests of the state, irrespective of which flag they were flying. But acting alone, this was not effective as it might be since incidents such as pollution may have originated in the waters of a nearby state.

In 1982 several European states reached agreement to form a regional group of nations co-operating in implementing PSC. The agreement was reached in Paris and as a result the group is known as the **Paris Memorandum of Understanding (MOU)**. Later Canada joined the group to extend PSC across the North Atlantic.

Ten years later a second regional group was formed by Latin American countries. Rapidly followed by Pacific (Tokyo MOU) and Caribbean Groups. Meantime the USA was also operating a PSC regime but outside of any regional group. Other groups have since been formed namely, the Indian Ocean, Mediterranean, West and Central Africa, The Black Sea and The Gulf MOUs

Ships are targeted using a number of criteria such as past record, flag, class, ship type and owner. Vessel selected are boarded by Inspectors who initially only check ships documents. If problems are uncovered by the document check or if the inspector judges the ship to require an expanded inspection he will begin a more thorough examination of all aspects of the ship including construction, navigation, safety and pollution prevention.

There is supposed to be a standardised procedure for inspections although understandably standards may vary. At the end of the inspection the PSC Officer will record details of any deficiencies found. If the deficiencies are sufficiently serious the vessel may be detained until they are rectified, otherwise the vessel will be allowed to sail but a time limit will be set for rectifying each identified deficiency.

Results of all reports are stored on a central computer by each MOU and in the USA. Ships that have been detained are recorded on the central computer and details are also publicised in newspapers and on Internet websites in an attempt to shame the owner/operators into improving conditions on the ships. The ultimate sanction is a complete ban of the vessel entering any port within the regional MOU.

2.7   SHIP CLASSIFICATION

It is important to have clear in your mind the difference between *registration*, and *classification*, which is the subject of this section. Registration, it will be recalled, is the establishing of a ship' nationality – its flag.

Classification is a way of a ship obtaining a certificate of quality without which no one will want to insure it or the cargo it carries and no wise person would want to entrust its cargo to such a ship. Classification is by no means mandatory in all countries but some states do insist upon it. Usually that is because the roles of flag inspection and classification society are combined within a single organisation. Russia and South Korea are both examples of this, India too has a similar system but most Indian shipowners choose also to class their ships with one of the European classification societies for commercial reasons.

Classification is provided by **Classification Societies,** some of which are extensions of governments and some commercial organisations. At one time all Classification societies were considered reputable but alongside the growth in FOC registration there has been a huge increase in the number of bodies calling themselves classification societies but operating to very dubious standards. It is difficult to say exactly how many classification societies there are because some of the poorest standard ones have short lives. The best estimates would be in the 30 – 50 range.

Class societies are so obviously linked to the condition of the vessels that they class, that Port State Control authorities actually target ships for inspection based on their classification. Those that have the worst record sometimes close and re-open under a new name to avoid this targeting strategy.

The largest and most reputable societies are all members or associate members of the **International Association of Classification Societies (IACS),** an organisation established to ensure consistent standards and to jointly develop regulations and undertake research into all aspects of ship design and construction. The current membership of IACS is:

Members	Symbol
ABS	ABS
Bureau Veritas	BV
CCS	CCS
DNV (Det Norske Veritas)	DNV
GL (Germanischer Lloyd)	GL
Indian Register of Shipping	IRS
KR (Korean Register)	KR
Lloyd's Register	LR
Class NK (Nippon Kaiji Kyokai)	NK
RINA	RINA
Russian Maritime Register of Shipping	RS

The Lloyd's Register Book is particularly valuable to shipping business practitioners because it includes *every* ship in the world over 100 tonnes deadweight regardless of whether it is classified by Lloyd's or not. For this reason, all those concerned with shipping should become familiar with the format and content of the Lloyd's Register volumes. Incidentally, it is of interest to note that the Lloyd's Register numbering of ships is so comprehensive that it has been adopted by the IMO to issue ships with official numbers used for identifying purposes on documents and carved into the ship itself. This number stays with the ship throughout its life and permits its history to be researched and investigated as necessary. Often owners of sub-standard ships change both their, and the ship's name after a string of poor port state control reports. The fact that the same IMO number remains, allows potential charterers and other users of the vessel to see beyond the deception.

Appendix 1 provides a sample of the manner in which Lloyd's Register is laid out.

The accepted classification with Lloyd's is **100A1** which indicates that the ship has been surveyed by Lloyds personnel and found to be complying with their standards of seaworthiness. Where a ship is shown to have a Maltese Cross symbol after the 100A1 (spoken of as Hundred A1 Star) it signifies that the ship was actually constructed under the supervision of Lloyd's surveyors.

To maintain its class a vessel must undergo periodical surveys which include inspections afloat and in dry dock. The 'special survey' has to take place every four years (or 5 years if the ship is on a Continuous Survey cycle). Each special survey tends to become more rigorous as the vessel ages. All parts of the ship are subject to survey, the hull of course, the machinery, boilers and tailshaft (the shaft linking the engine to the propellor) all have their own survey programme. In 2010 some classification societies introduced an extended drydocking programme for certain types of new ships (container, general cargo & multipurpose) built to specific standards and with agreed maintenance strategies in place. Ships accepted for these programmes are inspected alongside and need only dry dock every 7½ years until they are 15 years of age, when they revert to normal inspection regimes.

It was stressed at the beginning of this Chapter how important it is to keep Classification separate in your mind from Registration. This emphasis is made because most countries entrust some parts of their registration procedure to a classification society, particularly safety certification. Some flags leave the entire process of registration in the hands of a classification society which is why there is a risk of confusing the two processes.

2.8 SELF-ASSESSMENT AND TEST QUESTIONS

Attempt the following and check your answer from the text:

1. What three technological developments have had the greatest effect on world-wide merchant shipping?

2. What is the size of the largest tanker ever built?

3. How large do the experts consider container ships will become in the foreseeable future?

4. What speeds can modern container ships maintain?

5. What does 'intermodalism' mean?

Having completed Chapter Two, attempt the following and submit your essays to your Tutor.

1. Explain why ships have got larger and why some ships are larger than others?

2. Discuss the different tactics shipowners can and have adopted to protect themselves against periods of low freight rates. What could be some of the problems which may arise when some Governments help their merchant fleets excessively.

3. Refer to the page from Lloyd's Register (**Appendix 1**) and answer the following:

    (a) There are two ships called Amphion, what type of ship is the faster of the two?
    (b) Where would you expect the "Amro 2" to operate, doing what?
    (c) Where was the Amrado built and by whom?

Chapter 3

THE SHIP

The ship is obviously the fundamental tool of all commercially related shipping activities and although the finer points are beyond the scope of this book, there are certain basic aspects that need to be grasped by ALL working in the industry.

3.1   TONNAGE AND LOADLINES

When describing a ship it is quite common to hear people state that she is "so many tons" and leave it at that. In fact in shipping the word "ton" (or the metric equivalent "tonne") has many different meanings and ways of being calculated.

For instance, when referring to a ship's carrying capacity in volume terms the word "ton" does not refer to a weight ton at all. It was originally derived from the word "tun" and referred to the 252-gallon barrel used in the wine trade in the days of sail. Then a convenient way of estimating a ship's size was to calculate how many of these barrels she could carry and that figure was used as the ship's **register tonnage.**

From that tradition, and after engines were added to ships, there evolved **Gross Register Tonnage (GRT)** and **Nett Register Tonnage (NRT).** These were a measure of the enclosed space in the ship calculated on the basis of a ton being 100 cubic feet. **Gross** being the total space, while **Nett** was the total space less that used for machinery and accommodation.

There tended to be variations from country to country in the method of measuring ships for their GRT and NRT so that a new system of measurement was internationally agreed and came into full force in 1994. The size of the 'ton' now varies between 95 and 105 cubic feet depending on the size and the type of vessel. To differentiate between the old and the new system the word 'registered' was dropped so that we now have **Gross Tonnage (GT)** and **Net Tonnage (NT)**. Because the change is still relatively recent a lot of people, even seasoned professionals, still mistakenly refer to GRT or NRT when they mean GT or NT. But the old terms are not completely obsolete because some countries still calculate minimum manning levels based on the old figures.

These somewhat curious uses of the word "ton" are retained because entities such as port authorities, who seek to make their charges on some sort of size basis, see these measurement tonnages as a fairly reasonable way of charging according to an approximation of the revenue earning capacity of the ship. Gross tonnage is also the most popular way of referring to the sizes of **passenger** ships.

Despite world-wide discussion and agreement, the **Suez Canal** and the **Panama Canal** authorities decided to retain their respective unique methods of measuring ships for the purpose of calculating canal charges.

Ships do have other measurements that use weight as the basis of measurement. At one time the type of ton used depended upon the ship's nationality, today the metric tonne is used almost universally. Incidentally it should be noted that while the British use "tonne" to distinguish metric tonnes of 1,000 kg from imperial tons, other European countries simply use ton since they had no need to distinguish between the measurements.

3.1.1 Displacement Tonnage

This is the actual weight of the ship and the word displacement is used in reference to Archimedes Law, which states that the weight of a body is equal to the weight of water it displaces. Loaded displacement which is the total weight of the ship and all that it is carrying has no interest in merchant shipping but is commonly used as a way of referring to the size of warships.

3.1.2 Light Displacement

Is the actual weight of the empty ship, which is of interest to technical people and also to **ship sale and purchase brokers** when negotiating the sale of a ship to the scrap trade since it is a measure of the quantity of steel (and a few other metals) that is being sold.

3.1.3 Deadweight (dwt)

Coincidentally this is the difference in tons between the light and loaded displacement but its commercial importance is that it represents the total weight a ship can carry which includes cargo, fuel, stores, freshwater etc. To clarify, you may encounter the initials **DWAT** standing for **deadweight all told.**

More importantly to those concerned with the ship commercially are the initials **DWCC** standing for **deadweight cargo capacity.** This indicates the potential earning capacity of a ship but it is not a figure that is cast in stone. When quoted in a ship's description it assumes that the maximum quantity of stores and bunkers are on board. In practice the operator may increase the DWCC by carrying less bunkers.

3.1.4 Loadlines

The amount of a ship's deadweight is determined by its loadline and this varies slightly because a ship has a maximum depth (draft) to which it is permitted to be loaded. This differs according to the part of the world in which the ship is loading and what season of the year. When reference is being made to a ship's deadweight without any qualification it invariably refers to the amount that can be loaded on 'summer marks'.

The ship's maximum draft and its variations are determined according to an internationally established formula. This international convention was the first one dealing with ship safety and started life in **1876**. It was then that **Samuel Plimsoll** a campaigning British politician succeeded in persuading the government of the day to pass a Merchant Shipping Act. This gave the authorities several powers to detain unsafe ships and by an amendment drawn up in 1894 it particularly introduced a **loadline.** This was the deepest draft to which a ship could be loaded and was shown on the starboard side of the ship by a painted circular disc 12 inches in diameter with a line 18 inches long drawn horizontally through its centre to show the loadline. Because of Plimsoll's involvement, the loadline is sometimes referred to as a Plimsoll Mark.

The decision as to where the load line shall be situated is made at the time the ship is constructed and the decision process is overseen by the ship's Classification Society which issues the Load Line Certificate and supervises the placing of the loadline. This mark is situated approximately amidships on both sides of the vessel. The Classification Society's initials (e.g. LR, GL etc) are included in the loadline (see diagram page 23). The maximum draft allowed is calculated according to a formula laid down in the loadline convention but an owner can opt for a lesser draft and if he does so a lower NT can be assigned to the ship. An owner who intends to use his ship for carrying lightweight cargoes might choose this option because it means that port charges calculated on the ship's GT or NT will be lower.

Although, commercially, one associates the load line with the **draft** of the ship, the depth of the ship **in** the water, the safety aspect of the load line is concerned with the ship's **freeboard,** the amount of the ship's hull between the water level and the loadline deck. The level of the deck is indicated by a horizontal line painted on the ship's side above the loadline itself.

Different parts of the world and different seasons are considered to vary in their degree of danger and so vary in the amount of freeboard necessary for safety. International convention has divided the world into zones the least dangerous of which is titled 'Tropical' zone and the most dangerous is 'Winter, North Atlantic'. Furthermore, saltwater provides more buoyancy to a ship than freshwater so that if the ship loads in freshwater she may be loaded to a deeper draft as she will rise up to the correct draft when reaching the ocean.

For these reasons a ship's loadline can have as many as six marks, each of which has an initial against it which represents:

TF	=	Tropical Zone, Fresh Water
F	=	Fresh Water
T	=	Tropical Zone (Salt water)
S	=	Summer (in other zones)
W	=	Winter (in other zones)
WNA	=	Winter North Atlantic

The actual mark (the disc with a line through it) is the Summer Mark. On the line are placed the initials of the Classification Society that surveyed the ship to determine the positioning of the mark. In the illustration is LR (Lloyds Register) but there are several more such as AB (American Bureau) or RI (Registro Italiana) and so on.

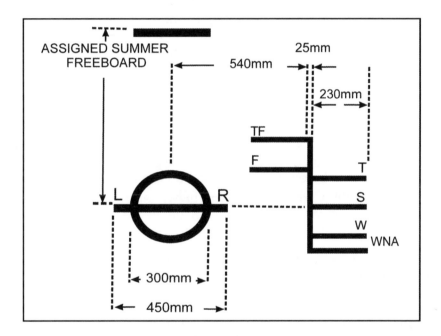

Ships used for carrying lumber (timber) can be granted an additional privilege because of the inherent buoyancy of the cargo and allowed to load deeper than ships carrying other cargoes. Additional loadline marks (corresponding to those mentioned above) are painted on the ship and prefixed with the letter L. If the ship happens not to be carrying timber on a particular voyage then the maximum draft will be in accordance with the standard marks.

3.1.5   Draft

This word, which can also be spelt 'draught', so far as this Chapter is concerned refers to the distance between the bottom of the ship (the **keel**) to the level of water on the ships side (the **waterline**).

The more cargo (weight) the ship loads the deeper the ship will lay in the water – the greater her draft.

Every ship has a characteristic progression of increase in draft with weight so that it is possible to produce a **deadweight scale** like the example shown in **Appendix 2**. From this will be seen that for every state of the ship's draft there is a corresponding total deadweight. The scale is such that if the ship knows that it can increase its draft by a certain amount it is possible to give a close approximation of the amount of cargo required. The formula used is the **TPC** (Tonnes per Centimetre) or **TPI** (Tons per Inch) in case of older British and most US ships.

For some bulk cargoes, the taking of a draft reading before commencement of loading and then again when loading is finished gives a good check on the weight of cargo that has been loaded. This is called a **draft survey** and when it is of critical importance it is usually carried out either jointly by personnel from the ship and from the terminal or by an independent surveyor.

The word draft (draught) is also used in reference to the **depth of water** available at a certain place in a sentence such as "the draft available at low tide is 6 metres".

3.1.6   Ship Measurement based on Volume

There is another important reason for knowing the measurement of the interior of the ship apart from Gross and Net Tonnage. Some cargoes are far bulkier than they are heavy. Visualise the difference in the space that would be occupied by a ton of feathers compared to a ton of steel. It would be pointless arranging for a quantity of cargo equivalent to the ship's DWCC if there was simply insufficient room in which to stow it.

For this reason it is vital to know the **stowage factor** of the cargo, that is the number of cubic metres or cubic feet to the tonne, **(see Appendix 3)** and to know the cubic capacity of the ship. A ship always has two cubic capacities one is referred to as the **grain cubic** which is the measurement of the total cargo space on the basis that materials like loose grain flow into all the spaces in the holds. The other figure, the smaller of the two, is the **bale cubic** that measures around rather than in and out of all the beams and girders in the hold. This, as the name implies, imagines the way bales of materials could not occupy the awkward corners. The difference between the two will vary according to the construction of the ship but in older vessels the bale cubic is very roughly ten percent lower than the grain cubic. More modern ships have an inner skin over the side beams so that the bale and grain cubic are much closer. The designed cubic capacity of a ship will depend upon the trade for which it is intended. If its life is to be exclusively in the iron ore trade it will not need to have so much space as if it were intended for grain, for example.

3.1.7   Stowage

All cargoes have their own characteristic density which for the purpose of shipping is referred to as the **stowage factor**. This was at one time always referred to as so many cubic feet to the ton (cuft/ton) and general purpose ships until well into the middle of the 20th century tended to have a cubic capacity with a ratio of about 40 cubic feet to the ton deadweight. For this reason, cargoes with a stowage factor of around 40 cuft/ton were referred to as **'deadweight cargo'**. Light cargoes, conversely are referred to as **'measurement cargo'**.

In more recent times two things have changed. First, most countries have now adopted the metric system and secondly, general-purpose ships now tend to have a rather more generous cubic capacity, nearer 50 than 40 cuft/ton. This means there is a rather wider range of cargoes with which a ship can be 'full and down', which is the expression seafarers use to refer to a ship which has its holds full to the top and the waterline level with its loadline.

Although cubic capacities are now measured in cubic metres many shipbrokers all around the world still use cubic feet when quoting stowage factors. Partly this is because it is easier to work with and remember stowage factors when quoted in cubic feet. Wheat for example has a stowage factor between 40 and 44 cubic feet/tonne, the equivalent in metric would be 1.133 to 1.246 m³/tonne. Of course the ship's cubic has to be converted into cubic feet but this involves just a single multiplication of the quoted figures although in most cases the owner will simply give the cubic in cubic feet when describing the ship.

Appendix 3 is a list giving examples of the stowage factors of a variety of cargoes and although you are not expected to memorise them, it is vital that you get an appreciation of the manner in which different cargoes can have widely differing stowage factors. When actively engaged in shipping business, knowing stowage factors becomes vitally important. An example of why this should be so concerns the time that Great Britain became more concerned with importing coal than exporting the material. British coal is mainly deep-mined and thus very dense so that shipowners were safe in assuming coal to be a 'deadweight' cargo. When coal from places like North America were being chartered, the market came to realise that shallow mined coal can stow considerably lighter than deadweight and some unhappy disputes arose before charterers and owners came to terms with realising that enquiring as to the stowage factor was important after all.

Note also in the appendix that there are comments alongside some commodities. Students should certainly acquire the habit of memorising any crucial characteristics about cargoes such as a tendency to spontaneous combustion, a tendency to contaminate the holds, or the need to take special care to keep the cargo dry, cool, well ventilated etc.

3.2   TYPES OF SHIPS

So far mention has been made of many different types of ships and how they have evolved. This section will take a closer look at some of them and their principle features.

3.2.1   The Bulk Carrier

These are, without doubt, the simplest of ships in terms of construction. As the name implies their purpose is to carry homogenous cargoes in bulk. What they will have in common is a single deck with clear holds and large hatches. Almost all existing bulk carriers are of single skin construction. Some ships with double hulls have been built and some new vessels are still being built although a move to make this method of construction mandatory was rejected by the IMO.

Bulk carriers vary in size from small coastal ships of a few thousand DWT up to ships capable of carrying well over 200,000 tonnes of cargo, there are at least five accepted terms that can be applied depending on size.

3.2.2   Capesize

Refers to any vessel too large to pass through the Suez or the Panama canals. The latter effectively puts a lower limit on the DWAT of around 76,000 tonnes. Anything above this size would be considered a Capesize vessel.

Typically a ship of this type would have nine cargo holds of approximately equal size. Capesize vessels are rarely if ever equipped with gear and are used mainly in the grain, coal and ore trades. A noticeable feature of most recently built vessels is the absence of a forecastle – a factor that many believe contributes to their vulnerability in heavy weather. The same dicsussions at the IMO that will lead to double hulls may also see a requirement to include a forecastle in new vessels.

3.2.3   Panamax

These ships are as the name suggests the largest size of ships able to pass through the Panama Canal. Effectively this puts a ceiling of around 75,500 DWT on ships, although vessels at the higher end may not be limited by length or beam, their draft when fully laden may make them too deep. Such ships will therefore need to be part loaded or full with high stowage factor cargo if they are to make use of the shorter routes made possible by the Panama canal. Panamax vessels typically have seven holds and are often also equipped with gear. In the main Panamax vessels participate in much the same markets as the Capesize ship but are more flexible being able to call at a wider range of ports.

3.2.4 Handy and Handymax

Such ships follow essentially the same designs with Handy size ships running from 20-35,000 DWT and above that being referred to as Handymax. Both classes will have five or six cargo holds and are much more likely to be geared than the Panamax and Capesize ships. Probably the most marked difference will be in the shape of the cargo holds, as both of the smaller types are usually square sectioned rather than hopper shaped. This factor reveals that aside from grain and ore cargoes, these ships are also highly active in the steel and forest product trades. As a consequence the hatches need to open to give access to as much of the hold as possible, and often extend virtually the full width of the ship – leading to them being referred to as "open hatch vessels" (not to be confused with open hold container ships which have no hatch covers whatsoever).

Ships below the sizes mentioned above are commonly referred to as **small bulkers** or in the case of the coastal ships **mini-bulkers**.

If you look at the cross-section of such a ship you will see the way in which they are 'self-trimmers' in that they are hopper-shaped at the top and bottom. The effect of this is that, as discharging proceeds, the cargo falls towards the centre and thus will be under the square of the hatch so that all the cargo is accessible to grabs without any manual labour being needed to 'trim' it from the sides. When loaded the shape reduces the free surface so that the extent to which the cargo is able to shift in bad weather is kept well within safe limits.

There is a further safety feature in this design because the sloping sections are water ballast tanks. More often than not, bulk-carriers have to travel long distances without any cargo in the holds. This would mean the ship would be so high out of the water that she would be almost unmanageable in even moderately rough weather with the propeller probably half out of the water. By filling those tanks with water the ship can be brought down to a safer draft with sufficient ballast above the water line as well as below to make for a comfortable passage.

Such a design, with cubic capacity adequate for most bulk commodities, is by no means ideal for one of the most common bulk cargoes – iron ore. Such material is extremely dense and so would only provide a relatively small heap in the bottom of each hold. Without going into the technicalities of stability diagrams, if all the weight is concentrated at the bottom, the ship will behave like a pendulum in any sort of rough sea. Such a movement, apart from being most uncomfortable for those on board, imposes undue stresses on the fabric of the ship.

The solution lies, of course, in purpose-built ore carriers which have a smaller cubic capacity than a general purpose bulk carrier. Such ships are also specially strengthened along the fore and aft line to cope with the strain that is imposed during loading and discharge, when parts of the ship are full while other parts are empty.

3.2.5 Tweendeckers

Typical General Cargo Ship

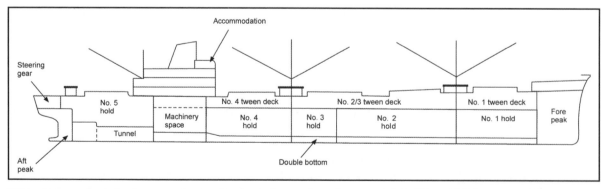

The above sketch shows a typical general purpose tramp ship of the 1970s and with so much emphasis today on specialised carriers the fact that there is a substantial proportion of the world's trade still being carried in such ships is inclined to be overlooked.

Today the tweendecker is more likely to be referred to as a multi-purpose ship a term that is quite vague and has different meanings to different people. While some do apply it to traditional tweendeckers others believe that for the term to be valid some additional feature must also be present. There are for instance vessels that have folding or moveable tween decks and some that also have a RORO ramp included into the design.

Virtually all multi-purpose ships are able to carry containers both in the holds and on deck. Almost certainly a multi-purpose ship will be equipped with cargo handling gear. Today most vessels are equipped with cranes although derricks are by no means obsolete. Crane capacity will vary, but around 30 tonnes is probably the most common choice unless the vessel is intended for trades where heavy lift cargo is frequently carried. As well as being employed in general cargo liner services, multi-purpose ships are often chartered for tramp voyages to carry cargo that is not easily containerised. They are used in the bulk trades for cargoes such as steel and forest products and, for vessels equipped with folding tween decks, grain, fertilisers and coal are also popular cargoes. To allow for the variation in stowage factors many multi-purpose ships also have moveable bulkheads that can be adjusted to prevent cargo shift or to allow separation.

The number of holds will vary between two and five and folding MacGregor hatches are the norm. Ships with a low number of holds often include a very long hold that can accommodate cargoes of exceptional length that needs under deck stowage.

Tween decks add to a ship's versatility because apart from the obvious need to have a simple way of separating consignments, there is a limit to how many bags, drums, crates etc one can place one on top of another before the bottom tiers collapse under the weight of those above.

3.2.6 Container Ships

Containership Typical Layout

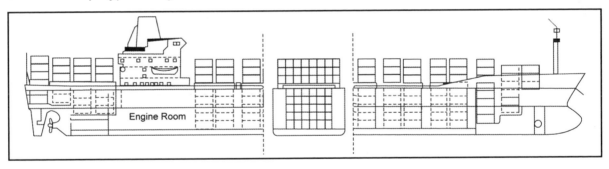

Are used mostly in the regular liner trades and carry most of the worlds trade in manufactured goods. This type of ship has already been well described in earlier chapters.

The large purpose-built container ships are 'fully cellular' which means that the holds have vertical metal guides into which containers can slide. Such a configuration obviates the need for any further securing of the containers in the ship as well as allowing loading to take place much more quickly. Such ships will load several tiers of containers on deck that will, of course, have to be secured by substantial methods of lashing.

The size of container ships is expressed in TEUs (twenty feet equivalent units) based on the standard ISO 20 feet long container. The largest vessels engaged in deep sea trade are around 13,000 TEU size but the vast majority of the container ship fleet are around 8,000 TEU.

3.2.7 Roll-on/Roll-off (Ro-Ro)

These ships as the name suggests are designed for any type of wheeled cargo. They range from small ferries for short-sea crossings, to trans-Atlantic ships well up into the 20,000 DWAT class. Common to all Ro-Ro ships is some form of ramp so that the cargo may be driven or towed on board. As well as cars, trucks, trailers and the like, Ro-Ro ships often operate on a conventional cargo route. The usual procedure for such an operation is for the cargo to be pre-loaded on to special trailers that are towed on by a specially designed tractor. Alternatively the cargo can be conveyed on to the vessel and stowed by forklifts.

RO-RO ships designed specifically for the carriage of new cars are easily distinguished from other types of ship by their slab sided construction and minimal superstructure. Frequently the bridge on these vessels is located in a forward position although the engine room remains aft. RO-RO ships for carrying cars are often referred to as Pure Car Carriers (PCCs) or Pure Car and Truck Carriers (PCTCs), ships that are used on freight ferry services are often called RO-PAX vessels today.

For the most part RO-RO ships are built with single hulls but there is an increasing tendency for ferries to be built with a catamaran hull. Some of these are what are termed "Fast Ferries" and are capable of speeds up to 40 knots, to help achieve this extensive use of aluminium is made in the superstructure and instead of propellers the ships are equipped with waterjet propulsion systems.

RORO vessels have been designed with their ramps in almost every conceivable position. Some have straight ramps that project directly forward or aft of the bow or stern respectively. Others have quarter ramps which project at an angle from on or other of the stern quarters whilst some have side access doors. Vessels with quarter or side access can usually berth alongside any normal quay whereas those with straight stern or bow ramps will require an 'L' shaped berth to work effectively. One advantage of the straight ramp is that extremely long loads can drive directly into the ship, something which is not possible with quarter or side access.

ROROs commonly have their capacity measured in lane metres. This measure gives an indication as to the total length of space available for vehicles of given widths.

The sketch below shows one of the larger types of Ro-Ro ships that would probably carry a mixed cargo of containers on deck and wheeled cargo under deck.

Typical Ro/Ro ship

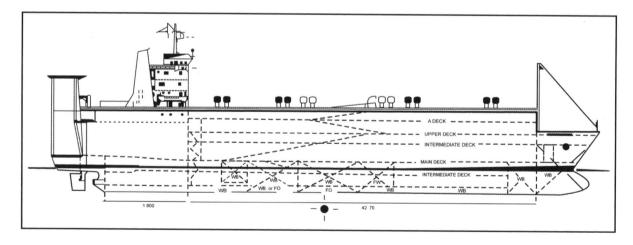

3.3 CARGO HANDLING GEAR

A means whereby cargo may be loaded in and discharged from a ship has to be available. With highly specialised ships like the larger bulk carriers and container ships, this process is carried out by appliances on the shore as the greater space and lack of need to worry about weight enables shore gear to be faster and have a greater capacity. Tankers, of course depend upon pumps, shore pumps to put the cargo in, shipboard pumps to discharge it. (its has to be this way because pumps can push very efficiently but only 'suck' rather poorly)

It is with the smaller bulk carriers, container feeder ships and general purpose ships that shipboard cargo handling equipment is found and if the trade needs a ship with cargo gear there are various features which have to be considered.

What type? At one time there was little choice, ships used winches and derricks. A **winch** is an electric or steam driven winding engine, and a **derrick** is a pole hinged to the mast near the deck over which runs hoisting wires which are linked to the winch. Crude though this system sounds it served the shipping industry extremely well for many generations, is very simple to maintain and operate which is why it is by no means obsolete yet.

More recently the trend has been towards **deck cranes** that are more expensive, need more sophisticated maintenance but operate at a far faster rate and as time is money to a ship the higher cost is offset by time saved. The other major question is its capability.

The principle factor here is the weight that it can safely lift – its **Safe Working Load (SWL)**. Heavy lift ships designed to carry specialist cargoes have much larger cranes. In this sector a 250-300 tonne crane was considered standard until recently and there are now ships with cranes of over 1,000 tonnes lifting capacity.

The SWL of cranes varies considerably depending upon the trade the owners have in mind. Usually they are in the range of 10-40 tonnes but there is a trend towards slightly higher capacity cranes of 60 tonnes. Heavy lift ships, such as those being introduced by the German operator, Rickmers on its specialised liner service are equipped with a variety of cranes including two 320-tonne cranes that can work in tandem to lift up to 640-tonne loads.

3.4 TANKERS

These are vessels which carry liquids in bulk and for the purposes of this Chapter we shall split them into two main categories:

a) Crude Oil and Product Tankers

and

b) Chemical and Specialist Tankers

3.4.1 Crude Oil and Product Tankers

The following terms are used to describe the various types of tankers which fall into this category.

i) ULCCs (Ultra Large Crude Carriers)

ii) VLCCs (Very Large Crude Carriers)

iii) MCCs (Medium Crude Carriers)

iv) Product Carriers.

The term ULCC describes tankers which range from 300/500,000 DWAT. They are mainly used for long haul operations between The Gulf and the Far East, Europe and North America discharging their cargo at terminals especially constructed to handle such large vessels.

VLCCs are vessels ranging from between 150/299,000 DWAT and are employed on similar routes to ULCCs but their relatively smaller size allows for greater flexibility. They can discharge at many terminals within the Mediterranean, North West Europe, West Africa, etc; they also have the advantage of being able to transit the Suez Canal in ballast condition.

MCCs range between 70/150,000 DWAT and are, in the main, used for short haul trips world wide. They have the advantage of being able to load at most terminals within the North Sea, North Africa and the Mediterranean, West Africa and the Far East. Their reduced size also gives flexibility within the ports they serve allowing many more options to Charterers and Shipowners. This type of vessel can use the Suez Canal in either fully laden or part laden condition depending on its size.

Product carriers can also be sub-divided into two main tonnage groups; the larger carrying products in quantities between 26,000 and 50,000 tonnes whilst the smaller, so-called 'Handy Size' loads between 12,000 and 25,000 tonnes; this latter type of vessel is often called a GP or General Purpose type.

Tankers are constructed to a simple but well tested system. The vessel is divided by longitudinal and lateral bulkheads that normally give vessels a series of centre tanks flanked by two wing tanks. In modern times some of the wing tanks are used only for water ballast and being segregated, do not become contaminated with oil. The ballast can then be discharged overboard into the sea thus enabling the vessel to call at terminals that do not have the facility to handle dirty or contaminated ballast water. Tanks designated purely for water ballast are referred to as 'segregated ballast tanks' or SBTs for short.

Tankers have traditionally been built with a single skinned hull, but there have been so many pollution incidents caused by ruptures to a tanker's hull that public opinion has forced authorities into taking some preventative action. As a result all new tankers now have to be built with a double hull and there is a programme in place to phase out all older single skin tankers within a relatively short period of time.

Tankers are invariably self-discharging and most are equipped with at least four pumps that operate at high speed enabling a fast turnaround in port. The rate of discharge is of course affected by local conditions such as climate, small shore lines, distance of receiving tanks from the berth, etc.

When carrying certain types of oils, tankers require heating coils within the tanks to keep the cargo fluid. Those coils, usually fitted in the bottom of the cargo tanks, can maintain a constant heat of up to approx. 50°C. Heating coils are not usually found in ULCCs or VLCCs as they are normally too large to load at terminals that supply the heavy and sticky crude oils.

3.4.2 Chemical and Parcel Tankers

In the last thirty years the expansion of the petro-chemical industry has seen the need for specialist vessels to carry the sophisticated products now produced. The smallest speck of rust or drop of water can in some cases ruin the specification of many petro-chemical cargoes. To counter this, modern Chemical Tankers are built with cargo tanks internally coated with types of epoxy, silicates or polyurethanes, and the different coatings are compatible (respectively incompatible) with different chemicals. The most sophisticated chemical carriers are those whose tanks, pipes and pumping systems are made of stainless steel.

Chemical/Parcel tankers are usually small in size ranging though up to a maximum of 50,000 DWAT. It has to be emphasised that the main requirement in this type of vessel is not only the ability to carry the maximum number of different products. It must be able to keep them so completely separate during loading, on passage and during discharging that there is no risk of one product contaminating another and, of course, no risk to human life or the environment.

3.4.3   Gas Carriers

The movement of gas, both Natural and Petroleum is now a major trade within the shipping industry.

As their names imply, Natural Gas is the gas which comes out of the ground in that form and can be used with little or no treatment. The North Sea gas which fuels most homes and many factories in the UK is a typical example. Petroleum Gas, on the other hand is a by-product of the refining process of crude oil. It has many uses, the ones with which we are probably most familiar are the small cylinders of Butane which are used in portable stoves for camp cooking or, smaller still, for cigarette lighters.

Both types of gas are carried in liquified form and, of course, both need purpose-built ships. They do, however, need quite different types of ship.

3.4.4   Liquid Petroleum Gas (LPG)

Diagram of LPG Carrier

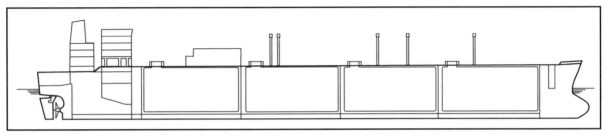

By kind permission of Syd Harris from *Fully Refrigerated LPG Carriers*

The two main types of LPG, Butane and Propane, have the advantage from the transportation point of view, that they can be kept in a liquid state so long as a high pressure is maintained. As with all gases in a liquid state, however, they are able to be kept that way more easily at a low temperature.

Gases can, therefore, be carried under any one of the following conditions either:

a)   at ambient temperature under pressure, or

b)   in insulated tanks at liquefaction temperature but at atmospheric pressure, or

c)   in a combination of liquefaction temperature under pressure.

For loading purposes the gases are liquefied by reducing their temperature by an amount dependent on the actual product involved; this operation is normally carried out by the shore installation. Most modern LPG carriers are, however, fitted with refrigeration equipment which allows them to reduce and maintain the cargo temperature as required usually to minus 50°C, thus any vapourising during the voyage or discharging can be liquefied by the internal system onboard the vessel. The size of the LPG carrier has increased over the past twenty years from vessels that carried 700 cubic metres to vessels carrying in excess of 70,000 cubic metres.

Cargo tanks in LPG carriers are normally cylindrical in shape constructed from aluminium alloy and are self-supporting and freestanding. Further they are insulated to keep the heat out by a coating of a suitable material such as polyurethane foam.

3.4.5   Liquid Natural Gas (LNG)

Natural gas cannot be liquefied by pressure alone and so has to be carried at very low temperatures. The main types of natural gas are Ethane and Methane. Ethane requires to be carried at minus 104°C and Methane at minus 163°C, both being carried at atmospheric pressure.

There are two very different systems used in the design on LNG ships although both of them rely on insulated tanks to store the cargo.

Firstly there is the Moss system named after its designer which is instantly recognisable by the spherical tanks protruding high above the ship's deck. The tanks themselves are made from an aluminium alloy surrounded by insulation and protected by a steel outer shell. The tanks are connected to the ship's hull but do not form part of it.

Diagram of LNG Carrier

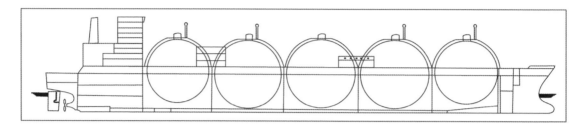

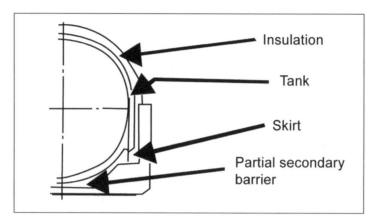

The second types of ship are referred to as membrane types. Unlike the spherical tanks of a Moss type LNG tanker, the prismatic tanks of a membrane LNG carrier are fully integrated into the hull. The cargo containment system is fitted inside the tanks, between the inner hull and the liquid cargo.

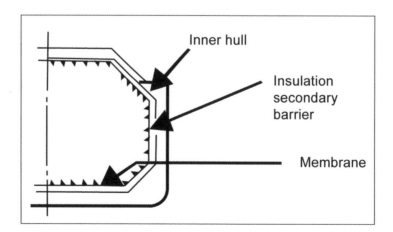

Neither type of storage system is fully effective and, the gas cargo boils off at the rate of around 0.15 per cent per day. Ordinarily this would be considered a negative factor but for the fact that most LNG ships are designed to make use of this tendency and are equipped with gas turbine engines that are mostly fuelled by the Boil Off Gas (BOG). For this reason LNG carriers only need to take on bunkers for auxiliary engines and for running the boilers for the turbines in port.

Most LNG carriers are built to service the needs of specific contracts as there is no spot trade in LNG. This is a situation that is likely to change very soon as the properties of LNG as an alternative fuel to petrol and diesel are being more and more appreciated. LNG consists of almost 96% Methane which when burnt produces very few so-called greenhouse gases. Although most LNG is extracted from underground reserves in the same way as oil (and in the same geographical locations), it can be produced ashore from waste materials. It is a fuel that is growing in importance and as such the demand for LNG carriers is also growing.

The vast majority of LNG carriers are between 135,000 and 145,000m³ (equal to about 60-70,000 DWAT) but new ships of 210,000m³ have already been built and ships up to 250,000m³ will be joining the world fleet in 2009.

3.5   SELF-ASSESSMENT AND TEST QUESTIONS

Attempt the following and check your answers from the text:

1.   What expression is used to denote how much cargo a ship can carry?

2.   What is the purpose of a Loadline?

3.   What is the approximate difference between grain and bale cubic capacities?

4.   How is oil pumped into and out of a tanker?

5.   What are ballast tanks used for?

6.   What do the initials SWL mean?

Having completed Chapter Three, attempt the following and submit your answers to your tutor:

1.   **Deadweight**

Refer to the deadweight scale in the **Appendix 2** and answer the following:

If the draft before loading was 3 metres and on completion of loading was 11 metres, approximately how much cargo had the ship loaded?

2.   **Stowages**

A 20ft container has a cubic capacity of approximately 30m³, referring to **Appendix 3**, estimate what weight of oranges in cases would fill it? Would this be a measurement or deadweight cargo?

3.   **Ships**

Discuss the factors which have influenced the development of ships during the second half of the twentieth century.

Chapter 4

THE DRY-CARGO CHARTERING MARKET

4.1 INTRODUCTION

The different sectors within shipping business are usually referred to as 'markets' because at some stage there is the sort of negotiation between two parties that is characteristic of a market. The bulk trades, especially, are essentially driven by the laws of supply and demand on an international basis. So free are these markets that economists refer to the chartering markets as "perfect competition".

Like the kind of market one might find in a country town, with its several different stalls, the dry-cargo chartering markets are comprised of their own different specialities such as grain, coal, iron ore etc. Where it differs from the town market, is the way that you will find the same trades being worked in different centres throughout the world. Not only the same trades but– such is the influence of international communication – at the same 'prices' or, to use a more appropriate shipping term, the same **rates**.

At one time the only significant market-place for dry cargo chartering was **London** because at that time, the world's largest merchant marine was under British flag. The actual place where this all took place was the **Baltic Exchange**, in a street called St Mary Axe which is in the heart of the City of London.

It might be argued that the origins of the 'Baltic' go back almost to the early part of the fifteenth century when there was an active import export trade between Britain and the countries surrounding the Baltic sea. A more tangible link is seen with the seventeenth century when in 1666 there was a catastrophic fire which destroyed much of the City of London including the then Royal Exchange which was a meeting place for all types of commercial activities. It was some years before a new (the present) Royal Exchange was built and during the interim, traders tended to meet in taverns. However they were not happy with this because they found they spent far too much on alcoholic beverages during a working day. As this was the time when coffee was becoming a very fashionable drink, coffee-houses became popular as merchants' meeting places and the first genuine foundation of the Baltic Exchange was when two coffee houses – the Virginia & Maryland and the Baltic Coffee houses – amalgamated with the specific intention of providing a meeting place for shipowners and merchants to come together to negotiate business. There is, of course, a wealth of history between that beginning and the establishment of an actual exchange in the middle of the nineteenth century from which today's exchange emerged. Paradoxically, there is now very little trade between Britain and the Baltic Sea conducted on the Baltic Exchange.

For many years, indeed until well past the middle of the twentieth century, the chartering of dry-cargo ships took place on the 'floor' of the Baltic, the business being conducted by word-of-mouth which is why the motto of the Baltic, which it shares with the Institute of Chartered Shipbrokers, is "Our Word Our Bond".

Of course the tremendous advances in electronic communication from the 1950s onwards has overtaken the face-to-face negotiation system and has encouraged the establishment of chartering markets in several other cities such as New York, Hong Kong, Hamburg, Oslo, Tokyo etc. Even so London is still by far the most active of all the market-places. The Baltic Exchange still exists although the wheel seems to have turned a full circle and now the trading floor has been rented out as offices while the 50-60 brokers who still come to the Exchange on a Monday morning have for some time held their meetings in the bar.

4.2   CHARTERING

The formal contract between a shipowner and the merchant seeking the use of his ship who is known as the **charterer** is called a **charter party**. The name is derived from the Latin *Charta Partita* (divided document). This dates from the time when an agreement was drawn up on a single sheet of parchment and then torn in two, one portion for each of the two parties. If they had a disagreement they had to bring the two halves together to attest that they were the original agreement.

There is nothing new about chartering ships, the earliest written voyage charter is in the British Museum and is dated AD 236. It contains all the basic elements of a modern charter party.

There are two basic ways a ship can be chartered:

4.2.1   Voyage Charter

By this means the merchant charters the ship to carry an agreed quantity of cargo from A to B. Payment is by means of **freight** which is usually expressed in terms of dollars per tonne but may sometimes be agreed as a 'lumpsum', a total amount rather than an amount per tonne.

In any case the actual level of rate of freight will be reached by negotiation, the dominant factor being the strength or weakness of the market at the time.

Voyage charters may be for a single voyage or can be several voyages of the same ship on a **consecutive voyage** basis. A variation of this is to ship an agreed quantity of cargo over a period of time. This is called a **contract of affreightment.** Such an agreement is of benefit both to the charterer, whose requirements will be covered for the period in question, and for the shipowner who can employ whichever of his ships is most conveniently placed rather than having to bring the one ship back in ballast on each occasion. Contracts of Affreightment can be of special benefit to 'pools' of shipowners

4.2.2   Time Charter

In this instance the charterer hires the vessel for a period of time and instead of paying a rate of freight per ton the charterer pays **hire rate per day**. During this time the shipowner still operates the ship and provides the crew. (There is an exceptional special sort of time charter, mentioned later in this section where this does not apply). The difference is that the charterer tells the ship where to go and what to do and pays for all the fuel (bunkers) consumed as well as the expenses incurred in entering and leaving ports and in loading and discharging cargo. Thus the charterer acts in many ways as if he were the owner and is known as the **disponent owner** which is the legal expression used for the entity that is "deemed to be the owner but not actually the owner".

All the terms of a time charter have to be negotiated in just the same way as for a voyage charter. The principal items to be agreed are, of course, the rate of hire and the period of the charter, which may be for a few months or for several years or even, on some occasions, for a **trip.** In this latter case the job the ship carries out is very similar to a voyage charter being from place A to place B but being paid at a rate of hire per day rather than a rate of freight per ton. The reason for a charterer preferring this way of chartering is that, although the charterer bears any risks of delays, it does give far more flexibility than could be easily built into a voyage charter.

The type of time charter where the shipowner does not take any part in operating the ship and does not supply the crew is called a **bareboat** charter or in more legal terminology a **demise** charter. In these cases the charterer really does act just as if he owns the ship and this method of chartering is only resorted to when a significant period is required. In fact bareboat chartering is perhaps more easily visualised if it is looked upon more as a way of financing the ownership of vessels without having to raise the capital to buy them.

It may help to perceive these different methods of chartering ships if you think of voyage charter being like hiring a taxi for a single journey, a time charter like hiring a car with a driver by the day and bareboat chartering like renting a self-drive car for a period of time. Naturally the extent to which these analogies may be stretched is rather limited.

Chartering, as has been stressed already, is achieved by negotiation of a commercial contract between charterer and owner, usually through the medium of shipbrokers, in a completely free international market governed only by the laws of supply and demand. Because in most countries, the law permits consenting adults to agree to anything that is not in itself illegal, there is considerable freedom of choice as to what is included in a charter party.

To avoid the chaos that such a scenario might suggest there is, first of all, a fair degree of self-regulation especially among practitioners who bind themselves to the motto "Our Word Our Bond".

Secondly there are many **standard forms** of charter party (abbreviated as C/P) many of them specific to individual trades and a representative list will be found in **Appendix 4.** Do not attempt to learn this list parrot fashion but study it sufficiently to grasp the following points:

1. There are very many forms and this list is far from complete as there are scores of private forms used exclusively by individual charterers or groups of charterers. Even the standard forms are rarely used exactly as they are printed because changes are made to reflect special conditions applying to some particular voyages and shippers and charterers both have favourite amendments which they like to incorporate into the standard forms.

2. Many of the forms are very old. Even those shown as fairly recently established are in many cases revisions of standard forms originally compiled in the nineteenth century. A typical example is the "Americanised Welsh" coal charterparty, which as the name implies, was derived from a Welsh Coal form. It was, in fact, based upon a form adopted by the Chamber of Shipping of the United Kingdom in 1896.

   Conservatism on the part of owners and charterers tends to favour well-established forms even though they may need many amendments to comply with modern conditions. The value of such tried and trusted documents is that almost every part of them has at some time been tested in Law courts.

3. Some forms for very specific trades were devised by the charterers and will tend to be biased in favour of the merchant. Conversely those that have been approved, adopted or actually compiled by The Baltic and International Maritime Council (BIMCO) an owners' organisation tend to favour the shipowner. Bias can, of course always be corrected by negotiation and amendment of the wording; to what extent this can be achieved in favour of one party or the other depends upon the strength of the market at the time.

Appendix 5 is a copy of one of the most famous time charter forms, the **"Baltime"** and shows an example of the 'box' layout.

Appendix 6 displays a copy of an extremely well-used voyage charter form, the **"Gencon"** which is the form used for any trade for which there is not a suitable (or acceptable) standard form.

Compare these two forms with the help of the summary in **Appendix 7** which highlights the major differences between voyage charters and time charters.

Note that **time charters** require more details of the ship including the speed and consumption of bunker fuel (for which the charterer pays). Owners will demand the inclusion of trading limits, and the exclusion of certain types of cargo. The place and time of delivery and re-delivery are important to both parties and of course the period and rate of hire are crucial.

In **voyage charters**, in addition to the obviously important items such as where from and where to, the cargo and the rate of freight, much attention is paid to **time**. First there is the time when the ship has to present to load.

Secondly the amount of time allowed for loading and discharging. "Time is money" is as true if not more so to a shipowner as it is in many trades. Too much time spent in port means less time for sailing and so less cargoes carried in a year. Thus many words are devoted in voyage charters to **Laytime,** which is the word used to cover loading and discharging time. If a charterer takes longer than the agreed amount of time to load or discharge, the charter will provide for a penalty called **demurrage** to be paid to the owner. In several dry cargo charters there is also provision for the charterer to be rewarded by a sort of bonus for taking *less* than the agreed amount of time, this is called **despatch money** and is usually based on half the amount per day as is agreed for demurrage.

One of the most important clauses gives details of how and when the **Notice of Readiness (NOR)** is to be given. An NOR is a statement given by the ship, or an agent acting on its behalf, to the charterer advising that the ship is ready to start loading or discharging. On the face of it this seems like quite a simple procedure, but it is complicated by events such as berth congestion, obtaining clearance for the ship by port authorities, confirmation from the charterer that the condition of the ship is acceptable and a whole host of other possible obstructions to starting work. Usually some time is also allowed to the charterer after receipt of the notice to arrange labour and equipment to work the vessel.

Despite all the attempts to make things clear as to when time commences to count and what periods are excepted, there are more legal disputes over laytime than any other element in chartering.

Appendix 8 gives a representative list of the abbreviations and acronyms used in chartering negotiations and it will be seen how many of these relate to laytime. Even these can be further complicated such as with SHEX which means that Sundays and Holidays do not count against the number of days allowed for loading/discharging. But what if the charterer decides to continue working during these excepted periods? To cover this eventuality one may find the letter "uu" added after SHEX which means "unless used". If the market is in charterers favour the added letters may be "eiu" meaning "even if used" which would allow the charterer to work over the weekend without any of that time counting. The overtime cost to the charterer might be more than compensated by the despatch money earned.

Somewhere in all voyage charter parties is a clause that details what form the **Bill of Lading** should take and how many are issued. A Bill of Lading is one of the most important documents that you will come across in the shipping business. A Bill of Lading is a document which carries information about the cargo, the terms on which it is being carried and who is entitled to take possession of the goods after discharge.

In legal terms it is a receipt for the goods, evidence of a contract and a document of title. The last makes it just as valuable as the goods themselves since the holder can sell the goods while they are at sea merely by transferring the Bill of Lading to the buyer. The functions of a bill of lading are explained in more detail in the section on liner trades.

Important as these are, all the foregoing probably only accounts for half of the total wording of the charter party. The rest comprises clauses that cover a number of other aspects that are either essential procedures or provision for unexpected eventualities.

Essential procedures includes things such as which party is to arrange and pay for the cargo handling or who has the choice of agents at the ports. The unexpected eventualities cover matters such as war, strikes, ice affecting navigation and also a clause that covers the cancelling procedure if the vessel is unable to arrive in time to commence the voyage.

There are also clauses that provide protection for either party in case the other side does something which causes additional expense or damage. Damage to the cargo is a common problem and the parties can agree beforehand what causes of damage are excluded or included. Most charter party forms also have a **clause paramount** that incorporates internationally agreed rules on cargo carriage, these rules are either the Hague rules or the Hague/Visby rules. Although they can apply to charter parties if specifically included they almost always apply to liner cargoes and they are discussed in greater detail in that section of the text.

An important clause from the owner's point of view is the **Lien** clause that sets out circumstances in which the owner can retain possession of, or even sell, the cargo if the charterer fails to pay freight or demurrage in due time.

4.3   THE CHARTERING NEGOTIATIONS

Like any other trading negotiations, chartering a ship begins with one side or the other making an offer; most frequently it is the shipowner who opens the 'bidding'.

Then will follow offers and counter-offers from each side until everything has been agreed when the contract is confirmed and is referred to in the chartering world as a **fixture**. The two sides usually come together through their respective brokers although many shipowners and charterers use departments in their own companies as brokers. Where the owners or charterers, referred to as the **principals**, use independent brokers they may be 'exclusive' brokers which is where the principal places its business on the market through only one broker, or they may use 'competitive' brokers which is where the principal broadcasts its business through many brokers who compete with each other to be the first to bring acceptable business to the principal.

The negotiations are opened by one side making a **firm offer** which will have a time limit. In these days of rapid communication this will only be a few hours but good sense will ensure that there will be enough time for the broker to pass the offer to his principal and to leave a reasonable period for it to be considered. The opening offer will include all the basic essentials which for a **voyage** charter would include:

- The ship's name and other details to identify her
- the cargo and the quantity
- loading and discharging ports
- rate of freight
- Laydays and Cancelling i.e. loading not to commence before the first date and the charterers having the option to cancel the charter if the ship does not present itself before the second date
- the rates of loading and discharging including a reference as to how time will count e.g. 12000/9000SHEX (Most bulk cargoes today are chartered on a Free In and Out (FIO) basis i.e. the charterers pay the cost of loading and discharging but in some cases the owner may be required to pay these costs in which case the amount per ton will be stated here)
- Demurrage and Despatch
- the charter party form to be used
- the commissions payable to all the brokers involved.

Usually in the early stages of negotiations the offers will state "otherwise subject to details" which allows the parties to leave it until they are sure they are both seriously intent upon the business before going into all the other terms and conditions which, although important, would not have a significant effect upon the financial aspects of the charter.

Quite often the broker, when replying, may use an expression such as "Accept-Except" and then set out those items that his principal seeks to alter. Despite this wording it is important to realise that a counter-offer is really saying "I decline your offer and I now make you the following firm offer". In other words the party making the first offer is under no obligation to continue with the negotiations if the other party fails to give a clean acceptance within the specified time and this applies throughout the negotiations until the two are able to agree when they will be able to say "That's a fixture".

Note that there is a fundamental difference between British and American law on the matter of "subject details". Under British law, if the details could not be agreed upon then there is no contract, however, under American law if the other party accepted the offer made subject to detail then there is a binding contract and the parties are obliged to continue to work out the details.

Once the negotiations seem serious, the charterer's broker will spell out all the details. These may be numerous because even the most recently devised standard charter party forms undergo many deletions and additions to the printed text and a page or so of typed additional clauses in order to cover the specific requirements of the parties.

The same routine would be followed in the case of a **time charter** but the content of the firm offer would be rather different, one would expect to see:

- Ship's name and other identifying details
- other details of the ship including such things as total deadweight; grain and bale cubic capacities; number of decks; number of holds and hatches; number and capacities of derricks or cranes etc
- period, e.g. 5/7 months or 2/3 years
- rate of hire stating whether it is to be paid monthly or semi-monthly (always in advance)
- where the ship is to be delivered to the charterer (often an exact place) and where to be re-delivered to the owners (often a range of ports)
- delivery dates which, like in a voyage charter state not before a certain date and the charterers option to cancel if later than a certain date
- the ship's speed and daily fuel consumption expressed as so many knots on so many tons of whatever type of fuel the ship uses
- the charter party form to be used
- the total commissions.

4.3.1 Voyage Charter or Time Charter?

There are many different reasons which influence a charterer's decision as to whether to charter on a voyage basis or to take ships on time charter. Voyage charter gives the charterer a fixed price per ton of material and passes almost all the risks, especially risks of delays due to bad weather, strikes etc onto the shoulders of the shipowner. The charterer does, however, have to pay for the privilege of being risk-free.

Time charter gives the charterer considerable flexibility as to where to send the ship and is spared the problems of demurrage. Time charter does, however, mean that if bad weather delays the ship or if workers in a chosen port decide to strike the daily rate of hire still has to be paid. Incidentally if the delay is caused through the ship breaking down then hire is not payable; the ship goes **off-hire.** As the charterer assumes many of the owner's risks and costs, the equivalent amount paid to the owner per ton of cargo carried is less than for a voyage contract.

Therefore if the charterer has a single commodity from one or a limited number of loading places to go to a single or limited number of discharging places and the rates of loading and discharging are well established, then voyage charter is the obvious choice.

If, however, the charterer has many different commodities from/to a variety of places so complex that it would be difficult if not impossible to include them all in a voyage charter, then time charter is a better idea. This is typified by time charter on a 'trip' basis where you could well see the business being quoted "Delivery Kobe, trip across Far East/West Coast North America redelivery Los Angeles – Vancouver Range expected duration 90 days"

Another regular reason for time chartering is when a liner company seeks temporarily to supplement its own fleet in order to cope with a seasonal increase in business. Time charter is often regularly used by container lines to cater for their 'feeder' business and there is a whole segment of the market devoted to relatively small container ships to fill the requirements of the feeder industry.

There are even speculators who think that they can trade ships more profitably than the owners themselves and will take ships on time charter and then re-let them on a voyage basis hoping to make a substantial profit between the cost of the time charter and the income from the voyage charter.

4.3.2   Chartering and the Internet.

There is a lot of history attached to the way the chartering market works and sometimes it may seem that the process is unnecessarily complicated, particularly the use of brokers as intermediaries to bring together shipowner and charterer. There have been several attempts to break with tradition and use the Internet as a platform for chartering whereby charterers and owners both subscribe to a site where details of cargoes or available ships can be matched and contracts concluded on-line. So far all attempts have failed although fresh attempts are made with monotonous regularity. Some sites are happy just to show details of cargoes and ships along with the contact details of the parties concerned, leaving it to brokers or the parties themselves to make the traditional negotiations. These sites seem to have a much longer life than the former type.

It is not hard to understand why this should be. Buying and selling goods and services on standard terms over the Internet is a well established method, but each combination of ship/ cargo/port/charterer and shipowner brings its own unique final charter party outcome and so is not best suited to the Internet business format.

Another reason why brokers are unlikely to be made redundant by the Internet is the very internationalism of the shipping business. With owners and charterers likely to be several thousand miles apart and perhaps unable to speak the same language, brokers who can negotiate for them and conclude an agreement, which might well be in a third language are an essential element. There is too the high degree of personal trust which exists in shipping markets and which cannot be replaced by computer screens.

While Internet broking may not be so attractive as IT enthusiasts anticipated, the use of electronic communications and e-mail has made chartering much easier. Not only are communications faster, but charter parties can be stored on computers and edited as required rather than having to be retyped each time.

4.4   SELF-ASSESSMENT AND TEST QUESTIONS

Attempt the following and check your answers from the text:

1.   How do economists describe the chartering market?

2.   In which city does most chartering take place?

3.   What is the motto of the Baltic Exchange?

4.   What basis is used for charging for the use of a ship under a time charter?

5.   What does the abbreviation SHEXuu mean?

6.   What is the penalty a charterer pays if too much time is used for loading/discharging?

7.   What is the title of the charter party form that is used for chartering ships for American coal?

Having completed Chapter Four attempt the following and submit your answers to your Tutor.

1. What major differences in conditions would you expect between a Time Charter and a Bareboat Charter and which would pay the higher rate?

2. What is the difference in laytime calculation between SHEXuu and SHEXeiu?

3. Explain what is meant by a firm offer and a counter-offer.

4. In a time charter, what would you negotiate concerning the hire money apart from how much? See **Appendix 5**.

5. Explain the cancelling clause shown in the "Gencon" charter. See **Appendix 6**.

6. What would be suitable charter forms for (a) coal; (b) sugar; (c) iron ore; (d) wood?

7. What type of charter party is known as the New York Produce Exchange C/P?

Chapter 5

THE TANKER CHARTERING MARKET

5.1 INTRODUCTION

Although oil has been found and used for many thousands of years its real commercial significance only began to emerge during the second half of the nineteenth century. This was in the USA where the first well specifically drilled for oil was in Pennsylvania in 1859. The chief interest at that time was in kerosene (paraffin oil) for lighting. Other products after extracting kerosene from the crude oil were simply burnt in furnaces and the lighter constituents like gasoline (petrol) were something of a problem. The automobile did not come on the scene until almost the end of that century but when internal combustion engines became more widely used, gasoline ceased to be a surplus commodity.

Prospecting for oil in the USA proceeded at a rapid pace and for many decades, America dominated the oil production market, which is why, even to this day, the multi-national oil companies are predominately American. The British and Dutch joined the race and oil fields were being developed in Latin America and South East Asia; Russia also discovered major oil reserves.

Although America, Britain and the Netherlands retained their dominance in *refining and distributing* petroleum products, by the 1930s the development of the vast oil deposits in the Middle East ensured that the Arab nations would, eventually, firmly dominate the oil *supply* market.

5.2 THE DEVELOPMENT OF TANKERS AND THE TANKER MARKET

For many years the demand for oil was small enough that it could be met by transporting it in metal receptacles usually packed in wooden crates and referred to as "case oil". The first steamship designed to carry oil in bulk was built in 1886 and had a deadweight capacity of 2,300 tons.

Initially oil refining took place close to where the oil wells were located but political as well as economic considerations made it wiser to site oil refineries near to the place of consumption rather than at its place of origin. Although this meant, in effect, that the oil would be "carried twice" it made a great deal of sense both at the time and subsequently.

Political sense, because a tendency was developing for some countries, having granted concessions to western nations for the exploration, extraction and refining of oil, later to nationalise these assets with minimal compensation.

Economic sense, because refining oil as near as possible to the area of most consumption simplifies the distribution of the many products of refining either by small specialist tankers, trucks or overland pipelines. The major advantage of carrying oil in its crude state is that it permits maximum **economies of scale** in terms of the ships used to transport it.

In the 1940s, when refined oil was the main cargo, 15,000 tonnes capacity was 'large' for a tanker, in the 1950s a so-called 'super-tanker' carried about 50,000 tonnes. By the mid-60s almost all oil refining was taking place near the areas of consumption and tankers carrying 200,000 tonnes emerged, these were given the name of **Very Large Crude Carriers (VLCCs)**.

Then, when the Suez Canal was closed as a result of the Arab-Israeli wars, not having to comply with canal dimensions there was no restriction on ship size but every incentive to maximise carrying capacity which resulted in ships around 350,000 tonnes becoming common. They gained the title of **Ultra-Large Crude Carriers (ULCCs)**. The ship was originally built in 1976 and named "Seawise Giant", she was severely damaged by an Exocet missile during the Iran-Iraq war. This was in fact the second time the vessel was rebuilt as its original contracting owner never took delivery of the vessel and when a new owner was found he required the vessel to be extended. In the latter stages of its life the vessel sailed under the name *Jahre Viking* but in 2004 was sold, renamed *Knock Nevis* and began undergoing conversion into a Floating Storage Offshore (FSO) unit.

For many years the major oil companies owned vast fleets of tankers so that they could move oil around with complete flexibility. Some independent tanker owning was encouraged because the oil companies enjoyed being able to supplement their own fleets from time to time. Nevertheless, to maintain the flexibility that was essential, they usually took these ships on time charter unless they had a specific port-to-port requirement when voyage chartering could be utilised.

The oil companies, however, later became anxious to reduce the sizes of their owned fleets as these tied up vast millions of dollars of company capital. For them the ideal situation would be to use some method of voyage chartering which was so devised as to continue to provide the flexibility for them to direct or re-direct the ships to the refinery with the most pressing demand.

The device was the creation of "scales" which first took place at the time of World War II. At that time the USA, through the United States Maritime Commission, developed their scale and the British, through the Ministry of Transport, developed theirs. This somewhat cumbersome system of two dissimilar scales continued until the 1960s when the American and British got together and created a single scale. The first of these combined scales was called **INTASCALE** and then, in 1966, it was further developed and given the name it bears today – **WORLDSCALE** – or, to give it its full title, **The New Worldwide Tanker Nominal Freight Scale**.

The system of Worldscale is to produce a freight rate in dollars for almost every conceivable oil tanker voyage (about 60,000 altogether). Each rate takes into consideration the distance, port costs, canal dues etc so that as far as is possible the same income per day would accrue regardless of the voyage performed. This enables charterers to take ships on charter with wide loading and discharging options with both sides being content with whatever load and discharge ports are finally declared.

The rates are listed in the Worldscale under the port of discharge showing the rate and the distance of the voyage in nautical miles for example:

PHILADELPHIA	USD/MT	Miles
Banias	8.38	10728
Bonny	8.28	10364
Cinta	17.63(C)	23998
Cinta	15.94(S)	20838

Note the different rates via the Cape of Good Hope (C) and via Suez Canal (S).

Of course the tanker market fluctuates just the same as any other chartering market and this is catered for by chartering at Worldscale followed by a number. Thus Worldscale 100 would be the flat rate as in the scale, Worldscale 175 would mean 175% of the flat rate and Worldscale 75 would be 75% of the flat rate. Market strength or weakness is not the only factor to influence the rate at which a ship may be fixed. The scale is calculated using an arbitrary ship size, speed and consumption as its basis so that if one's ship is widely different from that basis, a different rate will be sought.

The use of Worldscale is not only convenient for chartering single voyages but lends itself very conveniently to the use of **Contracts of Affreightment** which allows for a long term commitment and gives the charterer almost all the flexibility of time charter with none of the responsibilities for delays and no sudden gaps in supply in case of breakdown.

The ratio of tanker ownership has now reversed with the oil companies no longer having vast fleets of their own and the independents bearing the greater part of the benefits (and risks) of tanker ownership. Not surprisingly, they have their own dedicated international association – **INTERTANKO** – (The Independent Tanker Owners Association) which gives them a unified voice even to the extent of devising their own standard charterparty the **INTERTANKVOY.**

Independence is by no means confined to tanker owning. Reference has already been made to multi-national oil companies – the **oil majors** – of which there are several, probably the best known include EXXON (American), BP (British) and Shell (Anglo-Dutch). There are, however many smaller oil companies, some privately owned and some state-owned. These companies and countries are obviously reluctant to be dependent upon the majors for their supplies of crude oil or refined products. Their needs have encouraged the emergence of independent **oil traders** who buy the oil and charter the ships in their own names and then sell the cargo on to whichever oil company will pay the best price. Inevitably there is now a thriving oil market, the dominant centre being in Rotterdam. The stage has now been reached where the oil traders form a very significant segment of the tanker chartering market.

5.3   TYPES OF TANKERS

5.3.1   Crude Carriers

Most reference so far in this Chapter has been to those tankers designed to carry crude oil. Crude, as its name implies, is the oil just as it comes out of the ground. In that state it is a complex mixture ranging from heavy, dark coloured substances which are virtually solid at normal temperatures at one end to very volatile gases at the other. In between these two extremes is the fluid which, when processed through a series of refining processes, produces all the liquids which one tend to be associated with petroleum such as gasoline (petrol), kerosene (paraffin oil), diesel oil, fueloil and several more besides. In addition the refining process produces a large number of liquid chemicals with a host of uses from specialised solvents to the raw material from which plastics are made. Crude oils vary considerably depending upon their origins some, like that from the parts of Africa, are so thick and heavy that if allowed to cool becomes almost a solid. One the other hand crude oil from the offshore wells in the North Sea is lighter in colour and freely pourable at normal temperatures.

The crude oil is transported in the largest ships in the tanker group. And the sketch overleaf shows a typical crude carrier).

A typical crude carrier

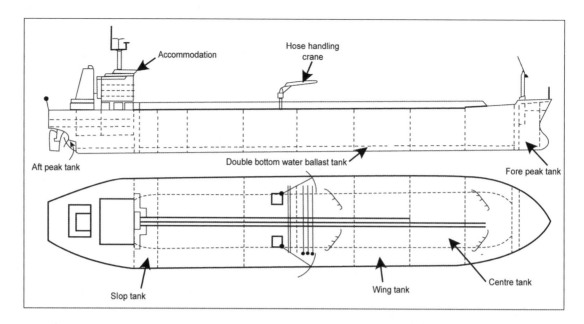

Reference was made earlier in this Chapter to VLCCs and ULCCs, these ships are relatively straightforward in their construction because there is no requirement to take elaborate precautions against contamination. Thus their division into a series of tanks is more for structural strength than for cargo segregation. The fact that these separations do exist naturally makes it possible for more than one discharging port to be served if necessary.

For many years, tankers were constructed with single plating, that is to say just one skin of metal between the cargo and the sea. However, some catastrophic instances of pollution of the sea and the sea shore through tanker accidents has led to increasing anti-pollution controls. The most stringent of these was the USA Oil Pollution Act of 1990 (OPA90) which required all tankers operating in United States waters to have 'double hulls'. That requirement has also been internationally adopted under the MARPOL convention so all new tankers are built with double hulls and an enforced scrapping programme means that by 2015 no single hull oil and chemical tankers will be trading.

The words "relatively straightforward" were used to describe the construction of crude carriers but they still include a fair amount of complex machinery and instrumentation. First there are cargo pumps which have to be capable of emptying the entire ship in no more than two days. Each tank must have its own set of pipelines with accompanying systems of valves and instruments to allow the right combination of tanks to be selected. Then there has to be a method of getting the heavy residues away from the sides of the tanks when discharging. This is usually achieved by a system known as **'Crude Oil Washing' (COW)** which comprises devices somewhat like huge, inverted lawn sprinklers which spray oil from the ship's own cargo around the insides of the tanks to wash the residues down.

Many types of crude oil are extremely viscous and would even become almost solid if cooled down, therefore crude carriers are equipped with 'heating coils' which, as the name implies, is a system of pipework in the tanks through which steam may be pumped to keep the oil at a pourable temperature.

Yet another set of pipelines is involved in providing the 'inert gas system'. Reference was made earlier to the fact that one component of crude oil is a volatile gas at normal temperatures. This gas when blended with air will produce a highly explosive mixture. To prevent air reaching it, the empty area above the level of the oil in the tanks is covered with a blanket of inert gas. The exhaust gases from the main engine supply some of this gas but most ships have an inert gas generator for the purpose.

As crude oil carriers invariably have to ballast to their loading ports, an efficient system of ballast tanks is also essential to enable this leg of the voyage to be carried out safely. In the early days of tankers, ballast water was simply run into the cargo tanks but this caused pollution of the sea when pumped out ready for loading. Tankers now, therefore, have 'segregated ballast tanks', that is tanks separated from the cargo tanks to avoid contamination of ballast water by cargo residues.

5.3.2 Product Carriers

Petroleum products, so far as the tanker market is concerned are divided into two categories, Clean products and Dirty products. Clean includes the lighter spirits and oils such as gasoline, kerosene, gas oil and diesel oil. Dirty covers the heavier oils such as the different types of fuel oil especially the so-called residual oils which are now the main type of bunker fuel for ships. (NB In chartering fixture reports the expression "Dirty" also covers crude oil.)

Tankers carrying clean products have to be meticulous in their cleanliness and cargo segregation because their cargoes are for use – often in delicate engines – without any further refining so that contamination would cause serious problems. Heavy fuel oils are not so sensitive but even so have to arrive in a satisfactory condition for immediate use.

Product carriers for clean cargoes are usually in the 40,000 tonne range whereas dirty product carriers can be any size even up to 150,000 tonnes.

5.3.3 Chemical Carriers

Cleanliness and freedom from contamination in the chemical trade has to be almost obsessive. Furthermore some of the chemicals are so corrosive that the tanks have to be coated in order that the cargo cannot make any contact at all with the metal. The coatings vary widely depending upon the intended cargoes. Load a cargo into a ship with the incorrect coating and the liquid could dissolve the coating and then start on the metal. There are even chemical carriers with tanks constructed of stainless steel.

5.3.4 Parcel Tankers

These are a very specialised type of chemical carrier which have an extremely high degree of segregation with each tank having not only its own pipeline system but its own pumps. These tankers are almost the 'liners' of the tanker trade as they are able to load several different parcels for different shippers. In this way quantities of chemicals can be shipped that in themselves would be insufficient to comprise a full cargo for even the smallest tanker. The specialist knowledge of the operators of parcel tankers and that of their seafarers has to be of the very highest order.

5.3.5 Gas Markets

There are two distinct types of gas regularly carried in ships as liquids. The first is **Liquid Natural Gas (LNG)** which is **methane** and as the name suggests, is gas as it comes out of the ground. This has to be carried in insulated tanks with a very powerful refrigerating system to keep it in liquid form. LNG is the gas that is piped to factories and homes replacing the town gas that used to be made from coal.

The other type is **Liquid Petroleum Gas (LPG)** – **propane** and **butane** – which are gases produced as a by-product of oil refining. They only require a modest amount of cooling but have to be kept under very high pressure to maintain a liquid state. These gasses are used where fixed connections are not usually available such as remote facilities and housing, camping and caravanning fuels and lighter fuels.

The gas markets are very closely connected to the crude oil trades since natural gas is found in the same sort of locations as crude oil and LPG is, as already stated, a by product of refining. Most of the gas supplies are controlled by the same major energy companies that produce crude oil and, since the ships required to carry it are highly specialised and hugely expensive to build, they are not built speculatively.

LNG particularly is seen as a very clean fuel because when burnt it only produces water vapour and carbon dioxide and not the more harmful acidic pollutants that oil does. For this reason there is a growing demand for it; as the fuel for power stations to produce electricity, for direct burning to supply heat and hot water and more recently as a fuel for vehicles and ships themselves.

As a consequence there will be an increase in the number of ships that can carry it and, most probably a growing spot market for them which may encourage speculative building.

The major reserves of natural gas are located near the crude oil reserves but there are also many places where, although extracting the crude oil would be uneconomic, taking out the gas is easier and this opens up the possibility to revisit some of the "worked out" crude deposits. Natural gas also occurs in places where crude oil has not yet been located.

There are gas fields in the North Sea, Mediterranean North Africa, The Middle East, Caribbean, US Gulf, Canada, Alaska, Indonesia, Australia and West Africa. Consumption tends to be in the nearest densely populated area with Europe and the US being the largest importers.

Since most of the ships now in existence are carrying cargo for their owners, there is not a huge charter market for them and when they are chartered it is usually on time charter or bareboat terms. However, there is one voyage charter party form "Gasvoy" published by BIMCO that is used regularly for shipping LPG and is readily adaptable to LNG cargoes.

Most ships are built for specific contracts (25 year charters are quite usual in this specialised sector) and the size will reflect the facilities in the ports. In 2005, *Excelsior* the first of a new type of LNG ship was commissioned. This ship has since been followed by another 8 or 9 ships with more on order. They are designated LNGRV (liquefied natural gas – regassification vessel) and have special equipment installed on deck that re-gassifies the cargo at the discharge point. Unusually this is not a port but an off-shore mooring where the ship is connected direct to a pipeline and becomes in effect the terminal. This method does away with the need for terminals on-shore which are not popular with the public because of the perceived risk associated with them. As the ships provide the initial pumping capacity, one ship has to be connected to the pipeline at all times.

5.3.6 Other liquid cargoes

Oil and the chemicals derived from oil are not the only liquids to be carried in tankers. Non-oil cargoes include chemicals such as phosphoric acid, sulphuric acid, liquid ammonia etc. There is also a separate market in edible liquids including vegetable oils, molasses even orange juice and wine.

With such cargoes areas of production are much more difficult to define than with oil and gas. The ships too may not follow the same design basics that apply to oil tankers. Juice carriers for example are much closer to dry-cargo ships and indeed some of them actually have provision to carry containers on deck as well as cargo in the removable tanks installed in the holds.

5.4 TANKER CHARTER PARTIES

There are, of course, many elements in tanker charters which follow the same lines as dry cargo forms but there are several significant differences. The tanker market has its own standard forms but with perhaps only two exceptions, these forms have been devised by the oil companies themselves.

Appendix 9 is an example of a "Shellvoy 6" voyage charter party and after the **preamble** giving the names of the parties, which is similar to any other standard form, the next clause "Description of Vessel" introduces some of the important differences. Lines 18/19 refer to a **heating system** which is a system of heating coils through which steam can be passed. The reason for their presence is because many crude oils would become solid and un-pumpable if allowed to cool to the sort of low ambient temperatures in, say, a north European winter.

The Shellvoy form is designed for use with any type of liquid cargo so that Line 20 refers to **tank-coating** which would not be of interest if the cargo was crude oil but vital if chemicals are involved.

It is interesting to note that lines 44/51 deal with the vessel's obligation to comply with latest guidelines and carry current publications covering best practice for certain important operations. This sort of requirement is rarely included into dry cargo charter parties.

Note that even tankers need winches or cranes (lines 21/22) but these are only needed to handle the hoses required for cargo handling.

Lines 23/28 are important as they deal with the capacity of the ship's **pumps**. Remember that the shore installation pumps the cargo **in** and the ship pumps it **out**. This is because pumps are very good at 'pushing' but not very efficient when 'sucking'.

If the ship is intended for loading clean products, her previous cargoes could leave a small amount of residue and some products could be contaminated by the merest trace of foreign matter. Thus lines 29/33 deal with the ship's **last cargoes**.

Mention was made earlier about **crude oil washing** and **inert gas systems**; these are covered by lines 34/38. The temperature of the cargo on loading is covered in clause 20 (lines 305-315 of part II of the c/p) which covers the ship's responsibility to heat the cargo.

The wording then follows more or less customary terms until line 85 where reference is made to the laytime. Note that this does not deal in so many tonnes per day loading and so many tonnes per day discharging but simply says **running hours** (i.e. SHINC) because almost always the agreed total length of time for loading and discharging is **72 hours** regardless of the size of the ship. The ship's pumps are invariably designed to match the size of the ship and shore pumps always have plenty of spare capacity. Running hours, as the words imply, mean no breaks for Sundays and Holidays because oil installations by their very nature work 24 hours a day and almost every day of the year.

Lines 86/87 deal with **demurrage** and it should be noted that tanker charters have **no provision** for despatch money.

Read through all the form in order to gain a general impression. Most of the clauses are not dissimilar from a dry cargo form but you will see reference to oil pollution, which, despite some very damaging and highly publicised incidents, is in fact quite rare.

Older versions of the c/p contain reference to TOVALOP (the Tanker Owners Voluntary Agreement concerning Liability for Oil Pollution) which was a fund to which most tanker owners subscribed to ensure that there was always a huge sum of money available should it be needed to deal with a major oil spill. This voluntary agreement is now defunct having been made obsolete by stricter regulatory regimes.

Shellvoy 5 now contains the **Shell ITOPF Clause** which replaces lines 561-565 and reads:

Owners warrant that throughout the duration of this charter the vessel will be:

1. owned or demise chartered by a member of the International Tanker Owners' Pollution Federation Limited and

2. entered in the Protection and Indemnity Club stated in part 1(A) 1 (xii) of SHELLVOY 5 as amended December 1996

5.4.1 The Civil Liability and Fund Conventions

The international compensation regime for damage caused by spills of persistent oil from laden tankers was based initially on two IMO conventions – the 1969 International Convention on Civil Liability for Oil Pollution Damage (1969 CLC) and the 1971 International Convention on the Establishment of an International Fund for Compensation for Oil Pollution Damage (1971 Fund Convention). This 'old' regime was amended in 1992 by two Protocols, which increased the compensation limits and broadened the scope of the original Conventions.

The 1969 CLC entered into force in 1975 and lays down the principle of strict liability (i.e. liability even in the absence of fault) for tanker owners and creates a system of compulsory liability insurance. Claims for compensation for oil pollution damage (including clean-up costs) may be brought against the owner of the tanker which caused the damage or directly against the owner's P&I insurer. The tanker owner is normally entitled to limit his liability to an amount that is linked to the tonnage of the tanker causing the pollution.

The 1971 Fund Convention provided for the payment of supplementary compensation to those who could not obtain full compensation for oil pollution damage under the 1969 CLC. The International Oil Pollution Compensation Fund (1971 IOPC Fund) was set up for the purpose of administering the regime of compensation created by the Fund Convention when it entered into force in 1978. By becoming Party to the 1971 Fund Convention, a country became a Member of the 1971 IOPC Fund. Payments of compensation and administrative expenses of the 1971 IOPC Fund were financed by contributions levied on companies in Fund Convention countries that received crude oil and heavy fuel oil after sea transport.

In 1992, a Diplomatic Conference adopted two Protocols amending the 1969 CLC and 1971 Fund Convention, which became the 1992 CLC and 1992 Fund Conventions. These 1992 Conventions, which provide higher limits of compensation and a wider scope of application than the original Conventions, entered into force on 30th May, 1996. As in the case of the original Conventions, the tanker owner and P&I insurer are liable for the payment of compensation under the 1992 CLC, and oil receivers in countries that are party to the 1992 Fund Convention are liable for the payment of supplementary compensation through the 1992 IOPC Fund. 1992 Fund Convention countries were required to denounce the 1969 CLC and 1971 Fund Convention, at midnight on 15th May 1998. As more States ratify or accede to the 1992 Conventions, the original Conventions have rapidly lost significance and the 1971 Fund Convention was terminated altogether on 24 May 2002.

In October 2000 the Contracting States to the 1992 CLC and 1992 Fund Convention approved a proposal to increase by about 50% (to about $260 million) the amount of compensation available under the terms of the Conventions. This came into effect on 1 November 2003.

Some countries that have not ratified the international compensation Conventions will have their own domestic legislation for compensating those affected by oil spills from tankers. Some of these may be highly specific, such as the Oil Pollution Act of 1990 in the USA, whereas other countries may rely on broader laws originally developed for other purposes.

5.5 NEGOTIATING THE CHARTER

Negotiation by means of offer and counter-offer are similar to those for dry cargo with a few significant differences. Reference has already been made to the way the majority of tanker fixtures, especially those for crude oil, are conducted according to **Worldscale** with the number being in line with the strength of the market at the time.

In almost all cases there tends to be only one broker between the charterer and the owner, unlike the dry cargo market where there is usually a charterer's agent and an owner's broker.

Negotiations in the tanker market tend to be far brisker than in dry cargo because both the charterers and the owners specialise in the oil business so that there are far fewer terms and conditions about which to haggle. Also, as the single broker is probably dealing directly with decision-makers on both sides, the time limits on offers and counter offers can be very short.

Unlike dry-cargo chartering which was, until recently, a face-to-face type of trading, tanker chartering always was (like all chartering now is) essentially desk-based. Tanker brokers have always been specialists and they usually tend to confine that specialisation to one segment of the market so that those working in crude oil are quite apart from those concentrating on refined petroleum products and chemical brokers are separate again.

5.6   SELF-ASSESSMENT AND TEST QUESTIONS

Attempt the following and check your answers from the text:

1. In which country are most multi-national oil companies based?
2. What is meant by saying oil is "carried twice"?
3. Where is the principle oil market used by oil traders?
4. What is the name of the independent tanker owners association?
5. What is COW?
6. Why do tankers have an inert gas system?
7. What are the two liquid gases called?
8. Why are some tanks coated?
9. How long are tankers normally allowed in which to load and discharge?
10. How many previous cargoes does the Shellvoy form wish to know about?
11. Who pays the cost of loading and discharging?
12. Who nominates the agents at ports of loading and discharge?

Having completed Chapter Five, attempt the following and submit your answers to your tutor.

1. Explain the reasons for oil companies deciding to base oil refining remotely from the areas of production.
2. From your study of the "Shellvoy" charter party and the text, analyse what owners undertake to do to ensure the minimum damage to the environment from oil pollution.
3. Explain the origins of Worldscale and the advantages arising from its use.

Chapter 6

LINERS

6.1   INTRODUCTION

A liner is a ship which is employed in a **service** between one port (or range of ports) and another port (or range of ports). It does this with a regularity and frequency which will conform to an **advertised schedule** which, in the main liner trades, is on a fixed day of the week basis. This in contrast to a tramp which follows no schedule and may trade among a wide variety of ports according to the market at the time.

A liner is a **common carrier**. If one recalls the analogy of the taxi in Chapter 4 one could then think in terms of a liner being the equivalent of a bus service. Common carrier means that any shipper may have his cargo carried so long as he is prepared to pay the rate quoted and abide by the liner operator's terms and conditions. This in contrast to a tramp which is a **private carrier** as the cargo carried under a charter is individually negotiated and an agreement signed. In some countries (e.g. the USA) the expression "common carrier" has strict legal connotations.

Whereas a tramp *almost always* carries raw materials, very often in bulk, a liner *almost always* carries manufactured goods, very often in small consignments. A tramp *almost always* carries the goods for one shipper whereas a liner always carries the goods of several, often very many, shippers; it is for this reason that goods carried by liners is referred to a **general cargo**.

Because a line carries many consignments the contract of carriage is not the subject of individual negotiation, the shipper accepts the line's standard conditions of carriage. These are set out in what is the most important document in liner business is the **Bill of Lading** which among other functions is the **evidence of a contract**.

If the lack of a formal contract signed by both parties is difficult to grasp, refer back to a bus service. The issue of a ticket in exchange for the fare and the passenger's acceptance of that ticket is evidence of a contract between the bus company and the passenger, subject to the bus company's terms and conditions. In the same way a Bill of Lading is evidence of a contract between the carrying line and the shipper and it is rare indeed to alter by negotiation any of the other terms and conditions of carriage laid down by the liner operator; unlike in chartering where almost anything can be negotiated.

The freight paid by the shipper for liner transportation (liner terms) includes the full cost of loading the cargo from the quay and discharging it to the quay at destination. This does not include the charges (usually called **terminal handling charges**) for handling the container into and out of the container terminal. With liner contracts there are no complex time counting provisions and no demurrage or despatch **except** demurrage will become payable if a container is delayed beyond the stipulated time by the shipper or consignee.

6.2   A BRIEF HISTORY OF LINERS

Regular lines did not really exist until steam propulsion enabled shipowners to predict voyage times with some accuracy as their ships were no longer totally dependent upon the wind (and somewhat less likely to become victims of adverse weather). The development of lines, as such, began in the second half of the nineteenth century.

The principal area to benefit from the improvement arising from steam propulsion was the carriage of passengers for whom the line operators competed with each other in the provision of comfort and (for the wealthy) luxury. This was the time that European nations were expanding their interests in their colonial empires so that links with these overseas territories were a prime objective for those governments who encouraged the development of liner companies for passengers, mail and cargo. As trades evolved, the lines developed separate services for cargo so that the passenger liners could concentrate on offering maximum luxury and fast passage times for mail services.

The importance of passenger carrying continued into the middle of the twentieth century when air transport took over this traffic. Passenger carrying today is largely confined to ferry services and to cruise liners, which continue the tradition of providing comfort and luxury.

6.3   CONTAINERISATION

It is debatable whether the advent of steam propulsion replacing sailing ships was a revolution in sea transport or merely evolution. However, the next development in the carriage of goods by sea was certainly revolutionary.

Cargo liners had steadily improved in their speed and efficiency with the regularity and frequency of services matching the demands of steadily increasing international trade. Further improvements were, however, hampered by the fact that general cargo came in all shapes and sizes. From massive crates of machinery to drums, bales, bags and cartons. Over a thousand separate consignments per sailing was not unusual and all these had to be stowed by hand. (This piece-by-piece cargo is now referred to as **break-bulk** or **conventional** cargo). Extraordinary skill was needed to ensure that the different consignments did not damage each other and were carried safely even in heavy weather. The time taken in port was such that there was no scope for any economies of scale because larger ships meant even longer in port. The cost of building faster ships would be lost as the time in port could not be improved.

An attempt was made to improve matters by **"unitising"** cargo, which was putting all cargo on to **pallets** or placing **"skids"** under heavy crates and cases. This process took place before the ship arrived – a rebate was offered to shippers who delivered their cargo already on pallets or skids. This meant all cargo could be handled by fork-lift trucks and even loaded into the ship through side ports accessed via ramps on the shore. Unitisation raised productivity in the docks from 1.7 tonnes per man-hour to 4.5 tonnes per man-hour.

Then, in the latter half of the 1960s, **containers** were introduced and this was, and still is, referred to and the "container revolution"; productivity in the docks shot up to 30 tonnes per man-hour and subsequently much more. This now meant that shipowners could think in terms of port stays being measured in hours and minutes rather than days and weeks.

Containerisation began in the United States where the first experiments took place in 1956. A year later a container service began operating across the North Atlantic and international discussions on standardising the dimensions of containers took place.

6.3.1   The Container

The first international standards were for a "box" measuring 8 feet wide, eight feet high (later increased to 8'6") and lengths of 10 feet, 20 feet, 30 feet and 40 feet. The 10' and 30' were never very much in demand and the 20' size was most popular in the early days which is why the TEU (Twenty feet Equivalent Unit) became the unit of reference; thus a 40' unit is measured as 2 TEU. Other standard sizes were later agreed but are generally in only limited use. In Europe there is growing use of the 45' pallet wide box with many ship designs being produced to accommodate it. In the USA, most land transport is done using 48 and 53' box lengths and at least one shipping line has proposed ships designed to accept these boxes on the Pacific trades to the US West Coast ports.

Other items were included in the standardisation including the security of doors etc. Probably the most important standard, however, is the **corner casting** which, by means of three oval holes on each corner of the container, standardised lifting, lashing and securing (e.g. to the bed of a road vehicle). This allows containers to be handled speedily anywhere in the world. (See **Appendix 10**)

Quite early in the container's history it went beyond simply being a box. Anything which could be fitted within those eight corner castings set at the standard dimensions was capable of carriage as a container (see **Appendix 11**) In addition to a general purpose container which is a sealed air and water-tight box there is also a **ventilated** container which is ideal for cargoes such a coffee beans which are still 'alive' and so must be ventilated. The ventilation ducts can be closed when used for cargo that does not need them. Still with sensitive cargoes in mind there is an **insulated** 'port hole' container which, as the name implies, is a container with insulating material top, bottom and sides and is used for cargo which has to be kept at a constant temperature. It has ports (round openings) in one end which can connect it to the ship's (and eventually shore-based) refrigeration plant. Similar to the insulated container is the **refrigerated** container (usually referred to as a **reefer** container) this one has its own refrigeration unit and can be set to sub-zero temperatures in necessary.

For pieces of cargo which are too heavy to be loaded horizontally by fork-lift and can only be handled by crane there is the **open top** container, which may have a removable tarpaulin providing a **soft top** (or tilt cover) or a steel roof giving a **hard top**. For more awkward shapes and sizes there is the **flat rack** and even a simple **platform**, several of which can be used side-by-side for really large items.

Bulk cargoes are not ignored as there is the **dry bulk** container, which has man-holes in the top for cargo to be poured in; these are ideal for cargoes like malt. Then for liquids there are **tank** containers which may be used for anything from sensitive liquid chemicals to liquid foodstuffs; they are, of course, dedicated to one type or the other.

The principal reason for containerisation was, of course, to reduce port time to a minimum and so allow liner operators to reap the same benefits from economies of scale as bulk carrier and tanker owners were enjoying. There was, however a considerable by-product which was **intermodalism**. The standard sizes and lifting/securing systems of containers allowed them to be carried with ease on rail wagons and road vehicles so that extolling the benefits of **door-to-door** transport was the main advertising ploy by the pioneers of containerisation.

6.3.2   Container Progress

It may be argued that the real "revolution" began in the late 1960s when a consortium of the lines operating between Europe and Australia formed Overseas Container Lines (OCL) and took delivery of six 29,000 tonners each initially capable of carrying 1250 twenty foot equivalent units (TEUs). Each of these ships could carry the equivalent of four or five conventional general cargo ships. It was many years before the proponents of containerisation admitted that they were so fearful that the conservatism of shippers might defeat the container concept that those first ships were designed so that they could become grain carriers if the idea failed, today it is difficult to believe such pessimism existed.

The Australian service was soon followed by the Europe/Far East services by which time shippers were beginning to prefer containers instead of having to be persuaded to accept them and all the major routes eventually became containerised. The word "revolution" is hardly an extravagant expression when it is realised that in no more than three decades the world's general cargo trade has changed from the old 'conventional' method to the situation where it is reckoned that 90% is now containerised and container ships of 12,000 TEU are trading with even larger ships in the design stages.

Shippers fondness for containers is such that more than 70%, on some services nearer 90%, of cargo is presented to the line as **Full Container Loads (FCLs)** but there is no problem for shippers with smaller consignments. These can be presented to the line a **Less than Container Loads (LCLs)** and the line consolidates such shipments into containers for the line's convenience. In the early years of containerisation, enterprising freight forwarders offered their services to shippers of LCL consignments, charging them rather more attractive rates than the line's minimum freight. These forwarders consolidated the shipments into containers which they then presented to the line a FCLs. Their profit came from the difference between what they paid the line for the FCL and the aggregate of what they charged the various shippers.

It was from these tentative beginnings that a whole new branch of shipping entrepreneurs evolved, these are the **Non-Vessel Operating Carriers (NVOCs)** who take the role of the actual carrier but do not operate their own ships. In some places (e.g. USA) these are referred to as **NVOCCs,** the extra "C" covers the word "common" because local regulations insist that these operators are Common Carriers in the eyes of the law.

Today, NVOCs specialise in house-to-house services on a worldwide basis, providing a value-added service to merchants, all as part of today's 'global market'. Some now handle more FCL units than quite important shipping lines. They buy space (often referred to as 'slots') in bulk and retail them on supply chain management basis. Although most still offer a service to FCL shippers at rates less than the lines themselves, some NVOCs no longer handle LCL business at all.

Containers and the intermodalism that they have allowed are such a feature of modern trading in manufactured goods that it is almost inconceivable to think that anything could restrict their use or hinder the productivity increases they have allowed in port working.

However because so many illegal immigrants are entering countries by stowing away in containers and the fact that it is so easy to smuggle goods and weapons inside sealed boxes have lead to moves by the US to insist on much more rigorous security checks. To this end some ports in other countries allow US Customs officials a presence in their ports to screen and inspect cargo in containers.

If these moves do not produce results there is every chance that a security conscious US may insist on all boxes being emptied in the ports rather than allowed to proceed inland unchecked. Scanning equipment and other security devices are being developed and installed by container terminals in an attempt to avoid the massive disruption that would result from official action.

6.4   CONFERENCES AND FREIGHT TARIFFS

Shortly after its opening, the Suez Canal 1869 proved so successful in reducing the passage time between Europe and South Asia that there was suddenly far too many ships. Shipowners started slashing rates to increase their cargo share but realised that this was benefitting no one. Thus, in 1875, the lines came together and formed the UK/Calcutta Conference which eventually became the India Pakistan Bangladesh Conference and as such it thrived for well over a century.

Eventually, virtually all liner routes had their conferences whose principal objectives were to regulate the number of lines in the trade and the frequency of their sailings. Also to produce a tariff of freight rates with which all the member lines undertook to charge. These tariffs became complex volumes because the aim always was to attract low-value cargo by charging inexpensive rates but compensating for any loss by charging high value goods much higher rates. This concept of charging "what the traffic would bear" seemed to suit everyone and helped to achieve what all owners wanted, a full ship providing an overall income that was profitable. Conferences also standardised bill of lading terms and conditions which all their member lines used.

Conferences only admitted members who could provide a service at the same standard as the other members and the cargo share and frequency for each member line was also agreed. This meant that a shipper using a conference service knew that regardless of which actual line it was, the rate and terms would be the same and the line concerned would be of reasonable quality. As no single line could offer the frequency and regularity that shippers needed, the conference system suited merchants as much as the shipowners.

The fact remains that liner conferences were price-fixing cartels. In the long-distance trades they had a virtual monopoly that they reinforced by giving rebates to shippers who were loyal to conference lines but cancelling such payments arbitrarily if a shipper dared to ship the smallest quantity in a non-conference ship. This stifling of competition was the subject of official enquiries and in the U.K. alone the government staged such investigations in 1909, 1923, and 1970 but on every occasion it was agreed that the advantage of conferences to merchants outweighed their disadvantages and they should not be outlawed.

The United Nations, on behalf of the world's developing nations, introduced a Code of Conduct for Liner Conferences. This was not so much to limit price-fixing but was an endeavour to ensure that the less developed countries, with their burgeoning national lines, would get a cargo share equal to the lines of the traditional maritime nations.

Paradoxically, by the time the UN Code became adopted as an international convention in 1982, containerisation had so altered the liner market that the conferences no longer enjoyed sufficient dominance in any trade and the Code became meaningless.

As has already been mentioned, prior to the advent of containers there was very little development in the basic design of liners, merely the natural evolution of propulsion machinery and hull design. The only real advance in shore-side practices was the reluctant acceptance by port labour of fork-lift trucks rather than hand barrows. There, was, therefore, no scope for any major reduction in freight rates.

Containers, however, provided room for massive economies of scale in a very short time, ship sizes increasing four-fold and with port times radically reduced voyage times were being halved. At about the same time the countries of South East Asia and the Far East were developing new merchant fleets. These were backed by their very high growth economies and large scale cheap ship building enabled shipowners from this region to enter liner trades, often outside the conference system. Even the most powerful conferences such as those for the Europe/Far East services found that these new operators, as well as new entrants from Europe, were competing successfully.

Conferences still exist in many trades and although they cannot exercise anything like the power they once had, they still strive to bring some order into liner routes. Their activities are constantly the subject of scrutiny by such anti-cartel regulatory bodies as the Federal Maritime Commission in the USA and the Directorate for Competition of the European Commission in Brussels.

Tariffs are still produced and regularly up-dated but in most trades a large measure of negotiation of freight rates is quite normal and these tend to be on a 'per box' structure irrespective of commodity.

6.4.1 Liner Consortium Agreements

Providing shippers with the frequency of sailings they require in a particular trade remains a problem as many lines cannot afford a large enough fleet to offer, say, a sailing on the same day every week. The solution these lines have found is to form joint services so that each line provides an agreed number of ships and then has a proportion of "slots" in every sailing regardless of whose ship it happens to be. There are cases where some consortium members may not contribute a vessel but as members still take a share of the slots available on each ship. These consortia emerge and disband according to the changes in the strength of the lines involved but the principle is now an integral part of container services.

6.4.2 Alliances

Consortia were originally formed by a group of lines operating in a particular trade such as Europe to the Far East. A line in that grouping might join with a total different set of partners in, say, the Europe to USA trade. With 'globalisation', the development of manufacturers selling to worldwide markets in the last decade of the 20th Century, these customers sought to make agreements with carriers on a world-wide basis. This led to the formations of **alliances** where groups of lines come together on all three of the worlds major trade routes, USA/Europe, Europe/Far East and Far East/USA to provide an integral service.

6.4.3 Profile of a Typical Major Liner Operator

Today's liner operator probably involves:

1. Membership of a consortium, alliance and possibly a Conference.

2. Fixed day sailings

3. Network of own offices and/or agents supplying service to customers with intense publicity and sales activity.

4. Engaged in major East-West trade(s) with subsidiary trades either direct or through feeder services North-South.

5. Inland and distribution operations by rail, road or barge so as to provide a full door-to-door service.

6.5 LINER DOCUMENTATION

The most important document concerned with cargo in liner shipping is the **Bill of Lading (B/L)**. A B/L comprises the front, which has a series of blank sections to be completed in accordance with the shipment in question, and the reverse which is a mass of small print that gives details of the terms and conditions of the contract of carriage. The shipper supplies the line or its agent with all the cargo details when the booking is made in the form of Shipping Instructions; and this information is usually stored on a computer and can be incorporated into the Bill of Lading at the touch of a button.

6.5.1 The Three Functions of a Bill of Lading

These have already been touched upon in the section on chartering when the importance and value of the Bill of Lading was stressed.

It is vital fix in one's mind that a B/L has three functions and if a mnemonic assists in this fixing process, think of a B/L being **RED**. A B/L is:

1. A **R**eceipt for cargo

2. **E**vidence of contract

3. A **D**ocument of title

Appendix 12 is the face of a typical **Combined Transport Bill of Lading**. It acquired its name to differentiate it from the type of B/L which was used for break-bulk cargo and although the latter is now seldom encountered because of the predominance of containerisation, the name "combined transport" is still applied because it stresses the fact that this B/L can cover the transport of the cargo from shipper's domicile to consignee's premises and this may involve road or rail transport before or after the ocean voyage and may include shipment in a **feeder vessel** before or after the ocean voyage. The important fact with a combined transport B/L is that the carrier's responsibility covers all the different modes of transport that may be involved even though some of these may have to be provided by sub-contractors.

6.5.2 Receipt for Cargo

The B/Ls role as a **receipt** for cargo is easy to see because it sets out who is the shipper (consignor), who is the receiver (consignee) (ignore "Notify Party" at this stage) where the cargo is first received into the carrier's custody, the actual port of loading, where it is to be discharged and the final destination. Then there is a large amount of blank space in which to describe the cargo.

Below all this is space for the signature on behalf of the Master of the ship but above that space are some very important printed words reading "Received by the Carrier from the Shipper **in apparent good order and condition** – - – -" and then goes on to incorporate the terms printed on the back of the form. A Combined Transport B/L is issued when the goods are received by the carrier. This will often be at some inland point and only later will the goods be shipped onboard the vessel. However, as will be seen later, contracts for the sale of goods often require the shipper to prove that the consignment has actually commenced the voyage to the buyer. This requires the B/L to give the actual date of shipment and in such cases the B/L is endorsed "Shipped on Board" with the date that occurred. Shipped on board B/Ls will also be issued for any goods which are received by the line at the port of shipment.

The B/L's function as a **receipt for cargo** is, therefore, twofold because it covers the **quantity** and the **condition** of the cargo and the consignee has the right to demand that he receives the same quantity in the same condition as it was when loaded.

With a **Full Container Load (FCL)** which has been **stuffed** by the shipper the description of the cargo will have the qualifying words "said to contain" so that the condition and quantity of the goods are outside the ship's control provided the exterior of the container is in good shape. In the case of **Less than Container Loads (LCL),** cargo where the container was stuffed by the line, the receipt as to condition and quantity are the same as for conventional cargo that is the actual number and type of packages.

Note that the expression for loading the goods into the container is **"stuffing"** in order to avoid confusion with **"loading"** which is the placing of the container in the ship. To avoid confusion with **"discharging"** which is taking the container off the ship, the expressions used for taking the goods out of the container are **"stripping"** or sometimes **"unstuffing"**.

6.5.3 Evidence of a Contract

Appendix 12 shows the reverse of the B/L which will be studied in a little more detail later in this lesson but at this stage it is sufficient to note that is comprises a mass of small print which gives details of the terms under which the goods are carried.

But the B/L is not the contract itself. It is not a document signed by both parties and in any case, the B/L is not drawn up until the custody of the goods passes from shipper to carrier. The actual contract, frequently no more than a simple verbal agreement, was made when the cargo was **booked** by the shipper with the line or the line's agent. Thus the B/L is the **evidence** of that contract.

Very rarely there will be a written contract for liner cargo and this will be in the form of a **booking note** an example of which may be found in **Appendix 13.** Booking notes are used in such instances as when a contractor for a major overseas civil engineering project wishes to arrange a fixed rate for all the materials involved rather than have the uncertainty of different rates for different materials, which could occur if the goods were shipped normally.

6.5.4   Document of Title

Title in this context is defined as **"the right to ownership of property with or without possession"** and this third function of a B/L is twofold.

"Right to ownership" simply means that whoever legally holds the B/L may claim the cargo and a unique feature of carriage in a ship, unlike surface transport is that once the cargo is shipped and the ship is at sea no one (except the crew of course) can get at the cargo. Therefore, if the B/L changes hands lawfully the right to ownership changes at that moment. In other words the B/L is a **negotiable document**. This permits the initial transfer of ownership from the consignor to the consignee and also permits subsequent transfers of ownership by handing over the B/L, suitably endorsed, to the new buyer. If he so wished, the new buyer could resell the cargo and this could go on any number of times while the ship is still at sea until the eventual buyer presents the B/L to the line or the line's agent at the discharging port and claims physical possession of the goods.

It will be easily seen that the seller of the B/L can delay passing the right to ownership until payment has been made so that the B/L's other function as a document of title is as **security for payment;** this role is almost indispensable to international traders.

When an exporter sells to an overseas buyer, only if the two parties are old and trusted friends can the matter of payment be an informal arrangement such as cash in advance or cash on delivery. Overseas trade is seldom like that and the problem is most often overcome by the system known as a **documentary credit**, often referred to as a **letter of credit.**

The buyer, having agreed price and other details with the seller, instructs his bank to arrange for a letter of credit to be made available at a bank in the shipper's country. When the cargo is shipped, the line or its agent gives a signed shipped B/L to the shipper who takes this to the bank holding the letter of credit together with all the other documents that the letter of credit may require. If the bank is satisfied that the documents comply exactly with the letter of credit the shipper is able to collect payment for the goods.

The bank in the shipper's country now has the B/L as security for payment by the buyer's bank to whom the B/L is now passed. Now the buyer's bank holds the B/L as security until the buyer has paid, at which point the buyer is in a position either to sell the cargo on, or to present the B/L to the line or its agent in order to claim the cargo.

Refer back to **Appendix 12** and look at the space just under the one marked "consignee", that box is titled **"notify address"** (some B/Ls show this as "notify party"). The point is that the bank involved does not wish to assume the position of actual consignee with all the responsibilities that may entail; the bank only wants the B/L as security. So, when a documentary credit is involved, the box marked "consignee" is completed with the one word **"Order"** which, after the shipper has endorsed it, makes the B/L 'open' (like a cheque drawn to 'cash'). The name of the buyer or his representative has been entered in the "notify" box so that the line or its agent knows who to communicate with even though that party will not have title to the goods until payment has been made to the bank and the B/L handed over.

Very rarely the buyer does not have the money and the bank is obliged to become the consignee rather than simply holding the B/L as security. It then disposes of the goods for as much cash as can be raised.

6.5.5   Sea Waybills

Today's more efficient liner services with just hours in port and high speed at sea present a new problem. The cargo can now arrive before the documents have filtered through the banking system because human hands and eyes still have to scrutinise the documents, that part cannot be rushed otherwise fraud would flourish.

One way to overcome this is for the buyer and the seller to agree to a different method of payment. If this is possible, and if the buyer has no intention to sell the goods on while the ship is on passage, a negotiable document is not necessary. In the circumstances a **Sea Waybill** can be used. Refer to **Appendix 14** from which you will see that a Sea Waybill is similar to a B/L in almost all respects except it is NOT negotiable. A Sea Waybill is not a document of title so that it does not have to be presented at discharging port. The line or its agent simply has to satisfy itself that it has properly identified the consignee and then hand the cargo over.

6.5.6   Electronic Bills of Lading

All container lines now use sophisticated computer systems to handle the large volumes of B/Ls, Waybills, Freight Invoices. Manifests and other documents needed and in most cases this information is exchanged between the lines office and agents by electronic means, either through dedicated information system providers or the Internet and e-mail. Furthermore, many liner ports have integrated port-community computer systems which provide data sharing among interested parties. The line or its local agent inputs the data relative to their import or export vessel and this can be accessed by authorised port users such as Customs, Terminal Operators, Harbour Masters etc.

The part of the problem that still has to be overcome is that of replacing the 'negotiable' aspect of the B/L electronically. A pilot scheme is in progress initiated by a group working under the acronym **"BOLERO"** and this is being closely watched by all parties but especially the banks who fear the risk of fraud may be too high. Students should keep a watch on the shipping journals for more news of this system. In its annual report in March 2004, the TT Club (which owns half of the company which runs BOLERO) reduced its valuation of the shares because of the overall lack of interest in the system. There are some committed customers using it but it has definitely not been a runaway success.

In 2010, a new electronic bill of lading system was established by a company called Electronic Shipping Solutions under the brand name 'CargoDocs Services'. Trials were carried out in the oil sector rather than the liner trade sector because much oil trading is already done electronically. The first electronic B/L was issued via CargoDocs in January 2010 for a shipment on the tanker Bro Deliverer from the Ineos Finnart Terminal to BP's terminal in Belfast.

The CargoDocs system incorporates trade finance practices and allows for the electronic presentation of documents to banks when trading under documentary credits. The system provides a simple and secure web-based interface with a central 'registry' where key documents such as B/Ls are stored under security. There is also a 'lite' version of the system's web interface for use on board ships where internet bandwidth restrictions may prevent the use of the full system. The 'lite' version allows Masters full access to documents and the ability to digitally sign B/Ls and, where necessary, issue a letter of protest.

In future, ESS plans to extend the system beginning with the tanker sector cross Europe, the US Gulf Coast and the Caribbean. The company also has plans to extend the system to liner and dry bulk shipping in 2011.

6.6   BILL OF LADING TERMS AND CONDITIONS

Refer again to **Appendix 13** which is the reverse of a typical B/L. Read through all the clauses and endeavour to understand as much as possible but in particular note clauses dealing with **carrier's responsibility.** Almost all countries have adopted one of three international conventions concerning the carriage of goods under a bill of lading and incorporated it into its own law under a title such as **Carriage of Goods by Sea Act**. These conventions, Rules they are called, will be dealt with in more detail in the lesson concerned with the **law of carriage** but for this lesson is it sufficient to be aware of the fact that such rules strictly lay down the carrier's obligations especially the extent to which the carrier's liability for loss or damage can be limited. It is limited because there has to be a point where the contract states "this is where the carrier's insurance policy stops so this is where the merchant's insurance policy should start".

Such conventions are also in existence for the international carriage of goods by road and by rail. The responsibility clauses in a B/L explain that when combined transport is involved, if damage or loss takes place other than at sea the convention covering the mode of transport involved (road or rail) will apply. When it is not known where the problem arose then the convention covering sea transport will always apply.

(N.B. the documents in the appendices of this lesson are those devised and printed by the Baltic and International Maritime Council (BIMCO) and are included as examples only. Most regular lines have their own B/Ls with their own house style in the top right hand corner and their own clauses on the back of the form. Whilst these may differ from line to line the fundamentals are similar because so many of the clauses have to comply with whichever international "Rules" apply).

6.6.1 Differences Between Liner and Charter Party Bills of Lading

A bill of lading has the same three essential elements whether it is a liner bill of lading or a charter party Bill of Lading. The major difference between them is in the function as evidence of a contract. The liner bill contains the contract within the written clauses printed on the bill. There are no other documents, except perhaps a tariff for the freight amount payable, that would be needed for a court to decide what rights and responsibilities each party had under the contract. But a Bill of Lading issued under a charter party will contain a clause stating that it was issued in accordance with the charter party and contained all the terms and conditions therein. So in the case of a dispute the two parties would also have to produce the charter party before the courts could come to a decision.

Clearly any party who buys the goods covered by a liner Bill of Lading while they are at sea and who receives the Bill of Lading in exchange for payment, will be able to see immediately what the terms of the contract are. But when the same transaction occurs under a voyage charter, whilst the Bill of Lading may change hands it is unlikely that the c/p will so the new owner of the bill may not be fully aware of the terms of the c/p. The law recognises this and in some cases extends protection to the new owner of the bill that was not available to the original holder because of some clause in the charter party itself.

6.7 SELF-ASSESSMENT AND TEST QUESTIONS

Attempt the following and check your answers from the text:

1. What are the dimensions of the most commonly used general purpose container?
2. Which were the first two European container services?
3. How many TEUs can the latest container ships carry?
4. What do the initials FCL and LCL stand for?

Having completed Chapter 6 attempt the following and submit you answers to your tutor.

1. Why has containerisation become the dominant method of liner cargo carrying in preference to other unitised methods or break-bulk?
2. What are the roles of an NVOCC?
3. Using a diagram to illustrate your answer, explain the progress of a Bill of Lading drawn to "order" from its blank state, via a documentary credit, to the completion of its life. Show also the progress of the goods themselves and of the funds used to pay for them.
4. Distinguish between Conferences, Consortia and Alliances and discuss the importance of the role of each form of co-operation today.

Chapter 7

THE PRACTITIONERS IN SHIPPING BUSINESS

7.1 INTRODUCTION – THE SIX "DISCIPLINES"

The basic 'disciplines' or areas of activity in the commercial shipping world which are now accepted as falling under the term '**Shipbroking**' can be conveniently divided into six categories of professional expertise.

They can be visualised as:

1. Buying (or selling) a ship – **Sale and Purchase Broking.**
2. Once purchased the ship has to be crewed, stored, maintained etc which involves **Ship Management,** after which it will require cargoes.
3. If the ship is a liner, the service must be marketed, the cargoes documented, arrangements made for loading and discharging these cargo all of which fall under the heading of **Liner Trades**, which will be carried out either within the liner operating company or by independent **Liner Agents.**
4. If the ship is a dry-cargo tramp, finding a cargo for the ship (or finding a ship for the cargo) will be the task of brokers in **Dry Cargo Chartering.**
5. A tanker will require a broker skilled in **Tanker Chartering.**
6. Whenever a dry-cargo tramp or a tanker calls at a port its interests will be entrusted to those who specialise in **Port Agency.**

There are, of course many other businesses involved in different aspects of commercial shipping. Two of these which interface most closely with the foregoing six 'disciplines' are the **exporters** and those that represent them, **freight forwarders**, both of these have their own professional institutes and are, therefore, outside the scope of this publication.

7.2 THE INSTITUTE OF CHARTERED SHIPBROKERS

In 1911, when the Institute was first formed, the world of shipping was a simpler place and the term 'shipbroker' in the United Kingdom referred to a person who arranged the chartering of ships, looked after them when they called in port and very occasionally became involved in sale and purchase negotiations. Liner services were in the hand of a relatively few major operators who used their own offices or exclusive 'loading brokers' to look after their business.

Since that time, the Institute has become a truly international organisation, retaining its title with all the tradition of professionalism it involves whilst fully recognising the way in which specialisation has created these six 'disciplines' within shipping business.

Furthermore it is recognised that the word 'shipbroker' means different things in different countries and in many there is a clear distinction made between brokers and agents. Indeed, several years ago the United Nations Conference on Trade and Development (UNCTAD) carried out a survey into the duties of the different intermediaries in shipping business in an attempt to find a single universal expression and eventually adopted the term "Shipping Agent" to cover everything including freight forwarders and forwarding agents. This survey was in connection with their devising a non-mandatory code of practice for shipping agents.

Although shipping business has become more specialised there are inevitably cases of overlapping with some people undertaking tasks which fall under more than one of the Institute's examination headings but in the interests of simplicity the six disciplines will be treated separately.

7.3   SHIP SALE AND PURCHASE

Almost all marine related property can be bought and sold, often for many millions of dollars, whether it be an order for a new vessel from a shipyard, an old ship to a scrapyard for demolition or a second-hand ship for further trading. It is this last named, the trade in second-hand ships, which forms the major part of the work of a ship Sale and Purchase broker.

Sale and Purchase broking is probably the most highly specialised sector of shipbroking, demanding as it does, all the usual attributes of a skilled negotiator with a wide range of knowledge of the technical aspects of ships.

It is customary for an S & P broker to be working specifically for one party or the other in a deal. When working for a potential buyer the broker has to be well versed in ship types as well as the vices and virtues of particular ship designs, builders and machinery in order to be able to advise clients appropriately. Advice on such matters as registration and classification even on sources of finance may even be called upon.

If working for a seller, the broker has to be able to place the ship before as many likely buyers via their brokers in the shortest possible time.

In both situations a thorough knowledge of the strength of the market is essential so that the buyer does not have to pay a penny more than the minimum necessary to secure the right ship and the seller gets the best price possible.

It is this market knowledge which enables leaders in the S & P field to act as **ship-valuers** when called upon for an expert opinion by such people as governments, financial institutions, insurance underwriters, probate lawyers, arbitrators and, of course, lawyers needing an expert witness.

As with many careers in shipbroking, ship Sale and Purchase demands many simultaneous skills. As well as an entrepreneurial flair and the technical knowledge the S & P broker needs a high degree of proficiency in gathering market information from every source possible. This has to include details of vessels in the market for sale and sales recently concluded as well as any factors such as freight market movements that might influence prices of ships. All this information has to be stored and in such a way that retrieval is rapid and accurate. Thus being up-to-date in the employment of computer technology is another vital faculty.

S & P brokers tend to specialise, some dealing exclusively in new ships where a close knowledge of the prices yards are quoting and the availability of building berths is needed together with knowing which yards are offering the best payment terms to buyers. Other brokers may operate at the opposite end of the scale and specialise in demolition when knowing which scrapyards are hungry for tonnage and which are over-stocked will dictate the prices available. Even among those working in the second hand for trading market may well specialise in tankers, or bulk carriers or in less regular areas such as oil exploration vessels, or smaller craft like dredgers or fishing vessels.

The sums of money involved in S & P are very great, but the ratio of deals which founder considerably outnumber those that succeed. An S & P broker must, therefore, be able to cope with a high level of frustration, although when a deal does succeed the rewards can be very attractive. S & P brokers' income arises from a commission on the price paid when the sale is concluded and all the brokers involved receive this commission from the seller. Rates of commission vary from 2½% for very small ships, down to 1% for larger sizes.

An S & P Broker is only as strong as his records allow him to be so that impeccable data, constantly up-dated is essential. Support staff are, therefore, vital and many Sale and Purchase brokers started their careers pounding the keys of a desk-top computer.

7.4   SHIP MANAGEMENT

Maintaining a ship as an operational unit requires a variety of specialist services. In a large shipowning enterprise these are carried out within the company. Where an owner has only a few ships (few in this context probably being somewhere between 1 and 10) it may be found more economical to use the services of a ship management company.

Ship management companies fall into two main categories, one being a shipowning company that manages its own ships and offers the same service to other shipowners. The other type are companies that have no ships of their own and solely provide ship management services to shipowners.

Whichever type its is the function is the same and falls under five main headings:

1.   Crewing

2.   Storing

3.   Technical

4.   Insurance

5.   Operations

Other services such as training and consultancy may also be offered.

Ship management appointments are individually negotiated according to the requirements of the principals but refer to **Appendix 15** which is a Standard Ship Management Agreement (SHIPMAN 2010) that sets out in greater detail all the different tasks a ship manager may be called upon to perform.

7.4.1   Crewing

It is not unusual for some shipowners to contract with a ship management company for crewing alone. This is particularly the trend among the traditional maritime nations where it is possible to register their ships under acceptable 'open registers'. One advantage of 'flagging out' (which is how this is often referred to) is that the national flag is retained but the regulations concerning the nationality of the ship's personnel are relaxed. Such shipowners, therefore, continue to carry out all other aspects of ship management but entrust the crewing to an offshore company. For the United Kingdom such places as the Isle of Man, Gibraltar and Bermuda have become popular, whilst several other countries, the Philippines is a typical example, provide a crew supply service as a form of 'invisible export'.

A crewing department will be responsible for checking the Certificates of Competency of the officers and take up references from previous employers. They will also ensure that the seamen are properly qualified for their positions in the ship.

Leave is often a significant factor in a seafarer's contract and the crewing department have to ensure that crew changes are carried out in such a way that ships are never delayed. All the travel arrangements for crew joining or leaving their ship will also be the responsibility of the crew department.

Last, but by no means least, ensuring all the crew receive their correct wages at the right time is a vital task for those in charge of crewing. Just as important (some might say more so) is ensuring that the portions of their wages to be sent to their dependents back home (called allotments) are promptly paid.

7.4.2 Storing

Stores fall into two classes, those items concerned with the crew and those concerned with the operation of the ship although some of the latter will be the responsibility of the technical department.

For the crew, the obvious items are food and drink. Still referred to a "victualling" by some traditionalists but now more usually called provisioning. This can be a demanding task as different nationalities have different food preferences, in many cases these are dictated as much by religious as by cultural needs. In many cases the ship's command has a high degree of control about buying supplies within budgetary limits but even in these cases close supervision is essential.

Other stores for the crew include such things as bed linen, cleaning materials, cooking utensils etc.

For the ship, one usually separates stores into two categories 'deck' and engine room'. Deck stores would include any materials needed for cargo operations such as ropes for lashing, timber for 'dunnage' etc. Specialist items such as tank cleaning and refrigeration materials as well as paints and other materials for routine maintenance also fall under the deck stores heading. Engine room stores will include such things as lubricants but spare parts are usually the responsibility of the technical people.

7.4.3 Technical

It is this department where one would be most likely to find former ship's officers with considerable sea-going experience. The technical department is often sub-divided into two sections, one under the management of the **marine superintendent**, who would be an ex-master mariner and the other managed by the **engineering superintendent,** who would be a former chief engineer.

The respective responsibilities of these two sections are probably self-evident. The engineers would be concerned with all the ship's machinery, probably including the cargo-handling equipment and possibly also the various electronic navigational devices. The marine superintendent would, in addition to his concern for the fabric of the ship, be responsible for keeping the classification surveys up to date.

The technical department also has one further vital rôle that is to respond instantly in the event of any ships under their control being involved in an accident. Technical department members are well accustomed to having to fly, perhaps to the other side of the world, at very short notice.

7.4.4 Insurance

Insurance is a shipowner's second biggest single item of cost so that the personnel dealing with this aspect need to be highly skilled. Marine insurance falls under two distinct headings. The first is the insuring of the ship itself, referred to as **hull and machinery insurance**. In view of the high value of ships today even a small reduction in the rate of premium can mean the saving of a substantial sum of money so that finding the best cover needs considerable expertise. The most famous provider of this type of insurance is **Lloyds of London** which is an organisation started in a City of London coffee house in the year 1687. Insurance with Lloyds is undertaken by individual **Underwriters** who group together in syndicates and can only be accessed through a **Lloyds broker.** Marine Insurance can also be arranged with insurance companies and it is for the ship manager's insurance department to ensure the best deal.

The other type of insurance is probably best described as **third party insurance** as it covers such things as claims against the ship by a port authority for damage done to a jetty; claims by ship's personnel for personal injury when negligence is alleged against the shipowner;

claims made by cargo owners when their goods do not arrive in the same "apparent good order and condition" as it was when loaded. In other words any claim made against the ship by another person or company.

For reasons which go right back into history, Lloyds of London were reluctant to offer this type of insurance and so shipowners joined together into groups and formed mutual associations which to this day are still referred to a **"P & I Clubs"**, their more formal title is **Protection and Indemnity Associations**, "Protection" being the legal help given to fight off unfair claims and "indemnity" covers repayment to the owners for any third party claims which have been legitimately made and settled. As there are inevitably several third party claims "in the pipeline" the Insurance department is always busy.

7.4.5   Operations

This is the department that runs the ship. It communicates with the commercial people and plans the voyages, decides upon bunkering, appoints port agents and generally does all that is necessary to convert the work of the other departments into a trading entity on the high seas.

Constantly close links have to be kept with the other departments. It would be hopeless if, for example, the operations department planned a long voyage just when the technical department had committed the ship to a spell in dry-dock.

In some companies, the commercial people are an integral part of the operations department so that the ultimate decision as to what trade to undertake are taken here and the brokers seeking cargoes would obtain their authority to negotiate business from the commercial people in the operations department.

The jobs in ship management vary from undemanding tasks to highly specialised work and many of the technical positions are the natural choice for ships' officers when the time comes for them to forsake the sea.

There is no set fee or percentage commission for ship management, the manager's remuneration is a matter for negotiation at the time of the appointment.

7.4.6   ISM Code

Regardless of whether a ship is managed by its true owner or a third party, the standard of management will have a profound effect upon the condition of the ship and how safely and effectively it is operated.

Bad shipowners and managers will run bad ships and it is those ships that are most often involved in incidents that lead to loss of life, injury and major pollution incidents. Even companies that would be expected to operate to the highest standards can allow bad practices to creep into their standard procedures.

It was in recognition of this fact the IMO incorporated a section into the SOLAS convention that requires ship operators to comply with a code of practice designed to reduce the number of dangerous incidents, this code is known as the International Safe Management Code (ISM).

Under the code operators have to have their management procedures on shore and at sea, audited and approved by inspectors acting on behalf of the flag state. If they satisfy the inspectors the company will be issued with a document of compliance (DOC) for the shore office and each ship will also be audited and inspected before being issued with a Safe Management Certificate (SMC).

Passing the inspections is not a mere formality and the company and its ships must be able to demonstrate full compliance with SOLAS, MARPOL and local regulations governing conditions and training onboard ships. All crew have to be properly trained for their jobs and in possession of appropriate certificates.

The ISM code was first introduced for companies operating passenger ships and tankers, bulkers followed soon after, and in July 2002 was extended to cover all ship types. Under the terms of the ISM code, every ship operator must appoint a **Designated Person Ashore (DPA)** whose role is to be a link between the ship and senior management. Usually the DPA is the senior superintendent but this is not cast in stone and individual companies may make their own arrangements. In very large management companies there may be several DPAs each dealing with a section of the fleet.

7.4.7 The ISPS Code

Or to give it its full name, the **International Ship and Port Facilities Security Code.** This is part of the SOLAS convention devised by the IMO as a response to concerns over security and terrorism.

The ISPS code is very much a reaction to the terrorist attacks on New York in September 2001 but it does include elements of two other problems, piracy and stowaways, that have been of concern for many years. Many within the shipping industry see the ISPS code as the product of politicians with little understanding of the way shipping works on a day-to-day basis. However it is a reality having come into force on July 1st 2004.

As the full name suggests the ISPS code works on two levels, ships (but only those over 500GT) and ports. Governments and maritime administrations must appoint **Recognised Security Organisations (RSOs)** to certify the security arrangements that have been made in ports, on ships and in the shore offices of shipping companies. Exactly what sort of organisation can become an RSO is entirely at the discretion of national governments. Within the UK, only the Maritime and Coastguard Agency (MCA) has the power to vet ships but many flag states have delegated the work to classification societies while Panama has awarded a monopoly to a specialist security company founded by former US intelligence and military people.

To comply with the code, ships and ports have to be subjected to a risk assessment after which a security plan is drawn up. The plan is then reviewed by the RSO and after a successful inspection and audit of the port or ship, a certificate is issued. After the coming into force of the code, port states will be able to deny entry to any ship which does not have a certificate, as well as ships coming from ports which have not been certified as complying with the code.

On a practical level both ports and ships will operate on a three stage security alert with the precautions taken dependant on the security threat assessed. This would mean that for the most part both would operate at the lowest level until some intelligence received makes a higher level desirable.

7.4.8 Liner Trades

The Institute refers to this sector of shipping business as Liner Trades rather than Liner Agency because whilst much of this work is carried out by independent liner agents, many liner operators now use departments in their own organisations to do this work. Whether "in house" or done by agents the work is the same and it will help if reference is made to **Appendix 16** which is a **Standard Liner Agency Agreement** a form devised by the international agents' association known as the **Federation of National Associations of Ship Brokers and Agents (FONASBA)** and recommended by the Baltic and International Maritime Council (BIMCO).

The agreement sets out in detail the duties of a liner agent, the important ones being:

(a)	Marketing and Sales	Sections	3.10 to 3.14
(b)	Documentation	"	3.15
(c)	Attending the Ship	"	3.20 to 3.29
(d)	Control of Equipment	"	3.30 to 3.38
(e)	Accounting and Finance	"	3.40 to 3.47

The Fonasba agreement is intentionally comprehensive in its summary of an agent's duties but there can be several variations. For example, the agent may only be called upon to deal with inward cargo arriving in the agent's territory or conversely only deal with outward cargo. The agent may even be involved only in sales and marketing (with no contact with the ship) which would be the case for an agent in, say, Switzerland, Austria, Zimbabwe or any other land-locked area; such agents are often referred to as **hinterland agents.**

Despite the rapid advance in electronic equipment, especially the computerisation of documentation and accounts, Liner work is the most labour-intensive sector of shipping business. That simple word "documentation" can involve the processing of many hundreds of separate consignments in a very short period of time. Each of these will involve several duties including, in the case of outward cargo, such items as taking cargo bookings including calculating the freight, checking the bills of lading, recording the container movement etc. With inward cargo there is the all-important task of ensuring the cargo is handed over to the legitimate bill of lading holder.

The prime advantage gained from containerisation was the reduction of the work to be done on the dockside but this inevitably meant radically increasing the amount of work in the liner agency office.

It will be seen from the foregoing that liner trades provides many types of work ranging from close links with the ship itself to jobs far remote from the dockside.

Independent liner agents' remuneration is a commission on the gross freight earned. In the days before containerisation there was a norm of 5% on outward freight (which was often considered to as 2½% for booking cargo and 2½% for handling cargo) and 2½% on inward freight. With the complex duties now involved with containers this simple formula has disappeared. It will be seen from the Schedule to the Standard Liner Agency Agreement that there can be negotiation around several aspects of the overall task of liner agency.

7.4.9 Dry Cargo Chartering

First assume that there is one broker representing the charterer looking for ships to carry his principal's cargoes and another broker representing the shipowner looking for cargoes to fill his principal's ships; this is not always so but is very often the case.

The brokers may be **exclusive brokers,** which means the principal channels all his business through that one broker whose job it is to advise the principal and to ensure the best possible deal in every case. Exclusivity may be total or may be exclusive to one part of the world so that the principal may use one broker in London another in New York another in Hong Kong and so on.

The other way is where the principal places his business through several brokers who are then referred to as **competitive brokers** because, of course, they compete with each other to bring suitable business to the principal.

There is another category that are referred to as **intermediate brokers** who may be part of a chain linking brokers on either side of them. This is far less common than it was because modern methods of communication make communication from one side of the world to another as easy as a local telephone call. An intermediate broker may also be used when that broker is the only one between the two principals.

The most exclusive broker is one who is part of the principal's company. This is quite common, for example almost all the 'London Greeks' have their own broking staff and many of the major grain companies have their own chartering departments.

When using an external broker the principal has what may be considered a dilemma. If using an exclusive broker, the principal will have a source of advice and service, a specific loyalty.

In cynical terms that loyalty is motivated by the knowledge that the entire connection is at risk if a poor service is given. You may argue, however, that in a given time there is a limit to how much of the market one broker can cover. On the other hand by placing his business in the hands of many brokers, the principal may feel that the market has been fully saturated and the incentive is for the brokers to work as hard and as fast as they can so as to be the first to the principal with suitable business. This does mean, however, that the principal is going to receive less in the way of objective advice. For example, in a competitive situation a broker is unlikely to be keen to offer advice such as "the market will be more in your favour if your delay fixing for a few days" which is certainly the type of advice an exclusive broker would provide in such circumstances.

Whether exclusive, competitive or intermediate and whether working on their own or for the charterer, all have one duty in common they have to **know their market**. That does not simply mean knowing the trade they are in but recognising, for example, how a sudden demand in a different part of the world for a totally different commodity can trigger a rise in rates in their own trade sooner or later.

Although the face-to-face negotiations on the 'floor' of the Baltic Exchange have been overtaken by electronic advances in communication, chartering is still essentially a person to person activity. It, therefore, demands a highly developed ability to inspire confidence. Fellow brokers will be looking for someone whose word they can trust whilst principals will, additionally, be seeking speed, efficiency and sound advice. One might add that stamina is also a necessity. Chartering is essentially an international activity with shipping markets in different time zones. New York, five hours behind London, Tokyo finishing work just as Europe's working day is starting so that a chartering broker cannot expect a nine-to-five job.

A brokerage (commission) of 1½% to each of the brokers involved in the fixture is usual in dry cargo chartering.

A chartering department does not consist entirely of brokers. Their back-up, generally referred to as the **post fixture department**, requires people who can translate the various notes, faxes, telexes etc into a written contract, the charter party, ready for principals to sign. Many brokers started their careers this way.

7.4.10   Tanker Chartering

Most of what has been said about dry cargo chartering applies to tankers except that tanker chartering is highly specialised. Many of the ships are limited to one commodity and the charterers are often major oil companies. The broker is generally between the two principals both of whom have a profound knowledge of the trade.

Urgency seems endemic in the crude oil world, the time lapse between business coming into the market and being fixed is usually very short. Thus the charterers tend to be more concerned with the sheer speed of finding the right ship. Exclusive brokers are rare in tankers.

There are, of course, many other liquids transported in tankers, each trade requiring its own particular expertise.

As with dry cargo chartering, 1¼% is the usual brokerage in tanker fixtures.

7.4.11   Port Agency

There is probably nowhere where the truth is more apparent that "time and tide wait for no man" than in Port Agency. It will be self evident that almost two thirds of all ships arrive and depart outside normal office hours. Nevertheless there is a special sort of job satisfaction in dealing physically with ships and their personnel.

When a tramp or a tanker calls at a port to load or discharge there s a considerable amount of work that has to be done before, during and after that call. The owner of the ship probably resides far away from the port concerned so that this work has to be entrusted to an agent who may be looked upon at the owner's 'extended right arm'.

The agent's first task will be to confer with the port authority who will demand payment (or a commitment to pay) large sums of money in dues for the use of the port and where appropriate, the dock. Duties may also include arranging a berth and will certainly entail liasing with the people involved in the actual loading or discharging who would be stevedores (dry cargo) or the jetty management (tankers). Then the tugs, pilot and mooring crew have to be ordered.

The agent usually meets the ship on arrival regardless of the time of day or night. In the past, except for a laconic exchange of radio telegrams, this would have been the first contact between the agent and the ship's Master (the Captain). Today, with the advances in radio-telephony, shipboard fax and telex machines, even mobile telephones there may have been several exchanges during which the arrangements made by the agent and the principal requirements of the ship will have been discussed. This first meeting is, however, an important one as there are several customs and immigration formalities to be dealt with. Important also will be the handing to the Captain the amount of cash he requires and almost as important, the handing over of the mail which will be eagerly awaited by the crew.

Delivery of stores and spares have to be arranged and cleared through customs, service engineers for ship's equipment may be needed and mundane tasks like organising laundry are all part of the agent's duties. Crew members may need medical or dental attention and it is even useful if the agent is skilled in the art of extricating from official custody any crew members who may have spent their time ashore unwisely. In fact there is no end to the activities in which the agent may be called upon to become involved and where the agent's local knowledge is invaluable.

Throughout this time the agent will be keeping the owner advised of the ship's progress and make any recommendations which might assist in the all-important task of turning the ship round in the shortest possible time.

The job is not finished when the ship has sailed. The parties will probably require a **Statement of Facts,** which is a record of how every minute of the ship's time in port was spent. From this the amount of demurrage or despatch, if any, will be calculated.

The final job, is to gather together all the accounts that have been paid on the ships behalf and compile the **disbursement account** for submission to the owner. A wise agent will have obtained substantial funds in advance and the disbursement account will denote what balance the agent requires or must refund to the owner.

The agent's remuneration is usually a fee, often based upon a tariff. These tariffs were at one time mandatory, some even had governmental support, but today in many countries any form of price-fixing is prohibited. The tariff is therefore no more than a guide and **Appendix 17** is an example of a scale of agency fees for dry cargo ships as currently produced by the Institute of Chartered Shipbrokers (this publication may eventually be disallowed by the European Commission). It will be seen that the scale tends to be based upon the size of the ship plus any more complex duties the agent may have to perform. Whilst the size of the ship may not determine the actual amount of work involved it has always been accepted that such scales reflect the concept that the larger the ship the greater the agent's responsibility, plus some element of 'what the traffic will bear'.

A problem a port agent may often face is that of conflict of interest. Quite frequently the charterers of a tramp or tanker will stipulate that the owner must appoint agents nominated by the charterers. For convenience in negotiations this is often referred to as **"charterers agents"** which gives an erroneous impression. In the eyes of the law the agent represents the owners of the ship (or the disponent owners if the ship is on time charter). It is perhaps easier to think in terms of the agent representing 'the ship'.

One may ask why charterers demand this right of nomination and there are several reasons. For example, in the case of tanker charterers there may be a combination of two reasons, first, is the need to maximise the efficient use of the oil jetty and having only one source of information about ships' positions from a known expert in whom they have confidence is valuable. Secondly, oil installations are extremely vulnerable places and limiting the number of people seeking access makes security easier. In other trades the owner might otherwise choose an agent with whom the charterer is anxious not to share knowledge of his business.

Not surprisingly in all cases of "charterers' agents" the charterer expects some *quid pro quo* from the agent in exchange for the nomination. The obvious one which in no way undermines the agent's loyalty to the owner is that the charterer will receive just as steady a stream of information about the ship's loading or discharging progress as the owner. Also the charterer can be confident that the handling of his cargo is in expert hands. Very occasionally the agent will be presented with a dilemma when a situation arises when the law of agency demands that the agent has to take the owner's side against the very people who insisted upon that agent being appointed. In such cases the agent's professionalism is rigorously tested.

As was mentioned earlier, the only occasion when the agent does not represent the owners of the ship is when the ship is on time charter when the agent represents the time charterer (the disponent owner) and under these circumstances the agent is expected to carry out all the normal duties for the ship. There are occasions when the owners want something extra done when it is quite usual for the owners to make an arrangement with the agent working for the time charterer to do this work which again is quite in order unless a conflict of interest is likely to arise.

There are rare occasions when the shipowner is simply not happy with the agent appointed by the charterer and in such circumstances the owner will appoint a **supervisory agent** sometimes called a **protecting agent** who will oversee the work done by the charterers appointed agents and will carry out any duties that the owner is not prepared to entrust to the charterers agent. You will see that the appointment of a supervisory agent is catered for in the scale of agency charges.

All the duties of a port agent are also carried out by a port-based liner agent and these are incorporated in the liner agency contract and are set out in clauses 3.20 to 3.29 of the Standard Liner Agency Agreement (**Appendix 16**).

Because of the essentially practical aspects of port agency work it can be the best possible basis for a career in any other branch of shipping business.

7.5   Conclusion

Except where any of the foregoing six 'disciplines' is carried out by a department in the principal's own office there is a principal/agent relationship and there have been occasional references to "the law of agency"; the legal aspects of this will be dealt with in a later Chapter.

Reference has also been made at different times to "skill"; "the ability to inspire confidence"; "professionalism" which tend to emphasise the point that an agent is only of value to a principal so long as he or she can do the job more efficiently that the principal could do it himself and to do the job as well or better than any other agent in the same locality. It has often been said the "the world does not owe a shipbroker a living".

7.6   TEST QUESTIONS

Having completed Chapter Seven, attempt the following and submit your answers to your tutor:

1.   Imagine you are a shipowning Principal wishing to appoint an Agent for ONE of the following tasks:

   (a)   Ship Sale and Purchase work

   (b)   Ship Management

   (c)   Liner Trade services

   (d)   Chartering Broker

   (e)   Tanker Broker

   (f)   Port Agent

   Give reasons why you would prefer to set up an 'In-House' department or appoint an independent agent for ONE of the above disciplines and describe the personal and professional qualities which you would be seeking.

2.   Repeat the exercise for a separate task within the range (a-f).

Chapter 8

MARITIME GEOGRAPHY

8.1 INTRODUCTION

The previous seven Chapters have set out the pieces and moves in the commercial game of shipping, this Chapter deals with the board upon which the game is played.

Readers should have a simple atlas to hand for reference, the object of this Chapter is to highlight those elements which have an influence upon maritime matters.

In conventional geography the tendency is to study the land and to look upon the oceans as merely the blue areas that separate the land masses. In shipping, the interest is concentrated upon the seas, the coastal areas and any other geographical factors which impinge upon the life of persons in the business of shipping.

8.2 OCEANS AND SEAS

One often hears reference to "the seven seas" which is a misnomer because there are very many "seas" for example the North Sea, the Mediterranean Sea, South China Sea, Red Sea etc. The "seven" refers to the seven **oceans**. Study **Appendix 18** which is an outline map of the world. There will be seen the:

> North Atlantic Ocean
> South Atlantic Ocean
> North Pacific Ocean
> South Pacific Ocean
> Indian Ocean
> Arctic Ocean
> Antarctic or Southern Ocean

8.3 CONTINENTS

Note also there are seven main land masses or **continents** which in descending order of area are:

> Asia
> Africa
> North America
> South America
> Europe
> Antarctica
> Australia

8.3.1 Latitude and Longitude

It will be noted also on the outline map of the world that some straight lines have been drawn but in order to consider the significance of those lines it is important first of all to understand how a mariner identifies **position** anywhere on the earth.

To establish a position on the surface of the earth it is necessary to refer to a universally accepted grid of lines which run East to West which are **Parallels of Latitude** and lines running North to South, from North Pole to South Pole, which are **Meridians of Longitude**.

There are 360 meridians of longitude each one being referred to as a **degree** and each degree is sub-divided into **60 minutes** and each minute into **60 seconds.** Refer now to the map and note the line running North to South cutting through England; it actually runs through a suburb of London called **Greenwich** where a famous astronomical observatory was once established. This line is nought degrees **(0°)** longitude and is referred to as the **Greenwich Meridian**. Longitude is therefore referred to as so many degrees, minutes and seconds East or West (of Greenwich).

The earth revolves on its axis once every twenty-four hours and mental arithmetic will reveal that the apparent movement of the sun in one hour will be 15° of longitude (360° ÷ 24hrs). This change of time with East-West travel will be referred to later when **time zones** are discussed.

It will be apparent that 180° West is the same as 180° East and further arithmetic will disclose that 180° of longitude is 12 hours (180 ÷ 15). This is why, on the map, there is another vertical line (although one which is not completely straight) this is the **International Date Line**. If you cross this line from East to West the date is put back so that there are two consecutive days of the same name and so if you cross it in the reverse direction a day is apparently 'lost'. The reason why this line is 'bent' is to coincide with national boundaries so as to avoid confusion for the populations of those countries.

In the case of **latitude**, the 0° line is the **Equator** positions are referred to as so many degrees North or South; therefore the North and South Poles are 90° North and South Latitude respectively. The parallels of latitude provide another purpose because it has been universally accepted that distances at sea should be referred to in **nautical miles**. A nautical mile is **one minute (1')** of latitude so that if you travel 60 miles due north or south your latitude will have increased by one degree (1°).

It should be firmly established in your mind that **speed** at sea is referred to as **knots** which is **nautical miles per hour.** (NEVER "knots per hour")

8.3.2   Charts

Because the earth is a sphere, depicting it on a flat page presented map-makers with a problem. There are several examples of solutions to this problem known as **projections**. The projection that you are most likely to encounter in shipping business is the **Mercator Projection,** named after the inventor, a sixteenth century geographer. Mercator's projection is based upon the idea of wrapping a cylinder of paper round the globe and projecting an image of the world's features on it. Its principal advantage is that it shows compass directions correctly which is vital for navigators, its disadvantage is the way that it distorts sizes because the further away from the equator, the larger things appear.

This is no problem for navigators because they measure distances according to the latitude scale, along the edge of the chart, which distorts at the same rate as other features.

Today a new ship is likely to be equipped with an electronic chart display and information system or ECDIS as it is known for short. This equipment permits the chart and radar information to be combined on a single screen assisting navigation and the chart information can be updated automatically using data broadcast over satellites. All ships are obliged by SOLAS to use official charts produced by national hydrographic bodies such as the UKHO. Electronic chart systems that can link data from a ship's GPS equipment to a chart displayed on a computer screen have been available for more than a decade now and in future a system known as ECDIS (electronic chart display and information system) will become mandatory under SOLAS on all ships. An ECDIS must be able to display official ENCs (electronic navigation charts) but it can also make use of unofficial charts that are produced for commercial purposes.

8.3.3 Time

Reference was made earlier to the way the rotation of the earth means that the time of day varies according to where you are situated.

Appendix 19 shows the different **time zones**. Most time zone charts use as the datum, the time of noon on the Greenwich (London) meridian known as **Greenwich Mean Time (GMT)** and although, for convenience, seafarers personal time pieces are altered as time zones are crossed, navigation is always carried on the basis of GMT. This follows the tradition established in the pre-electronic age when the ship's chronometer (a very accurate clock) was set at GMT and never altered.

Countries such as those in Europe and North America, experience a significant change in the amount of daylight depending upon the season i.e. long nights and short days in winter and the reverse in the summer. These countries change their clocks by advancing them one hour in the spring, this is often referred to as "Daylight Saving Time"; the clocks are put back again in the Autumn (Fall). (Memory aid for changing clocks – "Spring forward, fall back")

Time zones and any clock changes are important considerations for those in shipping business especially if negotiating a charter with the time limits which are an essential part of offers and counter offers. For example, the New York shipping market is five hours later than the London market so that a London broker wishing to impart some interesting piece of market gossip to his friend in New York would be ill-advised to do so as soon as the Londoner gets into the office (say 0930 London time) because his opposite number in New York will be fast asleep (0430 New York Time). On the other hand the London broker's Japanese counterpart may be on his way home as it will be 1830 (6.30 pm) in Tokyo. A country like the USA has its own problems because it has five time zones within its own borders.

8.3.4 Tides and Currents

The rise and fall of the tide are often important in shipping. Tides rise and fall as a result of the gravitational pull of the moon acting in conjunction with the earth's own gravity. In most places in the world there are two high tides and two low tides in each day. The gravitational pull of the sun also has an effect and when the sun's pull is working with the moon, the high tides are very high and the low tides very low; the are called **spring tides**. When the sun and the moon are not pulling together the **tidal range** is at its least and these are called **neap tides**. Spring tides occur approximately twice each month.

The difference between high and low tides varies from place-to-place. For example, in London the tidal range is about 6.5 metres between high and low on spring tides and 4.3 metres range on neap tides. Compare this with the Bay of Fundy (the inlet between Nova Scotia and New Brunswick in Canada) where the spring tide range is over 15 metres between high and low tide. Conversely in the Mediterranean the greatest range between high and low tide is less than a metre.

As the time of the rotation of the moon round the earth is not an exact day, the times of tides vary. This can be calculated precisely so that almost all the world's ports publish **tide tables.** Such tables can be of vital interest to shipping because the rise and fall of tides determines how deep the water will be in the port area during the course of the day and so dictates when ships can reach the port and when the water is too shallow to accommodate the ship's draft.

In some ports, the draft is deep enough at high water to allow the ship to enter but when the tide falls the ship goes aground, hence the abbreviation mentioned in the chartering terms (**Appendix 8**) NAABSA – Not Always Afloat But Safe Aground. The effect of neap tides can have a serious effect on NAABSA ports because a ship near the upper limit of the permitted draft may enter without difficulty on a reasonably high tide but may become trapped for several days if the neap tide occurs while the ship is at that berth.

One way that some ports have overcome the tidal problem and ensured that ships stay afloat throughout their stay is to construct **enclosed docks** which are large basins cut into the land which can be sealed from the tide by **lock gates.** Although this is an expensive solution the advantages outweigh the costs. Not only can large ships be accommodated without any risk of their going aground but as the water level within the dock is constant, the level of the ship relative to shore appliances also remains constant. The disadvantage is that the size of the dock and particularly the dimensions of the locks at its entrance impose a maximum size limitation which in many cases is far smaller than today's ships. It has been this tendency towards the ever-increasing size of ships that has caused many enclosed dock systems to become redundant.

Locks are simply short sections of canals with water-tight gates at each end. The water level is adjusted via sluice gates to match the level at the entrance side when that set of gates is opened. After the ship(s) have entered the lock, the gates are closed and the water level again adjusted, this time to match the level on the exit side when the exit gates are opened and the ships proceed. As well as being used to enter enclosed docks, locks can also be used to 'lift' ships over high ground in canal systems.

8.3.5   Currents

The effect of the flow of tides inevitably creates **currents**, that is the flow of water sometimes at appreciable speeds which can cause problems in estuaries (the wide entrances to rivers) and through narrow gaps between pieces of land. There is, for example, a gap called the Pentland Firth which is between the northern tip of the Scottish mainland and the Orkney Islands. The tidal current through this gap can flow at eight knots or more and some old small coasters in the past could find themselves making no headway against this flow.

There are other currents which are not related to tides but to the effect of prevailing winds. One of the most powerful of such currents is the **Gulf Stream** which flows diagonally across the Atlantic Ocean from South West (the Gulf of Mexico) to the North West corner of Europe. As this water is warm it has the effect of producing a mild climate in the British Isles and parts of North West Europe.

Various other factors play their part in the creation of ocean currents which can effect a navigator's task but fortunately the subject has been well researched and reference books produced which tell seafarers what currents to expect in any part of the world.

8.3.6   Wind and Weather

Far less predictable is the weather and even though modern ships are not dependent upon the wind as sailing ships were, very high winds and rough sea conditions are still responsible for delays, damage and actual loss of ships. Particularly severe are the tropical storms which have different names in different parts of the world but have the same devastating effect. In the area around the **Gulf of Mexico and the Caribbean Islands** they are called **hurricanes** which occur between June and November with the most severe time between August and October. In the **Far East** they are **typhoons** for which the season is May to January with maximum frequency between July and October. In the **Indian Ocean** they are **cyclones** which have various seasons in different parts of the region but the worst periods are during the middle and at the end of the year. When these cyclones reach the north-west corner of Australia they assume the somewhat whimsical name of "willy-willies".

These severe storms have been responsible for the loss of ships and in recent years, large bulk carriers have been the worst victims, a typical example being the bulk carrier "Derbyshire" which was loaded with iron ore and was lost with her entire crew in a typhoon. The disaster occurred so quickly that there was not even time for the ship to send a distress signal on the radio.

Even moderately strong winds and high seas can delay shipping and the strength of the wind is still referred to according to the **Beaufort Wind Scale** which was developed by Admiral Beaufort about 150 years ago. The Beaufort Scale is reproduced in **Appendix 20** from which it will be noted that the state of the sea at different wind strengths is also included.

The extent to which adverse weather can affect the performance of a ship can cause a problem when a time charter is involved. It will be recalled that the **speed and consumption** is an important term in a time charter because the time taken on a voyage and the amount of fuel consumed both have a considerable financial effect to the charterer. This has often been the cause of dispute between charterer and owner especially if the charterer has reason to doubt the accuracy of the entries in the ship's logbook. In more recent times disputes have been reduced by reference to meteorological specialists who maintain accurate records of weather conditions all over the world. Such **ocean routeing** companies can be engaged to advise the best route to avoid severe weather and in certain time charters the owners insist on an ocean routeing company being employed. The routeing companies keep up a two-way communication with ships which enables the masters to be advised of any changes in course needed to avoid storms while the routeing company receives feedback as to the actual weather conditions the ships are experiencing.

8.3.7   Ice

A hazard in some parts of the world, particularly the northern hemisphere is the risk of ships being immobilised through the sea freezing in winter. Most at risk are ports where timber is traditionally loaded in the Baltic Sea, White Sea and Gulf of Bothnia also ports in North West Russia. Another vulnerable area is the River St Lawrence and the whole of the Great Lakes. From time to time there is an air of concern verging on panic that some ships, which arrived late at Great Lakes ports, becoming trapped in the Great Lakes system because it is necessary to close the St Lawrence Seaway to avoid the lock gates being damaged by the formation of ice.

Port authorities in the Scandinavian region and in the St Lawrence River endeavour to keep some open water by the use of **ice breakers** which are specially designed ships some of which, notably those owned by the former Soviet Union, are nuclear powered. By this means some of the Scandinavian timber ports stay open all year round except during a particularly severe winter and in the St Lawrence, every effort is made to maintain access as far up river as Montreal.

Still a danger (although advance warnings and radar have lessened the hazard) are **icebergs**. These are pieces of the polar ice-cap which break free and can float into the shipping lanes. As in the days of the *"Titanic"* the North Atlantic is the area of greatest risk.

The Baltic and International Maritime Council (BIMCO) offer a service reporting weekly on the ice conditions. How to meet the problem of ice risk is covered in charter parties by an **ice clause** and an example of such a clause is shown in **Appendix 21**.

8.4   WATERWAYS

Two types of waterways are important in shipping, natural waterways such as rivers, estuaries and creeks and man-made waterways which are usually called canals.

Natural waterways provide the shelter from the weather that ships need when loading and discharging. Many major cities owe their very existence to the access afforded by a river. London is a typical example because it was founded by the Romans when they invaded Britain nearly two thousand years ago. London was as far up the river Thames that they could travel by ship and also the lowest point at which the river could be forded (crossed on foot).

Many other towns and cities began as ports, some typical examples are:

> Buenos Aires – River Plate
> Calcutta – Hooghly River
> Hamburg – River Elbe
> Lisbon – River Tagus
> Montreal – River St Lawrence
> Philadelphia – Delaware River

Man-made waterways are constructed for one of two reasons, either to reduce sailing time on a regularly used route, to cut off a corner so to speak, or to provide access to an inland region.

The most ambitious waterway to achieve access to a major inland region was the **St Lawrence Seaway (Appendix 22)**. Constructed in the 1950s, it enables ocean-going ships to penetrate North America as far west as Chicago and Duluth in the USA and Fort William in Canada which gives direct access to the vast grain producing areas in the centre of the North American Continent. Previously the St Lawrence was only navigable up to Montreal, although the Lachine Canal was dug which by-passed the Lachine Rapids and allowed small ships to reach Lake Ontario but the Niagara Falls prevented any further access. The Seaway, by a complex system of locks and canals opened up the Great Lakes to ocean ships with a draft limitation of 27 feet but many charters operate on the basis of loading to Seaway draft in the Lakes and then completing in Montreal.

A much older canal, constructed at the end of the 19th century, is the Manchester Ship Canal in North West England. This was principally designed to enable the ocean-going ships of the day to reach the industrial heartland of that part of the country. One of the main industries, due to its particularly humid climate and plentiful supplies of coal, was the spinning and weaving of cotton imported from the southern United States. The canal's size limitations no longer permit its use by deep sea liners but small ships still regularly call at ports along the canal as well as Manchester itself.

The first canal to reduce sailing time was the **Kiel Canal** which joins the North Sea to the Baltic sea **(Appendix 23)**. When it was first constructed in 1784 it was originally intended for use by the German navy which sought to avoid the stormy waters north of Denmark. In 1895 it was slightly re-routed and deepened to its present 11 metres and has since then been regularly used by commercial shipping.

Far more significant was the construction of the **Suez Canal** joining the Mediterranean Sea to the Red Sea **(Appendix 24).** You will have read in another Chapter what a tremendous change this shortening of the distance between Europe and South Asia had upon the trade with the Indian sub-continent and beyond, even to the extent of being the cause of the formation of first Liner Conference. Work on the Suez canal was commenced in 1859 and it was officially opened ten years later. Fortunately the difference in water levels between the Mediterranean and Red Seas never exceeds 1.25 metres so that there was no need to construct locks and thus it has been possible to widen and deepen the canal from time to time in tune with the increase in ship sizes.

More recent was the construction of the **Panama Canal** linking the Atlantic Ocean with the Pacific Ocean **(Appendix 25)**. People were toying with the idea of cutting through this very slim isthmus which links North America to South America as early as 1550 but it was not until 1908 that the United States Government obtained the concession to start construction and the canal was opened in 1914. Although the canal uses existing lakes and creeks for much of its length, there is a difference in sea levels between the two oceans. Furthermore the land rises considerably so that three sets of locks had to be constructed to raise and lower ships a total of 26 metres.

The Panama Canal is of vital importance for trade between Europe, America and the Far East as well, of course, for traffic between the East and West coasts of the USA itself.

8.5   PORTS

Ports form the beginning and end of a sea voyage and form the interface between the ship and the shore. Even today, ports vary widely in their degree of development and sophistication. Some are simply a reasonably sheltered inlet, creek or river mouth where a ship may lie at anchor and load or discharge into barges which ply between ship and shore. At the other end of the scale are highly developed systems of quays and terminals with the most technologically advanced systems of moving the cargo to or from the side of the ship and into or out of its holds or tanks. There are, of course an infinite variety of ports between those two extremes.

It is always interesting to discover why a port has developed in a particular location. In many cases, as was mentioned earlier in this Chapter, a port and then a town grew up because of the geographical convenience of the position. A position sheltered from rough seas plus a good depth of water has often been the reason for a port to develop; Southampton on England's south coast is a typical example of this.

In many cases the original purpose of the port has long since disappeared but because its original use created a centre of population the town has remained and new uses have been found for the port. Several ports in the United Kingdom are like this because they were first developed simply as coal export outlets but remain as ports with several functions even though coal exporting has almost entirely disappeared.

Ports are still created as outlets for particular commodities and the exports of coal and iron ore from places like Australia have prompted the building of huge automated loading terminals in places which may have no population nearby but which have the right amount of shelter and depth of water and are conveniently located as near as possible to the mineral extraction.

Mineral extraction is not the only reason for creating a port even where there is little or no local trade. Containerisation has seen a massive increase in ship sizes which means a commensurate increase in daily running costs. This encourages shipowners to make their voyage distances as short as possible and to depend upon feeders or land transport to deliver cargo to many places rather than call at several ports. This has resulted in development of ports like Felixstowe in England which has an almost entirely agricultural hinterland but is well positioned to despatch containers all over the UK and to work with feeders to many places on the European mainland.

Singapore, similarly has a very limited land area behind it but its strategic position enables its trans-shipment traffic to keep it always among the top three container ports in the world. The port of Colombo in Sri Lanka, originally built to serve the local tea, rubber and coconut trades, now has ambitions to emulate Singapore as a trans-shipment port for the Indian sub-continent region.

The owner of a less specialised ship, the general purpose 'tramp' has many factors to consider when contemplating a port involved in charter negotiations as many of these affect the financial outcome, some may even deter him from accepting. Typical among such considerations would be:

1.   The location of the loading port relating to the ship's present position (i.e how far would the ship have to sail in ballast to reach the loading port).

2.   Limitations such as:

    (a) Depth of water on approaches and alongside.
    (b) Size of locks if any.
    (c) Tides.
    (d) Any adverse weather problems.
    (e) Political problems.

3.   Costs, ports vary considerably in port, pilotage towage and other charges.

4.   Cargo handling systems and working schedules.

5. Facilities for repairs, and/or servicing of equipment.

6. Availability and cost of stores especially bunker fuel.

7. The location of discharging port relating to obtaining the ship's next cargo (again how far to sail in ballast).

8. A trustworthy agent.

8.6   GEOGRAPHY OF TRADE

8.6.1   Raw Materials

Readers of this Section should endeavour to obtain copies of shipping journals which report on chartering "fixtures" (An example is in **Appendix 26**). These will quickly display the major routes for raw materials especially the basic commodities.

Note that **coal** moves from such places as:

USA (e.g. Hampton Roads in Virginia) to Europe and to Japan and China.

South Africa (e.g. Richards Bay) also to the Far East and to Europe.

Australia (e.g Newcastle – New South Wales and Hay Point – Queensland) particularly to Japan.

Grain is shipped from such places as:

Canada (e.g. the Great Lakes and Montreal) to Europe.

USA (e.g. Gulf of Mexico ports) to Europe and to the Far East.

West Coast North America (e.g. Vancouver) to Japan.

South America (e.g. Buenos Aires in Argentina) to Europe and to the Far East.

Iron Ore is shipped from such places as:

Canada (e.g. ports in the province of Quebec), to Europe.

South America (Brazilian ports) to Europe and the Far East.

Australia (e.g Dampier – Western Australia) mainly to Japan and China.

Oil is shipped from such places as:

The Middle East, that is the countries around the Gulf between Iran and Saudi Arabia called by some the Arabian Gulf and by others the Persian Gulf and some the Middle East Gulf; politics influences the choice of name. These exports go to Europe, the Far East and many other places.

Latin America (e.g. Venezuela) to Europe and the Far East.

West Africa (Nigeria) mainly to Europe.

United Kingdom (Sullom Voe in the Shetland Isles).

Russia to Europe and the US. Shipment is presently done from terminals in the Baltic Sea and in future new terminals are expected to be built in the Arctic area. Russia has massive oil reserves and is expected to become a major exporter. This has led to a demand for ice-strengthened tankers and currently around half of all new tanker tonnage has an ice class of some type.

The oil from the North Sea oil fields (which are also drilled by the Netherlands and by Norway) produce a particularly light crude oil which provides quite different products and by-products from those derived from, for example the much heavier Middle East Crudes so that European oil-rich countries both export and import crude oil so that all the chemicals and other by-products can be produced in their refineries.

Other raw materials include:

Fertilizers	Timber	Other Forest Products
Agricultural Products	Cement	Minerals
Iron and Steel	Other Metals	Chemicals

These are examples and you should research into other seaborne trades specially those to and from their own locality.

8.6.2   Manufactured Goods

The trade in manufactured or semi-manufactured goods, liner trades, follow quite different routes. Whilst the movements in raw materials tend to be predominantly North to South, general cargo routes are predominately East to West. For example Transatlantic between Europe and North America, Transpacific, e.g. West Coast USA to and from the Far East, and Europe to and from the Indian sub-continent, South East Asia and the Far East.

The world-wide container trade, which is almost entirely made up of manufactured or partly manufactured goods, is expected to reach one billion (1,000,000,000) tonnes per annum by the early years of the 21st century.

Cars and Trucks, carried in specially designed ships, are also now a global trade especially since motor manufacturers construct vehicles in other countries as well as their home base. The network of lines carrying cars and trucks is almost as complex as that of the container trade.

8.7   SELF-ASSESSMENT AND TEST QUESTIONS

Attempt the following and check your answers from the text:

1.   From an atlas locate at least ten "seas" apart from those mentioned in the text.

2.   The location of the headquarters of TutorShip is:

510 30' 58" North Latitude and 00 05' 01" West Longitude

Determine the longitude and latitude of your present location and check the answer with a knowledgeable local person.

3.   Try to tune your radio to a shipping weather forecast and listen particularly to reference to the force of the wind.

4.   Look in your newspaper and see if, alongside the weather forecast, there is a prediction of when high tides will be on that day.

Having completed Chapter Eight, attempt the following and submit you assignment to your tutor.

1.   You have a bulk cargo to move from North West Europe to Australia. Taking as many factors as possible into consideration, discuss the advantages and disadvantages of the possible routes.

2.   Imagine you are a shipowner contemplating the carriage of a bulk raw material from the West Indies to Chicago. The charterer wants supplies spread evenly over the year. What problems do you envisage?

Chapter 9

ACCOUNTS

9.1 INTRODUCTION

The famous Greek shipowner, Aristotle Onassis, is once alleged to have said that "successful shipowning was 95% careful accounting". This view is perhaps reinforced when one considers how many prosperous Far East shipowners are, by background, financiers or bankers.

It is self-evident that if an enterprise spends more than it earns, it will not survive; unless, of course, it is subsidised from public funds such as a country bus service or an island ferry service which is run as a social service.

Whether intended as a profitable business or as a non-profit making undertaking it is necessary to produce records of income and expenditure more usually known as a "set of books". This Chapter does not attempt to be a training course in accounting or bookkeeping but seeks to provide an introduction into the basics of accounting matters in a shipping business context.

9.2 ACCOUNTING

Accounting is the complete package of all the planning and managing of the company's financial affairs. Bookkeeping is a part of accounting, its particular objects being:

1. To have a permanent record of all mercantile transactions.

2. To show the effect of each transaction and the combined effect of all the transactions upon the financial position of the enterprise.

The rest of the accounting process involves many other things including, for example, deciding what commercial activities are viable (i.e. practicable from an economic point of view), deciding what capital items to purchase, raising money to purchase capital items, ensuring there is always sufficient money (cash) available to pay accounts at the correct time, investing surplus money so that it earns interest when not needed for immediate use. In fact anything which affects the financial position of the company comes under the heading of "accounts".

9.3 CAPITAL

Capital in bookkeeping terms is the total value of all the company's **fixed assets**, **investments**, and **cash**, these are called **assets.** Assets are divided into fixed assets and current assets.

Capital is the money required to start a commercial enterprise and more may be required from time to time to maintain its momentum or to increase the range of its activities.

Capital is needed for two basic purposes, first to purchase any items of machinery or equipment i.e. anything which will become a **fixed asset** such as, for example, a ship. Capital is also required to run the company, to pay wages and salaries, to settle bills for rent etc this sort of capital is called **working capital.**

Capital, for whatever purpose, has to be **raised**. This can be by means of letting other people become owners of part of the company which will be dealt with later in this Chapter when the structure of companies is discussed. Or, capital can be raised by borrowing the money from a bank or other financial institution, this is often referred to as **loan capital** and the borrower has to pay the lender **interest** at an agreed percentage per annum as well as repay the loan in agreed instalments.

Interest is the percentage of the capital sum that the borrower pays the lender for the use of the money borrowed. Although borrowing among individuals may be frowned upon, borrowing and lending are an essential element of *commercial* life. A company may find it has, temporarily, more cash than it needs for its immediate purposes and will deposit this with a bank so that it earns interest rather than lying idle. On another occasion it may have a temporary shortage of ready cash which will require a short-term loan from the bank known as an **overdraft;** a well-run company can usually negotiate a substantial overdraft facility.

There is a special type of borrowing which is often used for buying such things as houses and **ships.** This is by means of a **mortgage** which is the name of the deed (agreement) signed by the owner of the ship which, in exchange for the loan of a substantial amount of its cost, pledges the ship as security for the loan. This means that if the owner, the borrower, cannot meet the loan repayments and interest charges the lender may **foreclose** on the mortgage which means the lender can take possession of the ship. It is important to note that it is the borrower who **gives** the mortgage to the lender so that the borrower, the shipowner, becomes the mortgagor and the bank or finance house who **takes** the mortgage becomes the mortgagee.

A ship, or a building or a piece of machinery is capital and is classified as a **fixed asset.** Many companies invest in associated businesses, for example a shipping company might invest in part of a terminal operating company. Such an investment, indeed any *long-term* investment, will also be classified as a fixed asset.

9.4 CREDIT

Goods and services in the commercial world are most frequently provided without immediate payment; the recipient of the goods is given **credit.** A most important function of bookkeeping is keeping track of this credit. When goods and/or services are supplied, an **account** is rendered, this may be called an **invoice.** This document gives details of the goods or services provided and the cost; there may be a reference on the invoice as to when payment should be made or the length of time permitted between supply and payment may be by mutual agreement between the two parties.

Those who have supplied goods or services and who are awaiting settlement of their invoices are **creditors.** When the accounts are paid, the outgoing money is referred to as **expenditure.**

Those who owe money against outstanding invoices are **debtors,** when they have settled their accounts the money received is referred to as **income** or **revenue.**

The function of bookkeeping is to record all outgoing and incoming accounts which are entered in **ledgers.** In years gone by these would have been large heavy books into which transactions were recorded in ink. Most major enterprises now keep all accounts by computer but the word "ledger" is still often use to refer to those parts of the system that record the issuing and/or receiving of invoices. The bookkeeping process then records when the invoices are settled and the traditional name for that record quite logically was the **cash book,** in computerised systems sometimes also referred to as **transaction lists.**

From time to time the totals of money received and money paid out and the totals of money owed by debtors and money owed to creditors are calculated and the result is either a **profit** or a **loss.** In most countries, such an account is simply called the **Profit and Loss Account** and such an account, covering the sum of all the transactions during the past year, has to be produced annually by limited companies, it has to be checked by an independent accountant called an **auditor** and then submitted to the government; it may eventually become available for public scrutiny.

At the same time as the Profit and Loss Account is published another account called the **Balance Sheet** also has to be produced. The Balance Sheet sets out the value of all the company's assets and liabilities at the end of that particular trading year. **Assets** as referred to earlier are the value of goods, investments, money due to be received from debtors and cash the company has at that moment in time. **Liabilities** include moneys due to be paid to creditors, loans which still have to be repaid and amounts due to the shareholders who subscribed the money with which the company was formed.

In the Balance Sheet assets are valued at the amount of money used to purchase them. Most fixed assets, such as cars and machinery, are worth substantially less than the original price once they are used. This progressive reduction in value has to be reflected in the company's accounts otherwise they would show a very misleading picture. The device used is to record a percentage of the value of such items as an expense each year under the heading of **depreciation** and the application of depreciation is referred to as **writing down** the asset.

Different rates of depreciation are applied to different types of capital goods, a ship may be considered to have a life of 20 years and so be written down by 5% per year whilst an office desk may be written down at 25% per annum.

You cannot leave the subject of how the value of an asset is shown in the company's books without touching on the subject of **revaluation** of assets. In shipping, perhaps more than most industries, the market is constantly fluctuating and occasionally these fluctuations are very great. Such fluctuations go beyond simply affecting the rates of freight being paid and spread their influence into the ship sale and purchase market. It would, therefore, be ridiculous if the owner steadily reduced the valuation of a ship in the balance sheet in accordance with a depreciation schedule while in the real world that ship had, perhaps, doubled in value.

Sadly the converse applies, the company would be lying to it's shareholders if a ship were shown in the books as only having reduced its value by, say, 10% when the recession was such that the ship had become worth only her value as scrap steel.

Revaluation of assets – up or down – is not carried out capriciously. A market trend has to be clearly expected to continue for a long time before any such action is taken and in may countries, company law has to be strictly observed.

To recapitulate, the Profit and Loss Account contains the sum of all the transactions over the previous year, the Balance Sheet shows what the company is worth at that particular moment.

9.5   MANAGEMENT ACCOUNTING

Reference to accounting so far, whether for use by the company or for official publication, has tended to look at the company's finances from a historical point of view i.e. what has happened. Management accounting looks at what is currently happening and what the company intends (or hopes) will happen in the future so that plans can be made to ensure continued or, better still, increased profitability.

Reference to the immediate past is still vital, you will often encounter the expression "same period last year" when seeking a foundation upon which to set a guide as to the expenses this week, month or year. This forward estimation of expenses is a vital part of **budgeting** as, of course, is the parallel but often much more difficult job of estimating future income. Conscientiously using such systems of planning and checking is referred to as **budgetary control.**

Apart from all the obvious advantages of having as accurate an estimate as possible of the company's future fortunes, the ability to compare "actual" with "budget" at frequent intervals will give an early warning of anything going awry. In particular budgeting permits the company to forecast **cash flow** so that it can be sure it will have money actually available to pay expenses, from the smallest invoice to the highest salary, when they become due.

Most companies prepare management accounts several times a year, often monthly. They include a profit and loss account for the year to date and comparisons with both the budget and the previous year. They will also include cash flow forecasts.

9.6 CASH FLOW

Earlier in this Chapter it was shown how, by comparing money due to come in with money due to be paid out plus money actually in hand, the company's profitability can be estimated. However, it does not matter how profitable the company is on paper, if the money is not physically available to pay vital things such as loan repayments, rentals, salaries etc. the company will fail, "become broke", "go bankrupt" or whatever term is chosen to describe total collapse.

It will be recalled that **creditors** are the people to whom your company owes money so, effectively, your company has some of **their** money in **its** account. Similarly **debtors** are those who owe your company money thus they have some of **your** company's money in **their** accounts.

If debtors have more of the company's money in their accounts than it has creditor's money in the company's account it will fast approach the stage when it has insufficient cash to meet immediate commitments, in other words it will reach a **cash-flow crisis**. Many otherwise profitable companies have failed due to mismanagement of their cash flow.

This is NOT a recommendation that a company should deliberately delay paying its bills well beyond their due date; a reputation as a "slow payer" can be damaging to future prospects. It is, however, important to negotiate the best possible payment terms with suppliers and to avoid conceding long credit periods with customers. Also important is having a person (or department) with the special responsibility for **credit control** because slow payers can so easily become non-payers resulting in **bad debts.**

It might be assumed, if a company's accounts show a considerable surplus of creditors over debtors, that its cash-flow is in a healthy state. This may well be the case although such a situation could well be the precursor of a very unhealthy state of affairs such as falling sales which will produce a trading loss next year. You should not judge by a single detail in a company's accounts but always study all the different items.

Being able to show convincingly how healthy a company's future cash-flow position will be, is an exercise companies may often be called upon to do. If a bank or finance house is asked for a loan, the lender is primarily anxious to ensure that the borrower has the ability to repay the loan and meet the interest payments. Although a mortgage may be taken on, say, the ship as security for the loan, the finance house wants to "buy and sell money" not become a shipowner. Thus before the loan is agreed the lender will wish to study a **cash-flow forecast** or **cash-flow projection** which will have to persuade the lender that he can be confident the borrower will be able to earn enough in order to meet his obligations under the loan.

9.7 COSTS

A capital asset (e.g. a ship), once purchased, must be put to work in order to earn revenue and therefore profit. To do so will require expenditure on a wide range of items, all of which will have to be forecast as accurately as possible for budgeting purposes. To assist in this process, costs are divided into two basic categories: **fixed costs** and **variable costs.**

In the case of a ship you would easily distinguish between the two because fixed costs, as the name implies, are those costs which would occur even if the ship were standing idle. Loan repayments and interest on the loan are certainly fixed costs (you will often hear this process referred to a **amortization**) and a cost which also continues regardless of what is happening is **depreciation** because, as an asset grows older, so its value decreases (subject to any revaluation of course).

The expression 'variable costs' is similarly self-explanatory. However, as your studies progress more deeply into the world of ship operations it will be seen that variable costs subdivide into **running costs** and **voyage costs.** Running costs are those that occur all the time a ship is operational, such as crews' wages, maintenance, insurance etc. Voyage costs are those that apply uniquely to the voyage being undertaken at the particular time and will include, bunker fuel, port costs, stevedoring, agency fees etc.

Whilst fixed costs are there to stay, variable costs give wide scope for the skills of those concerned with budgetary control; careful 'housekeeping' can make a considerable difference to the company's profitability.

9.8   DIFFERENT TYPES OF COMPANIES

9.8.1   Sole Traders and Partnerships

There is nothing to prevent an individual going into business on his or her own. In that way all the profit is retained (less what the Government takes as tax) but the individual has to raise all the money necessary to operate the business which may mean borrowing money against a security such as his or her own house. Furthermore all the risks fall on the individual with the ultimate risk of losing everything, and even bankruptcy.

Two or more people may decide to pool their resources of money and skills and so form a partnership. Usually they draw up a **partnership agreement** which formalises the arrangement. The same benefits and risks apply to partnerships as to sole traders except, of course, they are shared according to the agreed terms. Note, however that if one partner is unable to fulfil his or her obligations, the other partner is obliged to bear full responsibility.

A partnership is usually referred to as a **firm** and partnerships are by no means always small affairs. Many firms of accountants, stock brokers and lawyers are very substantial but are still essentially partnerships.

9.8.2   Limited Companies

One way of avoiding some of the risks of sole trading or partnerships is to form a limited company. The thing that is limited is the **liability.** Those forming the company are **shareholders** rather than partners and their liability is limited to their shareholding; if the company collapses all they lose is what they paid for their shares.

Someone has to bear the rest of the loss and they are, of course, those to whom the company owed money. This seems hardly fair to any suppliers who provided goods on credit but it is a risk that is run when dealing with a limited company. However, this risk is lessened by the fact that limited companies are, in most countries, strictly controlled by law. They have to keep proper books of accounts and publish these each year via an official body (In the U.K. this is the **Registrar of Companies**).

Limited companies have to have **Directors** (at least two) who may or may not be major shareholders. The same set of laws that insist on accounts being published also set out certain terms of conduct to be adhered to by directors.

A limited company may be owned by a small group of shareholders in which case it is referred to as a **private company** and its name has to include certain prescribed words or initials after its name (the word 'Limited' or the initials 'Ltd' are used in the U.K.).

Larger companies owned by a substantial number of shareholders are known as **public companies** and a different name and/or initials have to appear after their names appear (in the U.K. the initials 'plc' standing for public limited company are used). As the name implies, public companies shares are available to anyone who wishes to buy them and they are traded on the stock exchange at whatever price the market puts on that company at the time of the sale or purchase.

Large companies may buy, or form, subsidiary companies which may themselves be quite large but as they will only have a few actual shareholders they are still private limited companies (Ltd).

9.8.3 Conglomerates and Multi-national Companies

Large companies can become what are known as **conglomerates**, which means that in addition to having several branch offices and/or factories they buy or create a substantial number of subsidiary companies. These subsidiaries may be in a line of business related to that of the parent or in quite a different trade. One reason for forming a conglomeration is for **integration**, for example a shipowner may have in its group of companies a trucking company so that it does not have to buy inland transport from another company. It may well have other subsidiaries such as a chain of agency offices so that it uses its experience to gain income from others.

Other conglomerates may be a group of quite diverse operations such as a shipping company, an engineering division, a timber division and so on. They may trade with each other but this is not the main reason for this type of integration. The object is usually to spread the risk. One year shipping may be good but the building trade poor so that timber is not so profitable. Another year may be a boom time for engineering but the shipping market rather weak. In this way the total profitability is maintained because it does not depend on just one 'market'

A conglomerate which establishes branches and subsidiaries both in the country where the parent is registered and in other countries enables it to trade throughout the world but retain the trade and the profits from that trade within its own organization. This earns it the title of a **multi-national** and perhaps the best examples of such multi-nationals are the major oil companies as well as many of the liner shipping companies.

As referred to earlier in this Chapter, to run successfully a company needs **capital** which has to be raised. The principal way to raise capital is to sell **shares** in the company. The shareholders will only invest in the company if they are sure of receiving income in the form of **dividends** which is the term used to refer to the distribution of profits to the shareholders.

9.9 EXCHANGE RATES

Each country has its own currency and each currency has its value in comparison with the currency of another country. Furthermore these relative values fluctuate. Later in your studies you may encounter references to a country's **balance of trade** which is the difference between what a country earns abroad (with exports and/or services) and what it spends abroad on imports. You could look upon the balance of trade as the country's profit (or loss) and this measure of its prosperity will have a significant (but not the only) effect on the value of its currency against those of other countries. Other factors which impinge upon the complex foreign exchange markets are beyond the scope of this publication.

Those in shipping, being essentially an international business, constantly have to be aware of the effect that rates of exchange will have. For example, a company may have crews wages to pay in British Sterling, capital repayment in Japanese Yen, bunker and port costs in a wide variety of currencies and freight being earned in U.S. Dollars. Any of these currencies becoming either much stronger or weaker (worth more, respectively less, against your own currency) could have a profound effect on profitability.

This effect is just as important to, say, a chartering broker whose own salary and communications costs are in the currency of its own country but as the freight is payable in, say, U.S. dollars the broker's commission (brokerage), being a percentage of the freight, will also be in dollars. There is, of course, the paradox that if your own country is particularly prosperous just at that time and is enjoying a high rate of exchange in the world's markets, then the incoming dollar payment will yield less local currency than may have been hoped for at the time the deal was done.

When collecting freight on behalf of an overseas principal the effect of exchange rate fluctuations can cause a problem. If the agent in slow in remitting collected freight and the rate of exchange goes against the principal's country in the interim, the principal will suffer a loss, blame this on the agent's tardiness and demand recompense.

One can cite problem areas relating to exchange rates in all aspects of shipping business which means that it is a topic demanding constant vigilance.

9.10 COMPANY ACCOUNTS

Several references have been made to a company's "published accounts" and **Appendices 27 and 28** provide an example of how the basic elements of such a set of accounts might look. In practice a set of published accounts may also contain such things as a **Cash Flow Statement** as well as a list of **Explanatory Notes** which will include a description of the depreciation principles applied, the way in which assets have been valued and various other items.

Most of the terms used in the appendices should be self-evident but if there are any that are not clear please refer to Dictionary of Shipping International Business Trade Terms and Abbreviations (Published by Witherby Seamanship International Ltd).

9.11 TEST QUESTIONS

Having completed Chapter Nine and having studied the Appendices, attempt the following and submit your answers to your Tutor.

1. From the Balance Sheet comment upon how well (badly) the XYZ Group is managing its cash-flow. Is this better or worse than last year?

2. Assuming no ships are bought or sold, very approximately how much would you expect to see shown in XYZ's balance sheet next year as the asset value of the ships (explain how you reached your estimation, assume a useful life of 20 years).

3. Based upon the data in the appendices discuss, in approximately 250 words, XYZ's trading performance this year as compared with last.

4. From sources outside this text find two examples used by other countries of the initials and words used to indicate a private limited company and two examples of a public limited company.

Chapter 10

LAW OF CARRIAGE

10.1 INTRODUCTION

In any area of business there are legal rules and there are legal remedies should any of the rules be transgressed or should any problems arise.

This is especially so in shipping business where many transactions are only able to take place because of long-established legal customs and practices. It is vital, therefore, that students should be aware of the fundamental elements of the law of carriage of goods by sea which now includes those additional factors which the door-to-door aspects of containerisation have introduced.

Among the fundamentals, this Chapter will discuss the important principles governing agreements as well as liabilities arising even where there is no actual agreement or contract.

Different countries have different legal systems and it is beyond the scope of this publication to examine closely those differences. A great deal of shipping law is, however, based upon **English Law** which will tend to dominate in this Chapter.

In any case, shipping is essentially an international business and the majority of the maritime nations of the world have agreed to conform to wide-ranging **International Conventions** by incorporating those conventions into their own legal systems.

10.2 FUNDAMENTALS OF ENGLISH LAW

English Law is a **Common Law** system which is to be contrasted with **Civil Law** systems which have all the law enacted as a set of codified legal principles. In a Common Law system, whilst there are, of course, many pieces of legislation enacted by the government, much of English Law is contained in a set of principles and rules taken from earlier decisions made by judges in court cases. You will often hear common law being referred to as **Case Law.**

Whenever one reads a report on a court case it is almost inevitable that there will be references to previous cases, perhaps even some going back to the nineteenth century. This is because no two cases are likely to be exactly similar and the judge, in reaching his decision, must consider the most comparable past cases in order to form a new decision.

10.2.1 The Civil Court Structure

In England there are three basic levels of courts.

1. The courts of **'First Instance'** comprise (a) the **County Courts**, which deal in minor disputes, and (b) the **High Courts** for all other cases. The high courts have three divisions and the one dealing with commercial and maritime matters is called the **Queen's Bench Division.**

2. Above the courts of first instance is the **Court of Appeal** to which the losing party may go if it feels the first judge was wrong in reaching the decision. The Court of Appeal decisions are binding upon the courts of first instance.

3. The **House of Lords** is the ultimate court of appeal and only very controversial cases are decided at that level. House of Lords decisions are binding on all lower courts. It may overrule its own previous decisions although this rarely happens.

Also based in London is the **Judicial Committee of the Privy Council** which is the final court of appeal for the those United Kingdom dependent territories and those independent British Commonwealth countries which have retained this avenue of appeal upon achieving independence.

Those countries, including of course the United Kingdom, which are members of the **European Union** have an even higher court of appeal which is the **Court of Justice of the European Communities** whose purpose is to rule on any cases which may be held to violate the Community treaties.

10.2.2 Criminal Law

All the foregoing refers to civil law, that is disputes between individuals or groups of individuals. Quite separate from civil law is **Criminal Law** which deals with acts harmful to the population. Criminal law is beyond the scope of this course except to remark that some wrongful acts within shipping business, for example fraud, are crimes and would be dealt with in the criminal courts. The criminal courts have their own, tiered, structure similar to, but quite separate from, the civil courts.

10.3 ARBITRATION

Arbitration is a private means of settling a dispute. The parties choose their own arbitrator which may be a sole arbitrator, if they are so agree, or each party chooses his own arbitrator. Under some systems if the two arbitrators cannot agree they appoint an umpire. In other places the appointment of a third arbitrator to form a tribunal of three is automatic. There are several centres of maritime arbitration but the most active are London and New York.

Originally arbitration was a very cheap and speedy way of settling disputes with the arbitrators being themselves practising shipbrokers and their decisions being those of commercial men. Sadly, but perhaps inevitably, as the world has become a more complicated and more litigious place, arbitrations have involved professional lawyers arguing the case from both sides with the finer points of law appearing to be more important than a quick commercial settlement of an argument.

To overcome this problem and in an endeavour to regain arbitration's reputation for simplicity, both London and New York have introduced specific forms of arbitration which offer a quick and inexpensive alternative where the dispute is obviously suitable for a speedy solution.

Arbitration is not part of the country's public legal system although it is, of course, subject to governing legislation. With arbitration the parties are, in effect, "choosing their own judges". Arbitration awards are final and binding upon the parties, the only appeal to the courts would be for a judicial review on a question of law.

10.4 THE CONTRACT

Fundamental to any business act is a **contract** and it is vital to be clear as to what constitutes a legally binding contract and how it comes about. There are three distinct components to a contract:

1. **The Offer**

An offer is a specific expression of willingness to enter into a contract on specified terms.

2. Acceptance

The offer must be accepted on the exact stated terms. This converts to offer into an agreement.

3. Consideration

For the agreement to become a contract there has to be a consideration. The person to whom the offer is made must give (or promise to give) something in return for the offer.

4. Legality

In order to be valid a contract must also be legally enforceable; contracts cannot relate to an activity which is not in itself lawful.

These four elements have to be technically present whether you are buying a bar of chocolate or chartering a 150,000 tonne tanker for twenty years. Furthermore, there need not be a physical object involved because (as will be discussed later in this Chapter) a contract may be entered into to carry out a service such as a Port Agency.

Although there has to be a 'consideration' for a contract to exist, there are no rules as to how much must be involved. A contract to sell a vintage Rolls Royce for £100 would be just as valid as one for £100,000, provided the parties willingly agreed to it. Indeed there does not even have to be actual money involved, there are still some leases for property in existence for which the annual rent is one peppercorn.

The description of chartering negotiations set out in Lesson 4 are a perfect example of offer, acceptance and consideration (the freight rate).

10.5 REMEDIES FOR BREACH OF CONTRACT

If one party or the other in a contract does not perform in accordance to that which was agreed, a breach has been committed and the injured party may seek redress.

If the breach of contract is a major failure the injured party may simply withdraw from the contract and may seek damages. If the breach is a less important matter then the contract will continue to be valid but the injured party may seek damages.

Damages in this context mean the financial loss that has been suffered. In some cases, the amount of damages may be stipulated in the contract such as demurrage in a charter party in which case they are referred to as **liquidated damages.**

10.6 TORT

In the introduction it was mentioned that there may be liabilities even where no contract exists (and where no crime has been committed). Such a civil wrong is called a **tort** and it refers to an act or omission which causes another party damage in a situation where no contractual relationship exists. The party against whose person or property the tort was committed has the legal right to claim damages.

The type of tort which those in shipping business are most likely to encounter is **negligence** which is often described as a **failure of a duty of care.** A simple example would be where a ship allows an escape of oil which damages nearby property. The shipowner owed a duty of care to the nearby property owner, it was the oil spill that caused the damage and the property owner has the right to claim the cost of repairing that damage from the negligent shipowner.

Other torts include:

Trespass	– physical damage to another's property.
Defamation	– libel (written) or slander (spoken) statements which are held liable to damage a person's reputation.
Conversion	– allowing the possession of goods to pass into the hands of the wrongful owner (this could also be the crime of theft).
Deceit	– this would be fraud in a criminal case.

There are many instances in shipping business, for example, when an agent has control over what happens to goods even when they are not actually covered by a contract for which that agent is responsible, where a failure of a duty of care may occur and the agent may become liable for very heavy damages.

Another example could arise should a person be asked for information such as "You have done business with Mr So-and-So, is he all right financially?" If the answer given implies that Mr So-and-So is perfectly trustworthy financially without mentioning a suspicion that he is in fact a swindler, the enquirer could do business with Mr So-and-So and lose a lot of money. The enquirer could then have a legal case against the information provider who had a **duty of care** to give an honest and accurate reply.

Of course caution is needed here, the reply could have been "No, Mr So-and-So is a crook, have nothing to do with him" in which case the enquirer would not lose money but Mr So-and-So may get to hear what was said and sue the information giver for **defamation of character (slander or libel).**

The right way to deal with such a situation is of course to say something like "I had no trouble when I dealt with Mr So-and-So but you should make formal enquiries elsewhere"

One of the worst situations, which falls under the heading of the tort of **conversion,** is when the agent releases discharged cargo to the wrong party (i.e. some one who did not present a valid bill of lading). In such a case the legitimate bill of lading holder can claim for the full value of the goods from the errant agent who will have no defence and no one else to turn to (unless he is very fully insured).

10.7 CONTRACTS RELATING TO THE CARRIAGE OF GOODS BY SEA

10.7.1 General

The way in which transport by sea is unique is that, whilst the ship is on passage, the goods loaded in her are:

(a) the ship's sole responsibility and

(b) inaccessible to anyone (except of course the crew).

A great deal of the smooth operation of international trade depends upon taking proper advantage of these two facts.

10.7.2 Charter Parties

It will be recalled from earlier Chapters that there are two principal types of contracts for the carriage of goods by sea. Chapter four dealt with the **Charter Party**, which is a contract between **Charterer** and **Shipowner** with the rate and terms negotiated in an international market. Unless the parties choose specifically to incorporate any international conventions (such as the Hague-Visby Rules), a charterparty is a "stand-alone" contract in which virtually all the intentions of the parties are set out.

Chapter four covered the different types of charter with some detail about the standard forms used which, with any amendments and additions upon which the parties may agree, sets down in writing the full intentions of the parties which are legally referred to as the **express terms**.

There are, however, certain terms in a charter party which are implied under common law and are referred to as **implied terms.**

In the case of a voyage charter some basic implied terms are:

On the part of the shipowner:

    (a) that the ship is seaworthy.

    (b) that the ship will proceed "with reasonable despatch.

    (c) that the ship will make no unjustifiable deviation. (deviation to save life is always justifiable).

On the part of the charterer:

    (d) not to ship dangerous goods without the knowledge of the shipowner.

In the case of a time charter:

    (a) that the timecharterer will only use the vessel between good and safe ports.

    (b) that dangerous goods will not be shipped without the knowledge of the shipowner.

There are no international conventions covering ships under charter although the parties may choose to incorporate some such as:

    (a) stipulating that bills of lading covering the cargo carried will be subject to the **Hague Rules** or the **Hague-Visby Rules. See Appendix 29.** The incorporating clause is often referred to as the **Clause Paramount (Appendix 30).**

    (b) that **General Average** will be subject to the **York Antwerp Rules** which details how General Average should be applied and calculated.

        General Average is a centuries-old convention which agrees that if the ship takes action which avoids a peril or reduces the effects of a peril, all parties must contribute to the cost of this action (known as the "sacrifice") according to the value of their participation in the venture. The incorporating clause is often referred to as the **New Jason Clause. (Appendix 31)**

Other standard clauses which are not strictly speaking derived from international convention but have wide acceptance may also be included such as a **Both to Blame Collision Clause, (Appendix 32)** and/or a **War Risk Clause,** an example of such a clause is in **Appendix 33.**

10.8   LINER BILLS OF LADING

In the case of liner cargo, Chapter six explained how there is no equivalent of the charter party in the liner trade and whilst today there is often a degree of bargaining this tends almost always to be within the framework of the carrier's standard terms. Consequently it is rare for a written agreement to be produced for liner cargo and the vital document is the **Bill of Lading**. It was, therefore, stressed in Chapter six that the bill of lading was not an agreement but was **evidence of a contract;** the actual contract, very frequently only a verbal contract, having been made earlier.

Recall also from Chapter six the other functions of a Bill of Lading. It is a **receipt for goods** which covers both the **quantity** (which is set out in the body of the B/L) and the **quality** which is covered by the words "in apparent good order and condition". This enables the consignee to claim against the carrier if there is a shortage or if the cargo is damaged.

Today, most cargo is shipped in **containers** and in the case of Full Container Loads (FCLs) the question of quantity and quality is in the hands of the shipper and this part of the B/L will simply contain a Container number (together usually with the Seal number) and the words "said to contain" when describing the cargo. The consignee then has no claim against the carrier provided the container is undamaged and the seal is intact unless it can be proved that the contents had been damaged due to container having been badly handled.

With Less than Container Loads (LCL cargo) the carrier's responsibility as regards quantity and quality is the same as for break-bulk (conventional) cargo.

Note also in the case of break-bulk cargo, that technically, the B/L does not begin to operate until the cargo crosses the ship's rail at the time of loading. With container cargo, however, the receipt element of the B/L (and also the carrier's liability) comes into effect much sooner, possibly at the shipper's premises. For this reason, it will be recalled, a container B/L states "Received" rather than "Shipped" above the carrier's signature and the B/L needs a further endorsement to say when shipment actually took place in order to become a "shipped on board" B/L.

Finally the B/L is a **document of title**; the definition of "title" in this context is *the right to ownership of property with or without actual possession.*

Refer back to the preamble to this section of the Chapter where it was pointed out that no one has access to the cargo whilst it is afloat. Therefore, during this time the B/L is able to be a **negotiable document** enabling a named consignee to sell the cargo and to pass title to the cargo by endorsing the B/L by signing it on the back. There is no limit to the number of times a B/L, and also title to the cargo, can change hands in this manner so long as it takes place while the cargo is still on the ship.

Payment for the cargo may have been arranged via the banking system through the medium of a **documentary letter of credit** in which case the second part of the B/L's rôle as a document of title comes into play, this time as **security for payment.** In such a case, the B/L is not made out to a named consignee but in that part of the B/L the words **"To Order"** appear. Such a document has to be endorsed by the actual shipper and thereafter does not need any further endorsement because it is now 'open' and title to the goods belongs to anyone holding the B/L – theoretically he can claim the goods even if he found the B/L in the street. In the real world, shipping lines and their agents are very wary of handing goods to anyone who has obtained the B/L illegally. Most countries recognise the crime of stealing by finding.

Chapter six explains how the B/L is used in the letter of credit procedures.

Although title to the goods may be transferred from one to another, the actual contract remains between the original shipper and the carrier and a way had to be found to ensure that the rights and liabilities under the contract also pass to the new consignee (the endorsee). To achieve this the UK originally passed the *Bill of Lading Act 1855.* The evolution in liner shipping meant that this needed up-dating and it was replaced with the *Carriage of Goods by Sea Act 1992.*

Many find this title a misnomer because there is already a *Carriage of Goods by Sea Act 1971* which is the act with which the UK ratified the Hague/Visby rules. So it is vital to remember that the *1992 Act replaces the B/L Act of 1855 and does not affect the 1971 Act.*

The *Carriage of Goods by Sea Act 1992* (as did the 1855 B/L Act) empowers the consignee to sue the carrier and also subject the consignee to the liabilities in respect of the goods as if the contract had been made between the consignee and the carrier. The 1992 Act corrects various anomalies in the 1855 Act that the passage of time has revealed as well as taking Sea Waybills and Delivery orders into consideration.

10.9 THE HAGUE/VISBY RULES

Whereas there is some degree of equality of bargaining strength between an owner and a charterer which only varies according to the fluctuation of the market, liner shippers seldom have such power.

In the distant past, owners of ships carrying general cargo were able to exert their bargaining strength over shippers by imposing contract terms which allowed the shipowners to exempt themselves from all manner of negligence. Shippers rebelled and lobbied governments to introduce legislation in order to curb this abuse of shipowner power. This resulted in a hotchpotch of laws across the world which, in such an essentially international business as shipping created chaos.

Governments, therefore, came together to discuss the drafting of an international convention but it was not until 1921 that agreement was reached and the **Hague Rules** came into being. These were ratified by almost all the world's maritime nations; in the UK it was the *Carriage of Goods by Sea Act 1924.*

Then, largely due to the introduction of containerisation and changing values the Maritime Law Committee of the International Law Association agreed to amend the Hague Rules with the Brussels Protocol of 1958 and the amended Hague Rules became known as the **Hague/Visby Rules,** (refer again to **Appendix 29**). These rules again found favour with most maritime nations and the UK ratified the rules with the *Carriage of Goods by Sea Act 1971* which replaced (repealed) the 1924 Act.

The Hague/Visby Rules only apply to goods carried under a Bill of Lading or similar document, they do not apply to a charter party unless specifically incorporated into it.

In the Rules the term "carrier" is used throughout so that it includes owner or charterer who enters into a contract of carriage with a shipper. In the simplest terms, the Rules set out:

(a) the duties of the carrier to provide a seaworthy (and 'cargoworthy') ship at the beginning of the voyage. This is not an absolute liability, if the ship becomes unseaworthy during the course of the voyage "want of due diligence" has to be proved.

(b) the carrier must provide a bill of lading or similar document.

(c) there must be no unjustifiable deviation (saving life or property is considered 'reasonable' under the rules).

(d) the shipper guarantees the accuracy of the details of the cargo supplied by him.

(e) there is a list of things for which the carrier shall not be liable, these are matters which are clearly not under the carrier's control.

(f) there is a limit to the amount of compensation the carrier has to pay in the event of loss or damage. This is the equivalent of saying "This is where my insurance stops so this is where yours should start". The maximum amount is "per package" and in the Hague/Visby Rules the definition of package when containerisation is involved has been covered.

(g) there is a "Himalaya" clause incorporated in the rules (it was not in the original Hague Rules) which brings "a servant or agent of the carrier" under the protection of the bill of lading. (see below)

(h) a claim for loss or damage shall be time-barred "unless suit is brought within one year of delivery or the date when they should have been delivered".

Bear in mind that, now the vast majority of manufactured goods are being carried in containers, a Combined Transport B/L covers far more than simply carriage by sea. It now includes all the other ancillary transportation elements which comprise what is now termed **intermodalism.**

There are international conventions covering the carriage by road referred to as **The CMR Convention**. The initials stand for *Convention relative au contrat de transport des Marchandises par vois de Route.*

Similarly carriage by rail within Europe is covered by **The CIM Convention** and the translation in this case is *Convention International concernant le transport de Marchandises par chemin de fer.*

The details of these conventions are beyond the scope of this publication but in Chapter six it was explained that the rules and limitations of liability of these modes of transport come into effect if loss or damage occurs on road respectively on rail but that if the precise place where the problem arose is unknown then the Hague Visby Rules shall apply.

10.9.1 "Himalaya" clause

Reference was made earlier that the Hague-Visby Rules include a "Himalaya Clause" which brings agents and other servants of the owner under the protection of the Bill of Lading's limits of liability. The clause gets its title from a passenger ship of that name which created a legal landmark in the shipping world in 1954. A lady passenger – Mrs Adler – was injured when descending a gangway from the ship; the gangway had been inadequately secured. She found that, under the contract evidenced by her passenger ticket, she could not claim damages from the shipowner but she successfully sued the ship's Master (Captain Dickson) in *tort* in that he had failed in his duty of care. Not only was this a classic example of the law of *tort* in action but it was also a demonstration of **vicarious liability.** Securing the gangway was not part of the captain's own duties but it was the job of someone under his command going about his normal duties. (The definition of vicarious is "acting or done for another").

This case (*Adler v Dickson 1954*) sent a shockwave through the whole shipping business world because it was realised that the same device could be used to circumvent the limits of liability which the Hague Rules conferred upon the bill of lading. Therefore, it was that bills of lading were hastily re-drafted to include a clause which extended the protection of the B/L to all those directly working for the owner.

The reasonableness of such a clause was generally accepted throughout the shipping world so that, when the time came to up-date the Hague Rules by producing the Hague-Visby Rules, the situation was fully covered by the inclusion of the fours clauses which comprise Article IV*bis* in the Rules. Note that Clause 4 in that article does not protect the servant or agent "if it is proved that the damage resulted from an act – – – – – done with the intent to cause damage or recklessly – – –".

10.10 THE HAMBURG RULES

The United Nations Commission for Trade and Development (UNCTAD) whose brief is principally to look after the affairs of less developed nations, held a meeting in Hamburg in 1978 to consider the carriage of goods by sea. The meeting produced a rival to the Hague/Visby Rules entitled the **Hamburg Rules**.

The object of these rules was to favour non-maritime nations which tend to be cargo-owning countries and this is apparent when you see the limited number of nations which have ratified the Hamburg Rules.

Some of the principal differences include:

(a) Hague/Visby only operates as goods pass the ships rail in and out but Hamburg covers the whole period "during which the carrier is in charge of the goods" so for example applies before and after loading/discharge.

(b) the carriage of live animals and deck cargo are completely excluded from the provisions of Hague/Visby but there is a qualified inclusion in Hamburg.

(c) there is no provision for loss due to delay in Hague/Visby but with Hamburg the carrier is liable for losses due to delay unless he can prove the delay was entirely beyond his control.

(d) the amount of compensation for loss or damage is much higher in Hamburg under limitation of liability provision.

(e) the time bar is two years under Hamburg against one year in Hague/Visby.

(f) Hague Rules apply to goods loaded in a signatory state. Hamburg rules apply when goods are loaded or discharged in a signatory state. This may lead to conflicts under the B/L where the loading port is Hague-Visby and the discharging port is under Hamburg Rules.

The full text of the Hamburg Rules will be found in **Appendix 34**

10.11 THE ROTTERDAM RULES

The matter of international law relating to the carriage of goods by sea has never been straightforward and it is still somewhat confused today. In addition to the Hague, Hague/Visby and Hamburg rules there are a whole variety of domestic legislation around the world that picks parts from each or adds in elements from outside. In 2009 the UN completed work on a revised new text that will supersede the Hamburg rules and will address the argument that whereas the Hague rules were biased in favour of the shipowners, the Hamburg rules allowed the pendulum to swing too far the other way.

These new rules are referred to as 'The Rotterdam Rules' but the text needs to be ratified by nations and adopted in to national law before they will become effective. The Rotterdam Rules are the first to address the issue of multi-modal transport. While they have received an enthusiastic reception from many organisations around the world representing both shipowners and cargo interests, at least one body - The European Shippers' Council, has expressed concerns and in June 2009 were requesting that the rules should be reconsidered.

It is unlikely that the Rotterdam Rules will become the accepted standard for some time because of the protracted process of ratification and incorporating into statute. However, their existence should not be overlooked because it is conceivable that some parties may choose to adopt them as a freely negotiated contractual obligation. The final text of the Rotterdam Rules was agreed in 2009 and, in September that year, the rules were open for signatories. By the end of February 2010 there were 21 signatories, including the USA, Norway and the Netherlands and a number of more minor nations. The general feeling is that it will be at least 2015 before the Rules are fully ratified, even by the present signatories.

The text of the Rotterdam Rules is in Appendix 35.

10.12 AGENCY

All the "disciplines" referred to in Chapter seven are forms of agency that is to say carrying out work on behalf of a principal except, of course, where the work is done by a department in the principal's own office. An agent's function is to bring his principal into contractual relationships with third parties.

10.12.1 Creation of a Relationship of Agency

An agency can be created:

    (a) by express agreement.

    (b) by implication/conduct

    (c) by necessity, i.e. where a person is entrusted with another person's property and a definite and commercial necessity arises to deal with that property and it is impossible to obtain the property-owners's instructions.

10.12.2 Rights and Duties imposed as between Agent and Principal

Duties of an Agent:

    (a) to exercise due diligence in performance of his duties.

    (b) to apply any special skill which he professes to have.

    (c) to render account.

    (d) not to make a secret profit (doing so is a crime in many countries). An example could be where the agent agrees that the stevedore should inflate his account to the shipowner and pay the excess as a secret commission to the agent.

Duties of a Principal:

    (a) to remunerate the agent.

    (b) to indemnify the agent for liabilities incurred in the execution of his authority. This not only includes reimbursing for expenses incurred on the principal's behalf but also protecting the agent against "mis-directed arrows" i.e. legal action directed against the agent when it should have been directed against the principal.

10.13 BREACH OF WARRANTY OF AUTHORITY

When an agent deals on behalf of his principal the agent is **warranting** to the third party that he has his principal's **authority** to do so. If he deals without that authority (actual, implicit or of necessity) then he is in breach of the warranty of authority.

The agent can be in breach **deliberately**, that is he knew he was doing so, or was **reckless** as to whether or not he was in breach. He can also be in breach through **negligence.** For example, misreading the terms upon which he was authorised to offer a ship for a cargo and the subsequent fixture is not on the terms the owner intended.

In either of these cases the agent, by warranting he had authority to do what he did, will be liable to the third party for any loss so caused; mistakes have to be paid for.

There is another way that breach of warranty of authority operates which is less easy to understand. Imagine that you are a broker negotiating with a charterer on behalf of an owner based in another country. Now suppose that the authority to make an offer to the charterer comes not directly from the owner but from a broker in the owner's country and it is **that** broker who misreads the authority and passes to you a firm offer with a mistake in it. In good faith you make this offer to the charterer *warranting you have to owner's authority to do so.* If a fixture is concluded with this error in it and the charterer sustains a loss he will seek recompense and the law says you have to pay.

This may seem unfair because you have made no mistake but the view the law takes is that it would be quite wrong for the charterer to suffer. It would be equally wrong for the charterer to have to proceed against the foreign broker who made the mistake as the charterer had no direct contact with that broker. No, the faulty offer came from you so you have to pay the charterer's damages, this is breach of warranty of authority **without negligence**. All you can do is proceed against the overseas broker who made the error to recover what you have had to pay out. Fortunately agents and brokers can insure (usually through their P & I Club – see below) against breach of warranty of authority, with or without negligence and in view of the way one cannot otherwise protect oneself against a 'without negligence' situation, such insurance is a wise precaution.

10.14 PROTECTION AND INDEMNITY ASSOCIATIONS

P & I Clubs as they are called are principally concerned with providing shipowners with insurance against third party risks. They originated in the 19th century because commercial insurers and underwriters were not prepared to offer the full cover for these risks because of their open ended nature. P & I cover is arranged on a basis of "mutuality" which is to say that the clubs are non-profit making entities whose funds are contributed by the members and are named "calls". Members present their claims for sums which they have settled with the third party and what they have paid is reimbursed to them; this is the "indemnity" element of the clubs. Should the claims on the club exceed the funds available, the club will make a **supplementary call** to obtain the necessary extra money from the members.

The "protection" element involves providing legal advice to members and fighting claims which are considered to be wrong or excessive.

The main P & I Clubs are those of shipowners and the third party claims where they may be involved include such things as personal injury claims by people working on the ships and damage to property such as colliding with a jetty but probably the most active section is that dealing with cargo claims when consignees claim short delivery or damage to their cargo.

There are also P & I Clubs for charterers and for shipbrokers, the latter are principally concerned with professional indemnity insurance that is insuring people in shipping business against claims made against them for negligence.

Recently there has been a tendency among some owners to return to commercial insurance cover for their third party risks.

10.15 SELF-ASSESSMENT AND TEST QUESTIONS

Attempt the following and check your answer from the text:

1. Ascertain where the different courts are in your locality.

   If you live outside England, ensure that you have a clear idea of the different levels of courts in your own country.

2. What four components are essential to comprise a contract?

3. Name five types of tort.

4. What are the names given to the clauses which incorporate into a charter party?

   (a) the Hague/Visby Rules.

   (b) the York Antwerp Rules

5. What are the three functions of a Bill of Lading?

6. What is the definition of "title".

7. What are the three ways an agency can be created?

8. What types of claims do the shipowners' P & I Club deal with?

Having completed Chapter Ten, attempt the following and submit your answers to your Tutor:

1. Propose a Breach of Warranty of Authority situation different from those used in the text.

2. An FCL container which in the B/L is said to contain ten air conditioning units each weighing 150 kgs is lost. Referring to **Appendix 29** calculate how much compensation the consignee can expect to be paid by the carrier. Explain how you arrive at your answer.

3. What is the advantage to an agent of the "Himalaya" clause incorporated in the Hague/Visby Rules?

APPENDICES

Forms marked * reproduced by kind permission of BIMCO

Lloyd's Register Page Extract 2003-2004

7903328	AMPHION	53,898	Class: NV (NK)	1980-07 Sasebo Heavy Industries Co. Ltd.-Sasebo	Crude Oil Tanker	1 oil engine driving 1 CP propeller
9HGD5	exVenita-1996 exMegaVenita -1992	23,425		Yard, Sasebo Yd No: 282	COW IGS SBT	Total Power: 11,700kW(15.906hp)	13.0kn
5321	ex Venita-1990 ex Diana -1987	87,549		Loa 243.01 Br ex 42.04 Dght 12.722	Liq(Oil): 105,997	MAN	12V48/60
-	Amphion Shipping Co. Ltd.	T/cm		Lbp 230.03 Br md 42.03 Dpth 19.82	Cargo Heating Coils	1 x Vee 4 Stroke 12 Cy. 480 x 600 (new engine 1993)
	Paralos Maritime Corp. S.A.	88.4		Welded, 1 dk	3 Cargo Pumps	MAN B&W Diesel AG
	Valletta Malta				Manifold: Bow/CM: 122m	AuxGen: 1 x 560kW 450V 60Hz, 2 x 440kW 450V 60Hz
	SatCom: Inmarsat A					Fuel: 281.0(d.o.) 2773.5(hvf) 53 Opd
	MMSI: 249804000					

8407890	AMPHION	37,031	Class: AB	1987-10 Hyundai Heavy Industries Co., Ltd.-Ulsan	Bulk Carrier	1 oil engine driving 1 FP propeller
SXZP	ex Grischuna-1999	24,287		Yd No: 359	Str. heavy cargoes	Total Power: 8,799kW(11,963hp)	15.0kn
573	Panther Navigation Inc.	64,442		Loa 225.03 (BB) Br ex 32.26 Dght 13.101	SERS(LR)	B&W	5L70MC
-	Andriaki Shipping Co. Lid.	T/cm		Lbp 215.65 Br md 32.21 Dpth 18.01	Grain: 80,056	1 x 2 Stroke 5 Cy. 700x2,268
	Andros Greece MMSI:	65.8		Welded, 1 dk	Compartments: 7 Ho, ER 7	Hyundai Engine 8 Machinery Co., Ltd.
	239620000				Ha: ER	AuxGen 3 x 525kW 440V 60Hz
						Fuel:99.5(d.o.)1890.0(hvf)36.0pd

7226093	AMPHITRITE	2,478	Class: RS	1972 Sudostroitelnyy Zavod im. "Volodarskiy"-	General Cargo Ship	2 oil engines driving 2 FP propellers
UZCZ	ex Sovelskiy Sever -7998	917		Rybinsk YdNo:61	Ice strengthened	Total Power: 485kW(1,320hp)	10.5kn
712663	ex Viktor Koryakin-7993	3,135		Loa 113.90 Br ex 13.21 Dght 3.700	Bale: 4,125	S.K.L.	6NVD48A-U
-	Joint Stock Co "Amphitrite" (A/O "Amphitrite")	TV cm		Lbp 108.01 Br md - Dpth 5.54	Compartments: 4 Ho, ER	1 x 4 Stroke 6 Cy. 320 x 480 485kW(660bhp)
				Welded, 1 dk	4 Ha: (17.6 x 9.3) 3(18.1 x 9.3) ER	VEB Schwermaschinenbau "Karl Liebkneclit" (SKL)
	Kherson Ukraine					S.K.L.
	MMSI: 272151000					1 x 4 Stroke 6 Cy. 320 x 480 485kW(660bhp)
						VEB Schwermaschinenbau "Karl Liebknecht" (SKL
						AuxGen: 2 x 75kW. 1 x 50kW Fuel: 94.0(d.o.)

7224368	AMPLE HARVEST	4,275	Class: (CC) (NV)	1972 Kleven Mek. Verksted AS -Ulsteinvik	General Cargo Ship	1 oil engine driving 1 FP propeller
XU7MZ	ex Ample Route 1 -2001 ex Jin Tai -1999	2,400		Yd No: 23	Grain: 8,546; Bale: 7.795	Total Power: 3,383kW(4,600hp)	14 kn
0072334	ex Jia Fa -1996 ex Ocean Mercury -1986	5,919		Loa 106.80 Br ex 17.07 Dght 7.070	TEU 173 C.Ho 93/20' C.Dk	Werkspoor	8TM410
	ex Corona -1986 exFinnmaster-1982	T/cm		Lbp 10036 Br md 17.00 Dpth 9.00	80/20'(40')	1 x 4 Stroke 8 Cy. 410x470
	Tian Hua Maritime Transportation Corp. Ltd.	-		Welded, 2 dks	Compartments: 2 Ho, ER, 2 TwDk	Stork-Werkspoor Diesel B.V.
					2 Ha: 2(27.4 x 13.3) ER Cranes:	AuxGen: 3 x174kW 380V 60Hz
	Phnom-Penh Cambodia				2x12.5t,2x10t	Fuel: 236.0(d.o.) 386.0(hvf) 14 Opd
	SatCom: Inmarsat C					

9013177	AMPORELLE	345	Class: BV	1991-12 Soc. Francaise de Cons. Nav. -	Day-excursion Passenger Ship	2 oil engines with clutches, flexible couplings &Sr geared
FQHN		258		Villeneuve—la—Garenne Yd No: 869	Passengers: unberthed: 370	to sc. shafts driving 2 Water jets
125434	Government of The Republic of France (Regie	100		Loa 38.00 Br ex - Dght 1.350		Total Power: 3,398kW(4,620hp)	28.0kn
-	Departementale des Passages d'Eau de la	T/cm		Lbp 33.50 Br md 7 75 Dpth 3.40		MWM	TBD604BV16
	Vendee)	-		Welded, 1 dk		2 x Vee 4 Stroke 16 Cy. 170 x 195 each-
						1,699kW(2,310bhp)
	lie d'Yeu France MMSI:					Motoren Werke Mannheim AG (MWM)
	227004400					AuxGen: 2 x 60kW 380V 50Hz
						Fuel: 10.4(d.o.)

7102508	AMR	1.582	Class: .RS:	1970 Santierul Naval Constanta S.A. -Constanta	General Cargo Ship	1 oil engine driving 1 FP propeller
XUSF7	ex Cherepovets -1998	708		Yd No: 339	Ice strengthened	Total Power: 1,147kW(1,560hp)	12.0kn
9870089	Quantel Shipping Ltd.	1,857		Loa 80.27 Br ex 11.94 Dght 4.900	Bale: 2,450	Sulzer	6TAD36
	Romalex Marine S.A.E.	T/cm		Lbp 71.49 Br md - Dpth 5.69	Compartments: 3 Ho, ER	1 x 2 Stroke 6 Cy. 360 x 600
	Phnom-Penh Cambodia	-		Welded, 1 dk	3 Ha: (8.2 x 5 8) 2(8.2 x 7.9) ER	Tvornica Dizel Motora "Jugoturbina"
	MMSI: 514166000				Cranes: 3x5t	

5015294	AMRADO	201	Class: (LR)	1948-03 Ferguson Bros. (Port Glasgow) Ltd.-Port	Tug	2 Steam Recip. driving 2 FP propellers
-	Government of The Republic of Ghana (Ports	-	⊕ Classed LR until 10/48	Glasgow Yd No: 384		2 x Steam Recip Triple exp In-Line 6Cy. HP
-	Authority)	-		Loa 32.67 Br ex 7 47 Dght 3 277		IP1-(2)445 8 LP-(2)737 xStroke-559
-		T/cm		Lbp - Br md - Dpth -		Ferguson Bros. (Port Glasgow) Ltd.
	Takoradi Ghana	-		Welded,		

5138058	AMREET	999	Class ..LR:	1958-07 Valmet Oy -Helsinki Yd No: 191	General Cargo Ship	1 oil engine driving 1 FP propeller
YKBS	ex Al Schooner -1992 ex Rim -1988	504	⊕ Classed LR until 7/1/83	Loa 69.19 Br ex 10.83 Dght 4.242	Ice strengthened	Total Power: 706kW(960hp)	11.0 kn
39/LA	ex Mona Star-7978 ex Gullkrona -1976	1,408		Lbp 62.62 Br md 10.80 Dpth 4.42	Grain: 1,940: Bale: 1,743	Alpha	498R
-	Nazih Sidawi, Hussni Ammoun, Abdul Mouem	T/cm		Welded, 1 dk	2 Ha: (10.2 x 5.4) (16.2 x 6.0) ER	1 x 2 Stroke 8 Cy. 290 x 490
	Markabi & Mohi Eldin Kaak	-			Cranes: 2x3t	Alpha Diesel A/S
	Schooner Shipping					Fuel:71.0(d.o.)
	Laltakia Syria					

9081746	AMRIT KAUR	306	Class: (AB) (IR)	1993-03 Goa Shipyard Ltd. -Goa Yd No: 1150	Patrol Vessel	2 oil engines sr geared to sc. shaft driving 1 FT propeller
I'VXL		91		Loa 45.95 Br ex - Dght -	Search & Rescue	Total Power: 2.960kW(4.024hp)	23.0kn
225	Government of The Republic of India (Coast	-		Lbp 43.50 Br md 7.50 Dpth 4.30		M.T.U.	12V538TB82
-	Guard)	T/cm		Welded, 1 dk		2 x Vee 4 Stroke 12 Cy. 185 x 200 each-
		-				1,480kW(2,012bhp)
	India SatCom: Inmarsat C					MTU Friedrichshafen GmbH
						AuxGen:3x80kW415V50Hz

7102211	AMRITA I	173	Class: KI (GL)	1971 Handara Engineering & Shiprepairing Ltd.-	Tug	1 oil engine driving 1 CP propeller
YBYO		-		Hong Kong Yd No: 22		Total Power: 588kW(800hp)	11.2kn
172	P.T. Pelayaran Lokal Karunrung	10		Loa 29.04 Br ex 7.73 Dght 3.210		Alpha	408-26VO
		T/cm		Lbp 26.80 Br md 7.40 Dpth 3.41		1 x 2 Stroke 8 Cy. 260 x 400
	Jakarta Indonesia	-		Welded, 1 dk		Alpha Diesel A/S

5207615	AMROZ	396	Class: (LR)	1958-09 E.J. Smit & Zoon's Scheepswerven N.V.-	Livestock Carrier	1 oil engine driving 1 FP propeller
ODBX	ex RabunionV -1992 ex Croesus -1975	220	⊕ Classed LR until 1/1/95	Westerbroek Yd No: 746	Ice strengthened	Total Power: 552kW(750hp)	10.8kn
B2.795	ex Berta -1973 exLibertas-1972	1,315		Converted from: General Cargo Ship-1982	Bale: 1,744	Werkspoor	TMAB396
	Amro Z Shipping Co. SARL	T/cm		Loa 64.85 Br ex 9.91 Dght 4.560	Compartments: 2 Ho. ER	1 x 4 Stroke 6 Cy. 390 x 680
	Zeido Group			Lbp 59.75 Br md 9.81 Dpth 5.80	2 Ha: (8.0 x 4.0) (12.1 x 4.0) ER	N.V. Werkspoor
	Beirut Lebanon			Riveted/Welded, 2 dks	Derricks: 2x6t.4x3t: Winches: 6	AuxGen: 3 x25kW110V d.c.

8401755	AMRTA JAYA1	5,464	Class: NK	1984-05 Higakt Zosen K.K. -Imabari Yd No: 320	General Cargo Ship	1 oil engine driving 1 FP propeller
3FVN2		2,262		Loa 98.18 (BB) Br ex 18.01 Dght 7.544	Grain: 13,070; Bale: 12,097	Total Power: 2,427kW(3,300hp)	12.0kn
14189-84CH	Admiral Three Star S.A.	6,839		Lbp 89.95 Br md 18.00 Dpth 13.01	Compartments: 2 Ho, ER	Hanshin	6EL40
-	P.T. Pelayaran Samudera "Admiral Lines"	T/cm		Welded, 1 dk	2 Ha: (22.2 x 9.8) (24.7 x 9.8) ER	1 x 4 Stroke 6 Cy. 400 x 600
	Panama Panama				Cranes: 4x20t	The Hanshin Diesel Works Ltd.
	MMSI: 352112000					

8401834	AMRTA JAYA II	5,498	Class: NK	1984-08 Nishi Zosen K.K. -Imabari Yd No: 327	General Cargo Ship	1 oil engine driving 1 FP propeller
YFUS		3,836		Loa 98.18 (BB) Br ex 18.04 Dght 7.544	Grain: 13,070; Bale: 12,096	Total Power: 2.427kW(3,300hp)	12.0kn
-	P.T. Pelayaran Samudera "Admiral Lines"	6,840		Lbp 89.95 Br md 18.00 Dpth 13.00	Compartments: 2 Ho, ER	Hanshin	6EL41";
		T/cm		Welded, 2 dks	2 Ha: (22.2 x 9.8) (24.7 x 9.8) ER	1 x 4 Stroke 6 Cy. 400 x 600
	Jakarta Indonesia	-			Derricks: 4x20t	The Hanshin Diesel Works Ltd.
						AuxGen: 3 x280kWa.c.

9003988	AMRTA VII	5,473	Class: NK	1990-10 Murakami Hide Zosen K.K. -Hakata	General Cargo Ship	1 oil engine driving 1 FP propeller
3EKN8	ex Orient Queen -1997	1,999		Yd No: 318	Grain: 13,285; Bale: 12,611	Total Power: 2,427kW(3,300hp)	11.6kn
19238-90C	Admiral Three Star S.A.	7,018		Loa 99.92 (BB) Br ex - Dght 7.573	Compartments: 2 Ho, ER, 2 TwDk	Akasaka	A41
-	P.T. Pelayaran Samudera "Admiral Lines"	T/cm		Lbp 89.95 Br md 18.00 Dpth 13.00	2 Ha: (21.7 x 9.8) (24.5 x 9.8) ER	1 x 4 Stroke 6 Cy. 410x800
	Panama Panama			Welded,	Derricks: 4x20t	Akasaka Tekkosho K.K. (Akasaka Diesels Ltd.)
	SatCom: Inmarsat M MMSI: 353116000					AuxGen:4x167kWa.c.

9150080	AMRUM TRADER	5,941	Class: GL	1997-04 Peterswerft Wewetsfleth GmbH & Co.-	Container Ship (Fully Cellular)	1 oil engine with flexible couplings & reductiongeared to
V2LF	ex Seaboard Unity -1998	2,777		Wewelsfleth Yd No: 659	Grain: 9,259; Bale: 8.957	sc. shaft driving 1 FP propeller
	launched as Amnim Trader -	8,801		Loa 132.30 (BB) Br ex 19.50 Dght 6.921	TEU 624 C.Ho 170/20' (40')	Total Power: 5,940kW(8,075hp)
	Dreiunddreissigste Grosse Bleichen	T/cm		Lbp 123.40 Br md 19.20 Dpth 9.20	C.Dk 454/20'	Wartsila	9R38
	Schiffahrtsgesellschaft mbH & Co. KG			Welded, 1 dk	(40') incl. 80 ref C.	1 x 4 Stroke 9 Cy. 380x475
	Hermann Buss GmbH & Cie.				Compartments: 3 Cell Ho, ER	Stork-Wartsila Diesel B.V
	Leer Antigua & Barbuda				3 Ha: ER	AuxGen: 2 x 320kW 400V 50Hz
						Thrusters: 1 Thwart. FP thruster (f)
						Fuel:120.0(d.o.)560.0(i.f.o.)25.0pd

Appendix 1

Key to the Register of Ships 2008-2009

1. Registration

LR/IMO Number

A unique seven digit number printed in **bold type** which is used for data processing purposes, and which remains unchanged during the life of the ship.

The IMO (International Maritime Organization) identification number was adopted on 19th November 1987 in IMO Resolution A.600(15) and remains constant in the event of rebuilding or shiptype conversion. This unique number is assigned to the total or greater portion of the hull enclosing the machinery space and is the determining factor should additional hull sections be added. The LR/IMO Number is never reassigned to another vessel. This number is also utilised in respect of SOLAS XI 1/3 and 1/5.

> **Lloyd's Register – Fairplay Ltd is the sole authority for identifying and assigning an LR/IMO number.**

IMO Resolution A.600(15)

IMO Resolution A.600(15) applies to seagoing ships of 100 Gross Tonnage and above, with the exception of the following:-

- *Vessels solely engaged in fi shing;*
- *Ships without mechanical means of propulsion;*
- *Pleasure yachts;*
- *Ships engaged on special service (e.g. lightships, floating radio stations, search & rescue vessels);*
- *Hopper barges;*
- *Hydrofoils, hovercraft;*
- *Floating docks and structures classified in a similar manner;*
- *Ships of war and troop ships;*
- *Wooden ships in general.*

Call Sign

Signal letters or radio call sign assigned by the relevant national authority. This is shown in *italics*. A dash (-) will be displayed where confirmation is awaited.

Fishing Number

The identification number assigned by the relevant national authority to ships engaged in the fishing industry. The number is displayed, on the vessel's hull, for permanent identification. A dash (-) will be displayed for ships other than fishing vessels or where the information is awaiting confirmation.

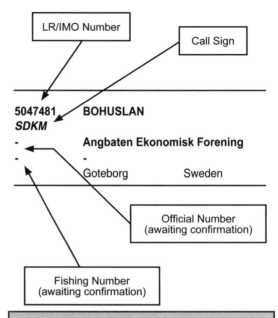

Radio Communications & Safety of Navigation

Subscribers seeking information should in the first instance refer to SOLAS chapters IV and V Chapter IV was revised in 1988 to incorporate amendments to introduce the Global Maritime Distress and Safety System (GMDSS) and details requirements for all passenger ships and all cargo ships of 300GT and upwards engaged on international voyages to carry equipment such as Satellite Emergency Positioning Indicating Radio Beacons (EPIRBs) and Search and Rescue Transponders (SARTs).

Chapter V references, inter alia, the carriage of Voyage Data Recorders (VDRs) and Automatic Ship Identification Systems (AIS) for certain ships.

2. Names & Owners

Ship's Name

The current ship's name is displayed in **bold type**. Ships are listed in the Register in alphabetical order, with numeric entries appearing after the end of the letter 'Z'.

Former Names

The figures following the former name of a ship indicate the year, where known, in which the change of name occurred and are listed in chronological order. The year of change is displayed in italics and is preceded by a dash (-). Where a name changes prior to the ship being commissioned, a 'Launched as' or 'Completed as' entry will be displayed.

(In the absence of date changes being advised, an estimated date has been included)

Owners

The registered owners are recorded in **bold type**. The underlined letter in each owner's name indicates the sort letter under which the entry appears in the *List of Shipowners*. A dash (-) will be displayed where confirmation of registered owners is awaited.

This field represents the legal owner of the ship and the name that appears on the ship's papers. It may be an owner/manager or a wholly-owned subsidiary in a larger shipping group or a company created on paper to legally own a ship or ships and limit liability for the real owners. This may be a legal requirement of the flag state with which it is registered.

Managers

The managers are recorded in normal type. The underlined letter in each manager's name indicates the letter under which the entry appears in the *List of Shipowners*.

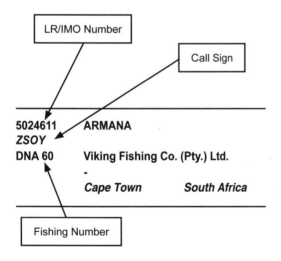

Appendix 1

Key to the Register of Ships 2008-2009

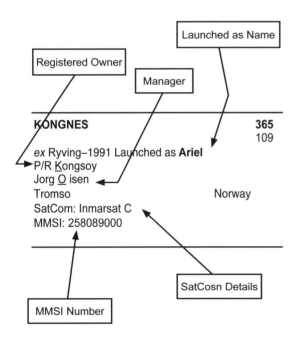

A dash (-) will be displayed where confirmation of the manager is awaited or is not applicable.

The company is responsible for the commercial decisions concerning the operation of a ship.

Port of Registry

The port of registry shown is that which is displayed on the ship and is published in *italics*.

Flag

This indicates the flag registry under which the ship normally operates and is displayed in *italics*.

A considerable number of ships now operate under Parallel Registry, which can result in confusedidentifi cation of a ship. Lloyd's Register – Fairplay's policy is to publish the Registry (flag and port), following verification, which is painted on the ship's stern.

Satellite Communication Data

Details of the service provider and the types of receiver are listed. The various types are as follows:-

• Inmarsat-A (Analogue system, supports voice, telex, fax and data)
• Inmarsat-B (Digital system, supports voice, fax, data & telex)
• Inmarsat-M (Digital system, capable of voice, fax & data)
• Inmarsat-Mini-M (Digital system, supports voice, fax, data and email)
• Inmarsat-C (Store & forward data, telex system)

MMSI Number

The Maritime Mobile Service Identity (MMSI) is displayed where known. These identifiers are supplied by National Authorities under the auspices of the International Telecommunications Union (ITU), which is based in Geneva.

The ITU is an international organisation within the United Nations System, where governments and the private sector co-ordinate global telecommunication networks and services. (web site address www.itu.org)

Each number is unique and used to identify an individual vessel (or shore-based) radio installation. It is used within GMDSS as a vessel code.

Official Number

The identification number assigned by the national registration authority. A dash (-) will be displayed where the information is awaiting confirmation.

3. Tonnage

Gross Tonnage

The Gross Tonnage printed in **bold type** indicates that the ship has been measured in accordance with the requirements of the 1969 International Convention on Tonnage Measurement of Ships. The Gross Tonnage generally comprises the moulded volume of all enclosed spaces of the ship, to which a formula is then applied in accordance with the Convention requirements. Accordingly, no unit of measurement is assigned and the figure attained is simply referred to as the ship's "Gross Tonnage" (GT). A dash (-) will be displayed where confirmation of the gross tonnage is awaited.

The Gross Tonnage printed in *italic type* indicates that the ship has been measured in accordance with tonnage regulations adopted prior to the 18th July 1982, when the 1969 Convention came into force. This tonnage is referred to as "Gross Registered Tonnage" (GRT).

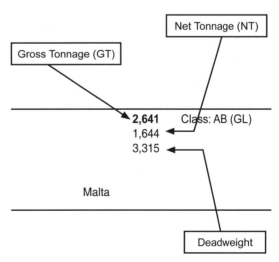

Appendix 1

Key to the Register of Ships 2008-2009

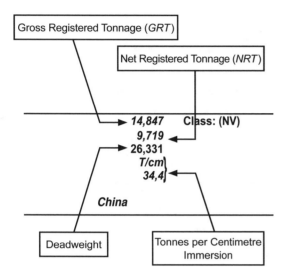

Net Tonnage

The Net Tonnage in normal type is derived in accordance with the requirements of the 1969 International Convention on Tonnage Measurement of Ships. The Net Tonnage generally comprises the moulded volume of all cargo spaces on board, to which a formula is then applied in accordance with the Convention requirements. The formula for Net Tonnage also takes account of the varying factors such as ships depth, draught, number of passengers but notwithstanding the above, will never be less than GT x 0.3. Accordingly, no unit of measurement is assigned and the figure attained is simply referred to as the ship's "Net Tonnage" (NT).

The Net Tonnage printed in *italic type* indicates that the ship has been measured in accordance with tonnage regulations adopted prior to the 18th July 1982, when the 1969 Convention came into force. This tonnage is referred to as "Net Registered Tonnage" (NRT).

The Net Registered Tonnage is derived by deducting spaces used for the accommodation of the master, officers, crew, navigation, and propelling machinery.

A dash (-) will be displayed where confirmation of the net tonnage is awaited.

Deadweight

The Deadweight is the weight in tonnes (1,000 kg) of cargo, stores, fuel, passengers and crew carried by the ship when loaded to the maximum summer loadline. In the case of vessels with more than 1 load line measurement, LRF record the higher deadweight and corresponding draught only.

A dash (-) will be displayed where confirmation of the deadweight is awaited.

Tonnes Per Centimetre Immersion

The Tonnes per Centimetre Immersion (T/cm), displayed in *italic type*, is the weight in tonnes (1,000 kg) required to immerse the hull of the ship by one centimetre at a particular draught. The value shown is that corresponding to the maximum summer draught.

4. Classification

General Class Details

If a ship is currently classed, the initial letters of the Society are recorded. In the event that a ship is disclassed the initial letters of the Society will be recorded in parentheses. Previous class history is recorded in sequence order.

Where a ship has applied for class which has not been confirmed '(Class Contemplated)' will be displayed immediately after the initials of the Society.

Lloyd's Register – Class Symbols (Hull & Equipment)

In the event that a ship is currently classed with Lloyd's Register (LR) then the following hull and equipment symbols may be displayed.

✠ The Maltese Cross denotes that the ship was constructed under LR's Special Survey in compliance with their Rules. This will be displayed in **bold** if applicable.

100 This character figure is assigned to ships considered suitable for sea-going service. This will be displayed in **bold** if applicable. (Prior to 1948 this figure was not included in the class notation of ships intended for limited sea-going service.

A The character letter is assigned to ships which have been constructed or accepted into class in accordance with LR's Rules and Regulations and which are maintained in good and efficient condition. This will be displayed in **bold** if applicable.

1 This character figure is assigned to:-(a) Ships having on board, in good and efficient condition, anchoring and/or mooring equipment in accordance with the Rules.

(b) Ships classed for special service, for which no specific anchoring and mooring Rules have been published, having on board, in good and efficient condition, anchoring and/or mooring equipment considered suitable and sufficient by LR for the particular service.

This will be displayed in **bold** if applicable.

– This character symbol, in the position usually occupied by the figure 1, is assigned to ships when the anchoring and mooring equipment is not in accordance with the requirements of the Rules, but is considered to be acceptable for the particular service. This symbol is no longer assigned.

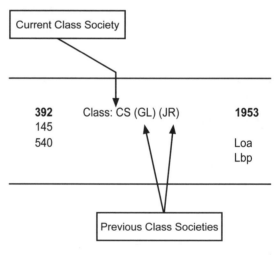

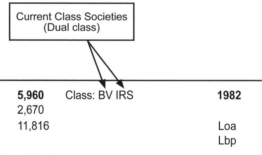

Appendix 1

Key to the Register of Ships 2008-2009

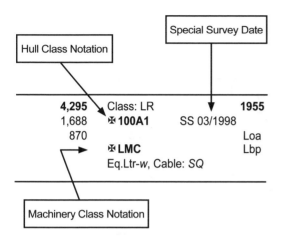

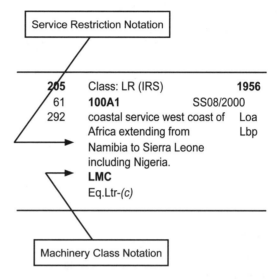

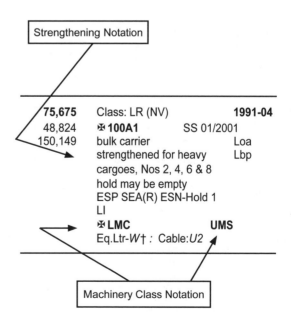

N This character letter is assigned to ships on which anchoring and mooring equipment need not be fitted in view of their particular service. This will be displayed in **bold** if applicable.

T This character letter is assigned to ships which are intended to perform their primary designed service function only while they are anchored, moored, towed or linked and which have in good and efficient condition, adequately attached anchoring, mooring, towing or linking equipment which has been approved as suitable and sufficient for the intended service. This will be displayed in bold if applicable.

OU/OI These character letters are assigned to offshore units classed with LR and can be assigned to self-propelled or non-propelled offshore units other than ships. This will be displayed in **bold** if applicable.

* Denotes that the ship was built under the supervision of the surveyors in accordance with the Rules of the British Corporation (BS).

BS Denotes that the hull and equipment of iron and steel ships classed in accordance to British Corporation Rules.

Lloyd's Register – Class Notations (Service Restrictions)
Service restriction notations will generally be assigned in one of the following forms but this does not preclude special consideration for other forms in unusual cases.

Protected Waters Service – Service in sheltered water adjacent to sand banks, reefs, breakwaters or other coastal features, and in sheltered water between islands.

Extended Protected Waters Service – Service in protected waters and also for distances (generally less than 15 nautical miles) beyond protected waters in reasonable weather. Reasonable weather is defined as Wind strengths of force 6 or less in the Beaufort scale, associated with sea states sufficiently moderate to ensure that green water is taken on board the ship's deck at infrequent intervals only or not at all.

'Fetch', 'sheltered water' and 'reasonable weather' are defined in LR's Rules and Regulations

Specified Coastal Service – Service along a coast, and for a distance out to sea not exceeding 21 nautical miles, unless some other distance is specified for "coastal service" by the Administration with which the ship is registered, or by the Administration of the coast off which it is operating, as applicable.

Specified Route Service – This notation means that the ship is intended for service between two or more ports, or other geographical features which are indicated.

Specified Operating Area Service – This notation means that the ship is intended for service within one or more geographical areas as indicated.

Short International Voyage – This expression means an international voyage in the course of which a ship is not more than 200 nautical miles from a port or place in which the

passengers and crew could be placed in safety, and which does not exceed 600 nautical miles in length between the last port of call in the country in which the voyage begins and the final port of destination. This notation is no longer assigned.

Lloyd's Register – Class Notations (Hull Strengthening)
Heavy Cargoes – When the scantlings and arrangements have been approved for the carriage of such cargoes a class notation 'Strengthened for heavy cargoes' is assigned.
As from January 1978 this notation is assigned to general cargo ships and bulk carriers, where applicable, but in the case of ore or oil carriers the class notation 'ore carrier' or 'ore or oil carrier' will be assigned.
'Strengthened for regular discharge by heavy grabs' is assigned at the owner's option where cargoes are regularly discharged by heavy grabs, and the thickness of the plating of the hold inner bottom, hopper and tranverse bulkhead bottom stool is increased in accordance with the requirements of the Rules.

Appendix 1

Key to the Register of Ships 2008-2009

Ice Strengthening – Iceclassifi cation notations and degrees of strengthening for navigation in ice are displayed within the class notation. Where a ship was previously assigned ice classification by the British Corporation this will be displayed as 'Ice strengthening'

The abbreviations and their descriptions can be found in the section 'Abbreviations used in the Register'

Lloyd's Register – Shipright Notation
Structural Design Assessment (SDA), Fatigue Design Assessment (FDA) and Construction Monitoring (CM) are notations assigned where a ship complies with the procedure for the Design, Construction and Lifetime Care of Ships.

The abbreviations and their descriptions can be found in the section 'Abbreviations used in the Register'

Lloyd's Register – Class Notations (Special Surveys)
SS-with date   Special Survey.
CS-with date   Continuous Survey of the hull
Lake SS   Periodical Survey of ship classed for Great Lakes service.

Lloyd's Register – Class Notations(Machinery)
✠LMC   Notation assigned when the propelling and essential auxiliary machinery has been constructed, installed and tested under LR's Special Survey and in accordance with the requirements of the Rules.

✠LMC   Notation assigned when the propelling and essential auxiliary machinery has been constructed under the survey of a recognised authority in accordance with the Rules and Regulations equivalent to those of LR and, in addition, the whole of the machinery has been installed and tested under LR's Special Survey in accordance with LR's Rules.

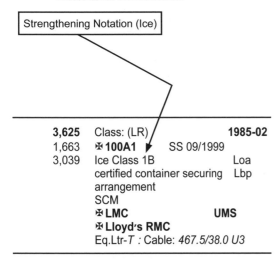

LMC   Notation assigned when the propelling and essential auxiliary machinery has neither been constructed nor installed under LR's Special Survey but the existing machinery, its installation and arrangement, have been tested and found to be acceptable by LR.

✠OMC   Notation

OMC   Denotes that the machinery was built and installed
MBS*   under the supervision of the surveyors to the Rules of the British Corporation or of LR respectively.

UMS   This notation may be assigned to a ship classed with LR which can be operated with the machinery spaces unattended and that the control equipment has been arranged, installed and tested in accordance with LR's Rules.

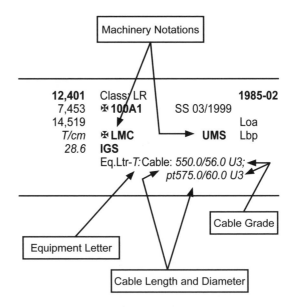

CCS   This notation may be assigned to a ship classed with LR which can be operated with the machinery spaces under continuous supervision from a centralised control station and that the control engineering equipment has been arranged, installed and tested in accordance with LR's Rules.

✠Lloyd's   Denotes that the refrigerated cargo installation of
RMC   a ship classed with LR and has been constructed, installed and tested under LR's Special Survey in accordance with the relevant requirements of the Rules.

Lloyd's   Denotes that the refrigerated cargo installation of a
RCM   ship is classed with LR and that the installation has been found to be equivalent to the re quirements of the Rules and has been tested in accordance with the relevant requirements of the Rules.

✠Lloyd's   This notation is assigned to a liquefied gas carrier
RCM (LG)   or tanker classed with LR in which reliquefaction or refrigeration equipment is approved and fitted for cargo temperature and pressure control, where the equipment has been constructed, installed and tested in accordance with the relevant requirements of the Rules.

Lloyd's   This notation is assigned to a liquefied gas carrier
RCM (LG)   or tanker classed with LR in which reliquefaction or refrigeration equipment is fitted for cargo temperature and pressure control, where the equipment has been found to be equivalent to the requirements of the Rules and tested in accordance with the relevant requirements of the Rules.

IGS   This notation will be assigned to a ship classed with LR when the ships is intended for the carriage of oil in bulk, or for the carriage of liquid chemicals in bulk and is fitted with an approved system for producing gas and for inerting the cargo tanks in accordance with the requirements of LR's Rules.

In all instances where the notation is shown in parentheses it denotes that the class has been temporarily suspended

Lloyd's Register – Class Notations (Equipment Letter, Cable Details)
The Equipment Letter (A, A†, B*, etc.), determined by LR's Rules, is displayed in *italics* prefixed by 'Eq.Ltr'. This is followed by the length (metres) and diameter (millimetres) of the chain cable, prefixed by 'Cable' and then the grade of chain cable. The dimensions and grade of cable are also displayed in *italics*. If the chain cable is made up of more than one part the dimension sets are displayed with a 'pt' separator.

Appendix 1

When shown in parentheses the Equipment Letter denotes that the actual equipment number permitted by the Rules differs from the calculated equipment number.
The character symbols U1, U2, U3 and U4 denote the grades of chain cable (other than wrought iron or mild steel fire-welded) as defined in LR's Rules.

Lloyd's Register – Class Withdrawal
When a ship becomes disclassed, either at owner's request or withdrawn by LR, the general class field will display LR in parentheses. All LR class related details will be deleted and in their place the notation '⊞ Classed LR until – date' or 'Classed LR until – date' will be displayed.

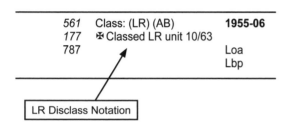

5. Hull

Date of Build
The date of build is displayed in bold and reflects the actual completion date or an estimate in the absence of confirmed data.
(In the absence of date changes being advised, an estimated date has been included).
In the event that there has been a significant interval between the launching and the completion and/or commissioning of the ship, dates may be recorded in parentheses after the shipbuilder prefixed by one of the following; 'launched', 'completed', 'commissioned', 'lengthened & completed', 'reassembled' 're-erected', ' assembled' or 're-built'.

Shipbuilder
The shipbuilder and place of build are displayed in bold type after the date of build. The underlined letter in each shipbuilder's name indicates the sort letter under which the entry appears in the Shipbuilder and Existing Ships Index. This normally records where the hull of the ship was built. Where a ship has major

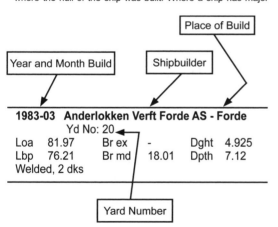

hull sections constructed by other builders, the date of build, shipbuilder and place of build, hull section, construction date detail and yard number are recorded.

IACS Procedural Requirements 1996 – No.11 It should be noted that where modifications, possibly extensive, have been carried out, the original 'Date of Build' shall remain assigned to the ship. Where a complete replacement or addition of a major portion

of the ship (e.g. forward section, after section, main cargo section) is involved then the 'Date of Build' associated with each major portion of the ship shall be indicated.

When the shipbuilder is unknown '...' is displayed. In the event that only the place, region or country is known this will be displayed prefixed by either 'in', 'at' or 'on'.

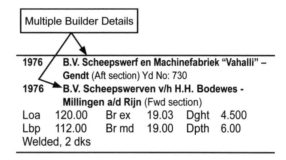

Yard Number
The Shipbuilder's number, known as yard or hull number, is displayed for the hull section, prefixed by 'Yd No:'. Where construction may involve more than one hull section or builder each shipbuilder's number is recorded.

Conversions
Details of ship conversions are recorded, listing the previous shiptype and date, prefixed by 'Converted from:'. Where a ship has been converted more than once the conversions will be recorded in reverse chronological order. (In the absence of date changes being advised, an estimated date has been included).

Alterations
Details of alterations (lengthened etc.) are recorded, listing the type of alteration and date. Where more than one alteration takes place at the same time these will be grouped together. (In the absence of date changes being advised, an estimated date has been included).

LENGTH OVERALL/REGISTERED LENGTH
The extreme length of the ship, recorded in metres to two decimal places, is displayed, prefixed by 'Loa'. A dash (-) will be displayed where confirmation of the length overall is awaited. Where the overall length is followed by the notation 'BB' this indicates that the ship has a bulbous bow. In these instance the recorded measurement includes any protrusion of that bow.

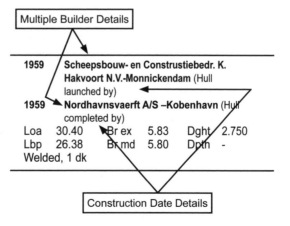

Appendix 1

Key to the Register of Ships 2008-2009

If the length overall is not available, the registered length, as given on the ship's certificates, may be recorded, prefixed by 'Lreg'.

Length Between Perpendiculars
The length between perpendiculars, recorded in metres to two decimal places, is displayed, prefixed by 'Lbp'. A dash (-) will be displayed where confirmation of the length between perpendiculars is awaited. This is the distance on the summer load waterline from the fore side of the stem to the after side of the rudder post, or to the centre of the rudder stock if there is no rudder post.

Extreme Breadth
The extreme breadth, recorded in metres to two decimal places, is displayed, prefixed by 'Brex'. A dash (-) will be displayed where confirmation of the extreme breadth is awaited. This is the maximum breadth to the outside of the ship's structure.

Moulded Breadth
The moulded breadth, recorded in metres to two decimal places, is displayed, prefixed by 'Brmd'. A dash (-) will be displayed where confirmation of the moulded breadth is awaited. This is the greatest breadth at amidships from heel of frame to heel of frame

Maximum Draught
The maximum draught, recorded in metres to three decimal places, is displayed, prefixed by 'Dght'. A dash (-) will be displayed where confirmation of the maximum draught is awaited. In most cases this is the maximum draught amidships, but in some ships of special construction the maximum draught is measured at the deepest point of the hull or any fixed appendages, and this measurement is recorded, where defined.

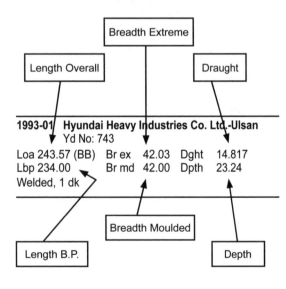

Moulded Depth
The moulded depth, recorded in metres to two decimal places, is displayed, prefixed by 'Dpth'. A dash (-) will be displayed where confirmation of the moulded depth is awaited. This is the vertical distance at amidships from the top of the keel to the top of the upper deck beam at side.

Construction
The construction of the ship is displayed and is recorded as one of the following:-

        Welded
        Riveted
        Riveted/Welded
        Bonded

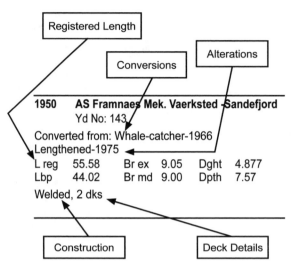

Decks
Details on the number and type of decks are displayed after the construction information.

> **The abbreviations and their descriptions can be found in the section 'Abbreviations used in the Register'**

6. Shiptype/Cargo Facilities

Shiptype
The description of the ship is displayed in **bold type** and indicates the basic type of the ship (i.e. tanker, tug, general cargo ship). It should be noted that these are not classification notations. (for further information on shiptypes please visit www.lrfairplay.com)

Hull Material
Hull material is displayed, prefixed by 'Hull material:', when a ship is constructed from a material other than steel. Unless otherwise stated, ships are of steel construction.

Hull Type
Details of specialised hull types are recorded where applicable. For instance 'Triple Hull' 'Split Hull'.

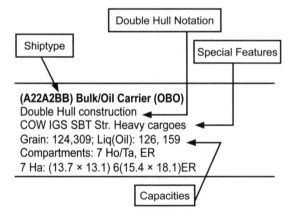

Ship Subtypes
The ship subtypes are displayed, where applicable, and indicate in more detail the known specific function of the ship.

Double Hull
Where ships have been constructed with double skin sides and double bottoms, the description 'Double Hull' will be displayed. For tankers where it is known that these comply

Appendix 1

Key to the Register of Ships 2008-2009

with the requirements of IMO Regulation 13F the description 'Double Hull (13F)' will be displayed.

Special Features

Special feature notations are displayed for ships with specific shiptype facilities or strengthening. For example 'F-S Ice Rules Notation', 'pt higher tensile steel', 'Str. Heavy cargoes', 'DB' (Double bottom), 'SBT' (Segregated ballast tanks), etc.

In addition Lloyd's Register Ship Right notations are displayed where a ship complies on a voluntary basis with the applicable requirements of the Procedures for the Design, Construction and Lifetime Care of Ships.

> **The abbreviations and their descriptions can be found in the section 'Abbreviations used in the Register'**

Passengers

Details of the number of passengers a ship is licensed to carry are recorded, prefixed by 'Passengers:' and are defined by 'deck', 'unberthed', 'berths' and 'driver berths'. Where confirmation of individual categories is awaited the total number of passengers is given.

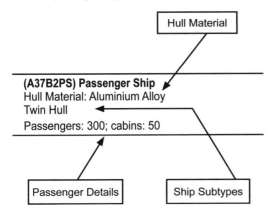

RO/RO Facilities

Details of ramps, lanes, vehicle counts are recorded for ships with Ro/Ro facilities.

Ramps – The number and type of ramps, position, length, width and safe working load are displayed where known. The dimensions for length, width and safe working load are prefixed with 'Len', 'Wid' and 'Swl' respectively. In the event

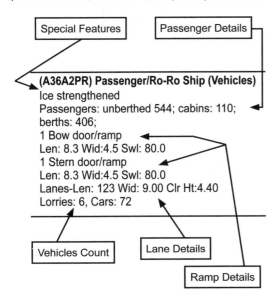

that a ship has ramps with different dimensions these will be displayed sequentially.

Lanes – The total maximum linear lane length, the maximum width of ro-ro lane and the maximum deck head clearance between adjacent fixed or movable decks are displayed, in metres, where known. The dimensions for length, width and clear height are prefixed with 'Len', 'Wid' and 'Clr Ht' respectively

Vehicle Counts – The details of vehicle counts are displayed, prefixed by the types of vehicle. For example 'Cars', 'Lorries', 'Trailers', 'Rail wagons' etc.

Capacities

Details of cargo capacities are recorded, prefixed by the appropriate types. The key definitions are as follows:-

Grain: The capacity of cargo spaces, measured to outside of frames, to top of ceiling and to top of beams, including hatchways. This does not include insulated spaces or spaces allocated to containers. Grain capacity is measured in cubic metres.

Bale: The capacity of cargo spaces, measure to inside of cargo battens, to top of ceiling and to underside of beams, including hatchways. This does not include spaces allocated to containers. Bale capacity is measured in cubic metres.

For insulated (Ins), liquid (Liq), liquid gas (Liq(Gas)), liquid oil (Liq(Oil)), asphalt (asphalt), ore (ore) and hopper (hopper) the capacities are also measured in cubic metres. Imperial equivalents are given to reflect industry standards, where appropriate.

Liquid and liquid oil capacities are recorded, where known as 98% of the total volume of the cargo carrying capacity, allowing 2% for expansion.

Where known information on cargo heating coils is recorded.

Container Details

For a container ship (fully cellular) or part container ship container details expressed in TEU (twenty foot equivalent units), are displayed as follows:-

C. Total carrying capacity in TEU. This information is only recorded when the separate number of laden containers carried in holds and those on deck is awaited.

C.Dk. Carrying capacity in TEU on weather deck.

C.Ho. Carrying capacity in TEU in holds.

Cell.Ho. Holds fitted with fixed cellguides for the carriage of laden containers.

> **Container Details**

(A33A2CC) Container Ship (Fully Cellular)
TEU 3484 C.3484/20' incl. 300 ref.C
Compartments: 7 Cell Ho, ER, 1 Cell Ho
15 Ha:ER

Hatch Details

Compartment Details

C.Ro-Ro Dk. Carrying capacity in TEU containers on internal decks accessed by doors and ramps.

In all instances the values are inclusive of any refrigerated units.

Compartments (Holds)

Details of the number and types of compartment are recorded, together with specific material where appropriate. Within the sequence of hold information 'ER' indicates the position of the engine room. Hold information is displayed prefixed by 'Compartment'.

Appendix 1

Key to the Register of Ships 2008-2009

> The abbreviations and their descriptions can be found in the section 'Abbreviations used in the Register'

Compartments (Tanks)

Details of the number, type, design, material, shape and alignment are recorded. Within the sequence of tank information 'ER' indicates the position of the engine room. Tank information is displayed prefixed by 'Compartment'.

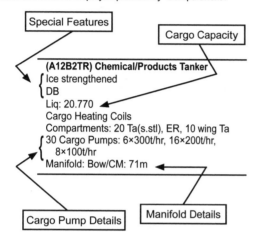

(A12B2TR) Chemical/Products Tanker
Ice strengthened
DB
Liq: 20.770
Cargo Heating Coils
Compartments: 20 Ta(s.stl), ER, 10 wing Ta
30 Cargo Pumps: 6×300t/hr, 16×200t/hr, 8×100t/hr
Manifold: Bow/CM: 71m

(labels: Special Features, Cargo Capacity, Cargo Pump Details, Manifold Details)

> The abbreviations and their descriptions can be found in the section 'Abbreviations used in the Register'

Hatches

Details of the number, position and dimensions of hatches are recorded. The hatches are given in order, commencing at No.1 from forward and are grouped by centreline (Ha) and wing (Wing Ha) and dimensions.
For tapered hatchways only the narrower breadth is recorded. Hatch dimensions are not recorded under 2 metres. For partial measurements the dimension under 2 metres is represented by '-'. Within the sequence of hatch information 'ER' indicates the position of the engine room

Cargo Gear

Details of the number and lifting capacity (SWL) of a ship's cargo gear are displayed, prefixed by the type (i.e cranes, derricks, etc.). The number of winches is also displayed.

Cargo Pumps

Details of the number and output of a ship's cargo pumps are displayed, grouped by output and prefixed by 'Cargo Pumps'. The output is recorded either in tonnes per hour 't/hr' or 'm³/hr'.

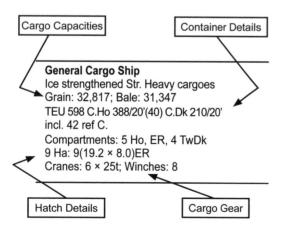

General Cargo Ship
Ice strengthened Str. Heavy cargoes
Grain: 32,817; Bale: 31,347
TEU 598 C.Ho 388/20'(40) C.Dk 210/20' incl. 42 ref C.
Compartments: 5 Ho, ER, 4 TwDk
9 Ha: 9(19.2 × 8.0)ER
Cranes: 6 × 25t; Winches: 8

(labels: Cargo Capacities, Container Details, Hatch Details, Cargo Gear)

Manifold

The distance between the bow and the centre manifold is recorded in metres, prefixed by 'Manifold: Bow/CM'.

7. Machinery

Summary

A summary, listing the number and prime mover type (in **bold**), gearing information, number of shafts and the number and propeller type, is displayed. For diesel electric installations the number of main generators and electric motors are recorded. Main generator output for each unit is displayed in kilowatts (kW). The total electric motor output is displayed in shaft horsepower (shp) and kilowatts (kW).

Total Prime Mover Power

The total output of the prime movers is displayed in kilowatts (kW) and horsepower (hp), prefixed by 'Total Power'.

Speed

The ship's service speed is displayed to the right of the total power and is defined as the speed that the ship is capable of maintaining at sea in normal weather and at normal service draught.

Prime Mover Design

The design of each prime mover is displayed. Ships with more than one prime mover of the same design and designation will be grouped together, unless manufactured or fitted at different times. Where a ship has prime movers of different designs these will be recorded individually.

Prime Mover Designation

The designation of the prime mover is displayed to the right of the main engine design.

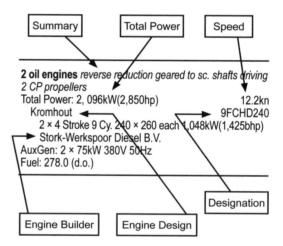

2 oil engines *reverse reduction geared to sc. shafts driving 2 CP propellers*
Total Power: 2, 096kW(2,850hp)   12.2kn
    Kromhout   9FCHD240
        2 × 4 Stroke 9 Cy. 240 × 260 each 1,048kW(1,425bhp)
        Stork-Werkspoor Diesel B.V.
AuxGen: 2 × 75kW 380V 50Hz
Fuel: 278.0 (d.o.)

(labels: Summary, Total Power, Speed, Engine Builder, Engine Design, Designation)

Prime Mover Details

Oil Engines – For each main engine group the number, configuration (if vee), stroke cycle, number of cylinders, bore and stroke dimensions, are displayed. In the event that the engine was manufactured significantly earlier than the ship then the date of manufacture is recorded. Similarly if the engine is replaced or re-conditioned dates of manufacture and fitting are recorded, where known.
(In the absence of date changes being advised, an estimated date has been included) The output of each engine is recorded in kilowatts (kW) and brake horsepower (bhp).

Appendix 1

Key to the Register of Ships 2008-2009

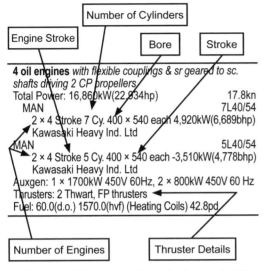

4 oil engines with flexible couplings & sr geared to sc. shafts driving 2 CP propellers.
Total Power: 16,860kW(22,934hp)   17.8kn
  MAN   7L40/54
    2 × 4 Stroke 7 Cy. 400 × 540 each 4,920kW(6,689bhp)
    Kawasaki Heavy Ind. Ltd
MAN   5L40/54
    2 × 4 Stroke 5 Cy. 400 × 540 each -3,510kW(4,778bhp)
    Kawasaki Heavy Ind. Ltd
Auxgen: 1 × 1700kW 450V 60Hz, 2 × 800kW 450V 60 Hz
Thrusters: 2 Thwart, FP thrusters
Fuel: 60.0(d.o.) 1570.0(hvf) (Heating Coils) 42.8pd

Gas Turbines – The number of gas turbines and relative outputs, recorded in kilowatts (kW) and shaft horsepower (shp), are displayed. In the event that the gas turbine was manufactured significantly earlier than the ship then the date of manufacture is recorded. Similarly if the gas turbine is replaced or re-conditioned dates of manufacture and fitting are recorded, where known.
(In the absence of date changes being advised, an estimated date has been included).
Steam Turbines – The number of steam turbines and relative outputs, recorded in kilowatts (kW) and shaft horsepower (shp), are displayed. In the event that the steam turbine was manufactured significantly earlier than the ship then the date of manufacture is recorded. Similarly if the steam turbine is replaced or re-conditioned dates of manufacture and fitting are recorded, where known.
(In the absence of date changes being advised, an estimated date has been included).
Steam Reciprocating Engines – For each steam reciprocating engine group the number, type, configuration, number of cylinders, bore of each cylinder (High, Intermediate and Low Pressure) and stroke dimension, are displayed. In the event that the engine was manufactured significantly earlier than the ship then the date of manufacture is recorded. Similarly if the

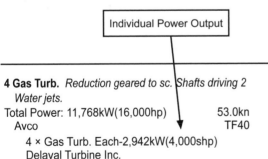

4 Gas Turb. *Reduction geared to sc. Shafts driving 2 Water jets.*
Total Power: 11,768kW(16,000hp)   53.0kn
  Avco   TF40
    4 × Gas Turb. Each-2,942kW(4,000shp)
    Delaval Turbine Inc.

engine is replaced or re-conditioned dates of manufacture and fitting are recorded, where known.
(In the absence of date changes being advised, an estimated date has been included).
The output of each engine is recorded in kilowatts (kW) and indicated horsepower (ihp)

Engine Manufacturer
The manufacturer of each engine group is displayed.

Auxiliary Generators
The number, rated power output and voltage for each auxiliary generator group is displayed. For 'a.c.' installations the frequency is recorded in hertz (Hz). Auxiliary generator details are prefixed by 'AuxGen:'. Emergency sources of power and sets used solely for harbour purposes are not recorded.

Boilers
Information on boilers is only recorded for vessels currently classed with Lloyd's Register and details are prefixed by 'Boilers:' For each boiler group the number, type, firing type, receiver (rcv) and heater (htr) details, pressures, superheater

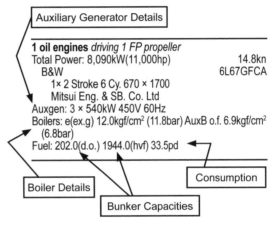

temperature and pressure details, and heating surface area (m²) are recorded. In the event that the boiler was manufactured significantly earlier than the ship then the date of manufacture is recorded. Similarly if the boiler is replaced or reconditioned dates of manufacture and fitting are recorded. Where details of boilers are recorded in parentheses this indicates that the boiler is temporarily out of use.

> **The abbreviations and their descriptions can be found in the section 'Abbreviations used in the Register'**

Thrusters
Details of special positioning units are recorded prefixed by 'Thrusters:'. For each type the number, type and position are displayed.

Bunkers
Bunker capacities, together with the daily fuel consumption, are recorded in tonnes, prefixed by 'Fuel'. Where a ship has heating coils fitted for bunker fuel these will be recorded after the fuel type.

Appendix 1

Abbreviations Used in the Register of Ships 2008-2009

Abbreviation	Column	Explanation
⊕	4 & 7	LR class character symbol (See Key for full explanation)
100	4	LR class character figure (See Key for full explanation)
⊕	4	LR class character symbol (See Key for full explanation)
A	4	LR class character letter (See Key for full explanation)
1	4	LR class character figure (See Key for full explanation)
–	4	LR class character symbol (See Key for full explanation)
N	4	LR class character letter (See Key for full explanation)
T	4	LR class character letter (See Key for full explanation)
*	4 & 7	British Corporation class character symbol (See Key for full explanation)
A, A†, B*, (A), (A†), (B*) etc.	4	Equipment Letters (See Key for full explanation)
a or (a)	4, 5, 6 & 7	aft
a.c.	7	Alternating current
ACT	2 & 5	Australian Capital Territory
AB	4	American Bureau of Shipping
AB	2 & 5	Alberta (Canada)
AK	2 & 5	Alaska
AH	2 & 5	Anhui
AL	2 & 5	Alabama
(alu)	6	Aluminium
AR	2 & 5	Arkansas
(Arg)	5	Argentina
aux	4, 5 & 7	Auxiliary
AuxB	7	Auxiliary Boiler(s) (LR) (See Key for full explanation)
AuxGen	7	Auxiliary generators
AZ	2 & 5	Arizona
B	4	Bridge
BB	5	Bulbous bow
BC	2 & 5	British Columbia (Canada)
BC	4	British Corporation (LR)
bhp	7	Brake horsepower (See Key for full explanation)
BJ	2 & 5	Beijing Municipality
Bow/CM	6	Distance from bow to centre manifold
BR	4	Bulgarian Register of Shipping
Br ex	5	Breadth extreme
Br md	5	Breadth moulded
BS	4	British Corporation class character letters – (LR) (See Key for full explanation)
btm	4 & 6	Bottom
BV	4	Bureau Veritas
BWMP	6	Ballast Water Management Plan (LR)
C	4	Diameter of wrought iron cable in sixteenths of an inch (BC Rules)
C	7	Compound expansion engine
C.	6	Total carrying capacity of containers
C. Dk	6	Containers carried on deck
C. Ho	6	Containers carried in hold(s)
C.Ro/Ro	6	Containers carried on internal decks
C.Ro/RoDk	6	Containers carried on internal decks
(CA)	4	Controlled Atmosphere denotes one or more cargo chambers enclosed in an air-tight envelope. (LR)
CA	4	Where ship is provided with a Controlled Atmosphere system which will maintain specified ranges of oxygen and carbon dioxide levels. (LR)
CA	2 & 5	California
CAC	4	Crew Accommodation Comfort (LR)
CASPPR	4	Canadian Arctic Shipping Pollution Prevention Regulations
CBT	6	Clean Ballast arrangements
CC	4	China Classification Society
CCS or (CCS)	4	Centralised Control System (LR) – (See Key for full explanation)
ccy	6	Conical cylindrical
Cell.Ho.	6	Cellular hold fitted with fixed cellguides
CG	4	Cargo gear on ships (LR)
Clr Ht	6	Clear height (RoRo ramps & lanes)
CM	4 & 6	Construction Monitoring (LR)
CO	2 & 5	Colorado
(Col)	5	Colombia
Comb. or comb.	5 & 6	Combined
COW or COW(LR)	6	Crude Oil Washing
CP	7	Controllable pitch (propellers or thrusters)
CQ	2 & 5	Chongqing Municipality
CR	4	Cargo ramps (LR)
CR	4	Corrosion Resistant material (LR)
CS	4	Continuous Survey of the Hull (LR)
CS	4	Croatian Register of Shipping
CSD	6	Closed Shelter Deck Ship
CT	2 & 5	Connecticut
Cy	7	Cylinders (engine)
cyl	6	Cylindrical
d.c.	7	Direct current
d.o.	7	Diesel oil
db	7	Domestic boiler
DB	5 & 6	Double bottom
DC	2 & 5	District of Columbia
dcc	6	Double cylindrical conical
dcy	6	Double-lobe cylindrical
DD	6	Double deck
DE	2 & 5	Delaware
Dght	5	Draught
Diam.	6	Diameter of manifold
Disch.	6	Discharge
dk or dks	4, 5 & 6	Deck(s)
DP (AA)	4	Dynamic Positioning with fully redundant automatic control system (LR)
DP (AAA)	4	Dynamic Positioning with fully redundant automatic control system and emergency automatic control system (LR)
DP (AM)	4	Dynamic Positioning with automatic and centralised remote manual control system (LR)
DP (CM)	4	Dynamic Positioning with centralised remote manual control system (LR)
Dp Ta	6	Deep tank
Dpth	5	Moulded depth
dr	7	Double reduction (gearing)
DS	4	Deutsche Schiffs –Revision und –Klassifikation GmbH
DSS	6	Double skin sides
DT or DTs or DTa	4, 5 & 6	Deep tank(s)
DTf	4, 5 & 6	Deep tank forward
DTm	4, 5 & 6	Deep tank midship
DTma	4, 5 & 6	Deep tank aft midship
DTmf	4, 5 & 6	Deep tank forward midship
dwt	6	Deadweight
econ	7	Economiser (Boilers – LR)
e(ex.g)	7	Exhaust gas economiser (Boilers – LR)
elec.	7	Electric
EP	4 & 6	Environmental Protection (LR)
Eq.Ltr	4	Equipment Letter (LR)
ER	5 & 6	Engine room
ES	4 & 6	Enhanced Scantlings (LR)
ESN	4	Enhanced Survivability Notation (LR)
ESN-Hold 1	4	Notation assigned to a ship that has been assessed for flooding No.1 hold and complies with or has been strengthened to comply with the requirements of the relevant LR Rules
ESN- Hold 1 with Loading Restrictions	4	Notation assigned to a ship that has been assessed for flooding No.1 hold and complies with the requirements of the relevant LR Rules by virtue of imposed loading restrictions.
ESN-All Holds		Notation assigned to a ship that has been assessed for fl ooding of all holds and complies with or has been strengthened to comply with the requirements of the relevant LR Rules
ESN-All Holds with Loading Restrictions		Notation assigned to a ship that has been assessed for flooding of all holds
in Hold(s) No….		and complies with the requirements of the relevant LR Rules by virtue of imposed loading restrictions.
ESP	4	Enhanced Survey Programme (LR)
Est.	5	Estimated
ETA	6	Emergency Towing Arrangements (LR)
(ex.g)	7	Exhaust gas (boilers)
exp	7	Expansion
f or (f)	4, 5, 6 & 7	Forward
F-S	6	Finish-Swedish Ice Rules notation
fcsa	6	Freight container securing arrangements (LR)
FDA	4 & 6	Fatigue Design Assessment (LR)
FEU	6	Forty Foot Equivalent Units (containers)
FJ	2 & 5	Fujian
FL	2 & 5	Florida
FP	4	Flash point (in degrees Celsius) (LR)
FP	7	Fixed pitch (propeller or thruster)
FSWR	4	Flexible Steel Wire Ropes (LR)
fwd	4, 5 & 7	Forward
G1 –G5	4	Service Limits (LR)
GA	2 & 5	Georgia
GD	2 & 5	Guangdong
Gen or gen	7	Generators
GL	4	Germanischer Lloyd AG
GS	2 & 5	Gansu
GX	2 & 5	Guangxi Zhuang AR
GZ	2 & 5	Guizhou
HA	2 & 5	Henan
Ha	6	Hatchways
HB	2 & 5	Hubei
HCM	6	Hull Condition Monitoring (LR)
HE	2 & 5	Hebei
HI	2 & 5	Hainan
HI	2 & 5	Hawaii
HL	2 & 5	Heilongjiang
HN	2 & 5	Hunan
Ho	6	Dry cargo hold
Ho/Ta	6	Hold/Tank(s)
Ho(comb)	6	Combined hold
hp	7	Horsepower

Appendix 1

Abbreviations Used in the Register of Ships 2008-2009

Abbreviation	Column	Explanation	Abbreviation	Column	Explanation	Abbreviation	Column	Explanation
HP	7	High Pressure	Liq(Oil)	6	Liquid oil capacity			
HR	4	Hellenic Register of Shipping	Lloyd's RMC	4	Refrigerated Cargo Installation Class	p	4, 5, 6 & 7	Port
HRS Level 1SS	6	Hull Renovation Scheme (LR)	or (Lloyd's RMC)		(LR) – (See Key for full explanation)	PA	2 & 5	Pennsylvania
						PAC	4	Passenger Accommodation Comfort (LR)
HRS Level 2SS	6	Hull Renovation Scheme (LR)	Lloyd's RMC (LG)	4	Class for refrigerating equipment for dealing with boil-off gas on a liquefied	PCR	4	Performance Capability Rating (LR)
hs	7	Heating surface (boilers)	or ((Lloyd's RMC (LG))		gas carrier (LR) – (See Key for full	PCWBT	6	Protective Coatings in Water Ballast Tanks (LR)
HSC	4	High Speed Craft			explanation)			
htr	7	Heater (boiler details)	LMA	4 & 6	Lloyd's Manoeuvring Assessment (LR)	pd	7	Per day (fuel consumption)
hvf	7	High viscosity fuel	LMC or	4	Machinery Class (LR) – (See Key for	PE	2 & 5	Prince Edward Island (Canada)
HWH	7	Hot Water Heater	(LMC)		full explanation)	Pmp rm	6	Pump room
Hz	7	Hertz	LN	2 & 5	Liaoning	PMS	6	Approved Planned Maintenance Scheme (LR)
*I.W.S.	4	Ship arranged for In Water Survey (LR)	LNG		Liquefied Natural Gas	PMS(CM)	6	Approved Planned Maintenance Scheme based on machinery
i.f.o.	7	Intermediate fuel oil	Loa	5	Length overall			condition monitoring (LR)
IA	6	Iowa	LP	7	Low Pressure			
IBS	4	Integrated Bridge Navigation System (LR)	LPG	5 & 6	Liquefied Petroleum Gas	PR	4	Polski Rejestr Statkow
ICC	4	Integrated Computer Control (LR)	LR	4 & 6	Lloyd's Register of Shipping	pri	7	Prismatic
Ice Class 1*, 1, 2 & 3	4	Ice Class Notations for general service (LR)	Lwr or lwr	5 & 6	Lower	PSMR	4	Propulsion and Steering Machinery Redundancy (LR)
Ice Class 1AS, A, B, C & D	4	Ice Class Notations for general service (LR)	m	4, 5 & 6	Midship	PSMR*	4	Propulsion and Steering Machinery Redundancy Located in Separate
			M.B.	2 & 5	Manitoba (Canada)			Machinery Spaces(LR)
Ice Class AC1, AC1-5, AC2 & AC3	4	Ice Class Notations for Arctic and Antarctic Service (LR)	m³/hr	6	Cubic metres per hour	pt	4, 5 & 6	Part
			MA	2 & 5	Massachusetts	pv	4	Pressure/vacuum relief valves for cargo tanks with positive setting
ID	2 & 5	Idaho	Mchy or mchy	5, 6 & 7	Machinery			where greater than 0.2 bar
IFP	4	Integrated Fire Protection (LR)	MD	2 & 5	Maryland			
IGS or IGS (LR)	6	Inert Gas System	ME	2 & 5	Maine	QC	2 & 5	Province of Quebec (Canada)
			(Mex)	5	Mexico	QH	2 & 5	Qinghai
IGS or (IGS)	4	Inert Gas System (See Key for full explanation)	MI	2 & 5	Michigan	QLD	2 & 5	Queensland (Australia)
			MN	2 & 5	Minnesota	RC	4	Registro Cubano de Buques
ihp	7	Indicated horsepower	MO	2 & 5	Missouri	rcv	7	Receiver (boiler details)
IL	2 & 5	Illinois	MS	2 & 5	Mississippi	rec	6	Rectangular
IN	2 & 5	Indiana	MT	2 & 5	Montana	Recip.	7	Reciprocating engine
incl.	5, 6 & 7	Including	N	4	Equipment not required (LR)	ref	6	Ships fitted with refrigerated cargo installation
Inmarsat-A	2	(See Key for full explanation)	NSW	2 & 5	New South Wales (Australia)			
Inmarsat-B	2	(See Key for full explanation)	NT	2 & 5	Northern Territory (Australian)	Ref C.	6	Refrigerated containers
Inmarsat-M	2	(See Key for full explanation)	NAV	4	Lloyd's Navigation Certificate (LR)	Retract.	7	Retractable
Inmarsat-Mini-M	2	(See Key for full explanation)	NAV1	4	Lloyd's Navigation Certificate for periodic One Man Watch (LR)	RI	4	Registro Italiano Navale
						RI	2 & 5	Rhode Island
Inmarsat-C	2	(See Key for full explanation)	NauxB	7	New Auxiliary Boilers (LR)	RN	4	Registrul Naval Roman
Ins	6	Insulated cargo capacity	NB	2 & 5	New Brunswick (Canada)	RoRo	6	Roll on Roll off
IP	4	Integrated Propulsion (LR)	NC	2 & 5	North Carolina	RP	4	Rinave Portuguesa
IP	7	Intermediate Pressure	ND	2 & 5	North Dakota	rpm	4	Revolutions per minute
IR	4	Indian Register of Shipping	NE	2 & 5	Nebraska	RS	4	Russian Maritime Register of Shipping
JL	2 & 5	Jilin	NH	2 & 5	New Hampshire	s	4, 5 & 7	Starboard
JR	4	Jugoslavenski Registar Brodova	Ni.stl	6	Nickel Steel	SA	2 & 5	South Australia
JS	2 & 5	Jiangsu	NJ	2 & 5	New Jersey	S.dk	5	Shelter deck
JX	2 & 5	Jiangxi	NK	4	Nippon Kaiji Kyokai	(s.stl) or s.stl	6	Stainless steel
KI	4	Biro Klasifikasi Indonesia	NL	2 & 5	Newfoundland & Labrador (Canada)	SB	7	Single-ended Main Boiler (LR)
kn	7	Knots	NM	2 & 5	Nei Menggu (Inner Mongolia AR)	SBP	6	Steady Bollard Pull (LR)
KR	4	Korean Register of Shipping	NM	2 & 5	New Mexico	SBT or SBT (LR)	6	Segregated Ballast Tanks
KS	2 & 5	Kansas	NR	7	Nuclear Reactor			
kW	4 & 7	Kilowatts	NS	2 & 5	Nova Scotia (Canada)	SBT/PL or SBT/PL(LR)	6	Segregated Ballast Tanks
KY	2 & 5	Kentucky	NT	2 & 5	Northwest Territories (Canada)			
L reg	5	Registered length	NU	2 & 5	Nunavut (Canada)	SC	4	Service Craft
L.S. 'O'.	4	Loading Sequence Accelerated (LR)	NV	2 & 5	Nevada	SC	2 & 5	South Carolina
L.S. 'T'.	4	Loading Sequence Normal (LR)	NV	4	Det Norske Veritas	SC	2 & 5	Sichuan
LA	4	Lifting Appliance (LR)	NX	2 & 5	Ningxia Hui AR	sc. shaft(s)	7	Screw shaft(s)
LA	2 & 5	Louisiana	NY	2 & 5	New York State	SCM	4 & 6	Screwshaft Condition Monitoring (LR)
Lake SS	4	Periodical Survey of ship classed for Great Lakes Service (LR)	(NZ)	6	New Zealand	SD	2 & 5	South Dakota
			o.f.	7	Oil fuel or oil-fired boilers	SD	2 & 5	Shandong
Lbp	5	Length between perpendiculars	OBO	5	Ore/Bulk/Oil	SDA	4 & 6	Structural Design Assessment (LR)
LDC	4	Light Displacement Craft	OH	2 & 5	Ohio	SDS or SDS(LR)	6	SOLAS Damage Stability
Len	6	Length (RoRo ramps & lanes)	OK	2 & 5	Oklahoma			
LI	4 & 6	Loading Instrument (LR)	ON	2 & 5	Ontario (Canada)	SEA	6	Ship Event Analysis (LR)
Liq	6	Liquid cargo capacity	OR	6	Oregon	SEA (HSS)	6	Sea Event Analysis (Hull Surveillance System) (LR)
Liq(Gas)	6	Liquid gas capacity Data Recording Capability (LR)	OSD	6	Open Shelter Deck Ship			
			OSD/CSD	6	Open & Closed Shelter Deck Ship	SEA(R)	6	Ship Event Analysis with Continuous
			OU/OI	4	LR class character letters (See Key for full explanation)			

119

Appendix 1

Abbreviations Used in the Register of Ships 2008-2009

Abbreviation	Column	Explanation
SEA(VDR)	6	Sea Event Analysis (Voyage Data Recorder System) (LR)
SERS or SERS(LR)	6	Ship Emergency Response Service
SG	4, 6 & 7	Specific gravity
SH	2 & 5	Shanghai Municipality
shp	7	Shaft horsepower
Ship Type 1, 2 & 3	4	Notations assigned to chemical tankers which comply with relevant requirements of LR's Rules. (LR)
Ship Type 1*, 2* & 3*	4	Notations assigned to chemical tankers which comply with relevant requirements of LR's Rules, where the International certificate of fitness is to be issued by an authority other than LR. (LR)
SK	2 & 5	Saskatchewan (Canada)
Slop Ta	6	Slop tank
SMR or SMR*	4	Steering Machinery Redundancy (LR)
SN	2 & 5	Shaanxi
(Sp)	5	Spain
sph	6	Spherical
SPM	4	Single Point Mooring
spt	7	Superheater (boilers) (LR)
SQ	4	Special Quality Steel Cable
sr	7	Single reduction (gearing)
SS	4	Special Survey (LR)
SSC	4	Special Service Craft
St or STs	6	Side Tank(s)
stbd	4, 5, 6 & 7	Starboard

Abbreviation	Column	Explanation
(stl) or stl	5 & 6	Steel
str	6	Strengthened
Swl	6	Safe working load (RoRo ramps)
SWATH	4 & 6	Small waterplane area twin-hull
SX	2 & 5	Shanxi
T	6 & 7	Tonnes (1000kg)
T/cm	3	Tonnes per centimetre immersion
T/hr	6	Tonnes per hour
T/m³	4	Tonnes per cubic metre
Ta	4 & 6	Cargo tank
Ta-Cln	6	Clean ballast tank
Ta-Seg	6	Segregated ballast tank
TAS	2 & 5	Tasmania (Australia)
TC	4	Temperature Control (LR)
TCM	6	Main steam Turbine Condition Monitoring (LR)
TEU	6	Twenty Foot Equivalent Units
TJ	2 & 5	Tianjin Municipality
TN	2 & 5	Tennessee
TOC	4	Transfer of Class
TOH	7	Thermal Oil Heater
Top Ho.	6	Dry cargo hold topside
Topside Ta	6	Cargo tank topside
tr	7	Triple reduction (gearing)
TL	4	Turk Loydu
turb.	7	Turbine
Twd	4 & 5	'Tween Deck Tank(s)
Twd	6	'Tween Deck Space
TX	2 & 5	Texas
Type A, B & C	4	Notations refer to chemical cargoes for the carriage of which the ship has been approved (LR)

Abbreviation	Column	Explanation
U1, U2, U3 or U4	4	Grades of chain cable (LR)
U dk	5	Upper deck
(UK)	6	United Kingdom
UMS or (UMS)	4	Unattended Machinery Space (LR) – (See Key for full explanation)
Upr. or upr	5 & 6	Upper
UT	2 & 5	Utah
V	7	Volts
VA	2 & 5	Virginia
VIC	2 & 5	Victoria (Australia)
VR	4	Vietnam Register
VT	2 & 5	Vermont
WA	2 & 5	Western Australia
WA	2 & 5	Washington State
WI	2 & 5	Wisconsin
WI	4	Wrought Iron cable
Wid	6	Width (RoRo ramps & lanes)
Wing Ha	6	Wing hatches
WTAuxB	7	Water Tube Auxiliary Boiler (LR)
WTB	7	Water Tube Main Boiler (LR)
Wtdb	7	Water tube domestic boiler (LR)
WV	2 & 5	West Virginia
WY	2 & 5	Wyoming
XJ	2 & 5	Xinjiang Uygur AR
XZ	2 & 5	Xizand (Tibet)
Yd No	5	Shipbuilder yard number
YN	2 & 5	Yunnan
YT	2 & 5	Yukon Territory (Canada)
ZJ	2 & 5	Zhejiang

Deadweight Scale

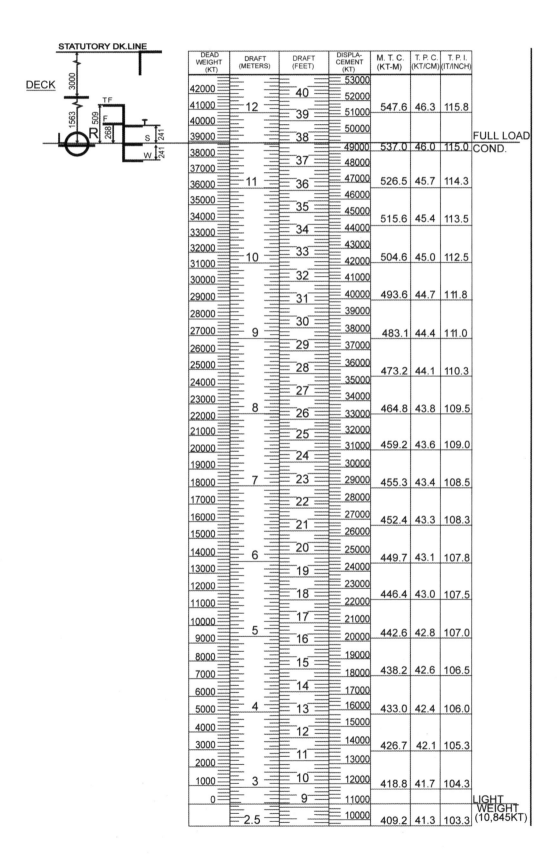

DEAD WEIGHT (KT)	DRAFT (METERS)	DRAFT (FEET)	DISPLA-CEMENT (KT)	M. T. C. (KT-M)	T. P. C. (KT/CM)	T. P. I. (IT/INCH)	
42000		40	53000 52000				
41000	12	39	51000	547.6	46.3	115.8	
40000			50000				
39000		38					FULL LOAD COND.
38000		37	49000	537.0	46.0	115.0	
37000			48000				
36000	11	36	47000	526.5	45.7	114.3	
35000		35	46000				
34000			45000	515.6	45.4	113.5	
33000		34	44000				
32000		33	43000	504.6	45.0	112.5	
31000	10		42000				
30000		32	41000				
29000		31	40000	493.6	44.7	111.8	
28000		30	39000				
27000	9		38000	483.1	44.4	111.0	
26000		29	37000				
25000		28	36000	473.2	44.1	110.3	
24000		27	35000				
23000			34000				
22000	8	26	33000	464.8	43.8	109.5	
21000		25	32000				
20000		24	31000	459.2	43.6	109.0	
19000			30000				
18000	7	23	29000	455.3	43.4	108.5	
17000		22	28000				
16000		21	27000	452.4	43.3	108.3	
15000			26000				
14000	6	20	25000	449.7	43.1	107.8	
13000		19	24000				
12000		18	23000	446.4	43.0	107.5	
11000			22000				
10000	5	17	21000	442.6	42.8	107.0	
9000		16	20000				
8000		15	19000	438.2	42.6	106.5	
7000			18000				
6000		14	17000				
5000	4	13	16000	433.0	42.4	106.0	
4000		12	15000				
3000			14000	426.7	42.1	105.3	
2000		11	13000				
1000	3	10	12000	418.8	41.7	104.3	
0		9	11000				LIGHT WEIGHT (10,845KT)
	2.5		10000	409.2	41.3	103.3	

Stowage Factors

Imperial – 40 cubic feet (Ft³)/t ton Metric – 1 Cubic metre (M³)/tonne

Conversion – 1 M³/Tonne = 35.314843 Ft³/ton

Commodity	Ft³/ton	M³/tonne	Remarks
Pig Iron	11	0.31	
Iron Ore	11 – 17	0.31 – 0.47	
Bauxite	20 – 32	0.56 – 0.89	
Sand	11 – 28	0.50 – 0.98	
Scrap Steel	20 – 40	0.56 – 1.11	
Salt	29 – 40	0.81 – 1.12	
Water	36	1.00	
Cement	23 – 29	0,67 – 0.99	
Sulphur	27 – 36	0.74 – 1.00	
China Clay	38 – 48	0.94 – 1.34	
Coal	40 – 58	1.11 – 1.53	If temperature exceeds 55º, head for nearest port. Do not use water at sea – use inert gas if available
Fertilizers	27 – 43	0.83 – 1.15	
Wheat in bulk	47 – 49	1.31 – 1.37	
Wheat in bags	52 – 54	1.45 – 1.50	
Urea	47 – 55	1.17 – 1.56	A form of fertilizer in granules, bead or prills
Petroleum Coke	48 – 55	1.25 – 1.67	Not hazardous if loaded below 54º
Canned Goods	55 – 60	1.53 – 1.61	
Oranges in cases	85 – 90	2.37 – 2.51	
Oranges in cartons	60 – 65	1.68 – 1.81	
Copra	70 – 78	1.95 – 2.18	Smell, infestation, risk of spontaneous combustion
Wood Chips	118 – 160	3.07 – 4.46	
Esparto Grass	180	4.00	
Cork	200	5.57	

Appendix 4

Examples of Standard Forms of Charterparties

VOYAGE CHARTERPARTIES

		Code Name
CEMENT	Standad Voyage Charterparty for the Transportation of Cement and Cement Clinker in Bulk	***CEMENTVOY**
COAL	Americanised Welsh Coal Charter	**AMWELSH 93**
	The Baltic & International Maritime Council Polish Coal Charter 1971	**POLCOALVOY**
	Japan Shipping Exchange Coal Charter	**NIPPONCOAL**
FERTILIZERS	UK Chamber of Shipping Fertilizer Charter 1942	**FERTICON**
	North American Fertilizer Charter 1978 Amended 1988	**FERTIVOY 88**
	Qatar Fertilizer Company Charter	**QAFCOCHARTER**
GENERAL	Baltic & International Maritime Council General Charter (Revised 1922, '74,'76,'94)	***GENCON**
	World Food Programme Charter	**WORLDFOOD**
GRAIN	Australian Wheat Charter 1990	**AUSTWHEAT**
	Continent Grain Charter (French)	**SYNACOMEX 90**
	North American Grain Charter 1973 Amended 1989. Issued by Association of Ship Brokers & Agents (ASBA) U.S.A.	**NORGRAIN 89**
	Grain Voyage Charter 1966 (Revised 1974)	***GRAINVOY**

Examples of Standard Forms of Charterparties (continued)

ORE	Japan Shipping Exchange, Iron Ore Charter	**NIPPONORE**
	Baltic & International Maritime Council Ore charter	***OREVOY**
STONE	UK Chamber of Shipping Stone Charter 1920 (Amended 1925, '59, '74, '95)	**PANSTONE**
WOOD	Baltic & International Maritime Council Baltic Wood Charter 1973 (Revised 1997)	***NUBALTWOOD**
	Russian Wood Charter	***RUSSWOOD**
	Japan Shipping Exchange, Charterparty for Logs	**NANYOZA 1997**

TIME CHARTERPARTIES

Baltic & International Maritime Council Uniform Time Charter (Amended 1950, 74)	***BALTIME1939**
Baltic & International Maritime Council Deep Sea Time Charter for Liners	***LINERTIME**
Baltic & International Maritime Council Time Charter for Container Ships	***BOXTIME**
New York Produce Exchange Time Charter	**NYPE 93**
Baltic & International Maritime Council Bareboat Charter	***BARECON 89**

N.B. This is a small selection of the many standard charterparty forms in circulation. All the above have either been Agreed or Adopted by The Baltic & International Maritime Council (BIMCO), those marked * actually compiled and published by BIMCO.

Appendix 5

Baltime

1. Shipbroker	THE BALTIC AND INTERNATIONAL MARITIME CONFERENCE UNIFORM TIME-CHARTER (Box Layout 1974) CODE NAME: "BALTIME" PART I
	2. Place and date
3. Owners/Place of business	4. Charterers/Place of business
5. Vessel's name	6. GRT/NRT
7. Class	8. Indicated horse power
9. Total tons d.w. (abt.) on Board of Trade summer freeboard	10. Cubic feet grain/bale capacity
11. Permanent bunkers (abt.)	
12. Speed capability In knots (abt.) on a consumption in tons (abt.) of	
13. Present position	
14. Period of hire (Cl. 1)	15. Port of delivery (Cl. 1)
	16. Time of delivery (Cl. 1)
17. (a) Trade limits (Cl. 2)	
(b) Cargo exclusions specially agreed	
18. Bunkers on re-delivery (state min. and max. quantity) (Cl. 5)	
19. Charter hire (Cl. 6)	20. Hire payment (state currency, method and place of payment; also beneficiary and bank account) (Cl. 6)
21. Place or range of re-delivery (Cl. 7)	22. War (only to be filled in if Section (C) agreed) (Cl. 21)
23. Cancelling date (Cl. 22)	24. Place of arbitration (only to be filled in if place other than London agreed) (Cl. 23)
25.. Brokerage commission and to whom payable (Cl. 25)	
	26. Numbers of additional clauses covering special provisions, if agreed

It Is mutually agreed that this Contract shall be performed subject to the conditions contained in this Charter which shall include Part well as Part II. In the event of a conflict of conditions, the provisions of Part I shall prevail over those of Part II to the extent of such conflict

Signature (Owners)	Signature (Charterers)

Appendix 5

PART II

"BALTIME 1939" Uniform Time-Charter (Box Layout 1974)

It is agreed between the party mentioned in Box 3 as Owners of the Vessel named in Box 5 of the gross/ net Register tonnage indicated in Box 6, classed as stated in Box 7 and of indicated horse power as stated in Box 8, carrying about the number of tons deadweight indicated in Box 9 on Board of Trade summer freeboard inclusive of bunkers, stores, provisions and boiler water, having as per builder's plan a cubic-feet grain/bale capacity as stated in Box 10, exclusive of permanent bunkers, which contain about the number of tons stated in Box 11, and fully loaded capable of steaming about the number of knots indicated in Box 12 in good weather and smooth water on a consumption of about the number of tons best Welsh coal or oil-fuel stated in Box 12, now in position as stated in Box 13 and the party mentioned as Charterers in Box 4, as follows:

1. **Period/Port *of* Delivery/Time of Delivery**
The Owners let, and the Charterers hire the Vessel for a period of the number of calendar months indicated in Box 14 from the time (not a Sunday or a legal Holiday unless taken over) the Vessel is delivered and placed at the disposal of the Charterers between 9 a.m. and 6 p.m., or between 9 a.m. and 2 p.m. if on Saturday, at the port stated in Box 15 in such available berth where she can safely lie always afloat, as the Charterers may direct, she being in every way fitted for ordinary cargo service.
The Vessel to be delivered at the time indicated in Box 16.

2. **Trade**
The Vessel to be employed in lawful trades for the carriage of lawful merchandise only between good and safe ports or places where she can safely lie always afloat within the limits stated in Box 17.
No live stock nor injurious. Inflammable or dangerous goods (such as acids, explosives, calcium carbide, ferro silicon, naphtha, motor spirit, tar, or any of their products) to be shipped.

3. **Owners to Provide**
The Owners to provide and pay for all provisions and wages, for insurance of the Vessel, for all deck and engine-room stores and maintain her in a thoroughly efficient state in hull and machinery during service.
The Owners to provide one winchman per hatch. If further winchmen are required, or if the stevedores refuse or are not permitted to work with the Crew, the Charterers to provide and pay qualified shore-winch men.

4. **Charterers to Provide**
The Charterers to provide and pay for all coals, including galley coal, oil-fuel, water for boilers, port charges, pilotages (whether compulsory or not), canal steersmen, boatage, lights, tug-assistance, consular charges (except those pertaining to the Master, Officers and Crew), canal, dock and other dues and charges, including any foreign general municipality or state taxes, also all dock, harbour and tonnage dues at the ports of delivery and re-delivery (unless incurred through cargo carried before delivery or after re-delivery), agencies, commissions, also to arrange and pay for loading, trimming, stowing (including dunnage and shifting boards, excepting any already on board), unloading, weighing, tallying and delivery of cargoes, surveys on hatches, meals supplied to officials and men in their service and all other charges and expenses whatsoever including detention and expenses through quarantine (including cost of fumigation and disinfection). All ropes, slings and special runners actually used for loading and discharging and any special gear, including special ropes, hawsers and chains required by the custom of the port for mooring to be for the Charterers' account. The Vessel to be fitted with winches, derricks, wheels and ordinary runners capable of handling lifts up to 2

5. **Bunkers**
The Charterers at port of delivery and the Owners at port of re-delivery to take over and pay for all coal or oil-fuel remaining in the Vessel's bunkers at current price at the respective ports. The Vessel to be re-delivered with not less than the number of tons and not exceeding the number of tons of coal or oil-fuel in the Vessels bunkers stated in Box 18.

6. **Hire**
The Charterers to pay as hire the rate stated in Box 19 per 30 days, commencing in accordance with Clause 1 until her re-delivery to the Owners.
Payment
Payment of hire to be made in cash, in the currency stated in Box 20, without discount, every 30 days, in advance, and in the manner prescribed in Box 20.
In default of payment the Owners to have the right of withdrawing the Vessel from the service of the Charterers, without noting any protest and without interference by any court or any other formality whatsoever and without prejudice to any claim the Owners may otherwise have on the Charterers under the Charter.

7. **Re-delivery**
The Vessel to be re-delivered on the expiration of the Charter in the same good order as when delivered to the Charterers (fair wear and tear excepted) at an ice-free port in the Charterers' option at the place or within the range stated in Box 21, between 9 a.m. and 6 p.m., and 9 a.m. and 2 p.m. on Saturday, but the day of re-delivery shall not be a Sunday or legal Holiday. *Notice*
The Charterers to give the Owners not less than ten days' notice at which port and on about which day the Vessel will be re-delivered, Should the Vessel be ordered on a voyage by which the Charter period will be exceeded the Charterers to have the use of the Vessel to enable them to complete the voyage, provided it could be reasonably calculated that the voyage would allow re-delivery about the time fixed for the termination of the Charter, but for any time exceeding the termination date the Charterers to pay the market rate if higher than the rate stipulated herein.

8. **Cargo Space**
The whole reach and burthen of the Vessel, including lawful deck-capacity to be at the Charterers' disposal, reserving proper and sufficient space for the Vessel's Master, Officers, Crew, tackle, apparel, furniture, provisions and stores.

9. **Master**
The Master to prosecute all voyages with the utmost despatch and to render customary assistance with the Vessel's Crew. The Master to be under the orders of the Charterers as regards employment, agency, or other arrangements. The Charterers to indemnify the Owners against all consequences or liabilities arising from the Master, Officers or Agents signing Bills of Lading or other documents or otherwise complying with such orders, as well as from any irregularity in the Vessel's papers or for over-carrying goods. The Owners not to be responsible for shortage, mixture, marks, nor for number of pieces or packages, nor for damage to or claims on cargo caused by bad stowage or otherwise. If the Charterers have reason to be dissatisfied with the conduct of the Master, Officers, or Engineers, the Owners, on receiving particulars of the complaint, promptly to investigate the matter, and, if necessary and practicable, to make a change in the appointments.

10. **Directions and Logs**
The Charterers to furnish the Master with all instructions and sailing directions and the Master and Engineer to keep full and correct logs accessible to the Charterers or their Agents.

11. **Suspension of Hire etc.**
(A) In the event of drydocking or other necessary measures to maintain the efficiency of the Vessel, deficiency of men or Owners' stores, breakdown of machinery, damage to hull or other accident, either hindering or preventing the working of the Vessel and continuing for more than twentyfour consecutive hours, no hire to be paid in respect of any time lost thereby during the period in which the Vessel is unable to perform the service immediately required. Any hire paid in advance to be adjusted accordingly.
(B) In the event of the Vessel being driven into port or to anchorage through stress of weather, trading to shallow harbours or to rivers or ports with bars or suffering an accident to her cargo, any detention of the Vessel and/or expenses resulting from such detention to be for the Charterers' account even if such detention and/or expenses, or the cause by reason of which either is incurred, be due to, or be contributed to by, the negligence of the Owners' servants.

12. **Cleaning Boilers**
Cleaning of boilers whenever possible to be done during service, but if impossible the Charterers to give the Owners necessary time for cleaning. Should the Vessel be detained beyond 48 hours hire to cease until again ready.

13. **Responsibility and Exemption**
The Owners only to be responsible for delay in delivery of the Vessel or for delay during the currency of the Charter and for loss or damage to goods onboard, if such delay or loss has been caused by want of due diligence on the part of the Owners or their Manager in making the Vessel seaworthy and fitted for the voyage or any other personal act or omission or default of the Owners or their Manager. The Owners not to be responsible in any other case nor for damage or delay whatsoever and howsoever caused even if caused by the neglect or default of their servants. The Owners not to be liable for loss or damage arising or resulting from strikes, lockouts or stoppage or restraint of labour (including the Master, Officers or Crew) whether partial or general.
The Charterers to be responsible for loss or damage caused to the Vessel or to the Owners by goods being loaded contrary to the terms of the Charter or by improper or careless bunkering or loading, stowing or discharging of goods or any other improper or negligent act on their part or that of their servants.

14. **Advances**
The Charterers or their Agents to advance to the Master, if required, necessary funds for ordinary disbursements for the Vessel's account at any port charging only interest at 6 per cent, p. a., such advances to be deducted from hire.

15. **Excluded Ports**
The Vessel not to be ordered to nor bound to enter: a) any place where fever or epidemics are prevalent or to which the Master. Officers and Crew by law are not bound to follow the Vessel
ice
b) any ice-bound place or any place where lights, lightships, marks and buoys are or are likely to be withdrawn by reason of ice on the Vessel's arrival or where there is risk that ordinarily the Vessel will not be able on account of ice to reach the place or to get out after having completed loading or discharging. The Vessel not to be obliged to force ice. If on account of ice the Master considers it dangerous to remain at the loading or discharging place for fear of the Vessel being frozen in and/or damaged, he has liberty to sail to a convenient open place and await the Charterers' fresh instructions. Unforeseen detention through any of above causes to be for the Charterers' account.

16. **Loss of Vessel**
Should the Vessel be lost or missing, hire to cease from the date when she was lost. If the date of loss cannot be ascertained half hire to be paid from the date the Vessel was last reported until the calculated date of arrival at the destination. Any hire paid in advance to be adjusted accordingly.

17. **Overtime**
The Vessel to work day and night if required. The Charterers to refund the Owners their outlays for all overtime paid to Officers and Crew according to the hours and rates stated in the Vessel's articles.

18. **Lien**
The Owners to have a lien upon all cargoes and sub-freights belonging to the Time-Charterers and any Bill of Lading freight for all claims under this Charter, and the Charterers to have a lien on the Vessel for all moneys paid in advance and not earned.

19. **Salvage**
All salvage and assistance to other vessels to be for the Owners' and the Charterers' equal benefit after deducting the Master's and Crew's proportion and all legal and other expenses including hire paid under the charter for time lost in the salvage, also repairs of damage and coal or oil-fuel consumed. The Charterers to be bound by all measures taken by the Owners in order to secure payment of salvage and to fix its amount.

20. **Sublet**
The Charterers to have the option of subletting the Vessel, giving due notice to the Owners, but the original Charterers always to remain responsible to the Owners for due performance of the Charter.

21. **War**
(A) The Vessel unless the consent of the Owners be first obtained not to be ordered nor continue to any place or on any voyage nor be used on any service which will bring her within a zone which is dangerous as the result of any actual or threatened act of war, war hostilities, warlike operations, acts of piracy or of hostility or malicious damage against this or any other vessel or its cargo by any person, body or State whatsoever. revolution, civil war, civil commotion or the operation of international law, nor be exposed in any way to any risks or penalties whatsoever consequent upon the imposition of Sanctions, nor carry any goods that may in any way expose her to any risks of seizure, capture, penalties or any other interference of any kind whatsoever by the belligerent or fighting powers or parties or by any Government or Ruler.
(B) Should the Vessel approach or be brought or ordered within such zone, or be exposed in any way to the said risks, (1) the Owners to be entitled from time to time to insure their interests in the Vessel and/ or hire against any of the risks likely to be involved thereby on such terms as they shall think fit, the Charterers to make a refund to the Owners of the premium on demand: and (2) notwithstanding the terms of Clause 11 hire to be paid for all time lost including any lost owing to loss of or injury to the Master, Officers, or Crew or to the action of the Crew in refusing to proceed to such zone or to be exposed to such risks.
(C) In the event of the wages of the Master. Officers and or Crew or the cost of provisions and or stores for deck and/or engine room and or insurance premiums being increased by reason of or during the existence of any of the matters mentioned in section (A) the amount of any increase to be added to the hire and paid by the Charterers on production of the Owners' account therefor, such account being rendered monthly.
(D) The Vessel to have liberty to comply with any orders or directions as to departure, arrival, routes, ports of call, stoppages, destination, delivery or in any other wise whatsoever given by the Government of the nation under whose flag the Vessel sails or any other Government or any person (or body) acting or purporting to act with the authority of such Government or by any committee or person having under the terms of the war risks insurance on the Vessel the right to give any such orders or directions.
(E) In the event of the nation under whose flag the Vessel sails becoming involved in war, hostilities, warlike operations, revolution, or civil commotion, both the Owners and the Charterers may cancel the Charter and, unless otherwise agreed, the Vessel to be re-delivered to the Owners at the port of destination or. if prevented through the provisions of section (A) from reaching or entering it, then at a near open and safe port at the Owners' option, after discharge of any cargo on board.
(F) If in compliance with the provisions of this clause anything Is done or is not done, such not to be deemed a deviation.
Section (C) is optional and should be considered deleted unless agreed according to Box 22.

22. **Cancelling**
Should the Vessel not be delivered by the date indicated in Box 23. the Charterers to have the option of cancelling.
If the Vessel cannot be delivered by the cancelling date, the Charterers, if required, to declare within 48 hours after receiving notice thereof whether they cancel or will take delivery of the Vessel.

23. **Arbitration**
Any dispute arising under the Charter to be referred to arbitration in London (or such other place as may be agreed according to Sox 24) one Arbitrator to be nominated by the Owners and the other by the Charterers, and in case the Arbitrators shall not agree then to the decision of an Umpire to be appointed by them, the award of the Arbitrators or the Umpire to be final and binding upon both parties.

24. **General Average**
General Average to be settled according to York' Antwerp Rules. 1974. Hire not to contribute to General Average.

25. **Commission**
The Owners to pay a commission at the rate stated in Box 25 to the party mentioned in Box 25 on any hire paid under the Charter, but in no case less than is necessary to cover the actual expenses of the Brokers and a reasonable fee for their work. If the full hire is not paid owing to breach of Charter by either of the parties the party liable therefor to indemnify the Brokers against their loss of commission. Should the parties agree to cancel the Charter, the Owners to indemnify the Brokers against any loss of commission but in such case the commission not to exceed the brokerage on one year's hire.

Appendix 6

Gencon

1. Shlpbroker	RECOMMENDED **THE BALTIC AND INTERNATIONAL MARITIME COUNCIL** **UNIFORM GENERAL CHARTER (AS REVISED 1922, 1976 and 1994)** **(To be used for trades for which no specially approved form is in force) CODE** **NAME: "GENCON"** PART I
	2. Place and date
3. Owners/Place of business (Cl. 1)	4. Charterers/Place of business (Cl. 1)
5. Vessel's name (Cl. 1)	6. GT/NT(Cl. 1)
7. DWT all told on summer load line in metric tons (abt.) (Cl. 1)	8. Present position (Cl. 1)
9. Expected ready to load (abt.) (Cl. 1)	
10. Loading port or place (Cl. 1)	11. Discharging port or place (Cl. 1)
12. Cargo (also state quantity and margin in Owners'option, if agreed; if full and complete cargo not agreed state "part cargo" (Cl. 1)	
13. Freight rate (also state whether freight prepaid or payable on delivery) (Cl. 4)	14. Freight payment (state currency and method of payment; also beneficiary and bank account) (Cl. 4)
15. State if vessel's cargo handling gear shall not be used (Cl. 5)	16. Laytime (if separate laytime for load, and disch. is agreed, fill in a) and b). If total laytime for load, and disch., fill in c) only) (Cl. 6)
17. Shippers/Place of business (Cl. 6)	(a) Laytime for loading
18. Agents (loading) (Cl. 6)	(b) Laytime for discharging
19. Agents (discharging) (Cl. 6)	(c) Total laytime for loading and discharging
20. Demurrage rate and manner payable (loading and discharging) (Cl. 7)	21. Cancelling date (Cl. 9)
	22. General Average to be adjusted at (Cl. 12)
23. Freight Tax (state if for the Owners' account (Cl .13 (c))	24. Brokerage commission and to whom payable (Cl. 15)
25. Law and Arbitration (state 19 (a), 19 (b) or 19 (c) of Cl. 19; if 19 (c) agreed also state Place of Arbitration) (if not filled in 19 (a) shall apply) (Cl. 19)	
(a) State maximum amount for small claims/shortened arbitration (Cl. 19)	26. Additional clauses covering special provisions, if agreed

It is mutually agreed that this Contract shall be performed subject to the conditions contained in this Charter Party which shall include Part I as well as Part II. In the event of a conflict of conditions, the provisions of Part I shall prevail over those of Part II to the extent of such conflict.

Appendix 6

PART II
"Gencon" Charter (As Revised 1922,1976 and 1994)

1. It is agreed between the party mentioned in Box 3 as the Owners of the Vessel named In Box 5, of the GT/NT indicated in Box 6 and carrying about the number of metric tons of deadweight capacity all told on summer loadline stated in Box 7, now In position as stated in Box 8 and expected ready to load under this Charter Party about the date indicated in Box 9, and the party mentioned as the Charterers in Box 4 that:
The said Vessel shall, as soon as her prior commitments have been completed, proceed to the loading port(s) or place(s) stated in Box 10 or so near thereto as she may safely get and lie always afloat, and there load a full and complete cargo (if shipment of deck cargo agreed same to be at the Charterers' risk and responsibility) as stated in Box 12, which the Charterers bind themselves to ship, and being so loaded the Vessel shall proceed to the discharging port(s) or place(s) stated in Box 11 as ordered on signing Bills of Lading, or so near thereto as she may safely get and lie always afloat, and there deliver the cargo.

2. **Owners' Responsibility Clause**
The Owners are to be responsible for loss of or damage to the goods or for delay in delivery of the goods only In case the loss, damage or delay has been caused by personal want of due diligence on the part of the Owners or their Manager to make the Vessel in all respects seaworthy and to secure that she is properly manned, equipped and supplied, or by the personal act or default of the Owners or their Manager.
And the Owners are not responsible for loss, damage or delay arising from any other cause whatsoever, even from the neglect or default of the Master or crew or some other person employed by the Owners on board or ashore for whose acts they would, but for this Clause, be responsible, or from unseaworthiness of the Vessel on loading or commencement of the voyage or at any time whatsoever.

3. **Deviation Clause**
The Vessel has liberty to call at any port or ports in any order, for any purpose, to sail without pilots, to tow and/or assist Vessels in all situations, and also to deviate for the purpose of saving life and/or property.

4. **Payment of Freight**
(a) The freight at the rate stated in Box 13 shall be paid in cash calculated on the intaken quantity of cargo.
(b) Prepaid. If according to Box 13 freight is to be paid on shipment, it shall be deemed earned and non-returnable, Vessel and/or cargo lost or not lost. Neither the Owners nor their agents shall be required to sign or endorse bills of lading showing freight prepaid unless the freight due to the Owners has actually been paid.
(c) On delivery. If according to Box 13 freight, or part thereof, is payable at destination It shall not be deemed earned until the cargo is thus delivered. Notwithstanding the provisions under (a), if freight or part thereof is payable on delivery of the cargo the Charterers shall have the option of paying the freight on delivered weight/quantity provided such option is declared before breaking bulk and the weight/quantity can be ascertained by official weighing machine, joint draft survey or tally.
Cash for Vessel's ordinary disbursements at the port of loading to be advanced by the Charterers, if required, at highest current rate of exchange, subject to two (2) per cent to cover insurance and other expenses.

5. **Loading/Discharging**
(a) Costs/Risks
The cargo shall be brought into the holds, loaded, stowed and/or trimmed, tallied, lashed and/or secured and taken from the holds and discharged by the Charterers, free of any risk, liability and expense whatsoever to the Owners. The Charterers shall provide and lay all dunnage material as required for the proper stowage and protection of the cargo on board, the Owners allowing the use of all dunnage available on board. The Charterers shall be responsible for and pay the cost of removing their dunnage after discharge of the cargo under this Charter Party and time to count until dunnage has been removed.
(b) Cargo Handling Gear
Unless the Vessel is gearless or unless it has been agreed between the parties that the Vessel's gear shall not be used and stated as such in Box 15, the Owners shall throughout the duration of loading/discharging give free use of the Vessel's cargo handling gear and of sufficient motive power to operate all such cargo handling gear. All such equipment to be in good working order. Unless caused by negligence of the stevedores, time lost by breakdown of the Vessel's cargo handling gear or motive power - pro rata the total number of cranes/ winches required at that time for the loading/discharging of cargo under this Charter Party - shall not count as laytime or time on demurrage. On request the Owners shall provide free of charge cranemen/winchmen from the crew to operate the Vessel's cargo handling gear, unless local regulations prohibit this, in which latter event shore labourers shell be for the account of the Charterers. Cranemen/winchmen shall be under the Charterers' risk and responsibility and as stevedores to be deemed as their servants but shall always work under the supervision of the Master.
(c) Stevedore Damage
The Charterers shall be responsible for damage (beyond ordinary wear and tear) to any part of the Vessel caused by Stevedores. Such damage shall be notified as soon as reasonably possible by the Master to the Charterers or their agents and to their Stevedores, failing which the Charterers shall not be held responsible. The Master shall endeavour to obtain the Stevedores' written acknowledgement of liability
The Charterers are obliged to repair any stevedore damage prior to completion of the voyage, but must repair stevedore damage affecting the Vessel's seaworthiness or class before the Vessel sails from the port where such damage was caused or found. All additional expenses incurred shall be for the account of the Charterers and anytime lost shall be for the account of and shall be paid to the Owners by the Charterers at the demurrage rate.

6. **Laytime**
* (a) Separate laytime tor loading and discharging
The cargo shall be loaded within the number of running days/hours as indicated in Box 16, weather permitting, Sundays and holidays excepted, unless used, in which event time used shall count.
The cargo shall be discharged within the number of running days/hours as indicated in Box 16, weather permitting, Sundays and holidays excepted, unless used, in which event time used shall count.
* (b) Total laytime for loading and discharging
The cargo shall be loaded and discharged within the number of total running days/hours as indicated in Box 16, weather permitting, Sundays and holidays excepted, unless used, in which event time used shall count.
(c) Commencement of laytime (loading and discharging)
Laytime for loading and discharging shall commence at 13.00 hours. If notice of readiness is given up to and including 12.00 hours, and at 06.00 hours next working day if notice given during office hours after 12.00 hours. Notice of readiness at loading port to be given to the Shippers named in Box 17 or If not named, to the Charterers or their agents named in Box 18. Notice of readiness at the discharging port to be given to the Receivers or, if not known, to the Charterers or their agents named in Box 19.
If the loading/discharging berth is not available on the Vessel's arrival at or off the port of loading/discharging, the Vessel shall be entitled to give notice of readiness within ordinary office hours on arrival there, whether In free pratique or not, whether customs cleared or not. Laytime or time on demurrage shall then count as if she were in berth and in all respects ready for loading/ discharging provided that the Master warrants that she is In fact reedy in all respects- Time used in moving from the place of wafting to the loading/ discharging berth shall not count as laytime.
If, after inspection, the Vessel is found not to be ready in all respects to load/ discharge time lost after the discovery thereof until the Vessel is again ready to load/discharge shall not count as laytime.
Time used before commencement of laytime shall count.
* Indicate alternative (a) or (b) as agreed, in Box 16.

7. **Demurrage**
Demurrage at the loading and discharging port Is payable by the Charterers at the rate stated in Box 20 in the manner stated in Box 20 per day or pro rata for any part of a day. Demurrage shall fall due day by day and shall be payable upon receipt of the Owners' invoice.
In the event the demurrage is not paid in accordance with the above, the Owners shall give the Charterers 96 running hours written notice to rectify the failure. If the demurrage is not paid at the expiration of this time limit and if the vessel is in or at the loading port, the Owners are entitled at any time to terminate the Charter Party and claim damages for any losses caused thereby.

8. **Lien Clause**
The Owners shall have a lien on the cargo and on all sub-freights payable in respect of the cargo, for freight, deadweight, demurrage, claims for damages and for all other amounts due under this Charter Party including costs of recovering same.

9. **Cancelling Clause**
(a) Should the Vessel not be ready to load (whether in berth or not) on the cancelling date indicated in Box 21, the Charterers shall have the option of cancelling this Charter Party.
(b) Should the Owners anticipate that, despite the exercise of due diligence, the Vessel will not be ready to load by the cancelling date, they shall notify the Charterers thereof without delay stating the expected date of the Vessel's readiness to load and asking whether the Charterers will exercise their option of cancelling the Charter Party, or agree to a new cancelling date.
Such option must be declared by the Charterers within 48 running hours after the receipt of the Owners' notice. If the Charterers do not exercise their option of cancelling, then this Charter Party shall be deemed to be amended such that the seventh day after the new readiness date stated In the Owners' notification to the Charterers shall be the new cancelling date.
The provisions of sub-clause (b) of this Clause shall operate only once, and In case of the Vessel's further delay, the Charterers shall have the option of cancelling the Charter Party as per sub-clause (a) of this Clause.

10. **Bills of Lading**
Bills of Lading shall be presented and signed by the Master as per the "Congenbill" Bill of Lading form, Edition 1994, without prejudice to this Charter Party, or by the Owners' agents provided written authority has been given by Owners to the agents, a copy of which Is to be furnished to the Charterers. The Charterers shall indemnify the Owners against all consequences or liabilities that may arise from the signing of bills of lading as presented to the extent that the terms or contents of such bills of lading impose or result in the imposition of more onerous liabilities upon the Owners than those assumed by the Owners under this Charter Party.

11. **Both-to-Blame Collision Clause**
If the Vessel comes into collision with another vessel as a result of the negligence of the other vessel and any act. neglect or default of the Master, Mariner, Pilot or the servants of the Owners in the navigation or In the management of the Vessel, the owners of the cargo carried hereunder will indemnify the Owners against all loss or liability to the other or non-carrying vessel or her owners in so far as such loss or liability represents loss of, or damage to, or any claim whatsoever of the owners of said cargo, paid or payable by the other or non-carrying vessel or her owners to the owners of said cargo and set-off, recouped or recovered by the other or non-carrying vessel or her owners as part of their claim against the carrying Vessel or the Owners. The foregoing provisions shall also apply where the owners, operators or those in charge of any vessel or vessels or objects other than, or In addition to, the colliding vessels or objects are at fault In respect of a collision or contact.

12. **General Average and New Jason Clause**
General Average shall be adjusted In London unless otherwise agreed in Box 22 according to York-Antwerp Rules 1994 and any subsequent modification thereof. Proprietors of cargo to pay the cargo's share in the general expenses even if same have been necessitated through neglect or default of the Owners' servants (see Clause 2).
If General Average is to be adjusted In accordance with the law and practice of the United States of America, the following Clause shall apply: "In the event of accident, danger, damage or disaster before or after the commencement of the voyage, resulting from any cause whatsoever, whether due to negligence or not, for which, or for the consequence of which, the Owners are not responsible, by statute, contract or otherwise, the cargo shippers, consignees or the owners of the cargo shall contribute with the Owners In General Average to the payment of any sacrifices, losses or expenses of a General Average nature that may be made or incurred and shall pay salvage and special charges incurred in respect of the cargo. If a salving vessel is owned or operated by the Owners, salvage shall be paid for as fully as if the said salving vessel or vessels belonged to strangers. Such deposit as the Owners, or their agents, may deem sufficient to cover the estimated contribution of the goods end eny salvage and special charges thereon shall, if required, be made by the cargo, shippers, consignees or owners of the goods to the Owners before delivery.".

13. **Taxes and Dues Clause**
(a) On Vessel -The Owners shall pay all dues, charges and taxes customarily levied on the Vessel, howsoever the amount thereof may be assessed.
(b) On cargo -The Charterers shall pay all dues, charges, duties and taxes customarily levied on the cargo, howsoever the amount thereof may be assessed.
(c) On freight -Unless otherwise agreed In Box 23, taxes levied on the freight shall be for the Charterers' account.

Appendix 6

PART II
"Gencon" Charter (As Revised 1922,1976 and 1994)

14. Agency
In every case the Owners shall appoint their own Agent both at the port of loading and the port of discharge.

15. Brokerage
A brokerage commission at the rate stated in Box 24 on the freight, dead-freight and demurrage earned Is due to the party mentioned in Box 24. In case of non-execution 1/3 of the brokerage on the estimated amount of freight to be paid by the party responsible for such non-execution to the Brokers as indemnity for the letter's expenses and work. In case of more voyages the amount of indemnity to be agreed.

16. General Strike Clause
(a) If there is a strike or lock-out affecting or preventing the actual loading of the cargo, or any part of it, when the Vessel is ready to proceed from her last port or at any time during the voyage to the port or ports of loading or after her arrival there, the Master or the Owners may ask the Charterers to declare, that they agree to reckon the laydays as if there were no strike or lock-out. Unless the Charterers have given such declaration in writing (by telegram, if necessary) within 24 hours, the Owners shall have the option of cancelling this Charter Party. If part cargo has already been loaded, the Owners must proceed with same, (freight payable on loaded quantity only) having liberty to complete with other cargo on the way for their own account.
(b) If there Is a strike or lock-out affecting or preventing the actual discharging of the cargo on or after the Vessel's arrival at or off port of discharge and same has not been settled within 48 hours, the Charterers shall have the option of keeping the Vessel waiting until such strike or lock-out is at an end against paying half demurrage after expiration of the time provided for discharging until the strike or lock-out terminates and thereafter full demurrage shall be payable until the completion of discharging, or of ordering the Vessel to a safe port where she can safely discharge without risk of being detained by strike or lock-out. Such orders to be given within 48 hours after the Master or the Owners have given notice to the Charterers of the strike or lock-out affecting the discharge. On delivery of the cargo at such port, ail conditions of this Charter Party and of the Bill of Lading shall apply and the Vessel shall receive the same freight as if she had discharged at the original port of destination, except that if the distance to the substituted port exceeds 100 nautical miles, the freight on the cargo delivered at the substituted port to be increased in proportion.
(c) Except for the obligations described above, neither the Charterers nor the Owners shall be responsible for the consequences of any strikes or lock-outs preventing or affecting the actual loading or discharging of the cargo.

17. War Risks ("Voywar 1993")
(1) For the purpose of this Clause, the words:
(a) The "Owners" shall include the shipowners, bareboat charterers, disponent owners, managers or other operators who are charged with the management of the Vessel, and the Master; and
(b) "War Risks" shall include any war (whether actual or threatened), act of war, civil war, hostilities, revolution, rebellion, civil commotion, warlike operations, the laying of mines (whether actual or reported), acts of piracy, acts of terrorists, acts of hostility or malicious damage, blockades (whether imposed against all Vessels or imposed selectively against Vessels of certain flags or ownership, or against certain cargoes or crews or otherwise howsoever), by any person, body, terrorist or political group, or the Government of any state whatsoever, which, in the reasonable judgement of the Master and/or the Owners, may be dangerous or are likely to be or to become dangerous to the Vessel, her cargo, crew or other persons on board the Vessel.
(2) If at any time before the Vessel commences loading, it appears that, in the reasonable judgement of the Master and/or the Owners, performance of the Contract of Carriage, or any part of it, may expose, or is likely to expose, the Vessel, her cargo, crew or other persons on board the Vessel to War Risks, the Owners may give notice to the Charterers cancelling this Contract of Carriage, or may refuse to perform such part of it as may expose, or may be likely to expose, the Vessel, her cargo, crew or other persons on board the Vessel to War Risks; provided always that if this Contract of Carriage provides that loading or discharging is to take place within a range of ports, and at the port or ports nominated by the Charterers the Vessel, her cargo, crew, or other persons onboard the Vessel may be exposed, or may be likely to be exposed, to War Risks, the Owners shall first require the Charterers to nominate any other safe port which lies within the range for loading or discharging, and may only cancel this Contract of Carriage If the Charterers shall not have nominated such safe port or ports within 48 hours of receipt of notice of such requirement.
(3) The Owners shall not be required to continue to load cargo for any voyage, or to sign Bills of Lading for any port or place, or to proceed or continue on any voyage, or on any part thereof, or to proceed through any canal or waterway, or to proceed to or remain at any port or place whatsoever, where it appears, either after the loading of the cargo commences, or at any stage of the voyage thereafter before the discharge of the cargo is completed, that, in the reasonable judgement of the Master and/or the Owners, the Vessel, her cargo (or any part thereof), crew or other persons on board the Vessel (or any one or more of them) may be, or are likely to be, exposed to War Risks. If it should so appear, the Owners may by notice request the Charterers to nominate a safe port for the discharge of the cargo or any part thereof, and if within 48 hours of the receipt of such notice, the Charterers shall not have nominated such a port, the Owners may discharge the cargo at any safe port of their choice (including the port of loading) in complete fulfilment of the Contract of Carriage. The Owners shall be entitled to recover from the Charterers the extra expenses of such discharge and, if the discharge takes place at any port other than the loading port, to receive the full freight as though the cargo had been carried to the discharging port and if the extra distance exceeds 100 miles, to additional freight which shall be.the same percentage of the freight contracted for as the percentage which the extra distance represents to the distance of the normal and customary route, the Owners having a lien on the cargo for such expenses and freight.
(4) If at any stage of the voyage after the loading of the cargo commences, it appears that, in the reasonable judgement of the Master and/or the Owners, the Vessel, her cargo, crew or other persons on board the Vessel may be, or are likely to be, exposed to War Risks on any part of the route (including any canal or waterway) which is normally and customarily used in a voyage of the nature contracted for, and there Is another longer route to the discharging port, the Owners shall give notice to the Charterers that this route will be taken. In this event the Owners shall be entitled, if the total extra distance exceeds 100 miles, to additional freight which shell be the same percentage of the freight contracted for as the percentage which the extra distance represents to the distance of the normal and customary route.
(5) The Vessel shall have liberty:-
(a) to comply with all orders, directions, recommendations or advice as to departure, arrival, routes, sailing in convoy, ports of call, stoppages, destinations, discharge of cargo, delivery or in any way whatsoever which are given by the Government of the Nation under whose flag the Vessel sails, or other Government to whose laws the Owners are subject, or any other Government which so requires, or any body or group acting with the power to compel compliance with their orders or directions;
(b) to comply with the orders, directions or recommendations of any war risks underwriters who have the authority to give the same under the terms of the war risks Insurance;
(c) to comply with the terms of any resolution of the Security Council of the United Nations, any directives of the European Community, the effective orders of any other Supranational body which has the right to issue and give the same, and with national laws aimed at enforcing the same to which the Owners are subject, and to obey the orders and directions of those who are charged with their enforcement;
(d) to discharge at any other port any cargo or part thereof which may render the Vessel liable to confiscation as a contraband carrier;
(e) to call at any other port to change the crew or any part thereof or other persons on board the Vessel when there is reason to believe that they may be subject to internment, imprisonment or other sanctions;
(f) where cargo has not been loaded or has been discharged by the Owners under any provisions of this Clause, to load other cargo for the Owners' own benefit and carry it to any other port or ports whatsoever, whether backwards or forwards or in a contrary direction to the ordinary or customary route.
(6) If in compliance with any of the provisions of sub-clauses (2) to (5) of this Clause anything is done or not done, such shall not be deemed to be a deviation, but shall be considered as due fulfilment of the Contract of Carriage.

18. General Ice Clause
Port of loading
(a) In the event of the loading port being inaccessible by reason of ice when the Vessel is ready to proceed from her last port or at any time during the voyage or on the Vessel's arrival or in case frost sets in after the Vessel's arrival, the Master for fear of being frozen in is at liberty to leave without cargo, and this Charter Party shall be null and void.
(b) If during loading the Master, for fear of the Vessel being frozen in, deems it advisable to leave, he has liberty to do so with what cargo he has on board and to proceed to any other port or ports with option of completing cargo for the Owners' benefit for any port or ports including port of discharge. Any part cargo thus loaded under this Charter Party to be forwarded to destination at the Vessel's expense but against payment of freight, provided that no extra expenses be thereby caused to the Charterers, freight being paid on quantity delivered (in proportion if lumpsum), all other conditions as per this Charter Party.
(c) In case of more than one loading port, and If one or more of the ports are closed by ice, the Master or the Owners to be at liberty either to load the part cargo at the open port and fill up elsewhere for their own account as under section (b) or to declare the Charter Party null and void unless the Charterers agree to load full cargo at the open port.
Port of discharge
(a) Should ice prevent the Vessel from reaching port of discharge the Charterers shall have the option of keeping the Vessel waiting until the re– opening of navigation and paying demurrage or of ordering the Vessel to a safe and immediately accessible port where she can safely discharge without risk of detention by ice. Such orders to be given within 48 hours after the Master or the Owners have given notice to the Charterers of the impossibility of reaching port of destination.
(b) If during discharging the Master for fear of the Vessel being frozen in deems it advisable to leave, he has liberty to do so with what cargo he has on board and to proceed to the nearest accessible port where she can safely discharge.
(c) On delivery of the cargo at such port, all conditions of the Bill of Lading shall apply and the Vessel shall receive the same freight as If she had discharged at the original port of destination, except that if the distance of the substituted port exceeds 100 nautical miles, the freight on the cargo delivered at the substituted port to be increased in proportion.

19. Law and Arbitration
* (a) This Charter Party shall be governed by and construed in accordance with English law and any dispute arising out of this Charter Party shall be referred to arbitration in London in accordance with the Arbitration Acts 1950 and 1979 or any statutory modification or re-enactment thereof for the time being in force. Unless the parties agree upon a sole arbitrator, one arbitrator shall be appointed by each party and the arbitrators so appointed shall appoint a third arbitrator, the decision of the three-man tribunal thus constituted or any two of them, shall be final. On the receipt by one party of the nomination In writing of the other party's arbitrator, that party shall appoint their arbitrator within fourteen days, failing which the decision of the single arbitrator appointed shall be final.
For disputes where the total amount claimed by either party does not exceed the amount stated in Box 25" the arbitration shall be conducted in accordance with the Small Claims Procedure of the London Maritime Arbitrators Association.
* (b) This Charter Party shall be governed by and construed in accordance with Title 9 of the United States Code and the Maritime Law of the United States and should any dispute arise out of this Charter Party, the matter in dispute shall be referred to three persons at New York, one to be appointed by each of the parties hereto, and the third by the two so chosen; their decision or that of any two of them shall be final, and for purpose of enforcing any award, this agreement may be made a rule of the Court. The proceedings shall be conducted in accordance with the rules of the Society of Maritime Arbitrators, Inc..
For disputes where the total amount claimed by either party does not exceed the amount stated in Box 25" the arbitration shall be conducted In accordance with the Shortened Arbitration Procedure of the Society of Maritime Arbitrators, Inc.. '
* (c) Any dispute arising out of this Charter Party shall be referred to arbitration at the place indicated In Box 25, subject to the procedures applicable there. The laws of the place indicated In Box 25 shall govern this Charter Party.
(d) If Box 25 in Part I is not tilled In, sub-clause (a) of this Clause shall apply.
* (a), (b) and (c) are alternatives; indicate alternative agreed in Box 25.
** Where no figure is supplied in Box 25 in Part I, this provision only shall be void but the other provisions of this Clause shall have full force and remain in effect.

Principle Clauses

PRINCIPLE CLAUSES COMMON TO BOTH VOYAGE AND TIME CHARTER PARTIES

1. Titles of the contracting parties (name of Shipowner and name of Charterer).
2. Name of ship with description including tonnage, classification, present position etc.
3. Warranty of seaworthiness. (Often "tight, staunch and strong").
4. Place of loading (of delivery in a time charter).
5. Type of cargo and quantity, (trading limits in a time charter).
6. Place of discharge (of redelivery in a time charter).
7. Rate of freight (of hire in a time charter).
8. When freight/hire to be paid (e.g. on loading or on discharge in a voyage charter, monthly or semimonthly in a time charter).
9. Laydays/Cancelling.
10. Arbitration.
11. Exceptions and exemptions from liability clauses.
12. Brokerages.

PRINCIPLE CLAUSES SPECIFIC TO VOYAGE CHARTERPARTIES

1. Rates of loading and discharging (tons per day or number of days/hours allowed).
2. When time commences to count including how and when notices of readiness to be given.
3. How laytime to be calculated e.g. SHEX.
4. Rate of demurrage (and despatch if any).
5. Who nominates port agents.

PRINCIPLE CLAUSES SPECIFIC TO TIME CHARTERPARTIES

1. Who pays for what especially fuel, fresh water, port charges etc.
2. Offhire clause (in case of breakdown, how soon hire ceases to become payable).
3. Owners option to drydock vessel during currency of charter.
4. Quantities of bunker fuel to be on board at time of delivery and redelivery.

Chartering Expressions and Abbreviations

Most chartering negotiations today will be conducted via some form of electronic written communication such as telex, fax, e-mail etc. Dating from the time when the only such medium was the telegraph many charterparty clauses were reduced to sets of initial letters. Because of their convenience they are still used.

It is vital that both parties in negotiations are fully aware of the meaning of these abbreviations and care should be taken to avoid ambiguity or misunderstanding.

Abbreviations concerning laytime

NOR
Notice of Readiness. The notice the ship gives to the shipper or receiver to say the ship is read to commence loading/discharging. This will determine when laytime commences to count.

SHEX
Sundays and Holidays excepted. Will follow the rate of loading/discharging and may be followed by 'uu' meaning 'unless used' or 'eiu' = 'even if used'. Would be FHEX (Fridays and Holidays) if Islamic countries involved.

SHINC
Sundays and Holidays included. Common when working at a dedicated bulk-cargo terminal which operates all day every day.

WWD
Weather Working Days ie days when bad weather does not interfere with loading/discharging.

Abbreviations concerning demurrage/dispatch

D1/2D
Despatch Half Demurrage may be followed by

BENDS
Meaning at Both Ends or

DLO
Despatch Loading Only or

DDO
Despatch Discharging Only

FD
Free of dispatch

Abbreviations concerning who pays for what

FIO
Free In and Out, means free of expense to the vessel, the shippers pay for loading and receivers pay for discharging.

FIOS
Free In and Out and Stowed. Shippers also pay for the stevedores working in the ship stowing the cargo in the holds.

FIOT
Free In and Out and Trimmed. With a bulk cargo the process of stowing, which will be that of levelling the material, is called trimming.

Gross Terms (or Liner Terms) means the ship pays all the cost of loading, stowing and discharging.

Appendix 8

Concerning the ship and cargo

DWAT   Deadweight All Told. The total weight of cargo, bunkers stores etc that the ship can carry.

DWCC   Deadweight Cargo Capacity. The total weight of cargo the ship can carry assuming an average quantity of bunkers and stores.

ETA   Estimated Time of Arrival.

ETD   Estimated Time of Departure.

ETS   Estimated Time of Sailing.

MOLOO   More of Less in Owners Option. Refers to the amount of cargo to be loaded where the owner seeks to allow the master some flexibility of depending upon the weight of fuel and stores he will have on board. The charterers may, however, insist on 'min/max' – an exact quantity.

aa   Always Afloat, the berth must be deep enough for the ship to be afloat at all states of the tide whether empty or loaded.

naabsa   Not Always Afloat But Safe Aground. At low tide there will not be enough water for the ship to be afloat but the bottom is sand or mud so the ship will not suffer damage.

SWAD   Salt Water Arrival Draft. The charterers cannot guarantee an accessible berth if the ship arrives on a deeper draft than stipulated.

Panamax   The dimensions of this ship are the maximum permissible for transmitting the Panama Canal. Usually about 60/80,000 tonnes dwat.

Capesize   Too large for Panama, usually over 100,000 dwat.

Handysize   An indeterminate size but currently around 30,000 dwat.

IWL   Institute Warranty Limits. The Institute in this case is the Institute of London Underwriters now called International Underwriters Association (IUA) who have published lists of geographical limits outside which the ship will not be insured unless additional premiums have been paid.

HHDW   Heavy Handy Deadweight. A method of referring to cargoes of scrap steel. As the name implies it will stow deadweight and there will be no awkward pieces.

HSS   Heavy grain/Sorghum/Soya refers to grain and gives charterers a range of options of types of grain to be loaded, typical method of chartering from the US Gulf.

TEU   Twenty Foot Equivalent Units, a way of describing the capacity of a ship intended for the container trade. Containers are either 20 feet or 40 feet long thus a 40 foot container is two Teus and known as an FEU.Beaufort Scale Wind Force Conversions.

Appendix 9

Shellvoy Charter Party

Code word for this Charter Party
"SHELLVOY 6"

Issued March 2005

VOYAGE CHARTER PARTY

LONDON,   20

PREAMBLE	1
IT IS THIS DAY AGREED between	2
of (hereinafter referred to as "Owners"), being owners 'disponent owners of the	3
motor/steam tank vessel called with an IMO number of	4
(hereinafter referred to as "the vessel")	5
and of	6
(hereinafter referred to as "Charterers"):	7
that the service for which provision is herein made shall be subject to the terms and conditions of this Charter which includes Part I, Part II and Part III. In the event of any conflict between the provisions of Part I, Part II and Part III hereof, the provisions of Part I shall prevail.	8 9

PART I   10

(A) Description of vessel	(I) vessel	Owners warrant that at the date hereof, and from the time when the obligation to proceed to the loadport(s) attaches, the	11 12
	(i)	Is classed	13
	(ii)(a)	Has a deadweight of tonnes (1000kg) on a salt-water draft on assigned summer freeboard of m. and if applicable,	14 15
	(b)	Has on board documentation showing the following additional drafts and deadweights	16
	(iii)	Has capacity lor cargo of m³	17
	(iv)	Is fully fitted with heating systems for all cargo tanks capable of maintaining cargo at a temperature of up to degrees Celsius and can accept a cargo temperature on loading of up to a maximum of degrees Celsius.	18 19
	(v)	Has tanks coated as follows:	20
	(vi)	Is equipped with cranes/derricks capable of lifting to and supporting at the vessel's port and starboard manifolds submarine hoses of up to tonnes (1000 kg) in weight.	21 22
	(vii)	Can discharge a full cargo (whether homogenous or multi grade) either within 24 hours, or can maintain a back pressure of 100 PSI at the vessel's manifold and Owners warrant such minimum performance provided receiving facilities permit and subject always to the obligation of utmost despatch set out in Part II, clause 3(1). The discharge warranty shall only be applicable provided the kinematic viscosity does not exceed 600 centistokes at the discharge temperature required by Charterers. If the kinematic viscosity only exceeds 600 centistokes on part of the cargo or particular grade(s) then the discharge warranty shall continue to apply to all other cargo/grades.	23 24 25 26 27 28
	(viii)	Has or will have carried, for the named Charterers, the following three cargoes (all grades to be identified) immediately prior to loading under this Charter:- Last Cargo/charterer 2ⁿᵈ Last Cargo/charterer 3ʳᵈ Last Cargo/charterer	29 30 31 32 33
	(ix)	Has a crude oil washing system complying with the requirements of the International Convention for the Prevention of Pollution from Ships 1973 as modified by the Protocol of 1978 ("MARPOL 73/78").	34 35
	(x)	Has an operational inert gas system and is equipped for and able to carry out closed sampling/ullaging/loading and discharging operations in full compliance with the International Safety Guide for Oil Tankers and Terminals ("ISGOTT") guidelines current at the date of this Charter.	36 37 38
	(xi)	Has on board all papers and certificates required by any applicable law, in force as at the date of this Charter, to enable the vessel to perform the charter service without any delay.	39 40

Appendix 9

Issued March 2005   **"SHELLVOY 6"**

(xii)	Is entered in the P&I Club, being a member of the International Group of P&I Clubs.	41
		42
(xiii)	Has in full force and effect Hull and Machinery insurance placed through reputable Brokers on Institute Time Clauses-Hull dated for the value of	43
(xiv)	Complies with the latest edition of the Oil Companies International Marine Forum ("OCIMF") standards for oil tankers' manifolds and associated equipment applicable to its size for cargo manifolds and vapour recovery systems.	44 / 45
(xv)	Is equipped to comply with, and is operated in accordance with, and has on board, the latest edition of the International Chamber of Shipping ("ICS") and/or OCIMF guidelines/publications covering:	46 / 47
	(a) Ship to Ship Operations	48
	(b) ISGOTT	49
	(c) Clean Seas Guide for Oil Tankers	50
	(d) Bridge Procedure Guide	51

(II)   Throughout the charter service. Owners shall ensure that the vessel shall be maintained, or that they take all steps necessary to promptly restore vessel to be, within the description in <u>Part I clause (A)(I)</u> and any questionnaires requested by Charterers or within information provided by Owners.   52 / 53 / 54

(III)   Owners warrant that any information provided on any Questionnaire(s) requested by Charterers or any other vessel information/details provided by Owners to Charterers is always complete and correct as at the date hereof, and from the time when the obligation to proceed to the loadport attaches and throughout the charter service. This information is an integral part of this Charter but if there is any conflict between the contents of the Questionnaire(s), or information provided by Owners, and any other provisions of this Charter then such other provisions shall govern.   55 / 56 / 57 / 58 / 59

(B) Position/ Readiness

Now   Expected ready to load   60

In addition to the above details on the position of the vessel Owners will advise Charterers of the known programme, including any contractual options available to the Charterers in Part I clause (A)(I) (viii) above between current position up to expected ready to load date at Charterers nominated or indicated first load port/area. Owners will not, unless with Charterers' prior consent, negotiate or enter into any business or give current Charterers any further options that may affect or alter the programme of the vessel as given in this clause.   61 / 62 / 63 / 64 / 65

(C) Laydays

Commencing Noon Local Time on   (Commencement Date)   66

Terminating Noon Local Time on   (Termination Date)   67

(D) Loading port(s)/ Range   68 / 69

(E) Discharging port(s)/ Range   70

(F) Cargo description   Charterers' option   71 / 72

Owners warrant that where different grades of cargo are carried pursuant to this Part I clause (F), they will be kept in complete segregation from each other during loading, transit, and discharge, to include the use of different pumps lines for each grade. If, however. Charterers so require it, the vessel may be required to: 73 / 74 / 75

(a) co-mingle different grades of cargo providing such grades fall within the cargo description set out in this Part I clause (F);   76

(b) otherwise breach the vessel's natural segregation;   77

(c) add dye to the cargo after loading, and/or

(d) carry out such other cargo operations as Charterers may reasonably require as long as the vessel is capable of such operations   78 / 79

provided that the Charterers will indemnify Owners for any loss damage delay or expense caused by following Charterers' instructions, except to the extent that such loss damage delay or expense could have been avoided by the exercise of due diligence by Owners.   80 / 81 / 82

(G) Freight rate

At   % of the rate for the voyage as provided for in the New Worldwide Tanker Nominal Freight Scale current at the date of commencement of loading (hereinafter referred to as "Worldscale") per ton (2240 lbs)/tonne (1000 Kg) or. if agreed, the following lumpsum amount(s)/or freight per tonne for named load and discharge area(s)/port(s) combinations   83

Appendix 9

Issued March 2005

"SHELLVOY 6"

(H) Freight payable to		84
(I) Laytime	running hours	85
(J) Demurrage per day (or pro rata)		86
		87
(K) ETAs	All radio/telex/e-mail messages sent by the master to Charterers shall be addressed to	
	All telexes must begin with the vessel name at the start of the subject line (no inverted commas, or use of MT/SS preceding the vessel name)	88 89
(L) Speed	The vessel shall perform the ballast passage with utmost despatch and the laden passage at ___ knots weather and safe navigation permitting at a consumption of ___ tonnes of Fueloil (state grade ___) per day.	90 91
	Charterers shall have the option to instruct the vessel to increase speed with Charterers reimbursing Owners for the additional bunkers consumed, at replacement cost.	92 93
	Charterers shall also have the option to instruct the vessel to reduce speed on laden passage. Additional voyage time caused by such instructions shall count against laytime or demurrage, if on demurrage, and the value of any bunkers saved shall be deducted from any demurrage claim Owners may have under this Charter with the value being calculated at original purchase price.	94 95 96 97
	Owners shall provide documentation to fully support the claims and calculations under this clause.	
(M) Worldscale	World scale Terms and Conditions apply/do not apply to this Charter. [delete as applicable]	98
(N) Casualty/ Accident contacts	In the event of an accident / marine casualty involving the vessel. Owners' technical managers can be contacted on a 24 hour basis as follows:	99 100
	Company Full Name:	101
	Contact Person:	102
	Full Address:	103
	Telephone Number:	104
	Fax Number:	105
	Telex Number:	106
	Email Address:	107
	24 Hour Emergency Telephone number:	108
		109
(O) Special provisions		
Signatures	IN WITNESS WHEREOF, the parries have caused this Charter consisting of the Preamble, Parts I, II and III to be executed as of the day and year first above written.	110 111
	By	112
	By	113

Appendix 9

Issued March 2005   **"SHELLVOY 6"**

PART II

Condition of vessel

1.   Owners shall exercise due diligence to ensure that from the time when the obligation to proceed to the loading port(s) attaches and throughout the charter service -

   (a)   the vessel and her hull, machinery, boilers, tanks, equipment and facilities are in good order and condition and in every way equipped and fit for the service required; and

   (b)   the vessel has a full and efficient complement of master, officers and crew and the senior officers shall be fully conversant in spoken and written English language

and to ensure that before and at the commencement of any laden voyage the vessel is in all respects fit to carry the cargo specified in Part I clause (F). For the avoidance of doubt, references to equipment in this Charter shall include but not be limited to computers and computer systems, and such equipment shall (inter alia) be required to continue to function, and not suffer a loss of functionality and accuracy (whether logical or mathematical) as a result of the run date or dates being processed.

Cleanliness of tanks

2.   Whilst loading, carrying and discharging the cargo the master shall at all times keep the tanks, lines and pumps of the vessel always clean for the cargo. Unless otherwise agreed between Owners and Charterers the vessel shall present for loading with cargo tanks ready and, subject to the following paragraphs, if vessel is fitted with Inert Gas System ("IGS"), fully inerted.

Charterers shall have the right to inspect vessel's tanks prior to loading and the vessel shall abide by Charterers' instructions with regard to tank or tanks which the vessel is required to present ready for entry and inspection. If Charterer's inspector is not satisfied with the cleanliness of the vessel's tanks. Owners shall clean them in their time and at their expense to the satisfaction of Charterers' inspector, provided that nothing herein shall affect the responsibilities and obligations of the master and Owners in respect of the loading, carriage and care of cargo under this Charter nor prejudice the rights of Charterers, should any contamination or damage subsequently be found, to contend that the same was caused by inadequate cleaning and/or some breach of this or any other clause of this Charter.

Notwithstanding that the vessel, if equipped with IGS, shall present for loading with all cargo tanks fully inerted, any time used for de-inerting (provided that such de-inerting takes place after laytime or demurrage time has commenced or would, but for this clause, have commenced) and/or re-inerting those tanks that at Charterers' specific request were gas freed for inspection, shall count as laytime or if on demurrage as demurrage, provided the tank or tanks inspected are found to be suitable. In such case Charterers will reimburse Owners for bunkers consumed for de-inerting/re-inerting, at replacement cost.

If the vessel's tanks are inspected and rejected, time used for de-inerting shall not count towards laytime or demurrage, and laytime or demurrage time shall not commence or recommence, as the case may be, until the tanks have been re-inspected, approved by Charterers' inspector, and re-incrted.

Voyage

3.   (1) Subject to the provisions of this Charter the vessel shall perform her service with utmost despatch and shall proceed to such berths as Charterers may specify, in any port or ports within Part I clause (D) nominated by Charterers, or so near thereunto as she may safely get and there, always safely afloat, load thecargo specified in Part I clause (F) of this Charter, but not in excess of the maximum quantity consistent with the International Load Line Convention for the time being in force and, being so loaded, proceed as ordered on signing bills of lading to such berths as Charterers may specify, in any port or ports within Part I clause (E) nominated by Charterers, or so near thereunto as she may safely get and there, always safely afloat, discharge the cargo.

Charterers shall nominate loading and discharging ports, and shall specify loading and discharging berths and, where loading or discharging is interrupted, shall provide fresh orders in relation thereto.

In addition Charterers shall have the option at any time of ordering the vessel to safe areas at sea for wireless orders. Any delay or deviation arising as a result of the exercise of such option shall be compensated by Charterers in accordance with the terms of Part II clause 26 (1).

(2) Owners shall be responsible for and indemnify Charterers for any time, costs, delays or loss including but not limited to use of laytime, demurrage, deviation expenses, replacement tonnage, lightening costs and associated fees and expenses due to any failure whatsoever to comply fully with Charterers' voyage instructions and clauses in this Charter which specify requirements concerning Voyage Instructions and/ or Owners'/masters' duties including, without limitation to the generality of the foregoing, loading more cargo than permitted under the International Load Line Convention, for the time being in force, or for not leaving sufficient space for expansion of cargo or loading more or less cargo than Charterers specified or for not loading/discharging in accordance with Charterers' instructions regarding the cargo quantity or draft requirements.

This clause 3(2) shall have effect notwithstanding the provision of Part II clause 32 (a) of this Charter or Owners' defences under the Hague-Visby Rules.

(3) Owners shall always employ pilots for berthing and unberthing of vessels at all ports and/or berths under this Charter unless prior exemption is given by correct and authorised personnel. Owners to confirm in writing if they have been exempt from using a pilot and provide Charterers with the details, including but not limited to, the authorising organisation with person's name.

(4) Without prejudice to the provisions of sub-clause (2) of this clause, and unless a specific prior agreement exists, if a conflict arises between terminal orders and Charterers' voyage instructions, the master shall stop cargo operations, and/or other operations under dispute, and contact Charterers immediately. Terminal orders shall never supersede Charterers' voyage instructions and any conflict

Appendix 9

Issued March 2005 **"SHELLVOY 6"**

PART II

shall be resolved prior to resumption of cargo, or other, operations in dispute. Where such a conflict arises the vessel shall not 62

sail from the port or resume cargo operations, and/or other operations under dispute, until Charterers have directed the vessel to 63

do so. 64

Time spent resolving the vessel/terminal conflict will count as laytime or demurrrage except that failure of Owners/master to comply 65

with the procedure set forth above shall result in the deduction from laytime or demurrage time of the time used in resolving the vessel/ 66/67

terminal instruction conflict. 68

(5) In this Charter, "berth" means any berth, wharf, dock, anchorage, submarine line, a position alongside any vessel or lighter or 69

any other loading or discharging point whatsoever to which Charterers are entitled to order the vessel hereunder, and "port" means any 70

port or location at sea to which the vessel may proceed in accordance with the terms of this Charter. 71

Safe berth 4. Charterers shall exercise due diligence to order the vessel only to ports and berths which are safe for the vessel and to 72

ensure that transhipment operations conform to standards not less than those set out in the latest edition of ICS/OCTMF Ship-to-Ship 73

Transfer Guide (Petroleum). Notwithstanding anything contained in this Charter, Charterers do not warrant the safely of any port, berth 74/75

or transhipment operation and Charterers shall not be liable for loss or damage arising from any unsafely if they can prove that due 76

diligence was exercised in the giving of the order or if such loss or damage was caused by an act of war or civil commotion within the 77

trading areas defined in Part I clauses (D/E). 78

Freight 5. (1) Freight shall be earned concurrently with delivery of cargo at the nominated discharging port or ports and shall be 79

paid by Charterers to Owners without any deductions, except as may be required in the Singapore Income Tax Act and/or under Part II 80

clause 48 and/or under clause 55 and/or under Part III clause 4(a), in United States Dollars at the rate(s) specified in Part I clause (G) 81

on the gross bill of lading quantity as furnished by the shipper (subject to Part II clauses X and 40). upon receipt by Charterers of notice 82/83

of completion of final discharge of cargo, provided that no freight shall be payable on any quantity in excess of the maximum quantity 84

consistent with the International Load Line Convention for the time being in force. 85

If the vessel is ordered to proceed on a voyage for which a fixed differential is provided in Worldscale, such fixed differential shall 86

be payable without applying the percentage referred to in Part I clause (G). 87

If cargo is carried between ports and/or by an agreed route for which no freight rate is expressly quoted in Worldscale, then 88

the parties shall, in the absence of agreement as to the appropriate freight rate, apply to Worldscale Association (London) Ltd., or 89/90

Worldscale Association (NYC) Inc., for the determination of an appropriate Worldscale freight rate. If Owners or master unilaterally 91

elect to proceed by a route that is different to that specified in Worldscale, or different to a route agreed between Owners and Charterers, 92

freight shall always be paid in accordance with the Worldscale rate as published or in accordance with any special rate applicable for 93

the agreed route. 94

Save in respect of the time when freight is earned, the location of any transhipment at sea pursuant to Part II clause 26(2) shall not 95

be an additional nominated port, unless otherwise agreed, for the purposes of this Charter (including this clause 5) and the freight rate 96/97

for the voyage shall be the same as if such transhipment had not taken place. 98

(2) If the freight in Part I clause (G) is a lumpsum amount and such lumpsum freight is connected with a specific number of load 99

and discharge ports given in Part I clause (L) and Owners agree that Charterers may order the vessel to additional load and/or discharge 100

ports not covered by the agreed lumpsum freight, the following shall apply: 101

(a) the first load port and the final discharge port shall be deemed to be the port(s) that form the voyage and on which the 102

lumpsum freight included in Part I clause (G) refers to; 103

(b) freight for such additional ports shall be calculated on basis of deviation. Deviation shall be calculated on the difference in 104

distance between the specified voyage (for which freight is agreed) and the voyage actually performed. 105

BP Shipping Marine Distance Tables (2004). produced by A to Briac shall be used in both cases. Deviation time/bunker 106/107

consumption shall be calculated using the charter speed and bunker consumption as per the speed and consumptions given in Part I 108

clause (L) of this Charter. 109

Deviation time and time spent in port shall be charged at the demurrage rate in Part I clause (J) of this Charter except that time used in 110

port which would otherwise qualify for half rate laytime and/or demurrage under Part II clause (15) (2) of this Charter will be charged 111/112

at half rate. 113

Additional bunkers consumed shall be paid at replacement cost, and actual port costs shall be paid as incurred. Such deviation costs shall 114

be paid against Owners' fully documented claim. 115

Claims, dues and other charges 6. (1) Dues and other charges upon the vessel, including those assessed by reference to the quantity of cargo loaded or 116

discharged, and any taxes on freight whatsoever shall be paid by Owners, and dues and other charges upon the cargo shall be paid by 117

Charterers. However, notwithstanding the foregoing, where under a provision of Worldscale a due or charge is expressly for the account 118

of Owners or Charterers then such due or charge shall be payable in accordance with such provision. 119

(2) Any costs including those itemised under applicable "Worldscale" as being for Charterers' account shall. 120/121

Issued March 2005   **"SHELLVOY 6"**

PART II

unless otherwise instructed by Charterers, be paid by Owners and reimbursed by Charterers against Owners' fully documented claim. 122 123

(3) Charterers shall be discharged and released from all liability in respect of any charges/claims (other than demurrage and Worldscale charges/dues and indemnity claims) including but not limited to additional bunkers, detention, deviation, shifting, heating, deadweight, speed up, slow down, drifting, port costs, additional freight, insurance. Owner may send to Charterers under this Charter unless any such charges/claims have been received by Charterer in writing, fully and correctly documented, within ninety (90) days from completion of discharge of the cargo concerned under this Charter. Part II clause 15 (3) of this Charter covers the notification and fully documented claim procedure for demurrage. 124 125 126 127 128 129

(4) If, after disconnection of hoses, the vessel remains at berth for vessel's purposes, Owners shall be responsible for all direct and indirect costs whether advised to Owners in advance or not. and including charges by Terminal Suppliers/ Receivers. 130 131 132 133

Loading and discharging cargo

7.   The cargo shall be loaded into the vessel at the expense of Charterers and, up to the vessel's permanent hose connections, at Charterers' risk. The cargo shall be discharged from the vessel at the expense of Owners and, up to the vessel's permanent hose connections, at Owners' risk. Owners shall, unless otherwise notified by Charterers or their agents, supply at Owners' expense all hands, equipment and facilities required on board for mooring and unmooring and connecting and disconnecting hoses for loading and discharging. 134 135 136 137 138

Deadfreight

8.   Charterers need not supply a full cargo, but if they do not freight shall nevertheless be paid as if the vessel had been loaded with a full cargo. 139 140

The term "full cargo" as used throughout this Charter means a cargo which, together with any collected washings (as defined in Part II clause 40) retained on board pursuant to the requirements of MARPOL 73/78, fills the vessel to either her applicable deadweight or her capacity stated in Part I clause (A) (I) (iii), whichever is less, while leaving sufficient space in the tanks for the expansion of cargo. If under Part I clause (F) vessel is chartered for a minimum quantity and the vessel is unable to load such quantity due to having reached her capacity as stated in Part I clause (A) (I) (iii), always leaving sufficient space for expansion of cargo, then without prejudice to any claims which Charterers may have against Owners, no deadweight between the quantity loaded and the quantity shown in Part I clause (F) shall be due. 141 142 143 144 145 146 147 148

Shifting

9.   Charterers shall have the right to require the vessel to shift at ports of loading and/or discharging from a loading or discharging berth within port limits and/or to a waiting place inside or outside port limits and back to the same or to another such berth/place once or more often on payment of all additional expenses incurred. For the purposes of freight payment and shifting the places grouped in Port and Terminal Combinations in Worldscale are to be considered as berths within a single port. If at any time before cargo operations are completed it becomes dangerous for the vessel to remain at the specified berth as a result of wind or water conditions. Charterers shall pay all additional expenses of shifting from any such berth and back to that or any other specified berth within port limits (except to the extent that any fault of the vessel contributed to such danger). 149 150 151 152 153 154 155

Subject to Part II clause 14(a) and (c) time spent shitting shall count against laytime or if the vessel is on demurrage for demurrage. 156 157 158

Charterers' failure to give orders

10.   If the vessel is delayed due to Charterers' breach of Part II clause 3 Charterers shall, subject to the terms hereof, compensate Owners in accordance with Part II clause 15(1) and (2) as if such delay were time exceeding the laytime. Such compensation shall be Owners' sole remedy in respect of such delay. 159 160

The period of such delay shall be calculated: 161

(i)   from 6 hours after Owners notify Charterers that the vessel is delayed awaiting nomination of loading or discharging port until such nomination has been received by Owners, or 162 163

(ii)   from 6 hours after the vessel gives notice of readiness at the loading or discharging port until commencement of loading or discharging, 164 165

as the case may be, subject always to the same exceptions as those set out in Part II clause 14. Any period of delay in respect of which Charterers pay compensation pursuant to this clause 10 shall be excluded from any calculation of time for laytime or demurrage made under any other clause of this Charter. Periods of delay hereunder shall be cumulative for each port, and Owners may demand compensation after the vessel has been delayed for a total of 20 running days, and thereafter after each succeeding 5 running days of delay and at the end of any delay. Each such demand shall show the period in respect of which compensation is claimed and the amount due. Charterers shall pay the full amount due within 14 days after receipt of Owners' demand. Should Charterers fail to make any such payments Owners shall have the right to terminate this Charter by giving written notice to Charterers or their agents, without prejudice to any claims which Charterers or Owners may have against each other under this Charter or otherwise. 166 167 168 169 170 171 172 173 174 175 176

Laydays/ Termination

11.   Should the vessel not be ready to load by noon local time on the termination date set out in Part I clause (C) Charterers shall have the option of terminating this Charter unless the vessel has been delayed due to Charterers' change of orders pursuant to Part II clause 26, in which case the laydays shall be extended by the period of such delay. 177 178 179 180

Appendix 9

Issued March 2005

"SHELLVOY 6"

PART II

181

As soon as Owners become aware that the vessel will not be ready to load by noon on the termination date, Owners will give notice to Charterers declaring a new readiness date and ask Charterers to elect whether or not to terminate this Charter.

Within 4 days after such notice. Charterers shall either:

(i)   declare this Charter terminated or,

(ii)   confirm a revised set of laydays which shall be amended such that the new readiness date stated shall be the commencement date and the second day thereafter shall be the termination date or.

(iii)   agree a new set of laydays or an extension to the laydays mutually acceptable to Owners and Charterers

The provisions of this clause and the exercise or non-exercise by Charterers of their option to terminate shall not prejudice any claims which Charterers or Owners may have against each other.

Laytime   12.   (1) The laytime for loading, discharging and all other Charterers' purposes whatsoever shall be the number of running hours specified in Part I clause (I). Charterers shall have the right to load and discharge at all times, including night, provided that they shall pay for all extra expenses incurred ashore.

(2) If vessel is able to. and Charterers so instruct, the vessel shall load earlier than the commencement of of laydays and Charterers shall have the benefit of such time saved by way of offset from any demurrage incured. Such benefit shall be the time between commencement of loading until the commencement of the original laydays.

Notice of readiness/ Running time   13.   (1) Subject to the provisions of Part II clauses 13(3) and 14,

(a)   Time at each loading or discharging port shall commence to run 6 hours after the vessel is in all respects ready to load or discharge and written notice thereof has been tendered by the master or Owners' agents to Charterers or their agents and the vessel is securely moored at the specified loading or discharging berth. However, if the vessel does not proceed immediately to such berth time shall commence to run 6 hours after (i) the vessel is lying in the area where she was ordered to wait or, in the absence of any such specific order, in a usual waiting area and (ii) written notice of readiness has been tendered and (iii) the specified berth is accessible. A loading or discharging berth shall be deemed inaccessible only for so long as the vessel is or would be prevented from proceeding to it by bad weather, tidal conditions, ice, awaiting daylight, pilot or tugs, or port traffic control requirements (except those requirements resulting from the unavailability of such berth or of the cargo). If Charterers fail to specify a berth at any port, the first berth at which the vessel loads or discharges the cargo or any part thereof shall be deemed to be the specified berth at such port for the purposes of this clause.

Notice shall not be tendered before commencement of laydays and notice tendered by radio shall qualify as written notice provided it is confirmed in writing as soon as reasonably possible.

Time shall never commence before six hours after commencement of laydays unless loading commences prior to this time as provided in clause 13 (3).

If Owners fail;

(i)   to obtain Customs clearance; and/or

(ii)   to obtain free pratique unless this is not customary prior to berthing; and/or

(iii)   to have on board all papers/certificates required to perform this Charter, either within the 6 hours after notice of readiness originally tendered or when time would otherwise normally commence under this Charter, then the original notice of readiness shall not be valid. A new notice of readiness may only be tendered when Customs clearance and or free pratique has been granted and/or all papers/certificates required are in order in accordance with relevant authorities' requirements. Laytime or demurrage, if on demurrage, would then commence in accordance with the terms of this Charter. All time, costs and expenses as a result of delays due to any of the foregoing shall be for Owners' account.

(b)   Time shall:

(i)   continue to run until the cargo hoses have been disconnected,

(ii)   recommence two hours after disconnection of hoses if the vessel is delayed for Charterers' purposes and shall continue until the termination of such delay provided that if the vessel waits at any place other than the berth, any time or part of the time on passage to such other place that occurs after two hours from disconnection of hoses shall not count.

(2) If the vessel loads or discharges cargo by transhipment at sea time shall commence in accordance with Part II clause 13 (I) (a), and run until transhipment has been completed and the vessels have separated, always subject to Part II clause 14.

(3) Notwithstanding anything else in this clause 13, if Charterers start loading or discharging the vessel before time would otherwise start to run under this Charter, time shall run from commencement of such loading or discharging.

(4) For the purposes of this clause 13 and of Part II clause 14 and Part II clause 15 "time" shall mean laytime

182
183
184
185
186
187
188
189
190
191
192
193
194
195
196
197
198
199
200
201
202
203
204
205
206
207
208
209
210
211
212
213
214
215
216
217
218
219
220
221
222
223
224
225
226
227
228
229
230
231
232
233
234
235
236
237
238
239
240

Appendix 9

Issued March 2005   **"SHELLVOY 6"**

PART II

or time counting for demurrage, as the case may be.	241

Suspension of time

14.   Time shall not count when: 242

    (a)   spent on inward passage from the vessel's waiting area to the loading or discharging berth specified by   243
Charterers, even if lightening occurred at such waiting area; or   244

    (b)   spent in carrying out vessel operations, including but not limited to bunkering, discharging slops and tank   245
washings, and handling ballast, except to the extent that cargo operations are carried on concurrently and are   246
not delayed thereby; or   247

    (c)   lost as a result of: 248

        (i)   breach of this Charter by Owners; or   249, 250

        (ii)   any cause attributable to the vessel, (including but not limited to the warranties in Part I (A) of this   251
Charter) including breakdown or inefficiency of the vessel; or   252

        (iii)   strike, lock-out, stoppage or restraint of labour of master, officers or crew of the vessel or tug boats or   253
pilot.   254

Demurrage

15.   (1) Charterers shall pay demurrage at the rate specified in Part I clause (J).   255

If the demurrage rate specified in Part I clause (J) is expressed as a percentage of Worldscale such percentage shall be   256
applied to the demurrage rate applicable to vessels of a similar size to the vessel as provided in Worldscale or, for the purpose   257
of clause 10 and/or if this Charter is terminated prior to the commencement of loading, in Worldscale current at the termination   258
date specified in Part I clause (C).   259

Demurrage shall be paid per running day or pro rata for part thereof for all time which, under the provisions of this   260
Charter, counts against laytime or for demurrage and which exceeds the laytime specified in Part I clause (I). Charterers'   261
liability for exceeding the laytime shall be absolute and shall not in any case be subject to the provisions of Part II clause 32.   262, 263

(2) If, however, all or part of such demurrage arises out of or results from fire or explosion or strike or failure/breakdown   264
of plant and/or machinery at ports of loading and/or discharging in or about the plant of Charterers, shippers or consignees of   265
the cargo (not being a fire or explosion caused by the negligence or wilful act or omission of Charterers, shippers or consignees   266
of the cargo or their respective servants or agents), act of God, act of war, riot, civil commotion, or arrest or restraint of princes,   267
rulers or peoples, the laytime used and/or the rate of demurrage shall be reduced by half for such laytime used and/or for such   268
demurrage or such parts thereof.   269

(3) Owners shall notify Charterers within 60 days after completion of discharge if demurrage has been incurred and   270
any demurrage claim shall be fully and correctly documented, and received by Charterers, within 90 days after completion of   271
discharge . If Owners fail to give notice of or to submit any such claim with documentation, as required herein, within the limits   272
aforesaid. Charterers' liability for such demurrage shall be extinguished.   273, 274

(4) If any part cargo for other charterers, shippers or consignees (as the case may be) is loaded or discharged at the same   275
berth, then any time used by the vessel waiting at or for such berth and in loading or discharging which would otherwise count   276
as laytime or if the vessel is on demurrage for demurrage, shall be pro-rated in the proportion that Charterers' cargo bears to   277
the total cargo to be loaded or discharged at such berth. If however, the running of laytime or demurrage, if on demurrage, is   278
solely attributable to other parties' cargo operations then such time shall not count in calculating laytime or demurrage, if on   279
demurrage, against Charterers under this Charter.   280

Vessel inspection

16.   Charterers shall have the right, but no duty, to have a representative attend on board the vessel at any loading and/   281
or discharging ports and the master and Owners shall co-operate to facilitate his inspection of the vessel and observation of   282
cargo operations. However, such right, and the exercise or non-exercise thereof, shall in no way reduce the master's or Owners'   283
authority over, or responsibility to Charterers and third parties for, the vessel and every aspect of her operation, nor increase   284
Charterers' responsibilities to Owners or third parties for the same.   285

Cargo inspection

17.   This clause 17 is without prejudice to Part II clause 2 hereof. Charterers shall have the right to require inspection   286
of the vessel's tanks at loading and/or discharging ports to ascertain the quantity and quality of the cargo, water and residues   287
on board. Depressurisation of the tanks to permit inspection and/or ullaging shall be carried out in accordance with the   288
recommendations in the latest edition of the ISGOTT guidelines. Charterers shall also have the right to inspect and take samples   289
from the bunker tanks and other non-cargo spaces. Any delay to the vessel caused by such inspection and measurement or   290
associated depressurising/repressurising of tanks shall count against laytime, or if the vessel is on demurrage, for demurrage.   291, 292

Cargo measurement

18.   The master shall ascertain the contents of all tanks before and after loading and before and after discharging, and   293
shall prepare tank-by-tank ullage reports of the cargo, water and residues on board which shall be promptly made available to   294
Charterers or their representative if requested. Each such ullage report shall show actual ullage/dips, and densities at observed   295
and standard temperature (15° Celsius). All quantities shall be expressed in cubic metres at both observed and standard   296
temperature.   297

Inert gas

19.   The vessel's inert gas system (if any) shall comply with Regulation 62, Chapter II-2 of the 1974 Safety of   298

Appendix 9

Issued March 2005

"SHELLVOY 6"

PART II

Life at Sea Convention as modified by the Protocol of 1978, and any subsequent amendments, and Owners warrant that such 299
system shall be operated (subject to the provisions of Part II clause 2), during loading, throughout the voyage and during 300
discharge, and in accordance with the guidance given in the IMO publication "Inert Gas System (1983)". Should the inert 301
gas system fail. Section 8 (Emergency Procedures) of the said IMO publication shall be strictly adhered to and time lost as a 302
consequence of such failure shall not count against laytime or, if the vessel is on demurrage, for demurrage. 303
304

Crude oil washing 20. If the vessel is equipped for crude oil washing Charterers shall have the right to require the vessel to crude
oil wash, concurrently with discharge, those tanks in which Charterers' cargo is carried. If crude oil washing is required 305
by Charterers any additional discharge time thereby incurred, always subject to the next succeeding sentences, shall count 306
against laytime or, if the vessel is on demurrage, for demurrage. The number of hours specified in Part I clause (A) (I) 307
(vii) shall be increased by 0.6 hours per cargo tank washed, always subject to a maximum increase of 8 hours. If vessel 308
fails to maintain 100 PSI throughout the discharge then any time over 24 hours, plus the additional discharge performance 309
allowance under this clause, shall not count as laytime or demurrage, if on demurrage. This clause 20 does not reduce 310
Owners' liability for the vessel to perform her service with utmost despatch as setout in Part II, Clause 3(1). The master 311
shall provide Charterers with a crude oil washing log identifying each tank washed, and stating whether such tank has been 312
washed to the MARPOL minimum standard or has been the subject of additional crude oil washing and whether requested 313
by Charterers or otherwise. 314
315

Overage insurance 21. Any additional insurance on the cargo required because of the age of the vessel shall be for Owners' account. 316
317

Ice 22. The vessel shall not be required to force ice or to follow icebreakers. If the master finds that a nominated port is
inaccessible due to ice, the master shall immediately notify Charterers requesting revised orders and shall remain outside the 318
ice-bound area; and if after arrival at a nominated port there is danger of the vessel being frozen in, the vessel shall proceed 319
to the nearest safe and ice free position and at the same time request Charterers to give revised orders. 320

In either case if the affected port is: 321
 (i) the first or only loading port and no cargo has been loaded. Charterers shall either nominate another port, 322
  or give notice cancelling this Charter in which case they shall pay at the demurrage rate in Part I clause (J) 323
  for the time from the master's notification aforesaid or from notice of readiness on arrival, as the case may 324
  be,until the time such cancellation notice is given; 325
 (ii) a loading port and part of the cargo has been loaded. Charterers shall either nominate another port, or order 326
  the vessel to proceed on the voyage without completing loading in which case Charterers shall pay for any 327
  deadfrcight arising therefrom; 328
 (iii) a discharging port, Charterers shall either nominate another port or order the vessel to proceed to or return 329
  to and discharge at the nominated port. If the vessel is ordered to proceed to or return to a nominated 330
  port, Charterers shall bear the risk of the vessel being damaged whilst proceeding to or returning to or at 331
  such port, and the whole period from the time when the master's request for revised orders is received by 332
  Charterers until the vessel can safely depart after completion of discharge shall count against laytime or, 333
  if the vessel is on demurrage, for demurrage. 334

If, as a consequence of Charterers revising orders pursuant to this clause, the nominated port(s) or the number or 335
rotation of ports is changed, freight shall nevertheless be paid for the voyage which the vessel would otherwise have 336
performed had the orders not been so revised, such freight to be increased or reduced by the amount by which, as a result of 337
such revision of orders. 338
339
 (a) the time used including any time awaiting revised orders (which shall be valued at the demurrage rate in 340
  Part I clause (J)), and 341
 (b) the bunkers consumed, at replacement cost and 342
 (c) the port charges 343
  for the voyage actually performed are greater or less than those that would have been incurred on the 344
  voyage which, but for the revised orders under this clause, the vessel would have performed. 345
346

Quarantine 23. Time lost due to quarantine shall not count against laytime or for demurrage unless such quarantine was in force
at the time when the affected port was nominated by Charterers. 347
348

Agency 24. The vessel's agents shall be nominated by Charterers at nominated ports of loading and discharging. Such
agents, although nominated by Charterers, shall be employed and paid by Owners. 349
350

Charterers' obligation at shallow draft port/ Lightening in port 25. (1) If the vessel, with the quantity of cargo then on board, is unable due to inadequate depth of water in the port 351
safely to reach any specified discharging berth and discharge the cargo there always safely afloat. Charterers shall specify a 352
location within port limits where the vessel can discharge sufficient cargo into vessels or lighters to enable the vessel safely 353
to reach and discharge cargo at such discharging berth, and the vessel shall lighten at such location. 354
 (2) If the vessel is lightened pursuant to clause 25(1) then, for the purposes of the calculation of laytime and demurrage, 355
the lightening place shall be treated as the first discharging berth within the port where such lightening occurs. 356

Appendix 9

Issued March 2005   **"SHELLVOY 6"**

PART II

| Charterers' orders/ Change of orders/Part cargo transhipment | 26. | (1) If, after loading and or discharging ports have been nominated. Charterers wish to vary such nominations or their rotation, Charterers may give revised orders subject to Part I clause (D) and/or (E), as the case may be. Charterers shall reimburse Owners at the demurrage rate provided in Part I clause (J) for any deviation or delay which may result therefrom and shall pay at replacement cost for any extra bunkers consumed. Charterers shall not be liable for any other loss or expense which is caused by such variation. | 357 358 359 360 361 |

(2) Subject to Part II clause 33(6), Charterers may order the vessel to load and/or discharge any part of the cargo by transhipment at sea in the vicinity of any nominated port or en route between two nominated ports, in which case unless Charterers elect, (which they may do at any time) to treat the place of such transhipment as a load or discharge port (subject to the number of ports and ranges in Part I clauses (D) and (E) of this Charter), Charterers shall reimburse Owners at the demurrage rate specified in Part I clause (J) for any additional steaming time and/or delay which may be incurred as a consequence of proceeding to and from the location at sea of such transhipment and, in addition. Charterers shall pay at replacement cost for any extra bunkers consumed.

(3) Owners warrant that the vessel, master, officers and crew are, and shall remain during this Charter, capable of safely carrying out all the procedures in the current edition of the ICS/OCIMF Ship to Ship Transfer Guide (Petroleum). Owners further warrant that when instructed to perform a ship to ship transfer the master Officers and crew shall, at all times, comply with such procedures. Charterers shall provide, and pay for, the necessary equipment and, if necessary, mooring master, for such ship to ship operation.

Heating of cargo   27.   If Charterers require cargo heating the vessel shall, on passage to and whilst at discharging port(s), Maintain the cargo at the loaded temperature or at the temperature stated in Part I clause (A) (I) (iv), whichever is the lower. Charterers may request that the temperature of the cargo be raised above or lowered below that at which it was loaded, in which event Owners shall use their best endeavours to comply with such request and Charterers shall pay at replacement cost for any additional bunkers consumed and any consequential delay to the vessel shall count against laytime or, if the vessel is on demurrage, for demurrage.

ETA   28.   (1) Owners shall give Charterers a time and date of expected arrival at the first load port or if the loading range is in the Arabian Gulf, the time of her expected arrival off Quoin Island (hereinafter called "load port" in this clause) at the date of this Charter. Owners shall further advise Charterers at any time between the Charter date and arrival at load port of any variation of 6 hours or more in vessel's expected arrival time/date at the load port.

(2) Owners undertake that, unless Charterers require otherwise, the master shall:

(a) advise Charterers immediately on leaving the final port of call on the previous voyage of the time and date of the vessel's expected arrival at the first loading port and shall further advise Charterers 72, 48, 36, and 24 hours before the expected arrival time/date.

(b) advise Charterers immediately after departure from the final loading port, of the vessel's expected time of arrival at the first discharging port or the area at sea to which the vessel has been instructed to proceed for wireless orders, and confirm or amend such advice not later than 72, 48, 36 and 24 hours before the vessel is due at such port or area;

(c) advise Charterers immediately of any variation of more than six hours from expected times of arrival at loading or discharging ports, Quoin Island or such area at sea to Charterers;

(d) address all messages as specified in Part I clause (K).

Owners shall be responsible for any consequences or additional expenses arising as a result of non-compliance with this clause.

(3) If at any time prior to the tender of notice of readiness at the first load port, the vessel ceases to comply with the description set out in Part I clause (A) and in any questionnaire(s), the Owners shall immediately notify Charterers of the same, providing full particulars, and explaining what steps Owners are taking to ensure that the vessel will so comply. Any silence or failure on the part of Charterers to respond to or any inaction taken in respect of any such notice shall not amount to a waiver of any rights or remedies which Charterers may have in respect of the matters notified by Owners.

Packed cargo   29.   Charterers have the option of shipping products and/or general cargo in available dry cargo space, the Quantity being subject to the master's discretion. Freight shall be payable at the bulk rate in accordance with Part II clause 5 and Charterers shall pay in addition all expenses incurred solely as a result of the packed cargo being carried. Delay occasioned to the vessel by the exercise of such option shall count against laytime or, if the vessel is on demurrage, for demurrage.

Subletting/ Assignment   30.   Charterers shall have the option of sub-chartering the vessel and/or of assigning this Charter to any person or persons, but Charterers shall always remain responsible for the due fulfilment of all the terms and conditions of this Charter. Additionally Charterers may novate this charter to any company of the Royal Dutch/Shell Group of Companies.

362 363 364 365 366 367 368 369 370 371 372 373 374 375 376 377 378 379 380 381 382 383 384 385 386 387 388 389 390 391 392 393 394 395 396 397 398 399 400 401 402 403 404 405 406 407 408 409 410 411 412 413 414

Appendix 9

Issued March 2005   **"SHELLVOY 6"**

PART II

Liberty	31. The vessel shall be at liberty to tow or be towed, to assist vessels in all positions of distress and to deviate for the purpose of saving life or property. On the laden voyage the vessel shall not take on bunkers or deviate or stop, except as allowed in this clause 31, without prior permission of Charterers, Cargo Insurers, and Owners' P&I Club.	415 416 417

Exceptions   32.   (1) The vessel, her master and Owners shall not, unless otherwise in this Charter expressly provided, be liable for any loss or damage or delay or failure arising or resulting from any act, neglect or default of the master, pilots, mariners or other servants of Owners in the navigation or management of the vessel; fire, unless caused by the actual fault or privity of Owners; collision or stranding; dangers and accidents of the sea; explosion. Bursting of boilers, breakage of shafts or any latent defect in hull, equipment or machinery; provided, however, that Part I clause (A) and Part II clauses 1 and 2 hereof shall be unaffected by the foregoing. Further, neither the vessel, her master or Owners, nor Charterers shall, unless otherwise in this Charter expressly provided, be liable for any loss or damage or delay or failure in performance hereunder arising or resulting from act of God, act of war, act of public enemies, seizure under legal process, quarantine restrictions, strikes, lock-outs, restraints of labour, riots, civil commotions or arrest or restraint of princes, rulers or people.

(2) Nothing in this Charter shall be construed as in any way restricting, excluding or waiving the right of Owners or of any other relevant persons to limit their liability under any available legislation or law.

(3) Clause 32(1) shall not apply to or affect any liability of Owners or the vessel or any other relevant person in respect of

    (a)   loss or damage caused to any berth, jetty, dock, dolphin, buoy, mooring line, pipe or crane or other works or equipment whatsoever at or near any port to which the vessels may proceed under this Charter, whether or not such works or equipment belong to Charterers, or

    (b)   any claim (whether brought by Charterers or any other person) arising out of any loss of or damage to or in connection with the cargo. Any such claim shall be subject to the Hague-Visby Rules or the Hague Rules, or the Hamburg Rules as the case may be, which ought pursuant to Part II clause 37 hereof to have been incorporated in the relevant bill of lading (whether or not such Rules were so incorporated) or, if no such bill of lading is issued, to the Hague-Visby rules unless the Hamburg Rules compulsory apply in which case to the Hamburg Rules.

418
419
420
421
422
423
424
425
426
427
428
429
430
431
432
433
434
435
436
437
438
439
440

Bills of
lading   33.   (1) Subject to the provisions of this clause Charterers may require the master to sign lawful bills of lading for any cargo in such form as Charterers direct.

(2) The signing of bills of lading shall be without prejudice to this Charter and Charterers hereby indemnify Owners against all liabilities that may arise from signing bills of lading to the extent that the same impose liabilities upon Owners in excess of or beyond those imposed by this Charter.

(3) All bills of lading presented to the master for signature, in addition to complying with the Requirements of Part II clauses 35, 36 and 37, shall include or effectively incorporate clauses substantially similar to the terms of Part II clauses 22, 33(7) and 34.

(4) All bills of lading presented for signature hereunder shall show a named port of discharge. If when bills of lading are presented for signature discharging port(s) have been nominated hereunder, the discharging port(s) shown on such bills of lading shall be in conformity with the nominated port(s). If at the time of such presentation no such nomination has been made hereunder, the discharging port(s) shown on such bills of lading must be within Part I clause (E) and shall be deemed to have been nominated hereunder by virtue of such presentation.

(5) Article III Rules 3 and 5 of the Hague-Visby Rules shall apply to the particulars included in the bills of lading as if Charterers were the shippers, and the guarantee and indemnity therein contained shall apply to the description of the cargo furnished by or on behalf of Charterers.

(6) Notwithstanding any other provisions of this Charter, Owners shall be obliged to comply with any orders from Charterers to discharge all or part of the cargo provided that they have received from Charterers written confirmation of such orders.

If Charterers by telex, facsimile or other form of written communication that specifically refers to this clause request Owners to discharge a quantity of cargo either:

    (a)   without bills of lading and/or

    (b)   at a discharge place other than that named in a bill of lading and/or

    (c)   that is different from the bill of lading quantity

then Owners shall discharge such cargo in accordance with Charterers' instructions in consideration of receiving the Following indemnity which shall be deemed to be given by Charterers on each and every such occasion and which is limited in value to 200 per cent of the C.I.F. value of the cargo on board:

    (i)   Charterers shall indemnify Owners, and Owners' servants and agents in respect of any liability loss or damage of whatsoever nature (including legal costs as between attorney or solicitor and client and associated expenses) which Owners may sustain by reason of delivering such cargo in accordance with Charterers' request.

    (ii)   If any proceeding is commenced against Owners or any of Owners' servants or agents in connection with the

441
442
443
444
445
446
447
448
449
450
451
452
453
454
455
456
457
458
459
460
461
462
463
464
465
466
467
468
469
470
471
472
473
474
475

Appendix 9

Issued March 2005

"SHELLVOY 6"

PART II

vessel having delivered cargo in accordance with such request, Charterers shall provide Owners or any of Owners' servants or agents from time to time on demand with sufficient funds to defend the said proceedings. 476 477 478

(iii) If the vessel or any other vessel or property belonging to Owners should be arrested or detained, or if the arrest or detention thereof should be threatened, by reason of discharge in accordance with Charterers' instruction as aforesaid. Charterers shall provide on demand such bail or other security as may be required to prevent such arrest or detention or to secure the release of such vessel or property and Charterers shall indemnify Owners in respect of any loss, damage or expenses caused by such arrest or detention whether or not the same may be justified. 479 480 481 482 483 484

(iv) Charterers shall, if called upon to do so at any time while such cargo is in Charterers' possession, custody or control, redeliver the same to Owners. 485 486

(v) As soon as all original bills of lading for the above cargo which name as discharge port the place where delivery actually occurred shall have arrived and/or come into Charterers' possession. Charterers shall produce and deliver the same to Owners, whereupon Charterers' liability hereunder shall cease. Provided however, if Charterers have not received all such original bills of lading by 24.00 hours on the day 36 calendar months after the date of discharge, then this indemnity shall terminate at that time unless before that time Charterers have received from Owners written notice that: 487 488 489 490 491 492

(a) some person is making a claim in connection with Owners delivering cargo pursuant to Charterers' request or 493 494

(b) legal proceedings have been commenced against Owners and/or carriers and/Charterers and/or any of their respective servants or agents and/or the vessel for the same reason. 495 496

When Charterers have received such a notice, then this indemnity shall continue in force until such claim or legal proceedings are settled. Termination of this indemnity shall not prejudice any legal rights a party may have outside this indemnity. 497 498

(vi) Owners shall promptly notify Charterers if any person (other than a person to whom Charterers ordered cargo to be delivered) claims to be entitled to such cargo and/or if the vessel or any other property belonging to Owners is arrested by reason of any such discharge of cargo. 499 500

(vii) This indemnity shall be governed and construed in accordance with the English law and each and any dispute arising out of or in connection with this indemnity shall be subject to the jurisdiction of the High Court of Justice of England. 501 502 503

(7) The master shall not be required or bound to sign bills of lading for any blockaded port or for any port which the master or Owners in his or their discretion consider dangerous or impossible to enter or reach. 504 505

(8) Charterers hereby warrant that on each and every occasion that they issue orders under Part II clauses 22, 26, 34 or 38 they will have the authority of the holders of the bills of lading to give such orders, and that such bills of lading will not be transferred to any person who does not concur therein. 506 507 508

(9) Owners hereby agree that original bill(s) of lading, if available, will be allowed to be placed on board. 509

If original bill(s) of lading are placed on board. Owners agree that vessel will discharge cargo against such bill(s) of lading carried on board, on receipt of receivers' proof of identity. 510 511

War risks   34.   (1) If 512

(a) any loading or discharging port to which the vessel may properly be ordered under the provisions of this Charter or bills of lading issued pursuant to this Charter be blockaded, or 513 514

(b) owing to any war, hostilities, warlike operation, civil commotions, revolutions, or the operation of international law (i) entry to any such loading or discharging port or the loading or discharging of cargo at any such port be considered by the master or Owners in his or their discretion dangerous or prohibited or (ii) it be considered by the master or Owners in his or their discretion dangerous or impossible or prohibited for the vessel to reach any such loading or discharging port, 515 516 517 518 519

Charterers shall have the right to order the cargo or such part of it as may be affected to be loaded or discharged at any other loading or discharging port within the ranges specified in Part I clause (D) or (E) respectively (provided such other port is not blockaded and that entry thereto or loading or discharging of cargo thereat or reaching the same is not in the master's or Owners' opinion dangerous or impossible or prohibited). 520 521 522 523

(2) If no orders be received from Charterers within 48 hours after they or their agents have received from Owners a request for the nomination of a substitute port, then 524 525

(a) if the affected port is the first or only loading port and no cargo has been loaded, this Charter shall terminate forthwith; 526 527

(b) if the affected port is a loading port and part of the cargo has already been loaded, the vessel may proceed on passage and Charterers shall pay for any deadfreight so incurred; 528 529

(c) if the affected port is a discharging port. Owners shall be at liberty to discharge the cargo at any port which they or the master may in their or his discretion decide on (whether within the range specified in Part I clause (E) or not) and such discharging shall be deemed to be due fulfilment of the contract or contracts of affreightment so far as cargo so discharged is concerned. 530 531 532 533

(3) If in accordance with clause 34(1) or (2) cargo is loaded or discharged at any such other port, freight shall be paid as for the voyage originally nominated, such freight to be increased or reduced by the amount by which, as a result of loading or discharging at such other port, 534 535 536

(a) the time on voyage including any time awaiting revised orders (which shall be valued at the demurrage rate in Part I clause (J)), and 537

Appendix 9

Issued March 2005   **"SHELLVOY 6"**

PART II

(b) the bunkers consumed, at replacement cost, and	538
(c) the port charges	539

for the voyage actually performed are greater or less than those which would have been incurred on the voyage originally 540
nominated save as aforesaid, the voyage actually performed shall be treated for the purpose of this Charter as if it were the 541
voyage originally nominated. 542

(4) The vessel shall have liberty to comply with any directions or recommendations as to departure, arrival, routes, 543
ports of call, stoppages, destinations, zones, waters, delivery or in any otherwise whatsoever given by the government of 544
the nation under whose Hag the vessel sails or any other government or local authority including any de facto government 545
or local authority or by any person or body acting or purporting to act as or with the authority of any such government or 546
authority or by any committee or person having under the terms of the war risks insurance on the vessel the right to give any 547
such directions or recommendations. If by reason of or in compliance with any such directions or recommendations anything 548
is done or is not done, such shall not be deemed a deviation. 549

If, by reason of or in compliance with any such directions or recommendations as are mentioned in clause 34 (4), 550
the vessel does not proceed to the discharging port or ports originally nominated or to which she may have been properly 551
ordered under the provisions of this Charter or bills of lading issued pursuant to this Charter, the vessel may proceed to any 552
discharging port on which the master or Owners in his or their discretion may decide and there discharge the cargo. Such 553
discharging shall be deemed to be due fulfilment of the contract or contracts of affreightment and Owners shall be entitled 554
to freight as if discharging had been effected at the port or ports originally nominated or to which the vessel may have been 555
properly ordered under the provisions of this Charter or bills of lading issued pursuant to this Charter. All extra expenses 556
involved in reaching and discharging the cargo at any such other discharging port shall be paid by Charterers and Owners 557
shall have a lien on the cargo for all such extra expenses. 558

(5) Owners shall pay for all additional war risk insurance premiums, both for annual periods and also for the specific 559
performance of this Charter, on the Hull and Machinery value, as per Part I clause (A)(1) (xiii) applicable at the date of this 560
Charter, or the date the vessel was fixed "on subjects" (whichever is the earlier), and all reasonable crew war bonus. The 561
period of voyage additional war risks premium shall commence when the vessel enters a war risk zone as designated by the 562
London insurance market and cease when the vessel leaves such zone. If the vessel is already in such a zone the period shall 563
commence on tendering notice of readiness under this Charter.

Any increase or decrease in voyage additional war risk premium and any period in excess of the first fourteen days 564
shall be for Charterers' account and payable against proven documentation. Any discount or rebate refunded to Owners 565
for whatever reason shall be passed on to Charterers. Any premiums, and increase thereto, attributable to closure insurance 566
(i.e. blocking and trapping) shall be for Owners' account. 567

**Both to
blame clause**   35.   If the liability for any collision in which the vessel is involved while performing this Charter falls to be 568
determined in accordance with the laws of the United States of America, the following clause, which shall be included in all 569
bills of lading issued pursuant to this Charter shall apply:

"If the vessel comes into collision with another vessel as a result of the negligence of the other vessel and any act, 570
neglect or default of the master, mariner, pilot or the servants of the Carrier in the navigation or in the management of the 571
vessel, the owners of the cargo carried hereunder will indemnify the Carrier against all loss or liability to the other or non- 572
carrying vessel or her owners in so far as such loss or liability represents loss of, or damage to, or any claim whatsoever 573
of the owners of the said cargo, paid or payable by the other or non-carrying vessel or her owners to the owners of the said 574
cargo and set off, recouped or recovered by the other or non-carrying vessel or her owners as part of their claim against the 575
carrying vessel or the Carrier. 576

The foregoing provisions shall also apply where the owners, operators or those in charge of any vessel or vessels or 577
objects other than, or in addition to, the colliding vessels or objects are at fault in respect of a collision or contact." 578
579

**General
average/
New Jason
clause**   36.   General average shall be payable according to the York/Antwerp Rules 1994, as amended from time to time,
and shall be adjusted in London. All disputes relating to General Average shall be resolved in London in accordance with 580
English Law. Without prejudice to the foregoing, should the adjustment be made in accordance with the Law and practice 581
of the United States of America, the following clause, which shall be included in all bills of lading issued pursuant to this 582
Charter, shall apply: 583

"In the event of accident, danger, damage or disaster before or after the commencement of the voyage, resulting 584
from any cause whatsoever, whether due to negligence or not, for which, or for the consequence of which, the Carrier is not 585
responsible, by statute, contract or otherwise, the cargo, shippers, consignees or owners of the cargo shall contribute with the 586
Carrier in general average to the payment of any sacrifices, losses or expenses of a general average nature that may be made 587
or incurred and shall pay salvage and special charges incurred in respect of the cargo. 588

If a salving vessel is owned or operated by the Carrier, salvage shall be paid for as fully as if the said salving vessel or 589
vessels belonged to strangers. Such deposit as the Carrier or its agents may deem sufficient to cover the estimated contribution 590
of the cargo and any salvage and special charges thereon shall, if required, be made by the cargo, shippers, consignees or 591
owners of the cargo to the Carrier before delivery." 592

**Clause
Paramount**   37.   The following clause shall be included in all bills of lading issued pursuant to this Charter:

(1) Subject to sub-clauses (2) or (3) hereof, this bill of lading shall be governed by, and have effect subject to 593
the rules contained in the International Convention for the Unification of Certain Rules relating to bills of lading signed at 594
Brussels on 25th August 1924 (hereafter the "Hague Rules") as amended by the Protocol signed at Brussels on 23rd February 595
1968 (hereafter the "Hague-Visby Rules"). Nothing contained herein shall be deemed to be either a surrender by the carrier 596
of any of his rights or immunities or any increase of any of his responsibilities or liabilities under the Hague-Visby Rules. 597

Appendix 9

Issued March 2005

"SHELLVOY 6"

PART II

(2) If there is governing legislation which applies the Hague Rules compulsorily to this bill of lading, to the exclusion of the Hague-Visby Rules, then this bill of lading shall have effect subject to the Hague Rules. Nothing herein contained shall be deemed to be either a surrender by the carrier of any of his rights or immunities or an increase of any of his responsibilities or liabilities under the Hague Rules. 598 599 600 601

(3) If there is governing legislation which applies the United Nations Convention on the Carriage of Goods By Sea 1978 (hereafter the "Hamburg Rules") compulsorily to this bill of lading to the exclusion of the Hague-Visby Rules, then this bill of lading shall have effect subject to the Hamburg Rules. Nothing herein contained shall be deemed to be either a surrender by the carrier of any of his rights or immunities or an increase of any of his responsibilities or liabilities under the Hamburg Rules. 602 603 604 605

(4) If any term of this bill of lading is repugnant to the Hague-Visby Rules, or Hague Rules or Hamburg Rules, if applicable, such term shall be void to that extent but no further. 606 607

(5) Nothing in this bill of lading shall be construed as in any way restricting, excluding or waiving the right of any relevant party or person to limit his liability under any available legislation and/or law. 608 609

Back loading 38. Charterers may order the vessel to discharge and/or backload a part or full cargo at any nominated port within the loading/discharging ranges specified within Part I clauses (D/H) and within the rotation of the ports previously nominated, provided that any cargo loaded is of the description specified in Part I clause (F) and that the master in his reasonable discretion determines that the cargo can be loaded, segregated and discharged without risk of contamination by, or of any other cargo. 610 611 612 613

Charterers shall pay in respect of loading, carrying and discharging such cargo as follows: 614

(a) a lumpsum freight calculated at the demurrage rate specified in Part I clause (J) on any additional port time used by the vessel; and 615 616

(b) any additional expenses, including bunkers consumed (at replacement cost) over above those required to load and discharge one full cargo and port costs which included additional agency costs: and 617 618

(c) if the vessel is fixed on a Worldscale rate in Part I clause (G) then freight shall always be paid for the whole voyage at the rate(s) specified in Part I clause (G) on the largest cargo quantity carried on any ocean leg. 619 620

Bunkers 39. Owners shall give Charterers or any other company in the Royal Dutch/Shell Group of Companies first option to quote for the supply of bunker requirements for the performance of this Charter. 621 622

Oil pollution prevention/ Ballast management 40. (1) Owners shall ensure that the master shall:

(a) comply with MARPOL 73/78 including any amendments thereof; 623

(b) collect the drainings and any tank washings into a suitable tank or tanks and, after maximum separation of free water, discharge the bulk of such water overboard, consistent with the above regulations; and 624 625

(c) thereafter notify Charterers promptly of the amounts of oil and free water so retained on board and details of any other washings retained on board from earlier voyages (together called the "collected washings"). 626 627

(d) not to load on top of such 'collected washings' without specific instructions from Charterers. 628

(e) provide Charterers with a slops certificate to be made up and signed by the master and an independent surveyor/terminal representative. The certificate shall indicate: 629 630

Origin and composition of slops, Volume, Free water and API measured in barrels at 60 deg F. 631

(2) On being so notified, Charterers, in accordance with their rights under this clause (which shall include without limitation the right to determine the disposal of the collected washings), shall before the vessel's arrival at the loading berth (or if already arrived as soon as possible thereafter) give instructions as to how the collected washings shall be dealt with. Owners shall ensure that the master on the vessel's arrival at the loading berth (or if already arrived as soon as possible thereafter) shall arrange in conjunction with the cargo suppliers for the measurement of the quantity of the collected washings and shall record the same in the vessel's ullage record. 632 633 634 635 636 637

(3) Charterers may require the collected washings to be discharged ashore at the loading port, in which case no freight shall be payable on them. 638 639

(4) Alternatively Charterers may require either that the cargo be loaded on top of the collected washings and the collected washings be discharged with the cargo, or that they be kept separate from the cargo in which case Charterers shall pay for any deadweight incurred thereby in accordance with Part II clause 8 and shall, if practicable, accept discharge of the collected washings at the discharging port or ports. 640 641 642 643

In either case, provided that the master has reduced the free water in the collected washings to a minimum consistent with the retention on board of the oil residues in them and consistent with sub-clause (l)(a) above, freight in accordance with Part II clause 5 shall be payable on the quantity of the collected washings as if such quantity were included in a bill of lading and the figure therefore furnished by the shipper provided, however, that 644 645 646 647

(i) if there is a provision in this Charter for a lower freight rate to apply to cargo in excess of an agreed quantity. freight on the collected washings shall be paid at such lower rate (provided such agreed quantity of cargo has been loaded) and 648 649 650

(ii) if there is provision in this Charter for a minimum cargo quantity which is less than a full cargo, then whether or not such minimum cargo quantity is furnished, freight on the collected washings shall be paid as if such minimum cargo quantity had been furnished, provided that no freight shall be payable in respect of any collected washings which are kept separate from the cargo and not discharged at the discharge port. 651 652 653 654

(5) Whenever Charterers require the collected washings to be discharged ashore pursuant to this clause. Charterers shall provide and pay for the reception facilities, and the cost of any shifting there for shall be for Charterers' account. Any 655 656

Issued March 2005   **"SHELLVOY 6"**

PART II

time lost discharging the collected washings and/or shifting therefore shall count against laytime or, if the vessel is on demurrage, for demurrage. 657 658

(6) Owners warrant that the vessel will arrive at the load port with segregated/ clean ballast as defined by Annex I of MARPOL 73/78 including any amendments thereof. 659 660 661

Oil response pollution and insurance

41. (1) Owners warrant that throughout the duration of this Charter the vessel will be:

    (i) owned or demise chartered by a member of the 'International Tanker Owners Pollution Federation Limited, and 662 663

    (ii) entered in the Protection and Indemnity (P&I) Club slated in Part I clause (A) I (xii). 664

(2) It is a condition of this Charter that Owners have in place insurance cover for oil pollution for the maximum on offer through the International Group of P&I Clubs but always a minimum of United States Dollars 1,000,000,000 (one thousand million). If requested by Charterers, Owners shall immediately furnish to Charterers full and proper evidence of the coverage. 665 666 667

(3) Owners warrant that the vessel carries on board a certificate of insurance as required by the Civil Liability Convention for Oil Pollution damage. Owners further warrant that said certificate will be maintained effective throughout the duration of performance under this Charter. All time, costs and expense as a result of Owners' failure to comply with the foregoing shall be for Owners' account. 668 669 670 671

(4) Owners warrant that where the vessel is a "Relevant Ship", they are a "Participating Owner", both as defined in the Small Tanker Oil Pollution Indemnification Agreement ("STOPIA") and that the vessel is entered in STOPIA, and shall so remain during the currency of this Charter, provided always that STOPIA is not terminated in accordance with Clause VIII of its provisions. 672 673 674 675

Lien

42. Owners shall have an absolute lien upon the cargo and all subfreights for all amounts due under this charter and the cost of recovery thereof including any expenses whatsoever arising from the exercise of such lien. 676 677

Drugs and alcohol

43. Owners are aware of the problem of drug and alcohol abuse and warrant that they have a written policy in force, covering the vessel, which meets or exceeds the standards set out in the "Guidelines for the Control of Drugs and Alcohol on board Ship" as published by OCIMF dated June 1995. 678 679 680

Owners further warrant that this policy shall remain in force during the period of this Charter and such policy shall be adhered to throughout this Charter. 681

ITWF

44. Owners warrant that the terms of employment of the vessel's staff and crew will always remain acceptable to the International Transport Workers Federation on a worldwide basis. All time, costs and expenses incurred as a result of Owners' failure to comply with foregoing shall be for Owners' account. 682 683 684

Letters of protest/ Deficiencies

45. It is a condition of this Charter that from the time the vessel sails to the first load port there will be no Letter(s) of Protest ("LOP"'s) or deficiencies outstanding against the vessel. This refers to LOP's or deficiencies issued by Terminal Inspectorate or similar Port or Terminal or Governmental Authorities. 685 686 687

Documentation

46. Owners shall ensure that the master and agents produce documentation and provide Charterers with copies of all such documentation relevant to each port and berth call and all transhipments at sea, including but not limited to: 688 689

Notice of Readiness/Statement of Facts/Shell Form 19x (if Charterers nominate agents under Part II clause 24)/Time sheet(s)/LOPs/Hourly pumping logs/COW performance logs by facsimile (to the number advised in the voyage instructions). These documents to be faxed within 48 hours from sailing from each load or discharge port or transhipment area. If the vessel does not have a facsimile machine on board the master shall advise Charterers, within 48 hours from sailing from each port under this Charter, of the documents he has available and ensure copies of such documents are faxed by agents to Charterers from the relevant port of call or at latest from the next port of call. Complying with this clause does not affect the terms of Part II clause 15(3) with regard to notification and submission of a fully documented claim for demurrage or a claim described in Part II clause 6(3) of this Charter. Any documents to be faxed under this clause may be, alternatively, scanned and e-mailed to Charterers. If any actions or facilities of Suppliers/Receivers/Terminal/Transhipment vessels or Charterers, as applicable, impinge on the vessel's ability to perform the warranties and/or guarantees of performance under this Charter the master must issue a LOP to such effect. If the master fails to issue such LOP then Owners shall be deemed to have waived any rights to claim. Master and agents shall ensure that all documents concerning port/berth and cargo activities at all ports/berths and transhipment at sea places are signed by both an officer of the vessel and a representative of either Suppliers/Receivers/ Terminal/Transhipment vessels or Charterers, as applicable. 690 691 692 693 694 695 696 697 698 699 700 701 702

If such a signature from Suppliers/Receivers/Terminal/Transhipment vessels or Charterers, as applicable, is not obtainable the master or his agents should issue a LOP to such effect. All LOP's issued by master or his agents or received by master or his agents must be forwarded to Charterers as per the terms of this clause. 703 704 705

Administration

47. The agreed terms and conditions of this Charter shall be recorded and evidenced by the production of a fixture note sent to both Charterers and Owners within 24 hours of the fixture being concluded. This fixture note shall state the name and date of the standard pre-printed Charter Party Form, on which the Charter is based, along with all amendments/additions/ deletions to such charter party form. All further additional clauses agreed shall be reproduced in the fixture note with full wording. This fixture note shall be approved and acknowledged as correct by both Owners and Charterers to either the Ship Broker through whom they negotiated or, if no Ship Broker was involved, to each other within two working days after fixture concluded. 706 707 708 709 710 711

No formal written and signed Charter Party will be produced unless specifically requested by Charterers or Owners or is required by additional clauses of this Charter. 712 713

Appendix 9

Issued March 2005   **"SHELLVOY 6"**

PART II

Cargo retention

48.   If on completion of discharge any liquid cargo of a pumpable nature remains on board (the presence and quantity 714
of such cargo having been established, by application of the wedge formula in respect of any tank the contents of which do not 715
reach the forward bulkhead, by an independent surveyor, appointed by Charterers and paid jointly by Owners and Charterers), 716
Charterers shall have the right to deduct from freight an amount equal to the FOB loading port value of such cargo, cargo 717
insurance plus freight thereon; provided, however, that any action or lack of action hereunder shall be without prejudice to any 718
other rights or obligations of Charterers, under this Charter or otherwise, and provided further that if Owners are liable to any 719
third party in respect of failure to discharge such pumpable cargo, or any part thereof, Charterers shall indemnify Owners against 720
such liability up to the total amount deducted under this clause. 721

Hydrogen sulphide

49.   Owners shall comply with the requirements in ISGOTT (as amended from time to time) concerning Hydrogen 722
Sulphide and shall ensure that prior to arrival at the load port the Hydrogen Sulphide (ppm by volume in vapour) level in all 723
bunker, ballast and empty cargo spaces is below the Threshold Limit Value ("TLV") - Time Weighted Average ("TWA"). 724
725

If on arrival at the loading terminal, the loading authorities, inspectors or other authorised and qualified personnel declare 726
that the Hydrogen Sulphide levels in the vessels' tanks exceed the TLV- TWA and request the vessel to reduce the said level to 727
within the TLV-TWA then the original notice of readiness shall not be valid. A valid notice of readiness can only be tendered 728
and laytime, or demurrage time, if on demurrage, to the relevant authorities can only start to run in accordance with Part II 729
clause 13 when the TLV-TWA is acceptable. 730

If the vessel is unable to reduce the levels of Hydrogen Sulphide within a reasonable time Charterers shall have the option 731
of cancelling this Charter without penalty and without prejudice to any claims which Charterers may have against Owners under 732
this Charter. 733

Port regulations

50.   Owners warrant that the vessel will fully comply with all port and terminal regulations at any named port in this 734
Charter, and any ports to which Charterers may order the vessel to under this Charter in accordance with Part I clauses (D/E) 735
provided that Owners have a reasonable opportunity to acquaint themselves with the regulations at such ports. 736
737

Port regulations

51.   (1) Owners wan-ant that: 738
    (a)   the vessel complies with the OCIMF recommendations, current at the date of this Charter, for equipment 739
          employed in the mooring of ships at single point moorings in particular for tongue type or hinged bar type 740
          chain stoppers and that the messenger from the Chain Stopper(s) is secured on a winch drum (not a dram 741
          end) and that the operation is totally hands free. 742
    (b)   the vessel complies and operates in accordance with the recommendations, current at the date of this 743
          Charter, contained in the latest edition of OCIMF's "Mooring Equipment Procedures" 744
745
(2) If requested by Charterers, or in the event of an emergency situation arising whilst the vessel is at a Single Buoy 746
Mooring ("SBM"), the vessel shall pump sea water, either directly from the sea or from vessel's clean ballast tanks, to flush 747
SBMs floating hoses prior to, during or/after loading and/or discharge of the cargo; this operation to be carried out at Charterers' 748
expense and with time counting against laytime, or demurrage, if on demurrage. Subject to Owners exercising due diligence in 749
carrying out such an operation Charterers hereby indemnify Owners for any cargo loss or contamination directly resulting from 750
this request. If master or Owners are approached by Suppliers/Receivers or Terminal Operators to undertake such an operation 751
Owners shall obtain Charterers' agreement before proceeding. 752

ISPS/MTSA

52.   (1) (a) From the date of coming into force of the International Code for the Security of Ships and of Port Facilities 753
and the relevant amendments to Chapter XI of SOLAS ("ISPS Code") and the US Maritime Transportation Security Act 2002 754
("MTSA") in relation to the vessel, and thereafter during the currency of this Charter, Owners shall procure that both the 755
vessel and "the Company" (as defined by the ISPS Code) and the "owner" (as defined by the MTSA) shall comply with the 756
requirements of the ISPS Code relating to the vessel and "the Company" and the requirements of MTSA relating to the vessel 757
and the "owner". Upon request Owners shall provide a copy of the relevant International Ship Security Certificate to Charterers. 758
Owners shall provide documentary evidence of compliance with this clause 52 (1) (a). (b) Except as otherwise provided in this 759
Charter, loss, damage, expense or delay caused by failure on the part of Owners or "the Company"/"owner" to comply with the 760
requirements of the ISPS Code/MTSA or this clause shall be for Owners' account. 761
762
(2) (a) Charterers shall provide the Owners with their full style contact details and other relevant information reasonably 763
required by Owners to comply with the requirements of the ISPS Code/MTSA. Additionally. Charterers shall ensure that the 764
contact details of any sub-charterers are likewise provided to Owners. Furthermore, Charterers shall ensure that all sub-charter 765
parties they enter into shall contain the following provision: 766
"The Charterers shall provide the Owners with their full style contact details and, where sub-letting is permitted under the 767
terms of the charter party, shall ensure that contact details of all sub-charterers are likewise provided to the Owners". 768
769
(b) Except as otherwise provided in this Charter, loss, damage, expense or delay caused by failure on the part of Charterers 770
to comply with this sub clause (2) shall be for Charterers' account. 771

Appendix 9

Issued March 2005   **"SHELLVOY 6"**

PART II

(3) (a) Without prejudice to the foregoing. Owners right to tender notice of readiness and Charterers' liability for demurrage in respect of any time delays caused by breaches of this clause 52 shall be dealt with in accordance with Part II clauses 13, (Notice of readiness/Running time), 14, (Suspension of Time), and 15, (Demurrage), of the charter. 772 773 774

(b) Except where the delay is caused by Owners and/or Charterers failure to comply, respectively, with clauses (1) and (2) of this clause 52, then any delay arising or resulting from measures imposed by a port facility or by any relevant authority, under the ISPS Code/MTSA, shall count as half rate laytime, or, if the vessel is on demurrage, half rate demurrage. 775 776 777

(4) Except where the same are imposed as a cause of Owners and/or Charterers failure to comply, respectively, with clauses (1) and (2) of this clause 52, then any costs or expenses related to security regulations or measures required by the port facility or any relevant authority in accordance with the ISPS Code/MTSA including, but not limited to, security guards, launch services, tug escorts, port security fees or taxes and inspections, shall be shared equally between Owners and Charterers. All measures required by the Owners to comply with the Ship Security Plan shall be for Owners' account. 778 779 780 781 782 783

(5) If either party makes any payment which is for the other party's account according to this clause, the other party shall indemnify the paying party. 784 785

Business principles   53.   Owners will co-operate with Charterers to ensure that the "Business Principles", as amended from time to time, of the Royal Dutch/Shell Group of Companies, which are posted on the Shell Worldwide Web (www.Shell.com), are complied with. 786 787 788

Law and litigation Arbitration   54.   (a)   This Charter shall be construed and the relations between the parties determined in accordance with the laws of England. 789 790

(b)   All disputes arising out of this Charter shall be referred to Arbitration in London in accordance with the Arbitration Act 1996 (or any re-enactment or modification thereof for the time being in force) subject to the following appointment procedure: 791 792

(i)   The parties shall jointly appoint a sole arbitrator not later than 28 days after service of a request in writing by either party to do so. 793 794

(ii)   If the parties are unable or unwilling to agree the appointment of a sole arbitrator in accordance with (i) then each party shall appoint one arbitrator, in any event not later than 14 days after receipt of a further request in writing by either party to do so. The two arbitrators so appointed shall appoint a third arbitrator before any substantive hearing or forthwith if they cannot agree on a matter relating to the arbitration. 795 796 797 798 799

(iii)   If a party fails to appoint an arbitrator within the time specified in (ii) (the "Party in Default"), the party who has duly appointed his arbitrator shall give notice in writing to the Party in Default that he proposes to appoint his arbitrator to act as sole arbitrator. 800 801 802 803

(iv)   If the Party in Default does not within 7 days of the notice given pursuant to (iii) make the required appointment and notify the other party that he has done so the other party may appoint his arbitrator as sole arbitrator whose award shall be binding on both parties as if he had been so appointed by agreement. 804 805 806 807

(v)   Any award of the arbitrator(s) shall be final and binding and not subject to appeal. 808

(vi)   For the purposes of this clause 54 any requests or notices in writing shall be sent by fax, e-mail or telex and shall be deemed received on the day of transmission. 809 810

(c)   It shall be a condition precedent to the right of any party to a stay of any legal proceedings in which maritime property has been, or may be, arrested in connection with a dispute under this Charter, that that party furnishes to the other party security to which that other party would have been entitled in such legal proceedings in the absence of a stay. 811 812 813 814

Small claims   (d)   In cases where neither the claim nor any counterclaim exceeds the sum of United States Dollars 50,000 (or such other sum as Owners/Charterers may agree) the arbitration shall be conducted in accordance with the London Maritime Arbitrators' Association Small Claims Procedure current at the time when the arbitration proceedings are commenced. 815 816 817 818

Address commission   55.   Charterers shall deduct address commission of 1.25% from all payments under this Charter. 819 820

Construction   56.   The side headings have been included in this Charter for convenience of reference and shall in no way affect the construction hereof. 821 822

Appendix 9

Issued March 2005   **"SHELLVOY 6"**

PART III

| Australia | (1) (a) | The vessel shall not transit the Great Barrier Reef Inner Passage, whether in ballast en route to a loadport or laden, | 1 |

Australia   (1) (a)   The vessel shall not transit the Great Barrier Reef Inner Passage, whether in ballast en route to a loadport or laden, between the Torres Strait and Cairns, Australia. If the vessel transits the Torres Strait, the vessel shall use the outer reef passage as approved by the Australian Hydrographer. Owners shall always employ a pilot, when transiting the Torres Strait and for entry and departure through the Reef for ports North of Brisbane,   1 2 3 4

(b)   The vessel shall discharge all ballast water on board the vessel and take on fresh ballast water, always in accordance with safe operational procedures, prior to entering Australian waters.   5 6

(c)   On entering, whilst within and whilst departing from the port of Sydney Owners and master shall ensure that the water line to highest fixed point distance does not exceed 51.8 (fifty one point eight) metres.   7 8 9

(d)   If Charterers or Terminal Operators instruct the vessel to slow the cargo operations down or stop entirely the cargo operations in Sydney during the hours of darkness due to excessive noise caused by the vessel then all additional time shall be for Owners' account.   10 11 12

Goods Services Tax   (e)(i)   Goods Services Tax ("GST") imposed in Australia has application to any supply made under this Charter, the parties agree that the Charterer shall account for GST in accordance with Division 83 of the GST Act even if the Owner becomes registered. The Owner acknowledges that it will not recover from the Charterer an additional amount on account of GST.   13 14 15 16

(ii)   The Owner acknowledges that it is a non-resident and that it does not make supplies through an enterprise carried on in Australia as defined in section 995-1 of the Income Tax Assessment Act 1997.   17 18

(iii)   The Charterer acknowledges that it is registered. Where appropriate, terms in this clause have the meaning set out in section 195-1 of the GST Act.   19 20

Brazil   (2) (a)   Owners acknowledge the vessel will have, if Charterers so require, to enter a port or place of clearance within mainland Brazil, to obtain necessary clearance from the Brazilian authorities and/or to pick-up personnel required to be on board during the loading of the cargo at Fluminense FPSO. The vessel then proeeeds to the Fluminense FPSO where she can tender her notice of readiness. Time at the port of clearance, taken from arrival at pilot station to dropping outward pilot to be for Charterers' account and payable at the agreed demurrage rate together with freight. However this time not to count as laytime or demurrage if on demurrage.   21 22 23 24 25 26 27

(b)   Freight payment under Part II clause 5 of this Charter shall be made within 5 banking days of receipt by Charterers of notice of completion of final discharge   28 29

Canada   (3) Owners warrant that the vessel complies with all the Canadian Oil Spill response regulations currently in force and that the Owner is a member of a certified oil spill response organisation and that the Owners/vessel shall continue to be members of such organisation and comply with the regulations and requirements of such organisation throughout the period of this Charter.   30 31 32 33

Egypt   (4) (a)   Any costs incurred by Charterers for vessel garbage or in vessel deballasting at Sidi Kerir shall be for Owners' account and Charterers shall deduct such costs from freight   34

(b)   Charterers shall have the option for the discharge range Euromed and/or United Kingdom/Continent (Gibraltar Hamburg range) to instruct the vessel to transit via Suez Canal. In the event that Charterers exercise this option the following shall apply:
Charterers option to part discharge Ain Sukhna and reload Sidi Kerir.
Charterers will pay the following with freight against Owners' fully documenled claim: 35 36 37 38 39

(c)   time incurred at the demurrage rate on the passage from the point at which the vessel deviates from the direct sailing route between last loadport and Port Suez, till the tendering of notice of readiness at Ain Sukhna, less any time lost by reason of delay beyond Charterers' reasonable control;   40 41 42 43

(d)   time incurred at the demurrage rate on the passage from disconnection of hoses at Sidi Kerir to the point at which the vessel rejoins the direct sailing route between Port Said and the first discharge port UK Continent or Mediterranean, less any time lost by reason of delay beyond Charterers' reasonable control;   44 45 46

(e)   time incurred at the demurrage rate between tendering of notice of readiness at Ain Sukhna and disconnection of hoses there;   47 48

(f)   time incurred at the demurrage rate between tendering of notice of readiness at Sidi Kerir and disconnection of hoses there: 49 50

(g)   all bunkers consumed during the periods (c) to (f) above at replacement cost;   51

(h)   all port charges incurred at Ain Sukhna and Sidi Kerir.
Freight rate via Suez shall be based on the Suez/Suez flat rate without the fixed Suez rate differential, other than as described below (the Worldscale rates in Part I clause (G) of this Charter to apply). All canal dues related to Suez laden transit, including Suez Canal port costs, agency fees and expenses, including but not limited to escort tugs and other expenses for canal laden transit, to be for Charterers' account and to be settled directly by them. Charterers' to pay Owners the 'ballast transit only' fixed rate differential as per Worldscale together with freight.   52 53 54 55 56 57 58

India   (5) (a)   In assessing the pumping efficiency under this Charter at ports in India, Owners agree to accept the record of pressure maintained as stated in receiver's statement of facts signed by the ship's representative.   59 60

Appendix 9

Issued March 2005   **"SHELLVOY 6"**

PART III

	(b) Owners shall be aware of and comply with the mooring requirements of Indian ports. All time, costs and expenses as a result of Owners' failure to comply with the foregoing shall be for Owners' account.	61 62
	(c) Charterers shall not be liable for demurrage unless the following conditions are satisfied:	63
	(i) the requirements of Part II clause 15 (3) are met in full; and	64
	(ii) a copy of this Charter signed by Owners is received by Charterers at least 2 (two) working days prior to the vessel's arrival in an Indian port.	65 66 67
	Charterers undertake to pay agreed demurrage liabilities promptly if the above conditions have been satisfied.	68 69

Japan

(6) (a) Owners shall supply Charterers with copies of:- 70

(i) General Arrangement/Capacity plan; and 71

(ii) Piping/Fire Fighting Diagrams 72

as soon as possible, but always within 4 working days after subjects lifted on this Charter. 73

(b) If requested by Charterers, Owners shall ensure a Superintendent, fully authorised by Owners to act on Owners' 74
and or master's behalf, is available at all ports within Japan to attend safety meetings prior to vessel's arrival at the port(s) 75
and be in attendance throughout the time in each port and during each cargo operation. 76

(c) Vessel to record and print out the position with date/time by Global Positioning System when vessel enters 77
Japanese Territorial Waters ("JTW") in order to perform vessel's declaration of entering JTW for crude oil stock piling 78
purpose. 79 80

(d) If under Part I clause (E) of this Charter Japan, or in particular ports or berths in Tokyo Bay and or the SBM 80
at UBE Refinery, are discharge options and if the vessel is over 220,000 metric tons deadweight and has not previously 81
discharged in Tokyo Bay or the SBM at UBE Refinery then: 82 83

(i) Owners shall submit an application of Safety Pledge Letter confirming that all safety measures will be 84
complied with: and 85

(ii) Present relevant ship data to the Japanese Maritime Safety Agency. 86

Owners shall comply with the above requirements as soon as possible but always within 4 working days after 87
subjects lifted on this Charter. 88

(e) If Charterers instruct the vessel to make adjustment to vessel's arrival date/time at discharge port(s) in Japan, any 89
adjustments shall be compensated in accordance with Part I clause (L) of this Charter. 90 91

If vessel is ordered to drift off Japan, at a location in Owners'/master's option, then the following shall apply:- 91 92

(i) Time from vessel's arrival at drifting location to the time vessel departs, on receipt of Charterers' instructions, 92 93
from such location shall be for Charterers' account at the demurrage rate stipulated in Part I clause (J) of this 94
Charter. 95

(ii) Bunkers consumed whilst drifting as defined in sub clause (e)(i) above shall be for Charterers' account at 96
replacement cost. Owners shall provide full documentation to support any claim under this clause. 97

New Zealand

(7) (a) Owners of vessels carrying Persistent Oil - as defined by the International Group of P&I Clubs - which shall 98
always incorporate Crude and Fuel Oil, Non Persistent Oil as defined by the International Group of P&I Clubs - which shall 99
always incorporate Petroleum Products: and Chemicals, warrant that the vessel shall comply at all times with the Maritime 100
Safety Authority of New Zealand's Voluntary Routeing Code for Shipping whilst transiting the New Zealand coast and/or en 101
route to or from ports in New Zealand and whether laden or in ballast, 102 103

(b) the following voyage routing will apply: 103 104

(i) vessel is to keep a minimum of 5 miles off the New Zealand coast (and outlying islands) until approaching 104 105
the port's pilot station, with the following exceptions: 106

a) to pass a minimum of 4 miles off the coast when transiting Cook Strait; 107

b) to pass a minimum of 5 miles to the east of Poor Knights Islands and High Peaks Rocks; 108

c) to pass a minimum of 3 miles from land when transiting the Colville or Jellicoe Channels. 109

If due to safe navigation and or other weather related reasons the vessel proceeds on a different route to those set out above, 110
the Owners and master shall immediately advise Charterers and Owner's agents in New Zealand of the route being followed 111
and the reasons for such deviation from the above warranted route. 112

Thailand

(8) If Part I clause (E) of this Charter includes option to discharge at a port/berth in Thailand then the following, which is 113
consistent with industry practice for ships discharging in Thailand, shall apply over and above any other terms contained 114
within this Charter:- 115 116

(a) Laytime shall be 96 running hours 116 117

(b) Freight payment under Part II clause 5 of this Charter shall be made within 15 days of receipt by Charterers of 117 118
notice of completion of final discharge of cargo. 119

(c) Cargo quantity and quality measurements shall be carried out at load and discharge ports by mutually appointed 120
independent surveyors, with costs to be shared equally between Owners and Charterers. 121

Appendix 9

Issued March 2005   **"SHELLVOY 6"**

PART III

	This is additional to any independent surveyors used for the Cargo Retention clause 48 in Part II of this Charter.	122
		123
United Kingdom	(9) (a) It is a condition of this Charter that Owners ensure that the vessel fully complies with the latest Sullom Voe	124
	regulations, including but not limited to:-	125
	(i) current minimum bulk loading rates; and	126
	(ii) pilot boarding ladder arrangements.	127
	Owners shall also comply with Charterers' instructions regarding the disposal of ballast from the vessel. Charterers shall accept	128
	any deadfreight claim that may arise by complying with such instructions.	129
		130
	(b) It is also a condition of this Charter that Owners ensure that the vessel fully complies with the latest Tranmere and	131
	Shellhaven regulations, including but not limited to:-	132
	(i) being able to ballast concurrently with discharge ; or	133
	(ii) maintaining double valve segregation at all times between cargo and ballast if the vessel has to part discharge,	134
	stop to ballast, then resume discharge.	135
	(c) In the event of loading or discharge at Tranmere, Shell U.K. Ltd. shall appoint tugs, pilots and boatmen on behalf of	136
	Owners. The co-ordinator of these services shall be OBC., who will submit all bills to Owners direct, irrespective of whether	137
	OBC are appointed agents or not. Owners warrant they will put OBC in funds accordingly.	138
		139

United Kingdom

(9) (a)   It is a condition of this Charter that Owners ensure that the vessel fully complies with the latest Sullom Voe regulations, including but not limited to:-

   (i)   current minimum bulk loading rates; and
   (ii)   pilot boarding ladder arrangements.

Owners shall also comply with Charterers' instructions regarding the disposal of ballast from the vessel. Charterers shall accept any deadfreight claim that may arise by complying with such instructions.

   (b)   It is also a condition of this Charter that Owners ensure that the vessel fully complies with the latest Tranmere and Shellhaven regulations, including but not limited to:-

   (i)   being able to ballast concurrently with discharge ; or
   (ii)   maintaining double valve segregation at all times between cargo and ballast if the vessel has to part discharge, stop to ballast, then resume discharge.

   (c)   In the event of loading or discharge at Tranmere, Shell U.K. Ltd. shall appoint tugs, pilots and boatmen on behalf of Owners. The co-ordinator of these services shall be OBC., who will submit all bills to Owners direct, irrespective of whether OBC are appointed agents or not. Owners warrant they will put OBC in funds accordingly.

United State of America

(10)(a)   It is a condition of this Charter that in accordance with U.S. Customs Regulations, 19 CFR 4.7a and 178.2 as amended, Owners have obtained a Standard Carrier Alpha Code (SCAC) and shall include same in the Unique Identifier which they shall enter, in the form set out in the above Customs Regulations, on all the bills of lading. Cargo manifest. Cargo declarations and other cargo documents issued under this Charter allowing carriage of goods to ports in the U.S.

Owners shall be liable for all time, costs and expenses and shall indemnify Charterers against all consequences whatsoever arising directly or indirectly from Owners' failure to comply with the above provisions of this clause.

Owners warrant that they are aware of the requirements of the U.S Bureau of Customs and Border Protection ruling issued on December 5th 2003 under Federal Register Part II Department of Homeland Security 19 CFR Parts 4, 103, et al. and will comply fully with these requirements for entering U.S ports.

Coastguard compliance

(b)   Owners warrant that during the term of this Charter the vessel will comply with all applicable U.S. Coast Guard (USCG) Regulations in effect as of the date the vessel is tendered for first loading hereunder. If waivers are held to any USCG regulation Owners to advise Charterers of such waivers, including period of validation and reason(s) for waiver. All time costs and expense as a result of Owners' failure to comply with the foregoing shall be for Owners' account.

(c)   Owners warrant that they will

   (i)   comply with the U.S. Federal Water Pollution Control Act as amended, and any amendments or successors to said Act

Laws and regulation

   (ii)   comply with all U.S. State Laws and regulations applicable during this Charter, as they apply to the U.S. States that Charterers may order vessel to under Part I clauses (D/E) of this Charter.

   (iii)   have secured, carry aboard the vessel, and keep current any certificates or other evidence of financial responsibility required tinder applicable U.S. Federal or State Laws and regulations and documentation recording compliance with the requirements of OPA 90, any amendments or succeeding legislation, and any regulations promulgated thereunder. Owners shall confirm that these documents will be valid throughout this Charter.

W-8BEN

(d)   If the recipient of the freight due under this Charter does not file taxes within the US, then such recipient shall complete an IRS Form W-8BEN and forward the original by mail to Charterers, attention "Freight Payments". Should this not be received in a timely manner, then Charterers shall not be liable for interest on late payment of freight, or be in default of this Charter for such late payment.

Vapour Recovery System

Owners warrant that the vessel's vapour recovery system complies with the requirements of the United States Coastguard.

Vietnam

(11)If required by Charterers, when loading Bach Ho crude oil. Owners will instruct the master to start the cargo heating system(s) prior to loading commencing.

Line numbers
140, 141, 142, 143, 144, 145, 146, 147, 148, 149, 150, 151, 152, 153, 154, 155, 156, 157, 158, 159, 160, 161, 162, 163, 164, 165, 166, 167, 168, 169, 170, 171, 172, 173

Typical Ship Structures

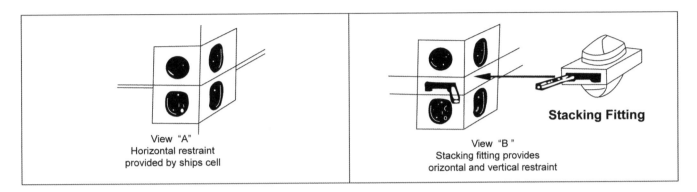

View "A"
Horizontal restraint
provided by ships cell

Stacking Fitting

View "B"
Stacking fitting provides
orizontal and vertical restraint

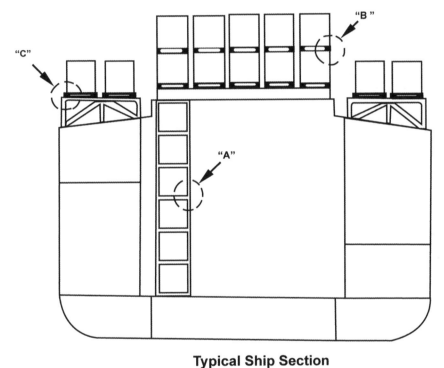

Typical Ship Section

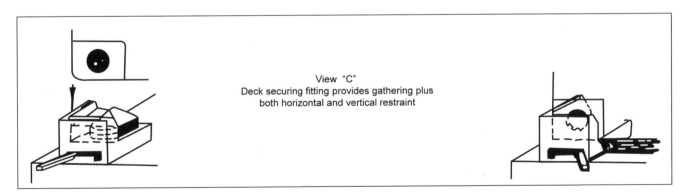

View "C"
Deck securing fitting provides gathering plus
both horizontal and vertical restraint

Typical use of corner fittings in shipload applications (in vertical container cells and on deck)

Containers

General Purpose Container 20´/40´

Ventilated-Container 20´
Especially for cargo which needs ventilation.

High Cube
General Purpose Container 40´
Especially for light-weight voluminous cargoes.

Insulated Container20´/40´
Especially for cargo which must be kept at a constant temperature.Temperature control via the ship's refrigeration plant, terminal refrigeration plant or a "Clip-On" refrigeration unit.

Hardtop Container 20´/40´
With removable steel roof. Especially for heavy or excessively high cargo. For loading from above or from the door with door header swung out.

Reefer Container 20´/40´
With integrated refrigeration unit. Especially for cargo which must be kept at a constant temperature above or below freezing point.

Open Top Container
With removable tarpaulin . Especially for overhight cargo.Loading either from top side or door side from swung out header

High Cube Refer Container 40´
With integrated refregeration unit.Especially for light weight, voluminous cargo which must be kept at a

Flat 20´/40´
Especially for heavy cargo and especially wide cargo.

Bulk Container 20´
Especially for bulk cargo e.g. Malt.

Platform 20´/40´
Especially for heavy loads and oversized cargo. Non-domestic shipments.

Tank Container 20´
Especially for liquid chemicals. Selected containers are used exclusively for the transport of liquid food stuffs.

Appendix 12

COMBINED TRANSPORT BILL OF LADING

Code Name: "COMBICONBILL"

Shipper

Reference No.

N e g o t i a b l e
COMBINED TRANSPORT BILL OF LADING

Revised 1995

Consigned to order of

Notify party/address

Place of receipt

Port of vessel	Port of loading		
Port of discharge	Place of delivery	Freight payable at	Number of original Bills of Lading
Marks and Nos	Quantity and description of goods		Gross weight, kg, Measurement, m^3

Particulars above declared by Shipper

Freight and charges

RECEIVED the goods in apparent good order and condition and, as far as ascertained by reasonable means of checking, as specified above unless otherwise stated.

The Carrier, in accordance with and to the extent of the provisions contained in this Bill of Lading, and with liberty to sub-contract, undertakes to perform and/or in his own name to procure performance of the combined transport and the delivery of the goods, including all services related thereto, from the place and time of taking the goods in charge to the place and time of delivery and accepts responsibility for such transport and such services.

One of the Bills of Lading must be surrendered duly endorsed in exchange for the goods or delivery order.

IN WITNESS whereof TWO (2) original Bills of Lading have been signed, If not otherwise stated above, one of which being accomplished the other(s) to be void.

Shipper's declared value of

subject to payment of above extra charge.

Note:
The Merchant's attention is called to the fact that according to Clauses 10 to 12 and Clause 24 of this Bill of Lading, the liability of the Carrier is, in most cases, limited in respect of loss of or damage to the goods and delay.

Place and date of issue

Signed for

....as Carrier

by...

As agent(s) only to the Carrier

155

Appendix 12

COMBINED TRANSPORT BILL OF LADING

Adopted by The Baltic and International Maritime Council in January, 1971 (as revised 1995)

Code Name: "COMBICONBILL"

I. GENERAL PROVISIONS

1. Applicability.
Notwithstanding the heading "Combined Transport", the provisions set out and referred to in this Bill of Lading shall also apply, if the transport as described in this Bill of Lading is performed by one mode of transport only.

2. Definitions.
"Carrier" means the party on whose behalf this Bill of Lading has been signed.
"Merchant" includes the Shipper, the Receiver, the Consignor, the Consignee, the holder of this Bill of Lading and the owner of the goods.

3. Carrier's Tariff.
The terms of the Carrier's applicable Tariff at the date of shipment are incorporated herein. Copies of the relevant provisions of the applicable Tariff are available from the Carrier upon request. In the case of inconsistency between this Bill of Lading and the applicable Tariff, this Bill of Lading shall prevail.

4. Time Bar.
All liability whatsoever of the Carrier shall cease unless suit is brought within 9 months after delivery of the goods or the date when the goods should have been delivered.

5. Law and Jurisdiction.
Disputes arising under this Bill of Lading shall be determined by the courts and in accordance with the law at the place where the Carrier has his principal place of business.

II. PERFORMANCE OF THE CONTRACT

6. Methods and Routes of Transportation.
(1) The Carrier is entitled to perform the transport and all services related thereto in any reasonable manner and by any reasonable means, methods and routes.
(2) In accordance herewith, for instance, in the event of carriage by sea, vessels may sail with or without pilots, undergo repairs, adjust equipment, drydock and tow vessels in all situations.

7. Optional Stowage.
(1) Goods may be stowed by the Carrier by means of containers, trailers, transportable tanks, flats, pallets, or similar articles of transport used to consolidate goods.
(2) Containers, trailers, transportable tanks and covered flats, whether stowed by the Carrier or received by him in a stowed condition from the Merchant, may be carried on or under deck without notice to the Merchant,

8. Hindrances etc. Affecting Performance.
(1) The Carrier shall use reasonable endeavours to complete the transport and to deliver the goods at the place designated for delivery.
(2) If at any time the performance of the contract as evidenced by this Bill of Lading is or will be affected by any hindrance, risk, delay, difficulty or disadvantage of whatsoever kind, and if by virtue of sub-clause 8 (1) the Carrier has no duty to complete the performance of the contract, the Carrier (whether or not the transport is commenced} may elect to:
(a) treat the performance of this Contract as terminated and place the goods at the Merchant's disposal at any place which the Carrier shall deem safe and convenient; or
(b) deliver the goods at the place designated for delivery.
(3) If the goods are not taken delivery of by the Merchant within a reasonable time after the Carrier has called upon him to take delivery, the Carrier shall be at liberty to put the goods in safe custody on behalf of the Merchant at the letter's risk and expense.
(4) In any event the Carrier shall be entitled to full freight for goods received for transportation and additional compensation for extra costs resulting from the Circumstances referred to above.

III. CARRIER'S LIABILITY

9. Basic Liability.
(1) The Carrier shall be liable for loss of or damage to the goods occurring between the time when he receives the goods into his charge and the time of delivery.
(2) The Carrier shall be responsible for the acts and omissions of any person of whose services he makes use for the performance of the contract of carriage evidenced by this Bill of Lading.
(3) The Carrier shall, however, be relieved of liability for any loss or damage if such loss or damage arose or resulted from:
(a) The wrongful act or neglect of the Merchant.
(b) Compliance with the instructions of the person entitled to give them.
(c) The lack of, or defective conditions of packing in the case of goods which, by their nature, are liable to wastage or to be damaged when not packed or when not properly packed.
(d) Handling, loading, stowage or unloading of the goods by or on behalf of the Merchant.
(e) Inherent vice of the goods.
(f) Insufficiency or inadequacy of marks or numbers on the goods, covering, or unit loads.
(g) Strikes or lock-outs or stoppages or restraints of labour from whatever cause whether partial or general.
(h) Any cause or event which the Carrier could not avoid and the consequence whereof he could not prevent by the exercise of reasonable diligence.
(4) Where under sub-clause 9 (3) the Carrier is not under any liability in respect of some of the factors causing the loss or damage, he shall only be liable to the extent that those factors for which he is liable under this Clause have contributed to the loss or damage.
(5) The burden of proving that the loss or damage was due to one or more of the causes or events, specified in (a), (b) and (h) of sub-clause 9 (3) shall rest upon the Carrier.
(6) When the Carrier establishes that in the circumstances of the case, the loss or damage could be attributed to one or more of the causes or events, specified in (c) to (g) of sub-clause 9 (3), it shall be presumed that it was so caused. The Merchant shall, however, be entitled to prove that the loss or damage was not, in fact, caused either wholly or partly by one or more of the causes or events.

10. Amount of Compensation
(1) When the Carrier is liable for compensation in respect of loss of or damage to the goods, such compensation shall be calculated by reference to the value of such goods at the place and time they are delivered to the Merchant in accordance with the contract or should have been so delivered.
(2) The value of the goods shall be fixed according to the commodity exchange price or, if there be no such price, according to the current market price or, if there be no commodity exchange price or current market price, by reference to the normal value of goods of the same kind and quality.
(3) Compensation shall not, however, exceed two Special Drawing Rights per kilogramme of gross weight of the goods lost or damaged.
(4) Higher compensation may be claimed only when, with the consent of the Carrier, the value for the goods declared by the Shipper which exceeds the limits laid down in this Clause has been stated on the face of this Bill of Lading at the place indicated. In that case the amount of the declared value shall be substituted for that limit.

11. Special Provisions for Liability and Compensation
(1) Notwithstanding anything provided for in Clauses 9 and 10 of this Bill of Lading, if it can be proved where the loss or damage occurred, the Carrier and the Merchant shall, as to the liability of the Carrier, be entitled to require such liability to be determined by the provisions contained in any international convention or national law, which provisions:
(a) cannot be departed from by private contract, to the detriment of the claimant, and
(b) would have applied if the Merchant had made a separate and direct contract with the Carrier in respect of the particular stage of transport where the loss or damage occurred and received as evidence thereof any particular document which must be issued if such international convention or national law shall apply.
(2) Insofar as there is no mandatory law applying to carriage by sea by virtue of the provisions of sub-clause 11 (1), the liability of the Carrier in respect of any carriage by sea shall be determined by the International Brussels Convention 1924 as amended by the Protocol signed at Brussels on February 23rd 1968 – The Hague/Visby Rules. The Hague/Visby Rules shall also determine the liability of the Carrier in respect of carriage by inland waterways as if such carriage were carriage by sea. Furthermore, they shall apply to all goods, whether carried on deck or under deck.

12. Delay, Consequential Loss, etc.
If the Carrier is held liable in respect of delay, consequential loss or damage other than loss of or damage to the goods, the liability of the Carrier shall be limited to the freight for the transport covered by this Bill of Lading, or to the value of the goods as determined in Clause 10, whichever is the lesser.

13. Notice of Loss of or Damage to the Goods
(1) Unless notice of loss of or damage to the goods, specifying the general nature of such loss or damage, is given in writing by the Merchant to the Carrier when the goods are handed over to the Merchant, such handing over is prima facie evidence of the Delivery by the Carrier of the goods as described in this Bill of Lading.
(2) Where the loss or damage is not apparent, the same *prima facie* effect shall apply if notice in writing is not given within three (3) consecutive days after the day when the goods were handed over to the Merchant.

14. Defences and Limits for the Carrier, Servants, etc.
(1) The defences and limits of liability provided for in this Bill of Lading shall apply in any action against the Carrier for loss or damage to the goods whether the action can be founded in contract or in tort.
(2) The Carrier shall not be entitled to the benefit of the limitation of liability provided for in sub-clause 10 (3), if it is proved that the loss or damage resulted from a personal act or omission of the Carrier done with intent to cause such loss or damage or recklessly and with knowledge that damage would probably result.
(3) The Merchant undertakes that no claim shall be made against any servant, agent or other persons whose services the Carrier has used in order to perform this Contract and if any claim should nevertheless be made, to indemnify the Carrier against all consequences thereof.
(4) However, the provisions of this Bill of Lading apply whenever claims relating to the performance of this Contract are made against any servant, agent or other person whose services the Carrier has used in order to perform this Contract, whether such claims are founded in contract or in tort. In entering into this Contract, the Carrier, to the extent of such provisions, does so not only on his own behalf but also as agent or trustee for such persons. The aggregate liability of the Carrier and such persons shall not exceed the limits in Clauses 10, 11 and 24, respectively.

IV. DESCRIPTION OF GOODS

15. Carrier's Responsibility.
The information in this Bill of Lading shall be prima facie evidence of the taking in charge by the Carrier of the goods as described by such information unless a contrary indication, such as "shipper's weight, load and count", "Shipper-packed container" or similar expressions, have been made in the printed text or superimposed on the Bill of Lading. Proof to the contrary shall not be admissible when the Bill of Lading has been transferred, or the equivalent electronic data interchange message has been transmitted to and acknowledged by the Consignee who in good faith has relied and acted thereon.

16. Shipper's Responsibility.
The Shipper shall be deemed to have guaranteed to the Carrier the accuracy, at the time the goods were taken in charge by the Carrier, of the description of the goods, marks, number, quantity and weight, as furnished by him, and the Shipper shall defend, indemnify and hold harmless the Carrier against all loss, damage and expenses arising or resulting from inaccuracies in or inadequacy of such particulars. The right of the Carrier to such indemnity shall in no way limit his responsibility and liability under this Bill of Lading to any person other than the Shipper. The Shipper shall remain liable even if the Bill of Lading has been transferred by him.

17. Shipper-packed Containers, etc.
(1) If a container has not been filled, packed or stowed by the Carrier, the Carrier shall not be liable for any loss of or damage to its contents and the Merchant shall cover any loss or expense incurred by the Carrier, if such loss, damage or expense has been caused by:
(a) negligent filling, packing or stowing of the container;
(b) the contents being unsuitable for carriage in container; or
(c) the unsuitability or defective condition of the container unless the container has been supplied by the Carrier and the unsuitability or defective condition would not have been apparent upon reasonable inspection at or prior to the time when the container was filled, packed or stowed.
(2) The provisions of sub-clause (1) of this Clause also apply with respect to trailers, transportable tanks, flats and pallets which have not been filled, packed or stowed by the Carrier.
(3} The Carrier does not accept liability for damage due to the unsuitability or defective condition of reefer equipment or trailers supplied by the Merchant.

18. Dangerous Goods.
(1) The Merchant shall comply with all internationally recognised requirements and all rules which apply according to national law or by reason of international Convention, relating to the carriage of goods of a dangerous nature, and shall in any event inform the Carrier in writing of the exact nature of the danger before goods of a dangerous nature are taken into charge by the Carrier and indicate to him, if need be, the precautions to be taken.
(2) Goods of a dangerous nature which the Carrier did not know were dangerous, may, at any time or place, be unloaded, destroyed, or rendered harmless, without compensation; further, the Merchant shall be liable for all expenses, loss or damage arising out of their handing over for carriage or of their carriage.
(3) If any goods shipped with the knowledge of the Carrier as to their dangerous nature shall become a danger to any person or property, they may in like manner be landed at any place or destroyed or rendered innocuous by the Carrier without liability on the part of the Carrier except to General Average, if any.

19. Return of Containers
(1) For the purpose of this Clause the Consignor shall mean the person who concludes this Contract with the Carrier and the Consignee shall mean the person entitled to receive the goods from the Carrier.
(2) Containers, pallets or similar articles of transport supplied by or on behalf of the Carrier shall be returned to the Carrier in the same order and condition as handed over to the Merchant, normal wear and tear excepted, with interiors clean and within the time prescribed in the Carrier's tariff or elsewhere.
(3) (a) The Consignor shall be liable for any loss of, damage to, or delay, including demurrage, of such articles, incurred during the period between handing over to the Consignor and return to the Carrier for carriage.
(b) The Consignor and the Consignee shall be jointly and severally liable for any loss of, damage to, or delay, including demurrage, of such articles, incurred during the period between handing over to the Consignee and return to the Carrier.

V. FREIGHT AND LIEN

20. Freight.
(1) Freight shall be deemed earned when the goods have been taken in charge by the Carrier and shall be paid in any event.
(2) The Merchant's attention is drawn to the stipulations concerning currency in which the freight and charges are to be paid, rate of exchange, devaluation and other contingencies relative to freight and charges in the relevant tariff conditions. If no such stipulation as to devaluation exists or is applicable the following shall apply:
If the currency in which freight and charges are quoted is devalued between the date of the freight agreement and the date when the freight and charges are paid, then all freight and charges shall be automatically and immediately increased in proportion to the extent of the devaluation of the said currency.
(3) For the purpose of verifying the freight basis, the Carrier reserves the right to have the contents of containers, trailers or similar articles of transport inspected in order to ascertain the weight, measurement, value, or nature of the goods,

21. Lien.
The Carrier shall have a lien on the goods for any amount due under this Contract and for the costs of recovering the same, and may enforce such lien in any reasonable manner, including sale or disposal of the goods.

VI. MISCELLANEOUS PROVISIONS

22. General Average.
(1) General Average shall be adjusted at any port or place at the Carrier's option, and to be settled according to the York-Antwerp Rules 1994, or any modification thereof, this covering all goods, whether carried on or under deck. The New Jason Clause as approved by BIMCO to be considered as incorporated herein.
(2) Such security including a cash deposit as the Carrier may deem sufficient to cover the estimated contribution of the goods and any salvage and special charges thereon, shall, if required, be submitted to the Carrier prior to delivery of the goods.

23. Both-to-Blame Collision Clause.
The Both-to-Blame Collision Clause as adopted by BIMCO shall be considered incorporated herein

24 U.S. Trade
(1) In case the contract evidenced by this Bill of Lading is subject to the Carriage of Goods by Sea Act of the United States of America, 1936 (U.S. COGSA), then the provisions stated in the said Act shall govern before loading and after discharge and throughout the entire time the goods are in the Carrier's custody.
(2) If the U.S. COGSA applies, and unless the nature and value of the goods have been declared by the shipper before the goods have been handed over to the Carrier and inserted in this Bill of Lading, the Carrier shall in no event be or become liable for any loss of or damage to the goods in an amount exceeding USD 500 per package or customary freight unit

Appendix 13

Liner Booking Note

Shipper (if known at time of booking)	**BIMCO BLANK BACK FORM OF LINER BOOKING NOTE**	
	Place and date	
Consignee (if known at time of booking)	Name of Merchant effecting the booking	
	Name of Carrier	
Notify address at place of delivery	Merchant's representatives at loading port	
	Time for shipment (about)	
Place of receipt by pre-carrier*	It is hereby agreed that this Contract shall be performed subject to the terms contained in this Booking Note and in the Carrier's Standard Conditions of Carriage, which shall prevail over any previous arrangements and which shall in turn be superseded (except as to deadweight and demurrage) by the terms of the Bill of Lading. Copies of Carrier's Standard Conditions of Carriage, if any, can be obtained upon request from the Carrier or his agents.	
Vessel / Port of loading**		
Port of discharge / Place of delivery by on-carrier*		

Marks and Nos. (if available)	Description of goods	Gross weight (if available)	Measurement (if available)

Freight details, charges, etc.	Special terms, if agreed	
Daily demurrage rate (if agreed)	Freight (state prepayable or payable at destination)	Signature (Merchant)
	Number of original Bs/L required	Signature (Carrier)

*Applicable only when Through Transport foreseen

**(or so near thereunto as the vessel may safely get and lie always afloat)

Sea Waybill

Consignee (not to order)

Notify address

Pre-carriage by*	Place of receipt by pre-carrier*
Vessel	Port of loading
Port of discharge	Place of delivery by on-carrier*

and Nos.   Number and kind of packages: description of goods   Gross weight   Measurement

Particulars furnished by the Merchant

Freight details, charges etc.	RECEIVED (or carriage the goods as specified above according to Shipper's declaration in apparent good order and condition - unless otherwise staled herein - weight, measure, marks, numbers, quality, contents and value unknown.

The goods shipped under this Liner Waybill will be delivered to the Party named as Consignee or Its authorised agent, on production of proof of identity without any documentary formalities. Carrier to excercise due care ensuring that delivery is made to the proper party. However, In case of Incorrect delivery, no responsibility will be accepted unless due to fault or neglect on the part of the Carrier.

This Liner Waybill which is not s document of title to the goods is deemed to be a contract of carriage which is subject to the exceptions, limitations, conditions and liberties {including those relating to pre-carriage and on-carriage) set out In the Carrier's Standard Conditions of Carriage applicable to the voyage covered by this Liner Waybill and operative on Its data of issue. If the Carrier does not have Standard Conditions of Carriage, this Liner Waybill is subject to the exceptions, limitations, conditions and liberties as set out on Page 1 of the "Conlinebill" Liner Bill of Lading operative on its date of issue.

The "Conlinebill" Liner Bill of Lading and the Carrier's Standard Conditions of Carriage incorporate or are deemed to incorporate the Hague Rules contained in the Brussels Convention dated 25th August 1924 and any compulsorily applicable national enactment of either the Hague Rules as such or as amended by the Hague-Visby Rules contained in the Brussels Protocol dated 23rd February 1968.

A copy of the Carrier's Standard Conditions of Carriage applicable hereto may be inspected or will be supplied on request at the office of the Carrier or the Carrier's Principal agents. Every reference in the Carrier's Standard Conditions of Carriage or in the "Conlinebill" Liner Bill of Lading to the words "Bill of Lading" shall be read and construed as a reference to the words "Non-Negotiable Liner Waybill" and the terms and conditions thereof shall be read and construed accordingly.

Daily demurrage rate (if agreed)	Freight payable at	Place and date of issue
		Signature

* Applicable only when document used as a Through

Appendix 15

SHIPMAN

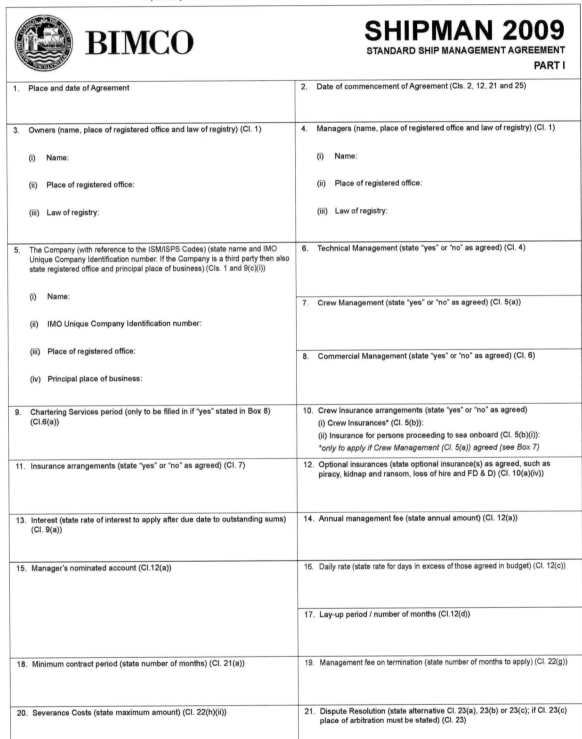

Appendix 15

SHIPMAN 2009
Standard ship management agreement

PART I

(continued)

22. Notices (state full style contact details for serving notice and communication to the Owners) (Cl. 24)	23. Notices (state full style contact details for serving notice and communication to the Managers) (Cl. 24)

It is mutually agreed between the party stated in Box 3 and the party stated in Box 4 that this Agreement consisting of PART I and PART II as well as Annexes "A" (Details of Vessel or Vessels), "B" (Details of Crew), "C" (Budget), "D" (Associated Vessels) and "E" (Fee Schedule) attached hereto, shall be performed subject to the conditions contained herein. In the event of a conflict of conditions, the provisions of PART I and Annexes "A", "B", "C", "D" and "E" shall prevail over those of PART II to the extent of such conflict but no further.

Signature(s) (Owners)	Signature(s) (Managers)

Appendix 15

PART II
SHIPMAN 2009
Standard ship management agreement

SECTION 1 – Basis of the Agreement

1. **Definitions**   1
In this Agreement save where the context otherwise requires, the following words and expressions shall have   2
the meanings hereby assigned to them: 3

"Company" (with reference to the ISM Code and the ISPS Code) means the organization identified in **Box 5**   4
or any replacement organization appointed by the Owners from time to time (see Sub-clauses 9(b)(i) or 9(c)   5
(ii), whichever is applicable).   6

"Crew" means the personnel of the numbers, rank and nationality specified in Annex "B" hereto.   7

"Crew Insurances" means insurance of liabilities in respect of crew risks which shall include but not be limited   8
to death, permanent disability, sickness, injury, repatriation, shipwreck unemployment indemnity and loss   9
of personal effects (see Sub-clause 5(b) (Crew Insurances) and Clause 7 (Insurance Arrangements) and   10
Clause 10 (Insurance Policies) and **Boxes 10** and **11**).   11

"Crew Support Costs" means all expenses of a general nature which are not particularly referable to any   12
individual vessel for the time being managed by the Managers and which are incurred by the Managers for the   13
purpose of providing an efficient and economic management service and, without prejudice to the generality   14
of the foregoing, shall include the cost of crew standby pay, training schemes for officers and ratings, cadet   15
training schemes, sick pay, study pay, recruitment and interviews.   16

"Flag State" means the State whose flag the Vessel is flying.   17

"ISM Code" means the International Management Code for the Safe Operation of Ships and for Pollution   18
Prevention and any amendment thereto or substitution therefor.   19

"ISPS Code" means the International Code for the Security of Ships and Port Facilities and the relevant   20
amendments to Chapter XI of SOLAS and any amendment thereto or substitution therefor.   21

"Managers" means the party identified in **Box 4**.   22

"Management Services" means the services specified in SECTION 2 - Services (Clauses 4 through 7) as   23
indicated affirmatively in **Boxes 6** through **8, 10 and 11,** and all other functions performed by the Managers   24
under the terms of this Agreement.   25

"Owners" means the party identified in **Box 3**.   26

"Severance Costs" means the costs which are legally required to be paid to the Crew as a result of the early   27
termination of any contracts for service on the Vessel.   28

"SMS" means the Safety Management System (as defined by the ISM Code).   29

"STCW 95" means the International Convention on Standards of Training, Certification and Watchkeeping   30
for Seafarers, 1978, as amended in 1995 and any amendment thereto or substitution therefor.   31

"Vessel" means the vessel or vessels details of which are set out in Annex "A" attached hereto.   32

2. **Commencement and Appointment**   33
With effect from the date stated in **Box 2** for the commencement of the Management Services and continuing   34
unless and until terminated as provided herein, the Owners hereby appoint the Managers and the Managers   35
hereby agree to act as the Managers of the Vessel in respect of the Management Services.   36

3. **Authority of the Managers**   37
Subject to the terms and conditions herein provided, during the period of this Agreement the Managers shall   38
carry out the Management Services in respect of the Vessel as agents for and on behalf of the Owners. The   39
Managers shall have authority to take such actions as they may from time to time in their absolute discretion   40
consider to be necessary to enable them to perform the Management Services in accordance with sound   41
ship management practice, including but not limited to compliance with all relevant rules and regulations.   42

Appendix 15

PART II
SHIPMAN 2009
Standard ship management agreement

SECTION 2 – Services

4. **Technical Management** 43
   *(only applicable if agreed according to **Box 6**).* 44
   The Managers shall provide technical management which includes, but is not limited to, the following 45
   services: 46

   (a) ensuring that the Vessel complies with the requirements of the law of the Flag State; 47

   (b) ensuring compliance with the ISM Code; 48

   (c) ensuring compliance with the ISPS Code; 49

   (d) providing competent personnel to supervise the maintenance and general efficiency of the Vessel; 50

   (e) arranging and supervising dry dockings, repairs, alterations and the maintenance of the Vessel to the 51
   standards agreed with the Owners provided that the Managers shall be entitled to incur the necessary 52
   expenditure to ensure that the Vessel will comply with all requirements and recommendations of the 53
   classification society, and with the law of the Flag State and of the places where the Vessel is required to 54
   trade; 55

   (f) arranging the supply of necessary stores, spares and lubricating oil; 56

   (g) appointing surveyors and technical consultants as the Managers may consider from time to time to be 57
   necessary; 58

   (h) in accordance with the Owners' instructions, supervising the sale and physical delivery of the Vessel 59
   under the sale agreement. However services under this Sub-clause 4(h) shall not include negotiation of the 60
   sale agreement or transfer of ownership of the Vessel; 61

   (i) arranging for the supply of provisions unless provided by the Owners; and 62

   (j) arranging for the sampling and testing of bunkers. 63

5. **Crew Management and Crew Insurances** 64
   (a) *Crew Management* 65
   *(only applicable if agreed according to **Box 7**)* 66
   The Managers shall provide suitably qualified Crew who shall comply with the requirements of STCW 95. 67
   The provision of such crew management services includes, but is not limited to, the following services: 68

   (i) selecting, engaging and providing for the administration of the Crew, including, as applicable, payroll 69
   arrangements, pension arrangements, tax, social security contributions and other mandatory dues related 70
   to their employment payable in each Crew member's country of domicile; 71

   (ii) ensuring that the applicable requirements of the law of the Flag State in respect of rank, qualification 72
   and certification of the Crew and employment regulations, such as Crew's tax and social insurance, are 73
   satisfied; 74

   (iii) ensuring that all Crew have passed a medical examination with a qualified doctor certifying that they are 75
   fit for the duties for which they are engaged and are in possession of valid medical certificates issued in 76
   accordance with appropriate Flag State requirements or such higher standard of medical examination 77
   as may be agreed with the Owners. In the absence of applicable Flag State requirements the medical 78
   certificate shall be valid at the time when the respective Crew member arrives on board the Vessel and 79
   shall be maintained for the duration of the service on board the Vessel; 80

   (iv) ensuring that the Crew shall have a common working language and a command of the English language 81
   of a sufficient standard to enable them to perform their duties safely; 82

   (v) arranging transportation of the Crew, including repatriation; 83

   (vi) training of the Crew; 84

Appendix 15

PART II
SHIPMAN 2009
Standard ship management agreement

(vii) conducting union negotiations; and 85

(viii) if the Managers are the Company, ensuring that the Crew, on joining the Vessel, are given proper 86
familiarisation with their duties in relation to the Vessel's SMS and that instructions which are essential 87
to the SMS are identified, documented and given to the Crew prior to sailing. 88

(ix) if the Managers are **not** the Company: 89

(1) ensuring that the Crew, before joining the Vessel, are given proper familiarisation with their duties 90
in relation to the ISM Code; and 91

(2) instructing the Crew to obey all reasonable orders of the Company in connection with the operation 92
of the SMS. 93

(x) Where Managers are **not** providing technical management services in accordance with Clause 4 94
(Technical Management): 95

(1) ensuring that no person connected to the provision and the performance of the crew management 96
services shall proceed to sea on board the Vessel without the prior consent of the Owners (such consent 97
not to be unreasonably withheld); and 98

(2) ensuring that in the event that the Owners' drug and alcohol policy requires measures to be taken 99
prior to the Crew joining the Vessel, implementing such measures; 100

(b) Crew Insurances 101
*(only applicable if Sub-clause 5(a) applies **and** if agreed according to **Box 10**)* 102
The Managers shall throughout the period of this Agreement provide the following services: 103

(i) arranging Crew Insurances in accordance with the best practice of prudent managers of vessels of a 104
similar type to the Vessel, with sound and reputable insurance companies, underwriters or associations. 105
Insurances for any other persons proceeding to sea onboard the Vessel may be separately agreed by 106
the Owners and the Managers (see **Box 10**); 107

(ii) ensuring that the Owners are aware of the terms, conditions, exceptions and limits of liability of the 108
insurances in Sub-clause 5(b)(i); 109

(iii) ensuring that all premiums or calls in respect of the insurances in Sub-clause 5(b)(i) are paid by their 110
due date; 111

(iv) if obtainable at no additional cost, ensuring that insurances in Sub-clause 5(b)(i) name the Owners as 112
a joint assured with full cover and, unless otherwise agreed, on terms such that Owners shall be under 113
no liability in respect of premiums or calls arising in connection with such insurances. 114

(v) providing written evidence, to the reasonable satisfaction of the Owners, of the Managers' compliance with 115
their obligations under Sub-clauses 5(b)(ii), and 5(b)(iii) within a reasonable time of the commencement 116
of this Agreement, and of each renewal date and, if specifically requested, of each payment date of the 117
insurances in Sub-clause 5(b)(i). 118

6. **Commercial Management** 119
*(only applicable if agreed according to **Box 8**).* 120
The Managers shall provide the following services for the Vessel in accordance with the Owners' instructions, 121
which shall include but not be limited to: 122

(a) seeking and negotiating employment for the Vessel and the conclusion (including the execution thereof) 123
of charter parties or other contracts relating to the employment of the Vessel. If such a contract exceeds the 124
period stated in **Box 9**, consent thereto in writing shall first be obtained from the Owners; 125

(b) arranging for the provision of bunker fuels of the quality specified by the Owners as required for the 126
Vessel's trade; 127

Appendix 15

PART II
SHIPMAN 2009
Standard ship management agreement

(c) voyage estimating and accounting and calculation of hire, freights, demurrage and/or despatch monies 128
due from or due to the charterers of the Vessel; assisting in the collection of any sums due to the Owners 129
related to the commercial operation of the Vessel in accordance with Clause 11 (Income Collected and 130
Expenses Paid on Behalf of Owners); 131

If any of the services under Sub-clauses 6(a), 6(b) and 6(c) are to be excluded from the Management Fee, remuneration 132
for these services must be stated in Annex E (Fee Schedule). See Sub-clause 12(e). 133

(d) issuing voyage instructions; 134

(e) appointing agents; 135

(f) appointing stevedores; and 136

(g) arranging surveys associated with the commercial operation of the Vessel. 137

7. Insurance Arrangements 138
*(only applicable if agreed according to **Box 11**).* 139
The Managers shall arrange insurances in accordance with Clause 10 (Insurance Policies), on such terms as 140
the Owners shall have instructed or agreed, in particular regarding conditions, insured values, deductibles, 141
franchises and limits of liability. 142

Appendix 15

PART II
SHIPMAN 2009
Standard ship management agreement

SECTION 3 – Obligations

8. Managers' Obligations 143

(a) The Managers undertake to use their best endeavours to provide the Management Services as agents 144
for and on behalf of the Owners in accordance with sound ship management practice and to protect and 145
promote the interests of the Owners in all matters relating to the provision of services hereunder. 146

Provided however, that in the performance of their management responsibilities under this Agreement, the 147
Managers shall be entitled to have regard to their overall responsibility in relation to all vessels as may from 148
time to time be entrusted to their management and in particular, but without prejudice to the generality of 149
the foregoing, the Managers shall be entitled to allocate available supplies, manpower and services in such 150
manner as in the prevailing circumstances the Managers in their absolute discretion consider to be fair and 151
reasonable. 152

(b) Where the Managers are providing technical management services in accordance with Clause 4 (Technical 153
Management), they shall procure that the requirements of the Flag State are satisfied and they shall agree 154
to be appointed as the Company, assuming the responsibility for the operation of the Vessel and taking over 155
the duties and responsibilities imposed by the ISM Code and the ISPS Code, if applicable. 156

9. Owners' Obligations 157

(a) The Owners shall pay all sums due to the Managers punctually in accordance with the terms of this 158
Agreement. In the event of payment after the due date of any outstanding sums the Manager shall be entitled 159
to charge interest at the rate stated in **Box 13**.
160
(b) Where the Managers are providing technical management services in accordance with Clause 4 (Technical 161
Management), the Owners shall:
162
(i) report (or where the Owners are not the registered owners of the Vessel procure that the registered 163
owners report) to the Flag State administration the details of the Managers as the Company as required 164
to comply with the ISM and ISPS Codes; 165

(ii) procure that any officers and ratings supplied by them or on their behalf comply with the requirements 166
of STCW 95; and 167

(iii) instruct such officers and ratings to obey all reasonable orders of the Managers (in their capacity as the 168
Company) in connection with the operation of the Managers' safety management system. 169

(c) Where the Managers are **not** providing technical management services in accordance with Clause 4 170
(Technical Management), the Owners shall: 171

(i) procure that the requirements of the Flag State are satisfied and notify the Managers upon execution of 172
this Agreement of the name and contact details of the organization that will be the Company by completing 173
Box 5; 174

(ii) if the Company changes at any time during this Agreement, notify the Managers in a timely manner of 175
the name and contact details of the new organization; 176

(iii) procure that the details of the Company, including any change thereof, are reported to the Flag State 177
administration as required to comply with the ISM and ISPS Codes. The Owners shall advise the Managers 178
in a timely manner when the Flag State administration has approved the Company; and 179

(iv) unless otherwise agreed, arrange for the supply of provisions at their own expense. 180

(d) Where the Managers are providing crew management services in accordance with Sub-clause 5(a) the 181
Owners shall: 182

(i) inform the Managers prior to ordering the Vessel to any excluded or additional premium area under 183
any of the Owners' Insurances by reason of war risks and/or piracy or like perils and pay whatever 184
additional costs may properly be incurred by the Managers as a consequence of such orders including, 185
if necessary, the costs of replacing any member of the Crew. Any delays resulting from negotiation 186
with or replacement of any member of the Crew as a result of the Vessel being ordered to such an area 187

Appendix 15

PART II
SHIPMAN 2009
Standard ship management agreement

shall be for the Owners' account. Should the Vessel be within an area which becomes an excluded or additional premium area the above provisions relating to cost and delay shall apply; 188
189

(ii) agree with the Managers prior to any change of flag of the Vessel and pay whatever additional costs may properly be incurred by the Managers as a consequence of such change. If agreement cannot be reached then either party may terminate this Agreement in accordance with Sub-clause 22(e); and 190
191
192

(iii) provide, at no cost to the Managers, in accordance with the requirements of the law of the Flag State, or higher standard, as mutually agreed, adequate Crew accommodation and living standards. 193
194

(e) Where the Managers are **not** the Company, the Owners shall ensure that Crew are properly familiarised with their duties in accordance with the Vessel's SMS and that instructions which are essential to the SMS are identified, documented and given to the Crew prior to sailing. 195
196
197

Appendix 15

SECTION 4 – Insurance, Budgets, Income, Expenses and Fees

10. Insurance Policies 198

The Owners shall procure, whether by instructing the Managers under Clause 7 (Insurance Arrangements) 199
or otherwise, that throughout the period of this Agreement: 200

(a) at the Owners' expense, the Vessel is insured for not less than its sound market value or entered for its 201
full gross tonnage, as the case may be for: 202

(i) hull and machinery marine risks (including but not limited to crew negligence) and excess liabilities; 203

(ii) protection and indemnity risks (including but not limited to pollution risks, diversion expenses and, 204
except to the extent insured separately by the Managers in accordance with Sub-clause 5(b)(i), Crew 205
Insurances; 206

NOTE: If the Managers are not providing crew management services under Sub-clause 5(a) (Crew 207
Management) or have agreed not to provide Crew Insurances separately in accordance with Sub-clause 208
5(b)(i), then such insurances must be included in the protection and indemnity risks cover for the Vessel (see 209
Sub-clause 10(a)(ii) above). 210

(iii) war risks (including but not limited to blocking and trapping, protection and indemnity, terrorism and crew 211
risks); and 212

(iv) such optional insurances as may be agreed (such as piracy, kidnap and ransom, loss of hire and FD & 213
D) (see **Box 12**) 214

Sub-clauses 10(a)(i) through 10(a)(iv) all in accordance with the best practice of prudent owners of vessels 215
of a similar type to the Vessel, with sound and reputable insurance companies, underwriters or associations 216
("the Owners' Insurances"); 217

(b) all premiums and calls on the Owners' Insurances are paid by their due date; 218

(c) the Owners' Insurances name the Managers and, subject to underwriters' agreement, any third party 219
designated by the Managers as a joint assured, with full cover. It is understood that in some cases, such as 220
protection and indemnity, the normal terms for such cover may impose on the Managers and any such third 221
party a liability in respect of premiums or calls arising in connection with the Owners' Insurances. 222

If obtainable at no additional cost, however, the Owners shall procure such insurances on terms such that 223
neither the Managers nor any such third party shall be under any liability in respect of premiums or calls arising 224
in connection with the Owners' Insurances. In any event, on termination of this Agreement in accordance 225
with Clause 21 (Duration of the Agreement) and Clause 22 (Termination), the Owners shall procure that the 226
Managers and any third party designated by the Managers as joint assured shall cease to be joint assured 227
and, if reasonably achievable, that they shall be released from any and all liability for premiums and calls 228
that may arise in relation to the period of this Agreement; and 229

(d) written evidence is provided, to the reasonable satisfaction of the Managers, of the Owners' compliance 230
with their obligations under this Clause 10 within a reasonable time of the commencement of the Agreement, 231
and of each renewal date and, if specifically requested, of each payment date of the Owners' Insurances. 232

11. Income Collected and Expenses Paid on Behalf of Owners 233

(a) Except as provided in Sub-clause 11(c) all monies collected by the Managers under the terms of this 234
Agreement (other than monies payable by the Owners to the Managers) and any interest thereon shall be 235
held to the credit of the Owners in a separate bank account. 236

(b) All expenses incurred by the Managers under the terms of this Agreement on behalf of the Owners 237
(including expenses as provided in Clause 12(c)) may be debited against the Owners in the account referred to 238
under Sub-clause 11(a) but shall in any event remain payable by the Owners to the Managers on demand. 239

(c) All monies collected by the Managers under Clause 6 (Commercial Management) shall be paid into a 240
bank account in the name of the Owners or as may be otherwise advised by the Owners in writing. 241

Appendix 15

PART II
SHIPMAN 2009
Standard ship management agreement

12. Management Fee and Expenses   242

(a) The Owners shall pay to the Managers an annual management fee as stated in **Box 14** for their services   243
as Managers under this Agreement, which shall be payable in equal monthly instalments in advance, the first   244
instalment (pro rata if appropriate) being payable on the commencement of this Agreement (see Clause 2   245
(Commencement and Appointment) and **Box 2**) and subsequent instalments being payable at the beginning   246
of every calendar month. The management fee shall be payable to the Managers' nominated account stated   247
in **Box 15**.   248

(b) The management fee shall be subject to an annual review and the proposed fee shall be presented in   249
the annual budget in accordance with Sub-clause 13(a).   250

(c) The Managers shall, at no extra cost to the Owners, provide their own office accommodation, office staff,   251
facilities and stationery. Without limiting the generality of this Clause 12 (Management Fee and Expenses) the   252
Owners shall reimburse the Managers for postage and communication expenses, travelling expenses, and   253
other out of pocket expenses properly incurred by the Managers in pursuance of the Management Services.   254
Any days used by the Managers' personnel travelling to or from or attending on the Vessel or otherwise used   255
in connection with the Management Services in excess of those agreed in the budget shall be charged at   256
the daily rate stated in **Box 16**.   257

(d) If the Owners decide to layup the Vessel and such layup lasts for more than the number of months   258
stated in **Box 17**, an appropriate reduction of the Management Fee for the period exceeding such period   259
until one month before the Vessel is again put into service shall be mutually agreed between the parties. If   260
the Managers are providing crew management services in accordance with Sub-clause 5(a), consequential   261
costs of reduction and reinstatement of the Crew shall be for the Owners' account. If agreement cannot be   262
reached then either party may terminate this Agreement in accordance with Sub-clause 22(e).   263

(e) Save as otherwise provided in this Agreement, all discounts and commissions obtained by the Managers   264
in the course of the performance of the Management Services shall be credited to the Owners.   265

13. Budgets and Management of Funds   266

(a) The Managers' initial budget is set out in Annex "C" hereto. Subsequent budgets shall be for twelve   267
month periods and shall be prepared by the Managers and presented to the Owners not less than three   268
months before the end of the budget year.   269

(b) The Owners shall state to the Managers in a timely manner, but in any event within one month of   270
presentation, whether or not they agree to each proposed annual budget. The parties shall negotiate in good   271
faith and if they fail to agree on the annual budget, including the management fee, either party may terminate   272
this Agreement in accordance with Sub-clause 22(e).   273

(c) Following the agreement of the budget, the Managers shall prepare and present to the Owners their   274
estimate of the working capital requirement for the Vessel and shall each month request the Owners in writing   275
to pay the funds required to run the Vessel for the ensuing month, including the payment of any occasional or   276
extraordinary item of expenditure, such as emergency repair costs, additional insurance premiums, bunkers   277
or provisions. Such funds shall be received by the Managers within ten running days after the receipt by the   278
Owners of the Managers' written request and shall be held to the credit of the Owners in a separate bank   279
account.   280

(d) The Managers shall at all times maintain and keep true and correct accounts in respect of the Management   281
Services in accordance with the relevant International Financial Reporting Standards or such other standard   282
as the parties may agree, including records of all costs and expenditure incurred, and produce a comparison   283
between budgeted and actual income and expenditure of the Vessel in such form and at such intervals as   284
shall be mutually agreed.   285

The Managers shall make such accounts available for inspection and auditing by the Owners and/or their   286
representatives in the Managers' offices or by electronic means, provided reasonable notice is given by the   287
Owners.   288

(e) Notwithstanding anything contained herein, the Managers shall in no circumstances be required to use   289
or commit their own funds to finance the provision of the Management Services.   290

Appendix 15

PART II
SHIPMAN 2009
Standard ship management agreement

SECTION 5 – Legal, General and Duration of Agreement

14. Trading Restrictions 291
If the Managers are providing crew management services in accordance with Sub-clause 5(a) (Crew 292
Management), the Owners and the Managers will, prior to the commencement of this Agreement, agree on any 293
trading restrictions to the Vessel that may result from the terms and conditions of the Crew's employment. 294

15. Replacement 295
If the Managers are providing crew management services in accordance with Sub-clause 5(a) (Crew 296
Management), the Owners may require the replacement, at their own expense, at the next reasonable 297
opportunity, of any member of the Crew found on reasonable grounds to be unsuitable for service. If the 298
Managers have failed to fulfil their obligations in providing suitable qualified Crew within the meaning of Sub- 299
clause 5(a) (Crew Management), then such replacement shall be at the Managers' expense. 300

16. Managers' Right to Sub-Contract 301
The Managers shall not subcontract any of their obligations hereunder without the prior written consent of 302
the Owners which shall not be unreasonably withheld. In the event of such a sub-contract the Managers 303
shall remain fully liable for the due performance of their obligations under this Agreement. 304

17. Responsibilities 305
(a) *Force Majeure* - Neither party shall be liable for any loss, damage or delay due to any of the following 306
force majeure events and/or conditions to the extent that the party invoking force majeure is prevented or 307
hindered from performing any or all of their obligations under this Agreement, provided they have made all 308
reasonable efforts to avoid, minimise or prevent the effect of such events and/or conditions: 309

   (i)   acts of God; 310

   (ii) any Government requisition, control, intervention, requirement or interference; 311

   (iii) any circumstances arising out of war, threatened act of war or warlike operations, acts of terrorism, 312
       sabotage or piracy, or the consequences thereof; 313

   (iv) riots, civil commotion, blockades or embargoes; 314

   (v) epidemics; 315

   (vi) earthquakes, landslides, floods or other extraordinary weather conditions; 316

   (vii) strikes, lockouts or other industrial action, unless limited to the employees (which shall not include the 317
       Crew) of the party seeking to invoke force majeure; 318

   (viii) fire, accident, explosion except where caused by negligence of the party seeking to invoke force majeure; 319
       and 320

   (ix) any other similar cause beyond the reasonable control of either party. 321

   (b) *Liability to Owners* 322
   (i)   Without prejudice to Sub-clause 17(a), the Managers shall be under no liability whatsoever to the Owners 323
       for any loss, damage, delay or expense of whatsoever nature, whether direct or indirect, (including but 324
       not limited to loss of profit arising out of or in connection with detention of or delay to the Vessel) and 325
       howsoever arising in the course of performance of the Management Services **UNLESS** same is proved 326
       to have resulted solely from the negligence, gross negligence or wilful default of the Managers or their 327
       employees or agents, or sub-contractors employed by them in connection with the Vessel, in which case 328
       (save where loss, damage, delay or expense has resulted from the Managers' personal act or omission 329
       committed with the intent to cause same or recklessly and with knowledge that such loss, damage, 330
       delay or expense would probably result) the Managers' liability for each incident or series of incidents 331
       giving rise to a claim or claims shall never exceed a total of ten (10) times the annual management fee 332
       payable hereunder. 333

   (ii) *Acts or omissions of the Crew* - Notwithstanding anything that may appear to the contrary in this 334
       Agreement, the Managers shall not be liable for any acts or omissions of the Crew, even if such acts 335

Appendix 15

PART II
SHIPMAN 2009
Standard ship management agreement

or omissions are negligent, grossly negligent or wilful, except only to the extent that they are shown to   336
have resulted from a failure by the Managers to discharge their obligations under Clause 5(a) (Crew   337
Management), in which case their liability shall be limited in accordance with the terms of this Clause   338
17 (Responsibilities).   339

(c) *Indemnity* - Except to the extent and solely for the amount therein set out that the Managers would be   340
liable under Sub-clause 17(b), the Owners hereby undertake to keep the Managers and their employees,   341
agents and sub-contractors indemnified and to hold them harmless against all actions, proceedings, claims,   342
demands or liabilities whatsoever or howsoever arising which may be brought against them or incurred or   343
suffered by them arising out of or in connection with the performance of this Agreement, and against and in   344
respect of all costs, loss, damages and expenses (including legal costs and expenses on a full indemnity   345
basis) which the Managers may suffer or incur (either directly or indirectly) in the course of the performance 346
of this Agreement.   347

(d) *"Himalaya"* - It is hereby expressly agreed that no employee or agent of the Managers (including every   348
sub-contractor from time to time employed by the Managers) shall in any circumstances whatsoever be   349
under any liability whatsoever to the Owners for any loss, damage or delay of whatsoever kind arising or   350
resulting directly or indirectly from any act, neglect or default on his part while acting in the course of or in 351
connection with his employment and, without prejudice to the generality of the foregoing provisions in this   352
Clause 17 (Responsibilities), every exemption, limitation, condition and liberty herein contained and every   353
right, exemption from liability, defence and immunity of whatsoever nature applicable to the Managers or to   354
which the Managers are entitled hereunder shall also be available and shall extend to protect every such   355
employee or agent of the Managers acting as aforesaid and for the purpose of all the foregoing provisions   356
of this Clause 17 (Responsibilities) the Managers are or shall be deemed to be acting as agent or trustee   357
on behalf of and for the benefit of all persons who are or might be their servants or agents from time to time   358
(including sub-contractors as aforesaid) and all such persons shall to this extent be or be deemed to be   359
parties to this Agreement.   360

18. General Administration   361
(a) The Managers shall keep the Owners and, if appropriate, the Company informed in a timely manner of   362
any incident of which the Managers become aware which gives or may give rise to delay to the Vessel or   363
claims or disputes involving third parties.   364

(b) The Managers shall handle and settle all claims and disputes arising out of the Management Services   365
hereunder, unless the Owners instruct the Managers otherwise. The Managers shall keep the Owners   366
appropriately informed in a timely manner throughout the handling of such claims and disputes.   367

(c) The Owners may request the Managers to bring or defend other actions, suits or proceedings related   368
to the Management Services, on terms to be agreed.   369

(d) The Managers shall have power to obtain appropriate legal or technical or other outside expert advice in   370
relation to the handling and settlement of claims in relation to Sub-clauses 18(a) and 18(b) and disputes and 371
any other matters affecting the interests of the Owners in respect of the Vessel, unless the Owners instruct   372
the Managers otherwise.   373

(e) On giving reasonable notice, the Owners may request, and the Managers shall in a timely manner make   374
available, all documentation, information and records in respect of the matters covered by this Agreement   375
either related to mandatory rules or regulations or other obligations applying to the Owners in respect of   376
the Vessel (including but not limited to STCW 95, the ISM Code and ISPS Code) to the extent permitted by   377
relevant legislation.   378

On giving reasonable notice, the Managers may request, and the Owners shall in a timely manner make   379
available, all documentation, information and records reasonably required by the Managers to enable them   380
to perform the Management Services.   381

(f) The Owners shall arrange for the provision of any necessary guarantee bond or other security.   382

(g) Any costs incurred by the Managers in carrying out their obligations according to this Clause 18 (General   383
Administration) shall be reimbursed by the Owners.   384

Appendix 15

PART II
SHIPMAN 2009
Standard ship management agreement

19.	**Inspection of Vessel**	385
	The Owners may at any time after giving reasonable notice to the Managers inspect the Vessel for any reason	386
	they consider necessary.	387

20.	**Compliance with Laws and Regulations**	388
	The parties will not do or permit to be done anything which might cause any breach or infringement of the	389
	laws and regulations of the Flag State, or of the places where the Vessel trades.	390

21. **Duration of the Agreement** 391

(a) This Agreement shall come into effect at the date stated in **Box 2** and shall continue until terminated by 392
either party by giving notice to the other; in which event this Agreement shall terminate upon the expiration 393
of the later of the number of months stated in **Box 18** or a period of two (2) months from the date on which 394
such notice is received, unless terminated earlier in accordance with Clause 22 (Termination). 395

(b) Where the Vessel is not at a mutually convenient port or place on the expiry of such period, this Agreement 396
shall terminate on the subsequent arrival of the Vessel at the next mutually convenient port or place. 397

22. **Termination** 398

(a) *Owners' or Managers' default.* 399
If either party fails to meet their obligations under this Agreement, the other party may give notice to the 400
party in default requiring them to remedy it. In the event that the party in default fails to remedy it within a 401
reasonable time to the reasonable satisfaction of the other party, that party shall be entitled to terminate this 402
Agreement with immediate effect by giving notice to the party in default. 403

(b) Notwithstanding Sub-clause 22(a): 404

(i) The Managers shall be entitled to terminate the Agreement with immediate effect by giving notice to the 405
Owners if any monies payable by the Owners and/or the owners of any associated vessel, details of 406
which are listed in Annex "D", shall not have been received in the Managers' nominated account within 407
ten days of receipt by the Owners of the Managers' written request, or if the Vessel is repossessed by 408
the Mortgagee(s). 409

(ii) If the Owners proceed with the employment of or continue to employ the Vessel in the carriage of 410
contraband, blockade running, or in an unlawful trade, or on a voyage which in the reasonable opinion 411
of the Managers is unduly hazardous or improper, the Managers may give notice of the default to the 412
Owners, requiring them to remedy it as soon as practically possible. In the event that the Owners fail to 413
remedy it within a reasonable time to the satisfaction of the Managers, the Managers shall be entitled 414
to terminate the Agreement with immediate effect by notice. 415

(iii) If either party fails to meet their respective obligations under Sub-clause 5(b) (Crew Insurances) and 416
Clause 10 (Insurance Policies), the other party may give notice to the party in default requiring them to 417
remedy it within ten (10) days, failing which the other party may terminate this Agreement with immediate 418
effect by giving notice to the party in default. 419

(c) *Extraordinary Termination* 420
This Agreement shall be deemed to be terminated in the case of the sale of the Vessel or, if the Vessel 421
becomes a total loss or is declared as a constructive or compromised or arranged total loss or is requisitioned 422
or has been declared missing or, if bareboat chartered, unless otherwise agreed, when the bareboat charter 423
comes to an end. 424

(d) For the purpose of Sub-clause 22(c) hereof: 425

(i) the date upon which the Vessel is to be treated as having been sold or otherwise disposed of shall be 426
the date on which the Vessel's owners cease to be the registered owners of the Vessel; 427

(ii) the Vessel shall be deemed to be lost either when it has become an actual total loss or agreement has 428
been reached with the Vessel's underwriters in respect of its constructive total loss or if such agreement 429
with the Vessel's underwriters is not reached it is adjudged by a competent tribunal that a constructive 430
loss of the Vessel has occurred; and 431

(iii) the date upon which the Vessel is to be treated as declared missing shall be ten (10) days after the Vessel 432

Appendix 15

PART II
SHIPMAN 2009
Standard ship management agreement

was last reported or when the Vessel is recorded as missing by the Vessel's underwriters, whichever 433
occurs first. A missing vessel shall be deemed lost in accordance with the provisions of Sub-clause 22(d) 434
(ii). 435

(e) In the event the parties fail to agree the annual budget in accordance with Sub-clause 13(b), or to agree 436
a change of flag in accordance with Sub-clause 9(d)(ii), or to agree to a reduction in the Management Fee in 437
accordance with Sub-clause 12(d), either party may terminate this Agreement by giving the other party not 438
less than one month's notice, the result of which will be the expiry of the Agreement at the end of the current 439
budget period or on expiry of the notice period, whichever is the later. 440

(f) This Agreement shall terminate forthwith in the event of an order being made or resolution passed 441
for the winding up, dissolution, liquidation or bankruptcy of either party (otherwise than for the purpose of 442
reconstruction or amalgamation) or if a receiver or administrator is appointed, or if it suspends payment, 443
ceases to carry on business or makes any special arrangement or composition with its creditors. 444

(g) In the event of the termination of this Agreement for any reason other than default by the Managers the 445
management fee payable to the Managers according to the provisions of Clause 12 (Management Fee and 446
Expenses), shall continue to be payable for a further period of the number of months stated in **Box 19** as 447
from the effective date of termination. If **Box 19** is left blank then ninety (90) days shall apply. 448

(h) In addition, where the Managers provide Crew for the Vessel in accordance with Clause 5(a) (Crew 449
Management): 450

(i)   the Owners shall continue to pay Crew Support Costs during the said further period of the number of 451
       months stated in **Box 19**; and 452

(ii)   the Owners shall pay an equitable proportion of any Severance Costs which may be incurred, not 453
       exceeding the amount stated in **Box 20**. The Managers shall use their reasonable endeavours to minimise 454
       such Severance Costs. 455

(i) On the termination, for whatever reason, of this Agreement, the Managers shall release to the Owners, 456
if so requested, the originals where possible, or otherwise certified copies, of all accounts and all documents 457
specifically relating to the Vessel and its operation. 458

(j) The termination of this Agreement shall be without prejudice to all rights accrued due between the parties 459
prior to the date of termination. 460

23. **BIMCO Dispute Resolution Clause** 461
(a) This Agreement shall be governed by and construed in accordance with English law and any dispute 462
arising out of or in connection with this Agreement shall be referred to arbitration in London in accordance with 463
the Arbitration Act 1996 or any statutory modification or re-enactment thereof save to the extent necessary 464
to give effect to the provisions of this Clause. 465

The arbitration shall be conducted in accordance with the London Maritime Arbitrators Association (LMAA) 466
Terms current at the time when the arbitration proceedings are commenced. 467

The reference shall be to three arbitrators. A party wishing to refer a dispute to arbitration shall appoint its 468
arbitrator and send notice of such appointment in writing to the other party requiring the other party to appoint 469
its own arbitrator within 14 calendar days of that notice and stating that it will appoint its arbitrator as sole 470
arbitrator unless the other party appoints its own arbitrator and gives notice that it has done so within the 471
14 days specified. If the other party does not appoint its own arbitrator and give notice that it has done so 472
within the 14 days specified, the party referring a dispute to arbitration may, without the requirement of any 473
further prior notice to the other party, appoint its arbitrator as sole arbitrator and shall advise the other party 474
accordingly. The award of a sole arbitrator shall be binding on both parties as if he had been appointed by 475
agreement. 476

Nothing herein shall prevent the parties agreeing in writing to vary these provisions to provide for the 477
appointment of a sole arbitrator. 478

In cases where neither the claim nor any counterclaim exceeds the sum of USD50,000 (or such other sum 479
as the parties may agree) the arbitration shall be conducted in accordance with the LMAA Small Claims 480
Procedure current at the time when the arbitration proceedings are commenced. 481

Appendix 15

PART II
SHIPMAN 2009
Standard ship management agreement

(b) This Agreement shall be governed by and construed in accordance with Title 9 of the United States Code   482
and the Maritime Law of the United States and any dispute arising out of or in connection with this Agreement   483
shall be referred to three persons at New York, one to be appointed by each of the parties hereto, and the   484
third by the two so chosen; their decision or that of any two of them shall be final, and for the purposes of   485
enforcing any award, judgment may be entered on an award by any court of competent jurisdiction. The   486
proceedings shall be conducted in accordance with the rules of the Society of Maritime Arbitrators, Inc.   487

In cases where neither the claim nor any counterclaim exceeds the sum of USD50,000 (or such other sum   488
as the parties may agree) the arbitration shall be conducted in accordance with the Shortened Arbitration   489
Procedure of the Society of Maritime Arbitrators, Inc. current at the time when the arbitration proceedings   490
are commenced.   491

(c) This Agreement shall be governed by and construed in accordance with the laws of the place mutually   492
agreed by the parties and any dispute arising out of or in connection with this Agreement shall be referred   493
to arbitration at a mutually agreed place, subject to the procedures applicable there.   494

(d) Notwithstanding Sub-clauses 23(a), 23(b) or 23(c) above, the parties may agree at any time to refer to   495
mediation any difference and/or dispute arising out of or in connection with this Agreement.   496

(i)   In the case of a dispute in respect of which arbitration has been commenced under Sub-clauses 23(a),   497
     23(b) or 23(c) above, the following shall apply: 498

(ii) Either party may at any time and from time to time elect to refer the dispute or part of the dispute to   499
     mediation by service on the other party of a written notice (the "Mediation Notice") calling on the other   500
     party to agree to mediation.   501

(iii) The other party shall thereupon within 14 calendar days of receipt of the Mediation Notice confirm that   502
     they agree to mediation, in which case the parties shall thereafter agree a mediator within a further 14   503
     calendar days, failing which on the application of either party a mediator will be appointed promptly by   504
     the Arbitration Tribunal ("the Tribunal") or such person as the Tribunal may designate for that purpose.   505
     The mediation shall be conducted in such place and in accordance with such procedure and on such   506
     terms as the parties may agree or, in the event of disagreement, as may be set by the mediator.   507

(iv) If the other party does not agree to mediate, that fact may be brought to the attention of the Tribunal   508
     and may be taken into account by the Tribunal when allocating the costs of the arbitration as between   509
     the parties.   510

(v)   The mediation shall not affect the right of either party to seek such relief or take such steps as it considers   511
     necessary to protect its interest.   512

(vi) Either party may advise the Tribunal that they have agreed to mediation. The arbitration procedure shall   513
     continue during the conduct of the mediation but the Tribunal may take the mediation timetable into   514
     account when setting the timetable for steps in the arbitration.   515

(vii) Unless otherwise agreed or specified in the mediation terms, each party shall bear its own costs incurred   516
     in the mediation and the parties shall share equally the mediator's costs and expenses.   517

(viii) The mediation process shall be without prejudice and confidential and no information or documents   518
     disclosed during it shall be revealed to the Tribunal except to the extent that they are disclosable under   519
     the law and procedure governing the arbitration.   520

(Note: The parties should be aware that the mediation process may not necessarily interrupt time limits.)   521

(e) If **Box 21** in Part I is not appropriately filled in, Sub-clause 23(a) of this Clause shall apply.   522

*Note: Sub-clauses 23(a), 23(b) and 23(c) are alternatives; indicate alternative agreed in **Box 21**. Sub-clause*   523
23(d) shall apply in all cases.   524

24. Notices   525
(a) All notices given by either party or their agents to the other party or their agents in accordance with the   526
provisions of this Agreement shall be in writing and shall, unless specifically provided in this Agreement to   527

Appendix 15

PART II
SHIPMAN 2009
Standard ship management agreement

the contrary, be sent to the address for that other party as set out in **Boxes 22** and **23** or as appropriate or to such other address as the other party may designate in writing.	528 529
A notice may be sent by registered or recorded mail, facsimile, electronically or delivered by hand in accordance with this Sub-clause 24(a).	530 531
(b) Any notice given under this Agreement shall take effect on receipt by the other party and shall be deemed to have been received:	532 533
(i) if posted, on the seventh (7th) day after posting;	534

(i)   if posted, on the seventh (7th) day after posting;   534

(ii) if sent by facsimile or electronically, on the day of transmission; and   535

(iii) if delivered by hand, on the day of delivery.   536

And in each case proof of posting, handing in or transmission shall be proof that notice has been given, unless proven to the contrary.   537
538

25. Entire Agreement   539
This Agreement constitutes the entire agreement between the parties and no promise, undertaking,   540
representation, warranty or statement by either party prior to the date stated in **Box 2** shall affect this   541
Agreement. Any modification of this Agreement shall not be of any effect unless in writing signed by or on   542
behalf of the parties.   543

26. Third Party Rights   544
Except to the extent provided in Sub-clauses 17(c) (Indemnity) and 17(d) (Himalaya), no third parties may   545
enforce any term of this Agreement.   546

27. Partial Validity   547
If any provision of this Agreement is or becomes or is held by any arbitrator or other competent body to be   548
illegal, invalid or unenforceable in any respect under any law or jurisdiction, the provision shall be deemed   549
to be amended to the extent necessary to avoid such illegality, invalidity or unenforceability, or, if such   550
amendment is not possible, the provision shall be deemed to be deleted from this Agreement to the extent   551
of such illegality, invalidity or unenforceability, and the remaining provisions shall continue in full force and   552
effect and shall not in any way be affected or impaired thereby.   553

28. Interpretation   554
In this Agreement: 555

(a) *Singular/Plural*   556
The singular includes the plural and vice versa as the context admits or requires.   557

(b) *Headings*   558
The index and headings to the clauses and appendices to this Agreement are for convenience only and shall   559
not affect its construction or interpretation.   560

(c) Day   561
"Day" means a calendar day unless expressly stated to the contrary.   562

Appendix 15

ANNEX "A" (DETAILS OF VESSEL OR VESSELS)
TO THE BIMCO STANDARD SHIP MANAGEMENT AGREEMENT
CODE NAME: SHIPMAN 2009

Appendix 15

ANNEX "B" (DETAILS OF CREW)
TO THE BIMCO STANDARD SHIP MANAGEMENT AGREEMENT
CODE NAME: SHIPMAN 2009

Date of Agreement:

Details of Crew:

Numbers	Rank	Nationality

Appendix 15

ANNEX "C" (BUDGET)
TO THE BIMCO STANDARD SHIP MANAGEMENT AGREEMENT
CODE NAME: SHIPMAN 2009

Date of Agreement:

Managers´ initial budget with effect from the commencement date of this Agreement (see **Box 2**):

Appendix 15

ANNEX "D" (ASSOCIATED VESSELS)
TO THE BIMCO STANDARD SHIP MANAGEMENT AGREEMENT
CODE NAME: SHIPMAN 2009

NOTE: PARTIES SHOULD BE AWARE THAT BY COMPLETING THIS ANNEX "D" THEY WILL BE
SUBJECT TO THE PROVISIONS OF SUB-CLAUSE 22(b)(i) OF THIS AGREEMENT.

Date of Agreement:

Details of Associated Vessels:

Appendix 15

ANNEX "E" (FEE SCHEDULE)
TO THE BIMCO STANDARD SHIP MANAGEMENT AGREEMENT
CODE NAME: SHIPMAN 2009

Appendix 16

Standard Liner and General Agency Agreement

The Federation of National Associations of Ship Brokers and Agents

STANDARD LINER AND GENERAL AGENCY AGREEMENT

Revised and adopted 2001

Approved by BIMCO 2001

It is hereby agreed between:

.... of...(hereinafter referred to as the Principal)

and

.... of...(hereinafter referred to as the Agent)

on the.. day of...20 ....

that:

1.00 The Principal hereby appoints the Agent as its Liner Agent for all its owned and/or chartered vessels including any space or slot charter agreement serving the trade between .... and ....

1.01 This Agreement shall come into effect on.....................and shall continue until...........................

Thereafter it shall continue until terminated by either party giving to the other notice in writing, in which event the Agreement shall terminate upon the expiration of a period of .....months from the date upon which such notice was given.

1.02 The territory in which the Agent shall perform its duties under the Agreement shall be ....

hereinafter referred to as the "Territory".

1.03 This Agreement covers the activities described in section 3 ....

1.04 The Agent undertakes not to accept the representation of other shipping companies nor to engage in NVOCC or such freight forwarding activities in the Territory, which are in direct competition to any of the Principal's transportation activities, without prior written consent, which shall not unreasonably be withheld.

1.05 The Principal undertakes not to appoint any other party in the Agent's Territory for the services defined in this Agreement.

1.06 The established custom of the trade and/or port shall apply and form part of this Agreement.

1.07 In countries where the position of the agent is in any way legally protected or regulated, the Agent shall have the benefit of such protection or regulation.

1.08 All aspects of the Principal's business are to be treated confidentially and all files and records pertaining to this business are the property of the Principal.

2.0 Duties of the Agent

2.01 To represent the Principal in the Territory, using his best endeavours to comply at all times with any reasonable specific instructions which the Principal may give, including the use of Principal's documentation, terms and conditions.

2.02 In consultation with the Principal to recommend and/or appoint on the Principal's behalf and account, Sub-Agents.

2.03 In consultation with the Principal to recommend and/or to appoint on the Principal's behalf and account, Stevedores, Watchmen, Tallymen, Terminal Operators, Hauliers and all kinds of suppliers.

2.04 The Agent will not be responsible for the negligent acts or defaults of the Sub-Agent or Sub-Contractor unless the Agent fails to exercise due care in the appointment and supervision of such Sub-Agent or Sub- Contractor. Notwithstanding the foregoing the Agent shall be responsible for the acts of his subsidiary companies appointed within the context of this Clause.

2.05 The Agent will always strictly observe the shipping laws and regulations of the country and will indemnify the Principal for fines, penalties, expenses or restrictions that may arise due to the failure of the Agent to comply herewith.

Appendix 16

Activities of Agent (Delete those which do not apply)

3.1 Marketing and Sales

3.11 To provide marketing and sales activities in the Territory, in accordance with general guidelines laid down by the Principal, to canvass and book cargo, to publicise the services and to maintain contact with Shippers, Consignees, Forwarding Agents, Port and other Authorities and Trade Organisations.

3.12 To provide statistics and information and to report on cargo bookings and use of space allotments. To announce sailing and/or arrivals, and to quote freight rates and announce freight tariffs and amendments.

3.13 To arrange for public relations work (including advertising, press releases, sailing schedules and general promotional material) in accordance with the budget agreed with the Principal and for his account.

3.14 To attend to conference, consortia and /or alliance matters on behalf of the Principal and for the Principal's account

3.15 To issue on behalf of the Principal Bills of Landing and Manifests, delivery orders, certificates and such other documents.

3.2 Port Agency

3.21 To arrange for berthing of vessels, loading and discharging of the cargo, in accordance with the local custom and conditions.

3.22 To arrange and co-ordinate all activities of the Terminal Operators, Stevedores, Tallymen and all other Contractors, •n the interest of obtaining the best possible operation and despatch of the Principal's vessel.

3.23 To arrange for calling forward, reception and loading of outward cargo and discharge and release of inward cargo and to attend to the transhipment of through cargo.

3.24 To arrange for bunkering, repairs, husbandry, crew changes, passengers, ship's stores, spare parts, technical and nautical assistance and medical assistance.

3.25 To carry out the Principal's requirements concerning claims handling, P & I matters, General Average and/or insurance, and the appointment of Surveyors.

3.26 To attend to all necessary documentation and to attend to consular requirements.

3.27 To arrange for and attend to the clearance of the vessel and to arrange for all other services appertaining to the vessel's movements through the port.

3.28 To report to the Principal the vessel's position and to prepare a statement of facts of the call and/or a port log

3.29 To keep the Principal regularly and timely informed on Port and working conditions likely to affect the despatch of the Principal's vessels.

3.3 Container and Ro/Ro Traffic

Where "equipment" is referred to in the following section it shall comprise container, flat racks, trailers or similar cargo carrying devices, owned, leased or otherwise controlled by the Principal.

3.31 To arrange for the booking of equipment on the vessel.

3.32 To arrange for the stuffing and unstuffing of LCL cargo at the port and to arrange for the provision of inland LCL terminals.

3.33 To provide and administer a proper system, or to comply with the principal's system for the control and registration of equipment. To organise equipment stock within the Territory and make provision for storage, positioning and repositioning of the equipment.

3.34 To comply with Customs requirements and arrange for equipment interchange documents in respect of the movements for which the Agent is responsible and to control the supply and use of locks, seals and labels.

3.35 To make equipment available and to arrange inland haulage.

3.36 To undertake the leasing of equipment into and re-delivery out of the system.

3.37 To operate an adequate equipment damage control system in compliance with the Principal's instructions. To arrange for equipment repairs and maintenance, when and where necessary and to report on the condition of equipment under the Agent's control.

General Agency

3.41 To supervise, activities and co-ordinate all marketing and sales activities of Port, Inland Agents and/or Sub-agents in the Territory, in accordance with general guidelines laid down by the Principal and to use every effort to obtain business from prospective clients and to consolidate the flow of statistics and information.

3.42 To supervise and co-ordinate all activities of Port, Inland Agents and/or Sub-agents as set forth in the agreement, in order to ensure the proper performance of all customary requirements for the best possible operation of the Principal's vessel in the G.A.'s Territory

3.43 In consultation with the Principal to recommend and/or appoint on the Principal's behalf and account Port, Inland Agents, and/or Sub-Agents if required.

3.44 To provide Port, Inland Agents and/or Sub-agents with space allocations in accordance with the Principal's requirements.

3.45 To arrange for an efficient rotation of vessels within the Territory, in compliance with the Principal's instructions and to arrange for the most economical despatch in the ports of its area within the scope of the sailing schedule.

3.46 To liaise with Port Agents and/or Sub-agents if and where required, in the Territory in arranging for such matters as bunkering, repairs, crew changes, ship's stores, spare parts, technical, nautical, medical assistance and consular requirements

3.47 To instruct and supervise Port, Inland Agents and/or Sub-Agents regarding the Principals requirements concerning claims handling. P & I matters and/or insurance, and the appointment of Surveyors. All expenses involved with claims handling other than routine claims are for Principal's account.

3.5   Accounting and Finance

3.5.1 To provide for appropriate records of the Principal's financial position to he maintained in the Agent's books, which shall be available for inspection and to prepare periodic financial statements.

3.52 To check all vouchers received for services rendered and to prepare a proper disbursement account in respect of each voyage or accounting period.

3.53 To advise the Principal of all amendments to port tariffs and other charges as they become known.

3.54 To calculate freight and other charges according to Tariffs supplied by the Principal and exercise every care and diligence in applying all terms and conditions of such Tariffs or other freight agreements. If the Principal organises or employs an organisation for checking freight calculations and documentation the costs for such checking to be entirely for the Principal's account.

3.55 To collect freight and related accounts and remit to the Principal all freights and other monies belonging to the Principal at such periodic intervals as the Principal may require. All bank charges to be for the Principal's account. The Agent shall advise the Principal of the customary credit terms and arrangements. If the Agent is required to grant credit to customers due to commercial reasons, the risk in respect of outstanding collections is for the Principal's account unless the Agent has granted credit without the knowledge and prior consent of the Principal.

3.56 The Agent shall have authority to retain money from the freight collected to cover all past and current disbursements, subject to providing regular cash position statements to the Principal.

3.57 The Agent in carrying out his duties under this Agreement shall not be responsible to the Principal for loss or damage caused by any Banker, Broker or other person, instructed by the Agent in good faith unless the same happens by or through the wilful neglect or default of the Agent. The burden of proving the wilful neglect of the Agent shall be on the Principal.

Principal's Duties

4.01 To provide all documentation, necessary to fulfil the Agent's task together with any stationery specifically required by the Principal.

4.02 To give full and timely information regarding the vessel's schedules, ports of call and line policy insofar as it affects the port and sales agency activities.

4.03 To provide the Agents immediately upon request with all necessary funds to cover advance disbursements unless the Agent shall have sufficient funds from the freights collected.

4.04 The Principal shall at all times indemnify the Agent against all claims, charges, losses, damages and expenses which the Agent may incur in connection with the fulfilment of his duties under this Agreement. Such indemnity shall extend to all acts, matters and things done, suffered or incurred by the Agent during the duration of this Agreement, notwithstanding any termination thereof, provided always, that this indemnity shall not extend to matters arising by reason of the wilful misconduct or negligence of the Agent.

Appendix 16

4.05   Where the Agent provides bonds, guarantees and any other forms of security to Customs or other statutory authorities then the Principal shall indemnify and reimburse the Agent immediately such claims are made, provided they do not arise by reason of the wilful misconduct or the negligence of the Agent.

4.06   If mutually agreed the Principal shall take over the conduct of any dispute which may arise between the Agent and any third party as a result of the performance of the Agent's duties.

5.0   Remuneration

5.01   The Principal agrees to pay the agent and the Agent accepts, as consideration for the services rendered, the commissions and fees set forth on the schedule attached to this Agreement Any fees specified in monetary units in the attached schedule shall be reviewed every 12 months and if necessary adjusted in accordance with such recognised cost of living index as is published in the country of the Agent.

5.02   Should the Principal require the Agent to undertake full processing and settlement of claims, then the Agent is entitled to a separate remuneration as agreed with the Principal and commensurate with the work involved.

5.03   The remuneration specified in the schedule attached is in respect of the ordinary and anticipated duties of the Agent within the scope of this Agreement. Should the Agent be required to perform duties beyond the scope of this Agreement then the terms on which the Agent may agree to perform such duties will be subject to express agreement between the parties. Without prejudice to the generality of the foregoing such duties may include e.g. participating in conference activities on behalf of the Principal, booking fare-paying passengers, sending out general average notices and making collections under average bonds insofar as these duties arc not performed by the average adjuster.

5.04   If the Tariff currency varies in value against the local currency by more than 10% after consideration of any currency adjustment factor existing in the trade the basis for calculation of remuneration shall be adjusted accordingly.

5.05   Any extra expenses occasioned by specific additional requirements of the Principal in the use of computer equipment and systems for the performance of the Agent's duties to the Principal shall be borne by the Principal.

5.06   The Principal is responsible for all additional expenses incurred by the Agent in connecting its computers to any national or local port community system.

6.0   Duration

6.01   This agreement shall remain in force as specified in clause 1.01 of this Agreement. Any notice of termination shall be sent by registered or recorded mail.

6.02   If the Agreement for any reason other than negligence or wilful misconduct of the Agent should by cancelled at an earlier date than on the expiry of the notice given under clause 1.01 hereof, the Principal shall compensate the Agent. The compensation payable by the Principal to the agent shall be determined in accordance with clause 6.04 below.

6.03   If for any reason the Principal withdraws or suspends the service, the Agent may withdraw from this agreement forthwith, without prejudice to its claim for compensation.

6.04   The basis of compensation shall be the monthly average of the commission and fees earned during the previous 12 months or if less than 12 months have passed then a reasonable estimate of the same, multiplied by the number of months from the dale of cancellation until the contract would have been terminated in accordance with clause 1.01 above. Furthermore the gross redundancy payments, which the Agent and/or Sub-Agent(s) is compelled to make to employees made redundant by reason of the withdrawal or suspension of the Principal's service, or termination of this Agreement, shall also be taken into account.

6.05   The Agent shall have a general lien on amounts payable to the Principal in respect of any undisputed sums due and owing to the Agent including but not limited to commissions, disbursements and duties.

7.0   Jurisdiction

7.01   a) This Agreement shall be governed by and construed in accordance with the laws of the country in which the Agent has its principle place of business and any dispute arising out of or in connection with this Agreement shall be referred to arbitration in that country subject to the procedures applicable there.

b) This Agreement shall be governed by and construed in accordance with the laws of...
and any dispute arising out of or in connection with this Agreement shall be referred to arbitration at ....,
subject to the procedures applicable there.

c) Any dispute arising out of this Agreement shall be referred to arbitration at..
subject to the law and procedures applicable there.

(subclauses [a] [b] & [c] are options. If [b] or [c] are not filled in then (a) shall apply.)

Appendix 16

REMUNERATION SCHEDULE BELONGING TO STANDARD LINER AND GENERAL AGENCY AGREEMENT

Between .... and ....date..........................
　　　　　(As Principal)　　　　　　　　　　(As Agent)

The Agent is entitled to the following remuneration based on all total freight earnings (including any surcharges,(eg BAF, CAF) handling charges (eg THC) and freight additionals including inland transport which may be agreed) of the Principal's liner service to and from the Territory to be paid in Agent's local currency. The total remuneration per call shall not in any case be lower than the local fee applicable

I　A.　Where the Agent provides all the services enumerated in this Agreement the Commission shall be:

Services outward .... %　[Min .... per cont or tonne/cbm]　　　} MIN

　　　inward .... %　[Min .... per cont or tonne/cbm]　} LUMP SUM
　　　　　　　　　　　　　　　　　　　　　　　　　　}
　2.　...................... % for cargo when only booking is involved.　[Min ... per cont]　} PER
　　　　　　　　　　　　　　　　　　　　　　　　　　　　　}
　3.　....................... % for cargo when only handling is involved.　[Min ... per cont]　} CALL ....

("only handling" in the remuneration schedule is so defined that the duties of an Agent are to call forward and otherwise arrange for the cargo to be loaded on board, where the specific booking has been made elsewhere and acknowledged as such by the shipper as nominated for the Principal's service.

　4.　In respect of movements of cargo outside the Agent's Territory .... % of the gross total freight is payable in cases where only collection of freight is involved.

　5.　An additional fee for containers and/or units entering or leaving the inventory control system of the Agent a fee of .... per unit.

II　A.　................................. % for cargo loaded on board in bulk.　[Min ..... per tonne/cbm]

　2.　................................. % for cargo discharged in bulk.　[Min ...... per tonne/cbm]

III　Where the Agent provides only the services as non-port agent the remuneration shall be:

When actually booked/originating from this area:

　1.　Services outward .... %　[Min........... per cont or tonne/cbm)

　　　inward .... %　[Min .... per cont or tonne/cbm]

　2.　An additional fee for containers and/or units entering or leaving the inventory control system of the Agent a fee of .... per unit.

IV　Where the Agent provides only the services as non-port agent the remuneration shall be:

　1.　.......................... % for cargo loaded on board in bulk.　[Min .... per tonne / cbm]

　2.　.......................... % for cargo discharged in bulk.　[Min ...... per tonne / cbm]

5.　Clearance and ship's husbandry fee shall be as agreed.

6.　A Commission of .... % shall be paid on all ancillary charges collected by the Agent on behalf of the Principal such as Depot Charges, Container Demurrage, Container Damage etc.

7.　Communications: The Principal will either pay actual communication expenses on a cost plus basis or pay a lumpsum monthly on an average cost plus basis, to be review able.

8.　Travelling expenses: When the Agent is requested by the Principal to undertake journeys of any significant distance and/or duration, all travel expenses including accommodation and other expenses will be for the Principal's account.

9.　Documentary and Administrative Charges: Such charges to be levied as appropriate by the Agent to cargo interests and to remain with the Agent even if related to the trade of the principal.

10.　In case of Transhipment Cargo, a transhipment fee of .... per cont / tonne /cbm is charged by the Agent.

....　　　　　　......................................
PRINCIPAL　　　　　　　　　　　　　AGENT

Appendix 17

Scale of Agency Charges for Dry Cargo Vessels

THE INSTITUTE OF CHARTERED SHIPBROKERS
85, Gracechurch Street, London EC3V 0AA
Tel: (020) 7623 1111; Fax: (020) 7623 8118; E-mail: federation@ics.org.uk
Founded 1911: Incorporated by Royal Charter 21 January 1920,
Supplemental Royal Charter 25 July 1984

SCALE OF AGENCY CHARGES FOR DRY CARGO VESSELS

Effective 1 January 2005

This scale applies only where agency services are rendered in respect of a vessel registered outside the EU and responsibility for payment rests with a Principal who is outside the EU.

For the purpose of the scale the following definitions apply:

SCALE OF AGENCY CHARGES	**means**	the fees applicable for services rendered to dry cargo vessels as from 1 January 2005.
OVERSEAS	**means**	vessels trading from or to the United Kingdom (including Northern Ireland) and all ports not otherwise specified.
COASTING	**means**	vessels trading between ports within the United Kingdom (including Northern Ireland).
DEADWEIGHT ALL TOLD (DWAT)	**means**	the weight in metric tonnes of cargo, stores and fuel carried by the vessel when loaded to her maximum summer load line as published in Lloyd's Register of Shipping or by vessel's classification society. Where the vessel has dual tonnages, the higher tonnage to apply.
APPROPRIATE FEE	**means**	the fee calculated under Section I modified by Section II, if applicable.

This Edition of the Scale of Agency Charges supersedes all previous editions and amendments thereto.

Institute of Chartered Shipbrokers Dry Cargo Scale of Agency Fees 2005

Appendix 17

DWAT	OVERSEAS 1A	COASTING IB
	£	£
UP TO 400	306	245
401 - 500	353	283
501 - 600	402	322
601 - 700	457	363
701 - 800	503	402
801 - 900	549	440
901 - 1000	605	483
1001- 1100	651	520
1101 - 1200	708	567
1201 - 1300	755	604
1301 - 1400	803	643
1401 - 1500	856	684
1501 - 1600	883	707
1601 - 1700	917	733
1701 - 1800	952	761
1801 - 1900	977	783
1901 - 2000	1012	811
2001 - 2200	1072	858
2201 - 2400	1134	907
2401 - 2600	1202	961
2601 - 2800	1263	1010
2801 - 3000	1324	1060
3001 - 3200	1358	1087
3201 - 3400	1398	1119
3401 - 3600	1432	1145
3601 - 3800	1474	1178
3801 - 4000	1508	1206
4001 - 4500	1568	1255
4501 - 5000	1630	1305
5001 - 5500	1696	1357
5501 - 6000	1766	1413
6001 - 6500	1826	1460
6501 - 7000	1887	1510
7001 - 8000	1982	1586
8001 - 9000	2106	1685
9001 - 10000	2273	1819
10001 - 12500	2450	1960
12501 - 15000	2619	2096
15001 - 17500	2796	2237
17501 - 20000	2965	2373
20001 - 22500	3142	2513
22501 - 25000	3319	2655
25001 - 27500	3488	2791
27501 - 30000	3665	2931
30001 - 40000	3828	3062
40001 - 50000	3941	3154
50001 AND OVER	4099	3279

Appendix 17

SECTION II
SUPPLEMENTAL AND MODIFIED FEES

A.   SPECIAL CARGO SUPPLEMENTS

   i)   Cargoes wholly or partly bagged, baled, banded, packaged, palletised, containerised or boxed; forest or steel products.   SECTION I plus 12.5%

   ii)   Mixed cargo, whether bulk, bagged, baled, banded, packaged, palletised, containerised or boxed; vehicles whether alone or with cased vehicles and/or spare parts.   SECTION I plus 25%

   iii)   Perishable vegetables and fruit; Refrigerated cargo.   SECTION I plus 50%

   iv)   Hazardous cargo (where extraordinary services are required).   SECTION I plus 100%

   v)   Ro-Ro Vehicle carriers.   SECTION I plus 150%

B.   MARITIME STATISTICS

   Where expenses are incurred in the collection of Maritime Statistics these will be passed on and a fee may be levied for the production of these statistics.

C.   EXTENDED PORT TIME

   i)   For ships in port and/or waiting at anchorage over 10 days; for each day or part thereof over 10 days.   5% of SECTION I

   ii)   Vessels detained in port once cargo operations have completed, for each day or part thereof   10% of SECTION I

D.   SHIP REQUIRED TO BE ENTERED WITH CUSTOMS INWARDS AND/OR CUSTOMS CLEARED OUTWARDS OUTSIDE NORMAL CUSTOMS HOURS, INCLUDING STATUTORY CUSTOMS BOARDING PROCEDURES   15% of SECTION IA (Maximum £ 372)

E   CALLING ONLY FOR BUNKERS AND/OR ORDERS AND/OR SHELTERING   50% of SECTION IA

F   REPAIRING AND/OR DRYDOCKING   75% of SECTION IA (Maximum fee £ 588)

   i)   For each week or part thereof, up to 8 weeks

   ii)   After 8 weeks   Subject to mutual agreement

G.   DELIVERY OR REDELIVERY OF TIME-CHARTERED SHIPS

   i)   Where an Agent earns also a loading and/or discharging and/or repairing fee from the same Principal.   20% of SECTION IA

   ii)   If for a different Principal or as an isolated operation.   50% of SECTION IA   Subject to mutual agreement

H.   ATTENDING DELIVERY OR NEWLY BUILT OR SECOND-HAND SHIPS OR LAID UP SHIPS

   i)   For each week or part thereof, up to 4 weeks.

   ii)   Thereafter for each week or part thereof.

   iii)   Attending laid-up ships.

I.   INWARD CUSTOMS REPORT OR OUTWARD CLEARANCE IN BALLAST OR CARGO R.O.B.* FROM/TO FOREIGN.   15% of SECTION IA

J.   APPOINTMENT AS SUPERVISORY AGENT.   50% of the appropriate fee

K.   OFFSHORE SUPPORT/SUPPLY/STANDBY VESSELS, TUGS. DUMB BARGES OR SIMILAR CRAFT OR ANY LIKE SERVICE VESSELS

   i)   For first 7 days, per day   £ 189

   ii)   Thereafter, for each day   £ 107

   Days spent solely awaiting orders not to count.

L.   GEOPHYSICAL SURVEY VESSELS. SUB-SEA SUPPORT VESSELS OR SIMILAR

   i)   For the first 7 days, per day Thereafter, for each day   £ 469

   ii)   Thereafter for each day   £ 234

Appendix 17

M. CREW ATTENDANCE AND OTHER
  i) Crew or persons missing/deserting ship or hospitalized
and requiring attention after vessel's departure.
Stowaways, refugees and illegal immigrants. £95 per person per week
  ii) Supervising crew or persons arriving/departing rail
stations or air terminals (in addition to (i), if applicable). £53 per person per week

N. EXTRA SHIPPERS OR RECEIVERS
For each one over 3. £38

O. ADDITIONAL SERVICES
Where an Agent is* called upon to give a Customs Bond on behalf of his Principal, and/or attends to the distribution and/or collection of Average Bonds and/or Valuations in cases of General Average and/or is involved in processing cargo claims, a charge may be made commensurate with the work involved.

P. AGENTS ANCILLARY EXPENSES
  (i) **The Scale Fee does not include agents out of office attendance (except as charged under Section C above); nor does it cover agents out of pocket expenses such as the cost of communications, car expenses, bank charges (including charges levied for cash advanced to Master) and other petties as incurred, together with statutory requirements for cargo and crew attendance, all of which are recoverable in addition to the agency fee.**

  (ii) The Owners or Disponents are to place the Agent in funds, in advance, to meet the ship's estimated total port disbursements, through freight collected by the Agent and/or by direct remittance if freight collected is insufficient. Where the Owners or Disponents are in default of such immediate advance payment they shall, without prejudice to the Agents' rights to immediate payment in advance, pay in addition a disbursement commission of 5% on any amount not covered by advance funds. One month after presentation of Accounts an additional charge of 2.5% compound interest per month or part of a month is payable.

Q. CANCELLATION FEE
Where an agent has spent time and incurred costs in
anticipation of vessel's arrival, subsequently diverted. 25% of SECTION IA

Appendix 18

Outline World Map

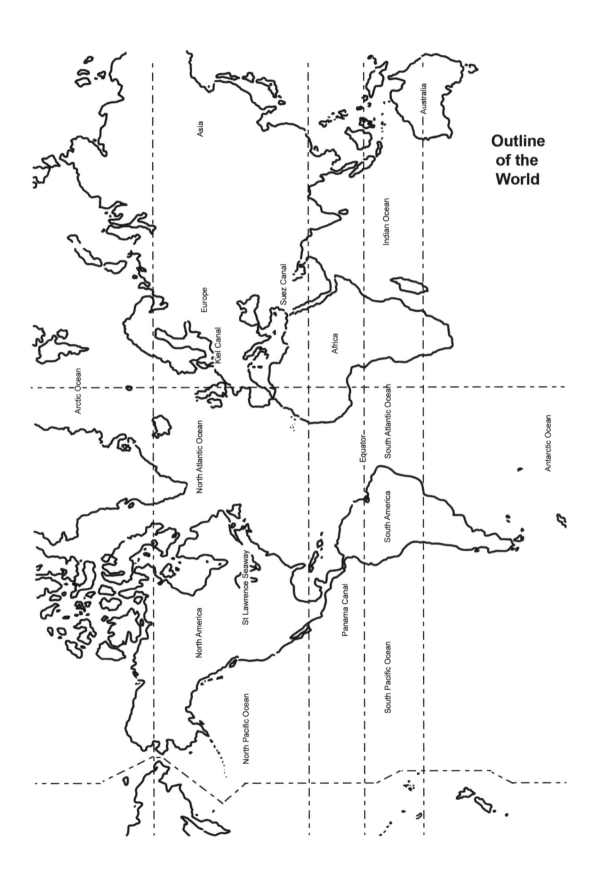

Outline
of the
World

Asia

Australia

Indian Ocean

Europe

Suez Canal

Kiel Canal

Africa

Arctic Ocean

North Atlantic Ocean

South Atlantic Ocean

Equator

Antarctic Ocean

St Lawrence Seaway

South America

North America

Panama Canal

North Pacific Ocean

South Pacific Ocean

Time Zones

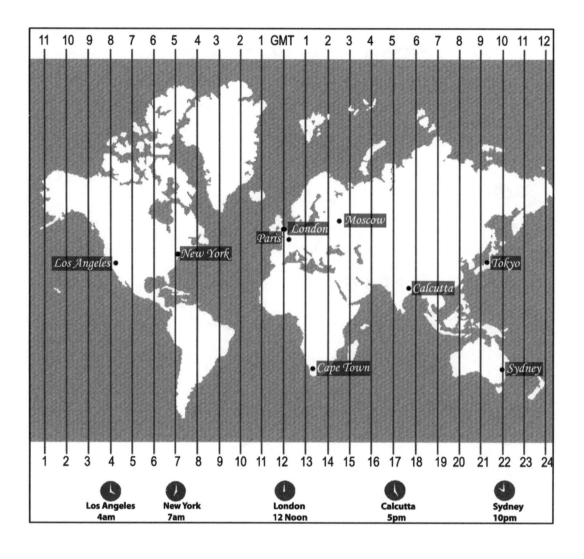

Appendix 20

Beaufort Scale Wind Force Conversions

Force	Type	Sea Conditions	Knots	Km/Hr	m/sec	mph
0	Calm	Sea like a mirror	Less than 1	Less than 1	Less than 1	Less than 1
1	Very light	Ripples with appearance of scales, no foam crests	1 - 3	1 - 5	1 - 2	1 - 3
2	Light breeze	Wavelets, small but pronounced. Crests with glassy appearance, but do not break.	4 - 6	6 - 11	2 -	4 - 7
3	Gentle breeze	Large wavelets, crests begin to break. Glassy looking foam, occasional white horses.	7 - 10	12 - 19	3 - 5	8 - 12
4	Moderate breeze	Small waves becoming longer, frequent white horses.	11 - 16	20 - 29	6 - 8	13 - 18
5	Fresh breeze	Moderate waves of pronounced long form. Many white horses, some spray.	17 - 21	30 - 39	9 - 11	19 - 24
6	Strong breeze	Some large waves, extensive white foam crests, some spray.	22 - 27	40 - 50	12 - 14	25 - 31
7	Near gale	Sea heaped up, white foam from breaking waves blowing in streaks with the wind.	28 - 33	51 - 61	14 - 17	32 - 38
8	Gale	Moderately high and long waves. Crests break into spin drift, blowing foam in well marked streaks.	34 - 40	62 - 74	17 - 21	39 - 46
9	Strong gale	High waves, dense foam streaks in wind, wave crests topple, tumble and roll over. Spray reduces visibility.	41 - 47	75 - 87	21 - 24	47 - 54
10	Storm	Very high waves with long overhanging crests. Dense blowing foam, sea surface appears white. Heavy tumbling of sea, shock-like, poor visibility.	48 - 55	88 - 101	24 - 28	55 - 63
11	Violent storm	Exceptionally high waves, sometimes concealing small and medium sized ships. Sea completely covered with long white patches of foam. Edges of wave crests blown into froth. Poor visibility.	56 - 63	102 - 117	28 - 3	64 - 73
12	Hurricane	Air filled with foam and spray, sea white with driving spray, poor visibility.	> 64	> 119	> 33	> 74

Ice Clause

BIMCO Special Ice Clause 1947 (Code Name: "Nordice")

I. Should during the time from the fixture of the contract until the Vessel leaves the loading port risk appear of the voyage - including the voyage to the loading port or ports - becoming impossible to perform without damage to the Vessel or substantial delay, or should such risk substantially increase, both the Carrier and the Charterers may cancel the contract without liability in damages.

If the contract is cancelled after the commencement of the loading, the cargo shall be discharged again and be received as fast as the Vessel can deliver. All discharging expenses above usual average discharging expenses for the Carrier's account under this contract, if any, shall be paid by the Charterers.

Should risk of freezing in arise at the loading port the Vessel may leave the port with such cargo as is onboard. The Carrier shall then have the option of completing from and to any port or ports for his own account unless the Charterers choose to pay deadweight.

II. Should such risk as mentioned in paragraph I exist or arise during the time of the voyage to the discharging port the Charterers shall upon request nominate to the Master an immediately accessible safe port for discharging which does not necessitate a voyage substantially longer than the one agreed upon under this contract.

Provided the Master has not received such nomination within 48 hours after Charterers' receipt of the request he may himself choose a discharging port, in the same country if possible.

III. Should risk arise of the Vessel being frozen in at the discharging port or ports, or of the Vessel being prevented by ice from getting to or out through the only fairway leading to open water, the Vessel may leave the port with such cargo as is onboard. With regard to the choice of discharging port for the cargo left onboard the stipulations in paragraph II shall apply.

IV. The Vessel is entitled to damages at the rate of demurrage entered in the contract of affreightment for any detention by reasons of ice. This shall apply even when the Vessel discharges her cargo at the loading port or if no accessible substitute discharging port is available and when the Vessel is frozen in. In case the Vessel becomes frozen in at the port where the Vessel is discharging but before the discharging is completed the loss of time shall be reckoned from the expiration of the discharging time until the Vessel shall be able to leave the port unhindered by ice.

Any loss of time awaiting the nomination of a substitute discharging port shall not be reckoned until 12 hours after Charterers' receipt of the request.

V. In case of alteration of destination the freight shall be adjusted according to the proportion between the voyage agreed upon and the distance performed. Regard shall also be taken to expenses being increased or saved.

VI. The Carrier shall have a lien on the cargo for all freight, demurrage, damages for detention and expenses due to him under this ice clause.

VII. The Vessel shall not be obliged to force ice or to follow icebreakers.

VIII. Anything done or not done by the Carrier in accordance with this clause shall be deemed to be within this contract.

St. Lawrence Seaway

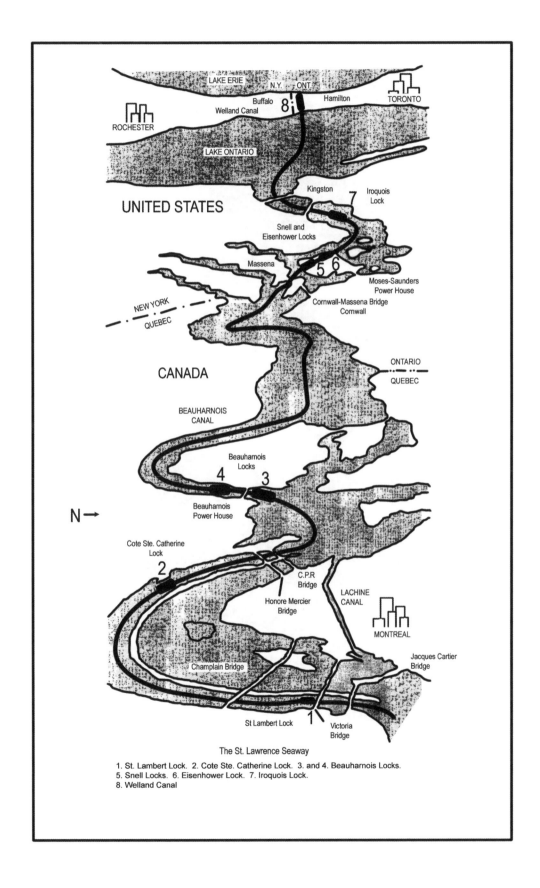

The St. Lawrence Seaway

1. St. Lambert Lock. 2. Cote Ste. Catherine Lock. 3. and 4. Beauharnois Locks.
5. Snell Locks. 6. Eisenhower Lock. 7. Iroquois Lock.
8. Welland Canal

Kiel Canal

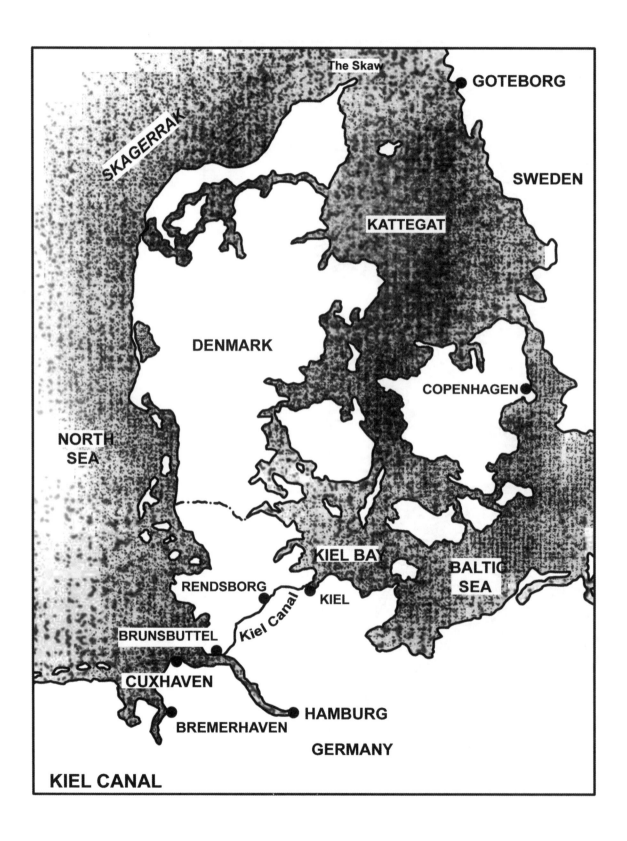

Suez Canal

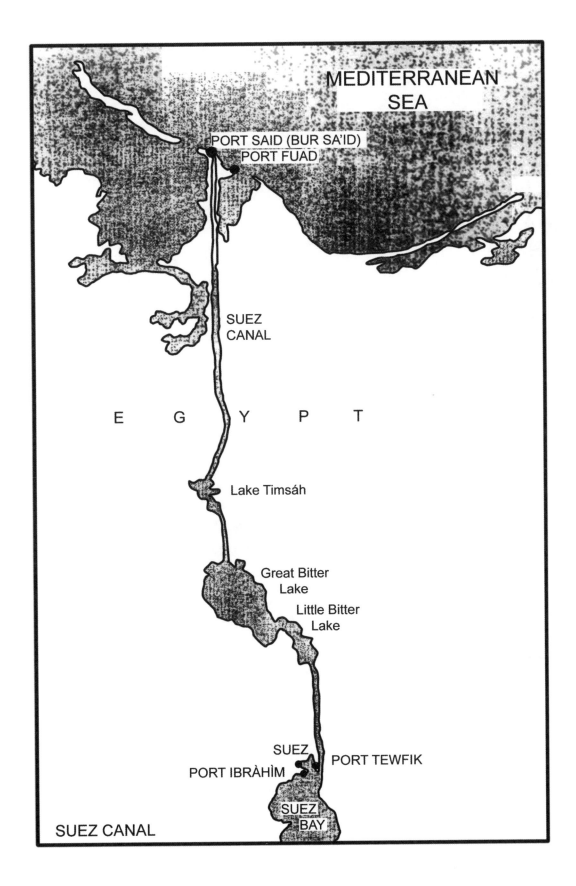

Panama Canal

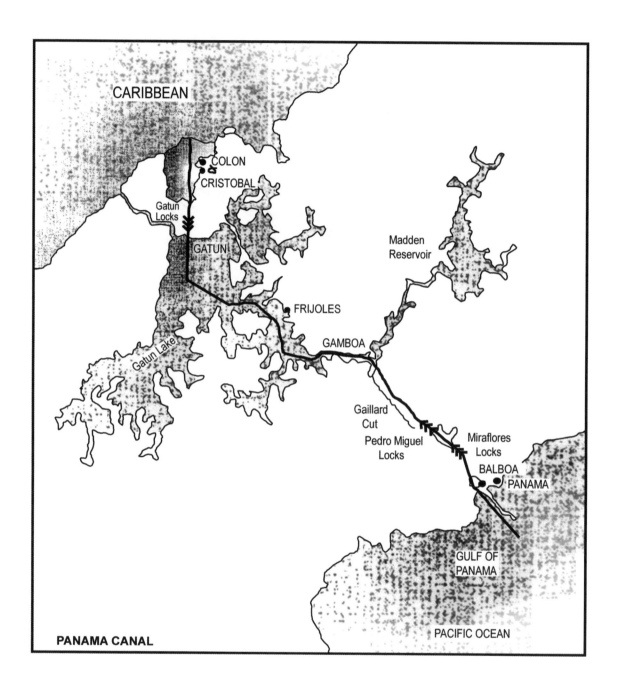

Appendix 26

Chartering and fixture Report

COMPANIES&MARKETS

End in sight for Oz mineral prices?

AUSTRALIA'S major commodity forecaster has dismissed suggestions that China's surging economic growth will continue to underpin high prices for iron ore and coal. The Australian Bureau of Agriculture and Resource Economics (Abare), in its latest commodity outlook, does predict that the Australian commodity export earnings will reach a record A$116Bn ($90.2Bn) for the 2005-6 financial year. But it also predicts that prices will soon start falling.

The report finds that increases in value of minerals and energy exports, to a record $66Bn, are largely caused by higher volumes and prices for metallurgical coal and thermal coal and iron ore. The total value of minerals and energy exports will increase during this year by 23%, it predicts, but prices for most minerals and energy will fall over the next six months. The reason is assumed weaker growth in global industrial activity, reduced Chinese demand for commodities and increases in world supply.

"Part of this forecast slowdown in China's

China Steel Express loads iron ore at Port Hedland, Australia: but will prices soon fall?

Photo: Southern Cross Maritime

demand for raw materials reflects lower growth in the demand for minerals and energy-intensive manufactured products in China's key export

markets," the report says. It dismisses suggestions by some market commentators that commodity prices are in a 'super-cycle', arguing that China's

Dry Fixtures

CARGO	VESSEL	FROM	TO	TONNES	DATE	RATE	CHART.	TERMS
Coal	Cape Kassos,04	Richards Bay	Rotterdam	150000-10%	Jul 5/20	10.00	Cargill	FIO;ScLd/25000tShinc
Coal	Ocean Cosmos,00	Richards Bay	Rotterdam	150000-10%	Jun 24/25	10.00	SwissMarin	PtC;FIO;ScLd/25OO0tShinc
Coal	Ingenious, 99	Richards Bay	Rotterdam	150000-10%	Jul 15/30	10.75	Cargill	FIO;ScLd/25000tShinc
Coal	Steamers, (Cosco)	Richards Bay	Tarragona	150000-10%Ea	2006/2007	11.50	Carboex	FI0;ScLd/24000tShex;7-9Cargoes
Hvy Grain	MassGlory,93	US Gulf	Egypt	65000-5%	Jun 25/27	27.00	ACTI	FIO;10000t/6000t
Wheat&Sorghums	Cynthia Fagan, 81	US Gulf	Mombasa & DarEsSalaam	3960 & 5930	Jul 1/10	210.36	WorldVisio	PtQBerthTerms
Iron Ore	Eternal Bright,81	Brazil	China	130000-10%	Jul 1/10	17.60	Cometals	FIO;ScLd/25000t
Iron Ore	Kerkis,82	Tubarao	Qingdao	170000-10%	Jul 10/20	19.00	Transfield	PtC;FIO;ScLd/25000t
Iron Ore	Steamer	Nouadhibou	Ghent	70000-10%	Jul 10/20	8.25	Sidmar	FI0;4Days
Iron Ore	Steamer, (NYK)	Cape Lambert	Ymuiden	150000-10%	Jul 10/17	11.25	Corus	FI0;6Days
Scrap	Fareast Sunny, 89	ECUS	Marmagoa	35000-5%	Jul 1/5	54.50	HugoNeu	FIO;10000t/3000t

Timecharter

CONSUMPTION	VESSEL	FROM	TO	TONNES	DATE	RATE	CHART.	TERMS
14kt/30t	Edfu,97	DelSkaw	Redel Portbury	71752dwt	Jul 5/10	22500 Day	Flame	TripOutviaVentspils
14kt/35t	Samjohn Liberty, 98	Del US Gulf	Redel Egyptian Med	74761 dwt	Jul 1/5	24000 Day	Cargill	TripOut+S450000Bonus
14.2kt/28.1t	KonkarGeorgios,97	Del Surabaya	RedelJapanviaIndo	46670dwt	Jul 7/15	21500 Day	GlobalBulk	Tripout
13.8kt/3l.8t	WadiAlArish,94	Del Kosichang	Redel Japan	64214dwt	Jul 1/3	11000 Day	Norden	PtHedlandRd
14.5kt/35.5t	IranKermanshah,01	Del Hong Kong	RedelTaiwan	75249dwt	Jul 1/5	13000 Day	Daebo	IndonesiaRd
13.7kt/49t	Hebei Angel, 93	Del Rizhao	Redel China	165133dwt	Jul 5/10	23000 Day	BHP-Billit	WAusRd
14.5kt/58t	Alpha Era, 00	DelBeilun	Redel China	170387dwt	Jul 5/10	27500 Day	BHP-Billit	WAusRd
14kt/31.5t	Captain Diamantis,00	DelGijon	Redel Fos	74757dwt	Jul 1/3	22500 Day	D'Amico	PrtoBolivarRd
14.3kt/32t	ArmiaKrajowa,91	Del So Korea	Redel Singapore/Japan	73505dwt	Jul 2/3	13500 Day	PanOcean	3020000GmBl;NoPacRd;DC
14.5kt/55t	Sa Fortius, 01	Del Japan	Redel Fos	172509dwt	Jul 15/20	16000 Day	SKShipp	TripOutviaAus&SoAfrica
14kt/31.5t	Christina Iv,00	Del Cape Passero	Redel FEviaECSoAm	72493dwt	Jun 24/26	25000 Day	Dreyfus	Tripout
14kt/52t	BulkAustralia,03	DelCapePassero	Redel FEviaBrazil	170578dwt	Jul 5/7	45000 Day	PanOcean	Tripout
13 5kt/28t	ClipperGem,90	DelJorfLasfar	Redel FEviaECSoAm	65619dwt	Jun 21/22	25000 Day	Dreyfus	2897000GmBl;Tripout
14kt/31.5t	HanjinNew0rleans,94	DelPtKelang	Redel MedviaRichardsBay	70337dwt	Jun 23/24	12500 Day	Daeyang	Tripout
14kt/40t	Stefania,81	DelTaiwan	Redel Skaw/Passero	61636dwt	Jun 29/30	9000 Day	Bunge	2640000GrnBl;TripOut

Appendix 26

Wet Fixtures

CARGO	VESSEL	FROM	TO	TONNES	DATE	RATE	CHART.	TERMS
Oil Dirty	Angelica Schulte, 05	WCUS	Far East	80000	Jul 1	1200000	CNR	PtC;Lump Sum
Oil Dirty	HellespTrader,96	St Lucia	Wilhelmshaven	130000	Jul 2	W75	PDVMarine	
Oil Dirty	SKSTyne,96	Trinidad	US Gulf	70000	Jul1	W161.25	ExxonMobil	Part cargo
Oil Dirty	Elisabeth Maersk, 99	Hound Point	US Gulf	280000	Jul 6	W67	Koch	Part cargo
Oil Dirty	Bravery, 94	Tallinn	USAtlanticUSGulf	80000	Jul 6	W165	Vital	Part cargo
Oil Dirty	Seatriumph/Racer02	Novorossiysk	UK/Continent Med	135000	Jul 8	W150	Lukoil	Part cargo
Oil Dirty	Minerva Eieonora, 04	Black Sea	Mediterranean	80000	Jun29	W130	Alpine	Part cargo
Oil Dirty	CapeAncona,98	Libya	Wilhelmshaven	80000	Jun29	W145	Dreyfus	Part cargo
Oil Dirty	Erviken,04	Arzew	Philadelphia	130000	Jul 14	W110	Sun	
Oil Dirty	Titan Glory, 00	Arzew	US Gulf	265000	Jul 20	W65	Valero	
Oil Dirty	African Ruby,94	W Africa	US Atlantic	130000	Jul 13	W132	Sun	
Oil Dirty	Bourgogne,96	WAfrica	Indonesia	260000	Jul 20	W65	Vital	
Oil Dirty	Arlene,03	MEGulf	US Gulf	130000	Jul 20	W100	Chevron	
Oil Dirty	Loul'watQatar,90	RasTanura	Chittagong	80000	JullO	W89	BSC	
Oil Dirty	Titan Neptune,88	MEGulf	Japan op Singapore	257500	Jul 18	W52opW55	ExxonMobil	
Oil Dirty	Front Lillo,91	Bushire	Far East	130000	Jul 11	W95	Arcadia	
Oil Dirty	Hebei Ambition, 90	Kharg Island	China	260000	Jul 13	W50	Zhenrong	
Oil Dirty	PoseidonM,95	Dumai	Taiwan	80000	Jul 4	465000	CPC	Lump Sum
Oil Clean	HansScholl,04	US Gulf	EC Mexico	30000	Jun 28	270000	PMI	Lump Sum
Oil Clean	AlamBitara,99	USGulf	UK/Continent	38000	Jun 29	W150	BP	
Oil Clean	Lion, 85	Caribbeans	Continent	38000	Jun 29	W150	CNR	
Oil Clean	Rosetta,03	UK/Continent	US Atlantic	37000	Jul 5	W265	CSSA	Part cargo
Oil Clean	Smooth Hound, 89	AntRottAmsterdam	Mediterranean	70000	Jun 25	W125	Shell	
Oil Clean	Seaexplorer,76	Black Sea	Mediterranean	30000	Jul 1	W290	Petraco	Part cargo
Oil Clean	ElkaHercules,02	Mediterranean	US Atlantic	37000	Jul 5	W270	Shell	
Oil Clean	Moming Glory Vii,99	MEGulf	Japan	55000	Jul 12	W179	SKShipp	Part cargo
Oil Clean	Dynamic Express, 93	Singapore	Japan	30000	Jul 14	W190	CNR	Part cargo
OilClean	DaQing453,02	NingBo	Ulsan	30000	Jul 7	300000	SKShipp	PtC;tump Sum

Source: Maritime Research Inc

Group Profit and Loss Account

For the year ended 31st March XXXX

	This Yr £M	Last Yr £M
Turnover	2920.2	1981.7
Net Operating Costs	(2620.9)	(1791.1)
	299.3	190.6
Share of pre-tax profits of Associated Companies	28.3	21.1
Operating Profit	327.6	211.7
Interest Payable less interest receivable	(45.6)	(33.2)
Profit on ordinary activities before Profit-share and taxation	282.0	178.5
Employee Profit-share	(7.3)	(4.4)
Profit on ordinary activities before taxation	274.7	174.1
Taxation on profit on ordinary activities	(79.5)	(49.4)
Profit on ordinary activities after taxation	195.2	124.7
Minority interests	(8.8)	(2.5)
Extraordinary and Capital Items	25.3	29.8
Profit for the financial year attributable to shareholders	211.7	152.0
Dividends	(91.8)	(70.3)
Profit transferred to other reserves	(41.1)	(30.2)
Profit for the year retained in this account	78.8	51.5
Dividends per £ of deferred stock	22.0p	19.0p
Earnings per £ of deferred stock	47.1p	41.7p

Balance Sheet

As at 31 st March XXXX

	This Yr £M	Last Yr £M
ASSETS EMPLOYED		
Fixed Assets		
Tangible Assets		
Ships	645.2	435.7
Properties	1068.7	855.9
Other fixed assets	252.4	118.8
Interest in leased assets	33.9	34.7
	168.5	139.6
Investments	2168.7	1584.7
Current Assets		
Stocks	309.9	226.6
Debtors	573.9	437.3
Investments	8.5	11.9
Cash at bank and in hand	57.0	54.8
	949.3	730.6
	3,118.0	2,515.3
Financed by		
CAPITAL AND RESERVES		
Called up share capital	545.0	376.7
Share premium	30.9	10.4
Revaluation reserve	232.7	142.7
Other reserves	373.1	357.6
Profit and Loss Account	284.7	225.3
Stockholders' Funds	1,446.4	1,112.7
Minority interests	32.4	34.5
Provsions for liabilities and charges	77.4	55.6
Loans	610.0	363.4
Creditors	931.8	749.1
	1,651.6	1,202.6
	3,118.0	2,315.3

The Hague Rules as Amended by the Brussels Protocol 1968

Commonly referred to as

The Hague-Visby Rules

Article I

In these Rules the following words are employed, with the meanings set out below:

(a) 'Carrier' includes the owner or the charterer who enters into a contract of carriage with a shipper.

(b) 'Contract of carriage' applies only to contracts of carriage covered by a bill of lading or any similar document of title, in so far as such document relates to the carriage of goods by sea, including any bill of lading or any similar document as aforesaid issued under or pursuant to a charter party from the moment at which such bill of lading or similar document of title regulates the relations between a carrier and a holder of the same.

(c) 'Goods' includes goods, wares, merchandise, and articles of every kind whatsoever except live animals and cargo which by the contract of carriage is stated as being carried on deck and is so carried.

(d) 'Ship' means any vessel used for the carriage of goods by sea.

(e) 'Carriage of goods' covers the period from the time when the goods are loaded on to the time they are discharged from the ship.

Article II

Subject to the provisions of Article VI, under every contract of carriage of goods by sea the carrier, in relation to the loading, handling, stowage, carriage, custody, care and discharge of such goods, shall be subject to the responsibilities and liabilities and entitled to the rights and immunities hereinafter set forth.

Article III

1. The carrier shall be bound before and at the beginning of the voyage to exercise due diligence to:

   (a) Make the ship seaworthy;

   (b) Properly man, equip and supply the ship;

   (c) Make the holds, refrigerating and cool chambers, and all other parts of the ship in which goods are carried, fit and safe for their reception, carriage and preservation.

2. Subject to the provisions of Article IV, the carrier shall properly and carefully load, handle, stow, carry, keep, care for, and discharge the goods carried.

3. After receiving the goods into his charge the carrier or the master or agent of the carrier shall, on demand of the shipper, issue to the shipper a bill of lading showing among other things:

   (a) The leading marks necessary for identification of the goods as the same are furnished in writing by the shipper before the loading of such goods starts, provided such marks are stamped or otherwise shown clearly upon the goods if uncovered, or on the cases or coverings in which such goods are contained, in such a manner as should ordinarily remain legible until the end of the voyage.

(b) Either the number of packages or pieces, or the quantity, or weight, as the case may be, as furnished in writing by the shipper.

(c) The apparent order and condition of the goods.

Provided that no carrier, master or agent of the carrier shall be bound to state or show in the bill of lading any marks, number, quantity or weight which he has reasonable ground for suspecting not accurately to represent the goods actually received, or which he has had no reasonable means of checking.

4. Such a bill of lading shall be prima facie evidence of the receipt by the carrier of the goods as therein described in accordance with paragraph 3 (a), (b) and (c). However, proof to the contrary shall not be admissible when the bill of lading has been transferred to a third party acting in good faith.

5. The shipped shall be deemed to have guaranteed to the carrier the accuracy at the time of shipment of the marks, number, quantity and weight, as furnished by him, and the shipper shall indemnify the carrier against all loss, damages and expenses arising or resulting from inaccuracies in such particulars. The right of the carrier to such indemnity shall on no way limit his responsibility and liability under the contract of carriage to any person other than the shipper.

6. Unless notice of loss or damage and the general nature of such loss or damage be given in writing to the carrier or his agent at the port of discharge before or at the time of the removal of the goods into the custody of the person entitled to delivery thereof under the contract of carriage, or, if the loss or damage be not apparent, within three days, such removal shall be prima facie evidence of the delivery by the carrier of the goods as described in the bill of lading.

The notice in writing need not be given if the state of the goods has, at the time of their receipt, been the subject of joint survey or inspection.

Subject to paragraph 6 bis the carrier and the ship shall in any event be discharged from all liability whatsoever in respect of the goods, unless suit is brought within one year of their delivery or of the date when they should have been delivered. This period, may however, be extended if the parties so agree after the cause of action has arisen.

In the case of any actual or apprehended loss or damage the carrier and the receiver shall give all reasonable facilities to each other for inspecting and tallying the goods.

6bis. An action for indemnity against a third person may be brought even after the expiration of the year provided for in the preceding paragraph if brought within the time allowed by the law of the Court seized of the case. However, the time allowed shall be not less than three months, commencing from the day when the person bringing such action for indemnity has settled the claim or has been served with process in the action against himself.

7. After the goods are loaded the bill of lading to be issued by the carrier, master, or agent of the carrier, to the shipper shall, if the shipper so demands be a 'shipped' bill of lading provided that if the shipper shall have previously taken up any document of title to such goods, he shall surrender the same as against the issue of the 'shipped' bill of lading, but at the option of the carrier such document of title may be noted at the port of shipment by the carrier, master, or agent with the name or names of the ship or ships upon which the goods have been shipped and the date or dates of shipment, and when so noted, if it shows the particulars mentioned in paragraph 3 of Article III, shall for the purpose of this article be deemed to constitute a 'shipped' bill of lading.

8. Any clause, covenant, or agreement in a contract of carriage relieving the carrier or the ship from liability for loss or damage to, or in connection with goods arising from negligence, fault, or failure in the duties and obligations provided in this article or lessening such liability otherwise than as provided in these Rules, shall be null and void and of no effect. A benefit of insurance in favour of the carrier or similar clause shall be deemed to be a clause relieving the carrier from liability.

Article IV

1. Neither the carrier nor the ship shall be liable for loss or damage arising or resulting from unseaworthiness unless caused by want of due diligence on the part of the carrier to make the ship seaworthy, and to secure that the ship is properly manned, equipped and supplied, and to make the holds, refrigerating and cool chambers and all other parts of the ships in which goods are carried fit and safe for their reception, carriage and preservation in accordance with the provisions of paragraph 1 of Article III. Whenever loss or damage has resulted from unseaworthiness the burden of proving the exercise of due diligence shall be on the carrier or other person claiming exemption under this article.

2. Neither the carrier nor she ship shall be responsible for loss or damage arising or resulting from:

    (a) Act, neglect, or default of the master, mariner pilot, or the servants of the carrier in the navigation or in the management of the ship.

    (b) Fire, unless caused by the actual fault or privity of the carrier.

    (c) Perils, dangers and accidents of the sea or other navigable waters.

    (d) Act of God.

    (e) Act of war.

    (f) Act of public enemies.

    (g) Arrest or restraint of princes, rulers or people, or seizure under legal process.

    (h) Quarantine restrictions.

    (i) Act or omission of the shipper or owner of the goods, his agent or representative.

    (j) Strikes or lockouts or stoppage or restraint of labour from whatever cause, whether partial or general.

    (k) Riots and civil commotions.

    (l) Saving of attempting to save life or property at sea.

    (m) Wastage in bulk of weight or any other loss or damage arising from inherent defect, quality or vice of the goods.

    (n) Insufficiency of packing.

    (o) Insufficiency of inadequacy of marks.

    (p) Latent defects not discoverable by due diligence.

    (q) Any other cause arising without the actual fault or privity of the carrier, or without the fault or neglect of the agents or servants of the carrier, but the burden of proof shall be on the person claiming the benefit of this exception to show that neither the actual fault or privity of the carrier nor the fault of neglect of the agents or servants of the carrier contributed to the loss or damage.

3. The shipped shall not be responsible for loss or damage sustained by the carrier or the ship arising or resulting from any cause without the act, fault or neglect of the shipper, his agents or his servants.

4. Any deviation in saving or attempting to save life or property at sea or any reasonable deviation shall not be deemed to be an infringement or breach of these Rules or of the contract of carriage, and the carrier shall not be liable for any loss or damage resulting therefrom.

5. **(a)** Unless the nature and value of such goods have been declared by the shipper before shipment and inserted in the bill of lading, neither the carriage nor the ship shall in any event be or become liable for any loss or damage to or in connection with the goods in an amount exceeding the equivalent of 666.67 units of account per package or unit or 2 units of account per kilo of gross weight of the goods lost or damaged, whichever is the higher.

(b) The total amount recoverable shall be calculated by reference to the value of such goods at the place and time at which the goods are discharged from the ship in accordance with the contract or should have been so discharged.

The value of the goods shall be fixed accordingly to the commodity exchange price, or, if there be no such price, according to the current market price, or, if there be no commodity price or current market price, by reference to the normal value of goods of the same kind and quality.

(c) Where a container, pallet or similar article of transport is used to consolidate goods, the number of packages or units enumerated in the bill of lading as packed in such article of transport shall be deemed the number of packages or units for the purpose of this paragraph as far as these packages or units are concerned. Except as aforesaid such article of transport shall be considered the package or unit.

(d) The unit of account mentioned in this Article is the special drawing right as defined by the International Monetary Fund. The amounts mentioned in h_visby/art/art/04_5a sub-paragraph (a) of this paragraph shall be converted into national currency on the basis of the value of that currency on a date to be determined by the law of the Court sized of the case.

(e) Neither the carrier nor the ship shall be entitled to the benefit of the limitation of liability provided for in this paragraph if it is proved that the damage resulted from an act or omission of the carrier done with intent to cause damage, or recklessly and with knowledge that damage would probably result.

(f) The declaration mentioned in sub-paragraph (a) of this paragraph, if embodied in the bill of lading, shall be prima facie evidence, but shall not be binding or conclusive on the carrier.

(g) By agreement between the carrier, master or agent of the carrier and the shipper other maximum amounts than those mentioned in sub-paragraph (a) of this paragraph may be fixed, provided that no maximum amount so fixed shall be less than the appropriate maximum mentioned in that sub-paragraph.

(h) Neither the carrier nor the ship shall be responsible in any event for loss or damage to, or in connection with, goods if the nature or value thereof has been knowingly mis-stated by the shipper in the bill of lading.

6. Goods of an inflammable, explosive or dangerous nature to the shipment whereof the carrier, master or agent of the carrier has not consented with knowledge of their nature and character, may at any time before discharge be landed at any place, or destroyed or rendered innocuous by the carrier without compensation and the shipper of such goods shall be liable for all damages and expenses directly of indirectly arising out of or resulting from such shipment. If any such goods shipped with such knowledge and consent shall become a danger to the ship or cargo, they may in like manner be landed at any place, or destroyed or rendered innocuous by the carrier without the liability on the part of the carrier except to general average, if any.

Article IV bis

1. The defences and limits of liability provided for in these Rules shall apply in any action against the carrier in respect of loss or damage to goods covered by a contract of carriage whether the action be founded in contract or in tort.

2. If such an action is brought against a servant or agent of the carrier (such servant or agent not being an independent contractor), such servant or agent shall be entitled to avail himself of the defences and limits of liability which the carrier is entitled to invoke under these Rules.

3. The aggregate of the amounts recoverable from the carrier, and such servants and agents, shall in no case excel the limit provided for in these Rules.

4. Nevertheless, a servant or agent of the carrier shall not be entitled to avail himself of the provisions of this article, if it is proved that the damage resulted from an act or omission of the servant or agent done with intent to cause damage or recklessly and with knowledge that damage would probably result.

Article V

A carrier shall be at liberty to surrender in whole or in part all or any of his rights and immunities or to increase any of his responsibilities and obligations under these Rules, provided such surrender or increase shall be embodied in the bill of lading issued to the shipper. The provisions of these Rules shall not be applicable to charter parties, but if bills of lading are issued in the case of a ship under a charter party they shall comply with the terms of these Rules. Nothing in these Rules shall be held to prevent the insertion in a bill of lading of any lawful provision regarding general average.

Article VI

Notwithstanding the provisions of the preceding articles, a carrier, master or agent of the carrier and a shipper shall in regard to any particular goods be at liberty to enter into any agreement in any terms as to the responsibility and liability of the carrier for such goods, and as to the rights and immunities of the carrier in respect of such goods, or his obligation as to seaworthiness, so far as this stipulation is not contrary to public policy, or the care or diligence of his servants or agents in regard to the loading, handling, stowage, carriage, custody, care and discharge of the gods carried by sea, provided that in this case no bill of lading has been or shall be issued and that the terms agreed shall be embodied in a receipt which shall be a non-negotiable document and shall marked as such.

An agreement so entered into shall have full legal effect.

Provided that this article shall not apply to ordinary commercial shipments made in the ordinary course of trade, but only to other shipments where the character or condition of the property to be carried or the circumstances, terms and conditions under which the carriage is to be performed are such as reasonably to justify a special agreement.

Article VII

Nothing herein contained shall prevent a carrier or a shipper from entering into any agreement, stipulation, condition, reservation or exemption as to the responsibility and reliability of the carrier or the ship for the loss or damage to, or in connection with, the custody and care and handling of goods prior to the loading on, and subsequent to the discharge from, the ship on which the goods are carried by sea.

Article VIII

The provisions of these Rules shall not affect the rights and obligations of the carrier under any statute for the time being in force relating to the limitation of the liability of owners of sea-going vessels.

Article IX

These Rules shall not affect the provisions of any international Convention or national law governing liability for nuclear damage.

Article X

The provisions of these Rules shall apply to every bill of lading relating to the carriage of goods between ports in two different States if:

- **(a)** the bill of lading is issued in a contracting State, or
- **(b)** the carriage is from a port in a contracting State, or
- **(c)** the contract contained in or evidenced by the bill of lading provides that these Rules or legislation of any State giving effect to them are to govern the contract;

whatever may be the nationality of the ship, the carrier, the shipper, the consignee, or any other interested person.

(The last two paragraphs of this Article are not reproduced. They require contracting States to apply the Rules to bills of lading mentioned in the Article and authorise them to apply the Rules to other bills of lading).

(Article 11 to 16 of the International Convention for the unification of certain rules of law relating to bills of lading signed at Brussels on August 25, 1974 are not reproduced. They deal with the coming into force of the Convention, procedure for ratification, accession and denunciation and the right to call for a fresh conference to consider amendments to the Rules contained in the Convention).

General Clause Paramount

The International Convention for the Unification of Certain Rules of Law relating to Bills of Lading signed at Brussels on 25 August 1925 ("the Hague Rules") as amended by the Protocol signed at Brussels on 23 February 1968 ("the Hague-Visby Rules") and as enacted in the country of shipment shall apply to this contract. When the Hague-Visby are not enacted in the country of shipment, the corresponding legislation of the country of destination shall apply, irrespective of whether such legislation may only regulate outbound shipments.

When there is no enactment of the Hague-Visby Rules in either the country of shipment or in the country of destination, the Hague-Visby Rules shall apply to this contract save where the Hague Rules as enacted in the country of shipment or if no such enactment is in place, the Hague Rules as enacted in the country of destination apply compulsorily to this Contract.

The Protocol signed in Brussels on 21 December 1979 ("the SDR Protocol 1979") shall apply where the Hague-Visby Rules apply, whether mandatorily or by the Contract.

The Carrier shall in no case be responsible for loss or damage to cargo arising prior to loading, after discharging, or while the cargo is in the charge of another carrier, or with respect to deck cargo and live animals.

New Jason Clause

In the event of accident, danger, damage or disaster before or after commencement of the voyage, resulting from any cause whatsoever, whether due to negligence or not, for which, or for the consequences of which, the carrier is not responsible. By statute, contract or otherwise, the goods, shippers, consignees or owners of the goods shall contribute with the carrier in general average to the payment of any sacrifice, losses or expenses of a general average nature that may be made or incurred, and shall pay salvage and special charges incurred in respect of the goods.

If a salving ship is owned or operated by the carriers, the salvage shall be paid for as fully as if such salving ship or ships belonged to strangers. Such deposit as the carrier or his agents may deem sufficient to cover the estimated contribution of the goods, and any salvage and special charges thereon shall, if required, be made by the goods, shippers, consignees or owners of the goods to the carrier before delivery.

Both to Blame Collision Clause

If the ship comes into collision with another ship as a result of the negligence of the other ship and any act, neglect or default of the master mariner, pilot or the servants of the carrier in the navigation or in the management of the ship, the owners of the goods carried hereunder will indemnify the carrier against all loss or liability to the other non-carrying ship or her owners in so far as such loss or liability represents loss of, or damage to, or any claim whatsoever of the owners of the said goods, paid or payable by the other non-carrying ship or her owners as part of their claim against the carrying ship or carrier.

The foregoing provisions shall also apply where the owners, operators or those in charge of any ship or ships or objects other than, or in addition to, the colliding ships or objects are the fault in respect to a collision or contract. Appendix 10:6.

War Risks Clauses

BIMCO Standard War Risks Clause for Voyage Chartering, 1993 Code Name: "Voywar 1993"

(1) For the purpose of this Clause, the words:

(a) "Owner" shall include the shipowners, bareboat charterers, disponent owners, managers or other operators who are charged with the management of the Vessel, and the Master; and

(b) "War Risks" shall include any war (whether actual or threatened), act of war, civil war, hostilities, revolution, rebellion, civil commotion, warlike operations, the laying of mines (whether actual or reported), acts of piracy, acts of terrorists, acts of hostility or malicious damage, blockades (whether imposed against all vessels or imposed selectively against vessels of certain flags or ownership, or against certain cargoes or crews or otherwise howsoever), by any person, body, terrorist or political group, or the Government of any state whatsoever, which, in the reasonable judgement of the Master and/or the Owners, may be dangerous or are likely to be or to become dangerous to the Vessel, her cargo, crew or other persons on board the Vessel.

(2) If at any time before the Vessel commences loading, it appears that, in the reasonable judgement of the Master and/or the Owners, performance of the Contract of Carriage, or any part of it, may expose, or is likely to expose, the Vessel, her cargo, crew or other persons on board the Vessel to War Risks, the Owners may give notice to the Charterers cancelling this Contract of Carriage, or may refuse to form such part of it as may expose, or may be likely to expose, the Vessel, her cargo, crew or other persons on board the Vessel to War Risks; provided always that if this Contract of Carriage provides that loading or discharging is to take place within a range of ports, and at the port or ports nominated by the Charterers the Vessel, her cargo,, crew, or other persons onboard the Vessel may be exposed, or may be likely to be exposed, to War Risks, the Owners shall first require the Charterers to nominate any other safe port which lies within the range for loading or discharging, and may only cancel this Contract of Carriage if the Charterers shall not have nominated such safe port or ports within 48 hours of receipt of notice of such requirement.

(3) The Owners shall not be required to continue to load cargo for any voyage, or to sign Bills of Lading for any port or place, or to proceed or continue on any voyage, or on any part thereof, or to proceed through any canal or waterway, or to proceed to or remain at any port or place whatsoever, where it appears, either after the loading of the cargo commences, or any stage of the voyage thereafter before the discharge of the cargo is completed, that, in the reasonable judgement of the Master and/or the Owners, the Vessel, her cargo (or any part thereof), crew or other persons on board the Vessel (or any one or all of them) may be, or are likely to be, exposed to War Risks. If it should so appear, the Owners may by notice request the Charters to nominate a safe port for the discharge of the cargo or any part thereof, and if within 48 hours of the receipt of such notice, the Charterers shall not have nominated such a port, the Owners may discharge the cargo at any safe port of their choice (including the port of loading) in complete fulfillment of the Contract of Carriage. The Owners shall be entitled to recover from the Charterers the extra expenses of such discharge and, if the discharge takes place at any port other than the loading port, to receive the full freight as though the cargo had been carried to the discharging port and if the extra distance exceeds 100 miles, to additional freight which shall be the same percentage of the freight contracted for as the percentage which the extra distance represents to the distance of the normal and customary route, the Owners having a lien on the cargo for such expenses and freight.

(4) If at any stage of the voyage after the loading of the cargo commences it appears that, in the reasonable judgement of the Master and/or the Owners, the Vessel, her cargo, crew or other persons on board the Vessel may be, or are likely to be, exposed to War Risks on any part of the route (including any canal or waterway) which is normally and customarily used in a voyage of the nature contracted for, and there is another longer route to the discharging port, the Owners shall give notice to the Charterers that this route will be taken. In this event the Owners shal lbe entitled, if the total extra distance exceeds 100 miles to additional freight which shall be the same percentage of the freight contracted for as the percentage which the extra distance represents to the distance of the normal and customary route.

(5) The Vessel shall have liberty:

(a) to comply with all orders, directions, recommendations or advice as to departure, arrival, routes, sailing in convoy, ports of call, stoppages, destinations, discharge of cargo, delivery or in any way whatsoever which are given by the Government of the Nation under whose flag the Vessel sails, or other Government to whose laws the Owners are subject, or any other Government which so requires, or any body or group acting with the power to compel compliance with their orders or directions;

(b) to comply with the orders, directions or recommendations of any war risks underwriters who have the authority to give the same under the terms of the war risks insurance;

(c) to comply with the terms of any resolution of the Security Council of the United Nations, and directives of the European Community, the effective orders of any other Supranational body which has the right to issue and give the same, and with national laws aimed at enforcing the same to which the Owners are subject, and to obey the orders and directions of those who are charged with their enforcement;

(d) to discharge at any other port any cargo or part thereof which may render the Vessel liable to confiscation as a contraband carrier;

(e) to call at any other port to change the crew or any part thereof or other persons on board the Vessel when there is reason to believe that they may be subject to internment, imprisonment or other sanctions;

(f) where cargo has been loaded or has been discharged by the Owners under any provisions of this Clause, to load other cargo for the Owners' own behalf and carry it to any other port or ports whatsoever, whether backwards or forwards or in a contrary direction to the ordinary or customary route.

(6) If in compliance with any of the provisions of sub-clauses (2) to (5) of this Clause anything is done or not done, such shall not be deemed to be a deviation, but shall be considered as due fulfilment of the Contract of Carriage.

Appendix 34

United Nations Convention on the Carriage of Goods by Sea (1978)

Hamburg Rules

PREAMBLE

THE STATES PARTIES TO THIS CONVENTION,

HAVING RECOGNIZED the desirability of determining by agreement certain rules relating to the carriage of goods by sea,

HAVING DECIDED to conclude a convention for this purpose and have thereto agreed as follows:

PART I. GENERAL PROVISIONS

Article 1. Definitions

In this Convention:

1. "Carrier" means any person by whom or in whose name a contract of carriage of goods by sea has been concluded with a shipper.

2. "Actual carrier" means any person to whom the performance of the carriage of the goods, or of part of the carriage, has been entrusted by the carrier, and includes any other person to whom such performance has been entrusted.

3. "Shipper" means any person by whom or in whose name or on whose behalf a contract of carriage of goods by sea has been concluded with a carrier, or any person by whom or in whose name or on whose behalf the goods are actually delivered to the carrier in relation to the contract of carriage by sea.

4. "Consignee" means the person entitled to take delivery of the goods.

5. "Goods" includes live animals; where the goods are consolidated in a container, pallet or similar article of transport or where they are packed, goods includes such article of transport or packaging if supplied by the shipper.

6. "Contract of carriage by sea" means any contract whereby the carrier undertakes against payment of freight to carry goods by sea from one port to another; however, a contract which involves carriage by sea and also carriage by some other means is deemed to be a contract of carriage by sea for the purposes of this Convention only in so far as it relates to the carriage by sea.

7. "Bill of lading" means a document which evidences a contract of carriage by sea and the taking over or loading of the goods by the carrier, and by which the carrier undertakes to deliver the goods against surrender of the document. A provision in the document that the goods are to be delivered to the order of a named person, or to order, or to bearer, constitutes such an undertaking.

8. "Writing" includes, inter alia, telegram and telex.

Article 2. Scope of application

1. The provisions of this Convention are applicable to all contracts of carriage by sea between two different States, if:

    (a) the port of loading as provided for in the contract of carriage by sea is located in a Contracting State, or

    (b) the port of discharge as provided for in the contract of carriage by sea is located in a Contracting State, or

    (c) one of the optional ports of discharge provided for in the contract of carriage by sea is the actual port of discharge and such port is located in a Contracting State, or

    (d) the bill of lading or other document evidencing the contract of carriage by sea is issued in a Contracting State, or

    (e) the bill of lading or other document evidencing the contract of carriage by sea provides that the provisions of this Convention or the legislation of any State giving effect to them are to govern the contract.

2. The provisions of this Convention are applicable without regard to the nationality of the ship, the carrier, the actual carrier, the shipper, the consignee or any other interested person.

3. The provisions of this Convention are not applicable to charter-parties. However, where a bill of lading is issued pursuant to a charter-party, the provisions of the Convention apply to such a bill of lading if it governs the relation between the carrier and the holder of the bill of lading, not being the charterer.

4. If a contract provides for future carriage of goods in a series of shipments during an agreed period, the provisions of this Convention apply to each shipment. However, where a shipment is made under a charter-party, the provisions of paragraph 3 of this article apply.

Article 3. Interpretation of the Convention

In the interpretation and application of the provisions of this Convention regard shall be had to its international character and to the need to promote uniformity.

PART II. LIABILITY OF THE CARRIER

Article 4. Period of responsibility

1. The responsibility of the carrier for the goods under this Convention covers the period during which the carrier is in charge of the goods at the port of loading, during the carriage and at the port of discharge.

2. For the purpose of paragraph 1 of this article, the carrier is deemed to be in charge of the goods

    (a) from the time he has taken over the goods from:

    (i) the shipper, or a person acting on his behalf; or

    (ii) an authority or other third party to whom, pursuant to law or regulations applicable at the port of loading, the goods must be handed over for shipment;

    (b) until the time he has delivered the goods:

    (i) by handing over the goods to the consignee; or

    (ii) in cases where the consignee does not receive the goods from the carrier, by placing them at the disposal of the consignee in accordance with the contract or with the law or with the usage of the particular trade, applicable at the port of discharge; or

    (iii) by handing over the goods to an authority or other third party to whom, pursuant to law or regulations applicable at the port of discharge, the goods must be handed over.

3. In paragraphs 1 and 2 of this article, reference to the carrier or to the consignee means, in addition to the carrier or the consignee, the servants or agents, respectively of the carrier or the consignee.

Article 5. Basis of liability

1. The carrier is liable for loss resulting from loss of or damage to the goods, as well as from delay in delivery, if the occurrence which caused the loss, damage or delay took place while the goods were in his charge as defined in article 4, unless the carrier proves that he, his servants or agents took all measures that could reasonably be required to avoid the occurrence and its consequences.

2. Delay in delivery occurs when the goods have not been delivered at the port of discharge provided for in the contract of carriage by sea within the time expressly agreed upon or, in the absence of such agreement, within the time which it would be reasonable to require of a diligent carrier, having regard to the circumstances of the case.

3. The person entitled to make a claim for the loss of goods may treat the goods as lost if they have not been delivered as required by article 4 within 60 consecutive days following the expiry of the time for delivery according to paragraph 2 of this article.

4. *(a)* The carrier is liable

    (i) for loss of or damage to the goods or delay in delivery caused by fire, if the claimant proves that the fire arose from fault or neglect on the part of the carrier, his servants or agents;

    (ii) for such loss, damage or delay in delivery which is proved by the claimant to have resulted from the fault or neglect of the carrier, his servants or agents in taking all measures that could reasonably be required to put out the fire and avoid or mitigate its consequences.

    (b) In case of fire on board the ship affecting the goods, if the claimant or the carrier so desires, a survey in accordance with shipping practices must be held into the cause and circumstances of the fire, and a copy of the surveyors report shall be made available on demand to the carrier and the claimant.

5. With respect to live animals, the carrier is not liable for loss, damage or delay in delivery resulting from any special risks inherent in that kind of carriage. If the carrier proves that he has complied with any special instructions given to him by the shipper respecting the animals and that, in the circumstances of the case, the loss, damage or delay in delivery could be attributed to such risks, it is presumed that the loss, damage or delay in delivery was so caused, unless there is proof that all or a part of the loss, damage or delay in delivery resulted from fault or neglect on the part of the carrier, his servants or agents.

6. The carrier is not liable, except in general average, where loss, damage or delay in delivery resulted from measures to save life or from reasonable measures to save property at sea.

7. Where fault or neglect on the part of the carrier, his servants or agents combines with another cause to produce loss, damage or delay in delivery, the carrier is liable only to the extent that the loss, damage or delay in delivery is attributable to such fault or neglect, provided that the carrier proves the amount of the loss, damage or delay in delivery not attributable thereto.

Article 6. Limits of liability

1. *(a)* The liability of the carrier for loss resulting from loss of or damage to goods according to the provisions of article 5 is limited to an amount equivalent to 835 units of account per package or other shipping unit or 2.5 units of account per kilogram of gross weight of the goods lost or damaged, whichever is the higher.

    (b) The liability of the carrier for delay in delivery according to the provisions of article 5 is

limited to an amount equivalent to two and a half times the freight payable for the goods delayed, but not exceeding the total freight payable under the contract of carriage of goods by sea.

(c) In no case shall the aggregate liability of the carrier, under both subparagraphs *(a)* and (b) of this paragraph, exceed the limitation which would be established under subparagraph *(a)* of this paragraph for total loss of the goods with respect to which such liability was incurred.

2. For the purpose of calculating which amount is the higher in accordance with paragraph 1 *(a)* of this article, the following rules apply:

(a) Where a container, pallet or similar article of transport is used to consolidate goods, the package or other shipping units enumerated in the bill of lading, if issued, or otherwise in any other document evidencing the contract of carriage by sea, as packed in such article of transport are deemed packages or shipping units. Except as aforesaid the goods in such article of transport are deemed one shipping unit.

(b) In cases where the article of transport itself has been lost or damaged, that article of transport, if not owned or otherwise supplied by the carrier, is considered one separate shipping unit.

3. Unit of account means the unit of account mentioned in article 26.

4. By agreement between the carrier and the shipper, limits of liability exceeding those provided for in paragraph 1 may be fixed.

Article 7. Application to non-contractual claims

1. The defences and limits of liability provided for in this Convention apply in any action against the carrier in respect of loss of or damage to the goods covered by the contract of carriage by sea, as well as of delay in delivery whether the action is founded in contract, in tort or otherwise.

2. If such an action is brought against a servant or agent of the carrier, such servant or agent, if he proves that he acted within the scope of his employment, is entitled to avail himself of the defences and limits of liability which the carrier is entitled to invoke under this Convention.

3. Except as provided in article 8, the aggregate of the amounts recoverable from the carrier and from any persons referred to in paragraph 2 of this article shall not exceed the limits of liability provided for in this Convention.

Article 8. Loss of right to limit responsibility

1. The carrier is not entitled to the benefit of the limitation of liability provided for in article 6 if it is proved that the loss, damage or delay in delivery resulted from an act or omission of the carrier done with the intent to cause such loss, damage or delay, or recklessly and with knowledge that such loss, damage or delay would probably result.

2. Notwithstanding the provisions of paragraph 2 of article 7, a servant or agent of the carrier is not entitled to the benefit of the limitation of liability provided for in article 6 if it is proved that the loss, damage or delay in delivery resulted from an act or omission of such servant or agent, done with the intent to cause such loss, damage or delay, or recklessly and with knowledge that such loss, damage or delay would probably result.

Article 9. Deck cargo

1. The carrier is entitled to carry the goods on deck only if such carriage is in accordance with an agreement with the shipper or with the usage of the particular trade or is required by statutory rules or regulations.

2. If the carrier and the shipper have agreed that the goods shall or may be carried on deck, the carrier must insert in the bill of lading or other document evidencing the contract of carriage by sea a statement to that effect. In the absence of such a statement the carrier has the burden of proving that an agreement for carriage on deck has been entered into; however, the carrier is not entitled to invoke such an agreement against a third party, including a consignee, who has acquired the bill of lading in good faith.

3. Where the goods have been carried on deck contrary to the provisions of paragraph 1 of this article or where the carrier may not under paragraph 2 of this article invoke an agreement for carriage on deck, the carrier, notwithstanding the provisions of paragraph 1 of article 5, is liable for loss of or damage to the goods, as well as for delay in delivery, resulting solely from the carriage on deck, and the extent of his liability is to be determined in accordance with the provisions of article 6 or article 8 of this Convention, as the case may be.

4. Carriage of goods on deck contrary to express agreement for carriage under deck is deemed to be an act or omission of the carrier within the meaning of article 8.

Article 10. Liability of the carrier and actual carrier

1. Where the performance of the carriage or part thereof has been entrusted to an actual carrier, whether or not in pursuance of a liberty under the contract of carriage by sea to do so, the carrier nevertheless remains responsible for the entire carriage according to the provisions of this Convention. The carrier is responsible, in relation to the carriage performed by the actual carrier, for the acts and omissions of the actual carrier and of his servants and agents acting within the scope of their employment.

2. All the provisions of this Convention governing the responsibility of the carrier also apply to the responsibility of the actual carrier for the carriage performed by him. The provisions of paragraphs 2 and 3 of article 7 and of paragraph 2 of article 8 apply if an action is brought against a servant or agent of the actual carrier.

3. Any special agreement under which the carrier assumes obligations not imposed by this Convention or waives rights conferred by this Convention affects the actual carrier only if agreed to by him expressly and in writing. Whether or not the actual carrier has so agreed, the carrier nevertheless remains bound by the obligations or waivers resulting from such special agreement.

4. Where and to the extent that both the carrier and the actual carrier are liable, their liability is joint and several.

5. The aggregate of the amounts recoverable from the carrier, the actual carrier and their servants and agents shall not exceed the limits of liability provided for in this Convention.

6. Nothing in this article shall prejudice any right of recourse as between the carrier and the actual carrier.

Article 11. Through carriage

1. Notwithstanding the provisions of paragraph 1 of article 10, where a contract of carriage by sea provides explicitly that a specified part of the carriage covered by the said contract is to be performed by a named person other than the carrier, the contract may also provide that the carrier is not liable for loss, damage or delay in delivery caused by an occurrence which takes place while the goods are in the charge of the actual carrier during such part of the carriage. Nevertheless, any stipulation limiting or excluding such liability is without effect if no judicial proceedings can be instituted against the actual carrier in a court competent under paragraph 1 or 2 of article 21. The burden of proving that any loss, damage or delay in delivery has been caused by such an occurrence rests upon the carrier.

2. The actual carrier is responsible in accordance with the provisions of paragraph 2 of article 10 for loss, damage or delay in delivery caused by an occurrence which takes place while the goods are in his charge.

PART III. LIABILITY OF THE SHIPPERS

Article 12. General rule

The shipper is not liable for loss sustained by the carrier or the actual carrier, or for damage sustained by the ship, unless such loss or damage was caused by the fault or neglect of the shipper, his servants or agents. Nor is any servant or agent of the shipper liable for such loss or damage unless the loss or damage was caused by fault or neglect on his part.

Article 13. Special rules on dangerous goods

1.   The shipper must mark or label in a suitable manner dangerous goods as dangerous.

2.   Where the shipper hands over dangerous goods to the carrier or an actual carrier, as the case may be, the shipper must inform him of the dangerous character of the goods and, if necessary, of the precautions to be taken. If the shipper fails to do so and such carrier or actual carrier does not otherwise have knowledge of their dangerous character:

   (a)   the shipper is liable to the carrier and any actual carrier for the loss resulting from the shipment of such goods, and

   (b)   the goods may at any time be unloaded, destroyed or rendered innocuous, as the circumstances may require, without payment of compensation.

3.   The provisions of paragraph 2 of this article may not be invoked by any person if during the carriage he has taken the goods in his charge with knowledge of their dangerous character.

4.   If, in cases where the provisions of paragraph 2, subparagraph (b), of this article do not apply or may not be invoked, dangerous goods become an actual danger to life or property, they may be unloaded, destroyed or rendered innocuous, as the circumstances may require, without payment of compensation except where there is an obligation to contribute in general average or where the carrier is liable in accordance with the provisions of article 5.

PART IV. TRANSPORT DOCUMENTS

Article 14. Issue of bill of lading

1.   When the carrier or the actual carrier takes the goods in his charge, the carrier must, on demand of the shipper, issue to the shipper a bill of lading.

2.   The bill of lading may be signed by a person having authority from the carrier. A bill of lading signed by the master of the ship carrying the goods is deemed to have been signed on behalf of the carrier.

3.   The signature on the bill of lading may be in handwriting, printed in facsimile, perforated, stamped, in symbols, or made by any other mechanical or electronic means, if not inconsistent with the law of the country where the bill of lading is issued.

Article 15. Contents of bill of lading

1.   The bill of lading must include, *inter alia*, the following particulars:

   (a)   the general nature of the goods, the leading marks necessary for identification of the goods, an express statement, if applicable, as to the dangerous character of the goods, the number of packages or pieces, and the weight of the goods or their quantity otherwise expressed, all such particulars as furnished by the shipper;

   (b)   the apparent condition of the goods;

   (c)   the name and principal place of business of the carrier;

   (d)   the name of the shipper;

(e) the consignee if named by the shipper;

(f) the port of loading under the contract of carriage by sea and the date on which the goods were taken over by the carrier at the port of loading;

(g) the port of discharge under the contract of carriage by sea;

(h) the number of originals of the bill of lading, if more than one;

(i) the place of issuance of the bill of lading;

(j) the signature of the carrier or a person acting on his behalf;

(k) the freight to the extent payable by the consignee or other indication that freight is payable by him;

(l) the statement referred to in paragraph 3 of article 23;

(m) the statement, if applicable, that the goods shall or may be carried on deck;

(n) the date or the period of delivery of the goods at the port of discharge if expressly agreed upon between the parties; and

(o) any increased limit or limits of liability where agreed in accordance with paragraph 4 of article 6.

2. After the goods have been loaded on board, if the shipper so demands, the carrier must issue to the shipper a "shipped" bill of lading which, in addition to the particulars required under paragraph 1 of this article, must state that the goods are on board a named ship or ships, and the date or dates of loading. If the carrier has previously issued to the shipper a bill of lading or other document of title with respect to any of such goods, on request of the carrier the shipper must surrender such document in exchange for a "shipped" bill of lading. The carrier may amend any previously issued document in order to meet the shippers demand for a "shipped" bill of lading if, as amended, such document includes all the information required to be contained in a "shipped" bill of lading.

3. The absence in the bill of lading of one or more particulars referred to in this article does not affect the legal character of the document as a bill of lading provided that it nevertheless meets the requirements set out in paragraph 7 of article 1.

Article 16. Bills of lading: reservations and evidentiary effect

1. If the bill of lading contains particulars concerning the general nature, leading marks, number of packages of pieces, weight or quantity of the goods which the carrier or other person issuing the bill of lading on his behalf knows or has reasonable grounds to suspect do not accurately represent the goods actually taken over or, where a "shipped" bill of lading is issued, loaded, or if he had no reasonable means of checking such particulars, the carrier or such other person must insert in the bill of lading a reservation specifying these inaccuracies, grounds of suspicion or the absence of reasonable means of checking.

2. If the carrier or other person issuing the bill of lading on his behalf fails to note on the bill of lading the apparent condition of the goods, he is deemed to have noted on the bill of lading that the goods were in apparent good condition.

3. Except for particulars in respect of which and to the extent to which a reservation permitted under paragraph 1 of this article has been entered:

(a) the bill of lading is prima facie evidence of the taking over or, where a "shipped" bill of lading is issued, loading, by the carrier of the goods as described in the bill of lading; and

(b) proof to the contrary by the earner is not admissible if the bill of lading has been transferred to a third party, including a consignee, who in good faith has acted in reliance on the description of the goods therein.

4. A bill of lading which does not, as provided in paragraph 1, subparagraph (k), of article 15, set forth the freight or otherwise indicate that freight is payable by the consignee or does not set forth demurrage incurred at the port of loading payable by the consignee, is prima facie evidence that no freight or such demurrage is payable by him. However, proof to the contrary by the carrier is not admissible when the bill of lading has been transferred to a third party, including a consignee, who in good faith has acted in reliance on the absence in the bill of lading of any such indication.

Article 17. Guarantees by the shipper

1. The shipper is deemed to have guaranteed to the carrier the accuracy of particulars relating to the general nature of the goods, their marks, number, weight and quantity as furnished by him for insertion in the bill of lading. The shipper must indemnify the carrier against the loss resulting from inaccuracies in such particulars. The shipper remains liable even if the bill of lading has been transferred by him. The right of the carrier to such indemnity in no way limits his liability under the contract of carriage by sea to any person other than the shipper.

2. Any letter of guarantee or agreement by which the shipper undertakes to indemnify the carrier against loss resulting from the issuance of the bill of lading by the carrier, or by a person acting on his behalf, without entering a reservation relating to particulars furnished by the shipper for insertion in the bill of lading, or to the apparent condition of the goods, is void and of no effect as against any third party, including a consignee, to whom the bill of lading has been transferred.

3. Such a letter of guarantee or agreement is valid as against the shipper unless the carrier or the person acting on his behalf, by omitting the reservation referred to in paragraph 2 of this article, intends to defraud a third party, including a consignee, who acts in reliance on the description of the goods in the bill of lading. In the latter case, if the reservation omitted relates to particulars furnished by the shipper for insertion in the bill of lading, the carrier has no right of indemnity from the shipper pursuant to paragraph 1 of this article.

4. In the case of intended fraud referred to in paragraph 3 of this article, the carrier is liable, without the benefit of the limitation of liability provided for in this Convention, for the loss incurred by a third party, including a consignee, because he has acted in reliance on the description of the goods in the bill of lading.

Article 18. Documents other than bills of lading

Where a carrier issues a document other than a bill of lading to evidence the receipt of the goods to be carried, such a document is prima facie evidence of the conclusion of the contract of carriage by sea and the taking over by the carrier of the goods as therein described.

PART V. CLAIMS AND ACTIONS

Article 19. Notice of loss, damage or delay

1. Unless notice of loss or damage, specifying the general nature of such loss or damage, is given in writing by the consignee to the carrier not later than the working day after the day when the goods were handed over to the consignee, such handing over is prima facie evidence of the delivery by the carrier of the goods as described in the document of transport or, if no such document has been issued, in good condition.

2. Where the loss or damage is not apparent, the provisions of paragraph 1 of this article apply correspondingly if notice in writing is not given within 15 consecutive days after the day when the goods were handed over to the consignee.

3. If the state of the goods at the time they were handed over to the consignee has been the subject of a joint survey or inspection by the parties, notice in writing need not be given of loss or damage ascertained during such survey or inspection.

4.   In the case of any actual or apprehended loss or damage, the carrier and the consignee must give all reasonable facilities to each other for inspecting and tallying the goods.

5.   No compensation shall be payable for loss resulting from delay in delivery unless a notice has been given in writing to the carrier within 60 consecutive days after the day when the goods were handed over to the consignee.

6.   If the goods have been delivered by an actual carrier, any notice given under this article to him shall have the same effect as if it had been given to the carrier; and any notice given to the carrier shall have effect as if given to such actual carrier.

7.   Unless notice of loss or damage, specifying the general nature of the loss or damage, is given in writing by the carrier or actual carrier to the shipper not later than 90 consecutive days after the occurrence of such loss or damage or after the delivery of the goods in accordance with paragraph 2 of article 4, whichever is later, the failure to give such notice is *prima* facie evidence that the carrier or the actual carrier has sustained no loss or damage due to the fault or neglect of the shipper, his servants or agents.

8.   For the purpose of this article, notice given to a person acting on the carriers or the actual carriers behalf, including the master or the officer in charge of the ship, or to a person acting on the shippers behalf is deemed to have been given to the carrier, to the actual carrier or to the shipper, respectively.

Article 20. Limitation of actions

1.   Any action relating to carriage of goods under this Convention is time-barred if judicial or arbitral proceedings have not been instituted within a period of two years.

2.   The limitation period commences on the day on which the carrier has delivered the goods or part thereof or, in cases where no goods have been delivered, on the last day on which the goods should have been delivered.

3.   The day on which the limitation period commences is not included in the period.

4.   The person against whom a claim is made may at any time during the running of the limitation period extend that period by a declaration in writing to the claimant. This period may be further extended by another declaration or declarations.

5.   An action for indemnity by a person held liable may be instituted even after the expiration of the limitation period provided for in the preceding paragraphs if instituted within the time allowed by the law of the State where proceedings are instituted. However, the time allowed shall not be less than 90 days commencing from the day when the person instituting such action for indemnity has settled the claim or has been served with process in the action against himself.

Article 21. Jurisdiction

1.   In judicial proceedings relating to carriage of goods under this Convention the plaintiff, at his option, may institute an action in a court which according to the law of the State where the court is situated, is competent and within the jurisdiction of which is situated one of the following places:

   (a)   the principal place of business or, in the absence thereof, the habitual residence of the defendant; or

   (b)   the place where the contract was made, provided that the defendant has there a place of business, branch or agency through which the contract was made; or

   (c)   the port of loading or the port of discharge; or

   (d)   any additional place designated for that purpose in the contract of carriage by sea.

2.   *(a)*   Notwithstanding the preceding provisions of this article, an action may be instituted in the courts of any port or place in a Contracting State at which the carrying vessel or any other vessel of the same ownership may have been arrested in accordance with applicable rules of the law of that State and of international law. However, in such a case, at the petition of the defendant, the claimant must remove the action, at his choice, to one of the jurisdictions referred to in paragraph 1 of this article for the determination of the claim, but before such removal the defendant must furnish security sufficient to ensure payment of any judgement that may subsequently be awarded to the claimant in the action.

      (b)   All questions relating to the sufficiency or otherwise of the security shall be determined by the court of the port or place of the arrest.

3.   No judicial proceedings relating to carriage of goods under this Convention may be instituted in a place not specified in paragraph 1 or 2 of this article. The provisions of this paragraph do not constitute an obstacle to the jurisdiction of the Contracting States for provisional or protective measures.

4.   *(a)*   Where an action has been instituted in a court competent under paragraphs 1 or 2 of this article or where judgement has been delivered by such a court, no new action may be started between the same parties on the same grounds unless the judgement of the court before which the first action was instituted is not enforceable in the country in which the new proceedings are instituted;

      (b)   For the purpose of this article, the institution of measures with a view to obtaining enforcement of a judgement is not to be considered as the starting of a new action;

      (c)   For the purpose of this article, the removal of an action to a different court within the same country, or to a court in another country, in accordance with paragraph 2 (a) of this article, is not to be considered as the starting of a new action.

5.   Notwithstanding the provisions of the preceding paragraphs, an agreement made by the parties, after a claim under the contract of carriage by sea has arisen, which designates the place where the claimant may institute an actions, is effective.

Article 22. Arbitration

1.   Subject to the provisions of this article, parties may provide by agreement evidenced in writing that any dispute that may arise relating to carriage of goods under this Convention shall be referred to arbitration.

2.   Where a charter-party contains a provision that disputes arising thereunder shall be referred to arbitration and a bill of lading issued pursuant to the charter-party does not contain special annotation providing that such provision shall be binding upon the holder of the bill of lading, the carrier may not invoke such provision as against a holder having acquired the bill of lading in good faith.

3.   The arbitration proceedings shall, at the option of the claimant, be instituted at one of the following places:

   (a)   a place in a State within whose territory is situated:

      (i)   the principal place of business of the defendant or, in the absence thereof, the habitual residence of the defendant; or

      (ii)   the place where the contract was made, provided that the defendant has there a place of business, branch or agency through which the contract was made; or

      (iii)   the port of loading or the port of discharge; or

   (b)   any place designated for that purpose in the arbitration clause or agreement.

4. The arbitrator or arbitration tribunal shall apply the rules of this Convention.

5. The provisions of paragraphs 2 and 4 of this article are deemed to be part of every arbitration clause or agreement, and any term of such clause or agreement which is inconsistent therewith is null and void.

6. Nothing in this article affects the validity of an agreement relating to arbitration made by the parties after the claim under the contract of carriage by sea has arisen.

PART VI. SUPPLEMENTARY PROVISIONS

Article 23. Contractual stipulations

1. Any stipulation in a contract of carriage by sea, in a bill of lading, or in any other document evidencing the contract of carriage by sea is null and void to the extent that it derogates, directly or indirectly, from the provisions of this Convention. The nullity of such a stipulation does not affect the validity of the other provisions of the contract or document of which it forms a part. A clause assigning benefit of insurance of goods in favour of the carrier, or any similar clause, is null and void.

2. Notwithstanding the provisions of paragraph 1 of this article, a carrier may increase his responsibilities and obligations under this Convention.

3. Where a bill of lading or any other document evidencing the contract of carriage by sea is issued, it must contain a statement that the carriage is subject to the provisions of this Convention which nullify any stipulation derogating therefrom to the detriment of the shipper or the consignee.

4. Where the claimant in respect of the goods has incurred loss as a result of a stipulation which is null and void by virtue of the present article, or as a result of the omission of the statement referred to in paragraph 3 of this article, the carrier must pay compensation to the extent required in order to give the claimant compensation in accordance with the provisions of this Convention for any loss of or damage to the goods as well as for delay in delivery. The carrier must, in addition, pay compensation for costs incurred by the claimant for the purpose of exercising his right, provided that costs incurred in the action where the foregoing provision is invoked are to be determined in accordance with the law of the State where proceedings are instituted.

Article 24. General average

1. Nothing in this Convention shall prevent the application of provisions in the contract of carriage by sea or national law regarding the adjustment of general average.

2. With the exception of article 20, the provisions of this Convention relating to the liability of the carrier for loss of or damage to the goods also determine whether the consignee may refuse contribution in general average and the liability of the carrier to indemnify the consignee in respect of any such contribution made or any salvage paid.

Article 25. Other conventions

1. This Convention does not modify the rights or duties of the carrier, the actual carrier and their servants and agents provided for in international conventions or national law relating to the limitation of liability of owners of seagoing ships.

2. The provisions of articles 21 and 22 of this Convention do not prevent the application of the mandatory provisions of any other multilateral convention already in force at the date of this Convention relating to matters dealt with in the said articles, provided that the dispute arises exclusively between parties having their principal place of business in States members of such other convention. However, this paragraph does not affect the application of paragraph 4 of article 22 of this Convention.

3. No liability shall arise under the provisions of this Convention for damage caused by a nuclear incident if the operator of a nuclear installation is liable for such damage:

    (a) under either the Paris Convention of 29 July 1960 on Third Party Liability in the Field of Nuclear Energy as amended by the Additional Protocol of 28 January 1964, or the Vienna Convention of 21 May 1963 on Civil Liability for Nuclear Damage, or

    (b) by virtue of national law governing the liability for such damage, provided that such law is in all respects as favourable to persons who may suffer damage as is either the Paris Convention or the Vienna Convention.

4. No liability shall arise under the provisions of this Convention for any loss of or damage to or delay in delivery of luggage for which the carrier is responsible under any international convention or national law relating to the carriage of passengers and their luggage by sea.

5. Nothing contained in this Convention prevents a Contracting State from applying any other international convention which is already in force at the date of this Convention and which applies mandatorily to contracts of carriage of goods primarily by a mode of transport other than transport by sea. This provision also applies to any subsequent revision or amendment of such international convention.

Article 26. Unit of account

1. The unit of account referred to in article 6 of this Convention is the special drawing right as defined by the International Monetary Fund. The amounts mentioned in article 6 are to be converted into the national currency of a State according to the value of such currency at the date of judgement or the date agreed upon by the parties. The value of a national currency, in terms of the special drawing right, of a Contracting State which is a member of the International Monetary Fund is to be calculated in accordance with the method of valuation applied by the International Monetary Fund in effect at the date in question for its operations and transactions. The value of a national currency, in terms of the special drawing right, of a Contracting State which is not a member of the International Monetary Fund is to be calculated in a manner determined by that State.

2. Nevertheless, those States which are not members of the International Monetary Fund and whose law does not permit the application of the provisions of paragraph 1 of this article may, at the time of signature, or at the time of ratification, acceptance, approval or accession or at any time thereafter, declare that the limits of liability provided for in this Convention to be applied in their territories shall be fixed as 12,500 monetary units per package or other shipping unit or 37.5 monetary units per kilogram of gross weight of the goods.

3. The monetary unit referred to in paragraph 2 of this article corresponds to sixty-five and a half milligrams of gold of millesimal fineness nine hundred. The conversion of the amounts referred to in paragraph 2 into the national currency is to be made according to the law of the State concerned.

4. The calculation mentioned in the last sentence of paragraph 1 and the conversion mentioned in paragraph 3 of this article is to be made in such a manner as to express in the national currency of the Contracting State as far as possible the same real value for the amounts in article 6 as is expressed there in units of account. Contracting States must communicate to the depositary the manner of calculation pursuant to paragraph 1 of this article, or the result of the conversion mentioned in paragraph 3 of this article, as the case may be, at the time of signature or when depositing their instruments of ratification, acceptance, approval or accession, or when availing themselves of the option provided for in paragraph 2 of this article and whenever there is a change in the manner of such calculation or in the result of such conversion.

PART VII. FINAL CLAUSES

Article 27. Depositary

The Secretary-General of the United Nations is hereby designated as the depositary of this Convention.

Article 28. Signature, Ratification, Acceptance, Approval, Accession

1. This Convention is open for signature by all States until 30 April 1979 at the Headquarters of the United Nations, New York.

2. This Convention is subject to ratification, acceptance or approval by the signatory States.

3. After 30 April 1979, this Convention will be open for accession by all States which are not signatory States.

4. Instruments of ratification, acceptance, approval and accession are to be deposited with the Secretary-General of the United Nations.

Article 29. Reservations

No reservations may be made to this Convention.

Article 30. Entry into force

1. This Convention enters into force on the first day of the month following the expiration of one year from the date of deposit of the twentieth instrument of ratification, acceptance, approval or accession.

2. For each State which becomes a Contracting State to this Convention after the date of the deposit of the twentieth instrument of ratification, acceptance, approval or accession, this Convention enters into force on the first day of the month following the expiration of one year after the deposit of the appropriate instrument on behalf of that State.

3. Each Contracting State shall apply the provisions of this Convention to contracts of carriage by sea concluded on or after the date of the entry into force of this Convention in respect of that State.

Article 31. Denunciation of other conventions

1. Upon becoming a Contracting State to this Convention, any State Party to the International Convention for the Unification of certain Rules relating to Bills of Lading signed at Brussels on 25 August 1924 (1924 Convention) must notify the Government of Belgium as the depositary of the 1924 Convention of its denunciation of the said Convention with a declaration that the denunciation is to take effect as from the date when this Convention enters into force in respect of that State.

2. Upon the entry into force of this Convention under paragraph 1 of article 30, the depositary of this Convention must notify the Government of Belgium as the depositary of the 1924 Convention of the date of such entry into force, and of the names of the Contracting States in respect of which the Convention has entered into force.

3. The provisions of paragraphs 1 and 2 of this article apply correspondingly in respect of States Parties to the Protocol signed on 23 February 1968 to amend the International Convention for the Unification of certain Rules relating to Bills of Lading signed at Brussels on 25 August 1924.

4. Notwithstanding article 2 of this Convention, for the purposes of paragraph 1 of this article, a Contracting State may, if it deems it desirable, defer the denunciation of the 1924 Convention and of the 1924 Convention as modified by the 1968 Protocol for a maximum period of five years from the entry into force of this Convention. It will then notify the Government of Belgium of its intention. During this transitory period, it must apply to the Contracting States this Convention to the exclusion of any other one.

Article 32: Revision and amendment

1. At the request of not less than one third of the Contracting States to this Convention, the depositary shall convene a conference of the Contracting States for revising or amending it.

2. Any instrument of ratification, acceptance, approval or accession deposited after the entry into force of an amendment to this Convention is deemed to apply to the Convention as amended.

Article 33. Revision of the limitation amounts and unit of account or monetary unit

1. Notwithstanding the provisions of article 32, a conference only for the purpose of altering the amount specified in article 6 and paragraph 2 of article 26, or of substituting either or both of the units defined in paragraphs 1 and 3 of article 26 by other units is to be convened by the depositary in accordance with paragraph 2 of this article. An alteration of the amounts shall be made only because of a significant change in their real value.

2. A revision conference is to be convened by the depositary when not less than one fourth of the Contracting States so request.

3. Any decision by the conference must be taken by a two-thirds majority of the participating States. The amendment is communicated by the depositary to all the Contracting States for acceptance and to all the States signatories of the Convention for information.

4. Any amendment adopted enters into force on the first day of the month following one year after its acceptance by two thirds of the Contracting States. Acceptance is to be effected by the deposit of a formal instrument to that effect with the depositary.

5. After entry into force of an amendment a Contracting State which has accepted the amendment is entitled to apply the Convention as amended in its relations with Contracting States which have not within six months after the adoption of the amendment notified the depositary that they are not bound by the amendment.

6. Any instrument of ratification, acceptance, approval or accession deposited after the entry into force of an amendment to this Convention is deemed to apply to the Convention as amended.

Article 34. Denunciation

1. A Contracting State may denounce this Convention at any time by means of a notification in writing addressed to the depositary.

2. The denunciation takes effect on the first day of the month following the expiration of one year after the notification is received by the depositary. Where a longer period is specified in the notification, the denunciation takes effect upon the expiration of such longer period after the notification is received by the depositary.

Done at Hamburg, this thirty-first day of March, one thousand nine hundred and seventy-eight, in a single original, of which the Arabic, Chinese, English, French, Russian and Spanish texts are equally authentic.

In witness whereof the undersigned plenipotentiaries, being duly authorized by their respective Governments, have signed the present Convention.

Common understanding adopted by the United Nations Conference on the Carriage of Goods by Sea.

It is the common understanding that the liability of the carrier under this Convention is based on the principle of presumed fault or neglect. This means that, as a rule, the burden of proof rests on the carrier but, with respect to certain cases, the provisions of the Convention modify this rule.

Rotterdam Rules

General Assembly

Distr.: General
2 February 2009

Sixty-third session
Agenda item 74

Resolution adopted by the General Assembly

[*on the report of the Sixth Committee (A/63/438)*]

63/122. **United Nations Convention on Contracts for the International Carriage of Goods Wholly or Partly by Sea**

The General Assembly,

Recalling its resolution 2205 (XXI) of 17 December 1966, by which it established the United Nations Commission on International Trade Law with a mandate to further the progressive harmonization and unification of the law of international trade and in that respect to bear in mind the interests of all peoples, in particular those of developing countries, in the extensive development of international trade,

Concerned that the current legal regime governing the international carriage of goods by sea lacks uniformity and fails to adequately take into account modern transport practices, including containerization, door-to-door transport contracts and the use of electronic transport documents,

Noting that the development of international trade on the basis of equality and mutual benefit is an important element in promoting friendly relations among States,

Convinced that the adoption of uniform rules to modernize and harmonize the rules that govern the international carriage of goods involving a sea leg would enhance legal certainty, improve efficiency and commercial predictability in the international carriage of goods and reduce legal obstacles to the flow of international trade among all States,

Believing that the adoption of uniform rules to govern international contracts of carriage wholly or partly by sea will promote legal certainty, improve the efficiency of international carriage of goods and facilitate new access opportunities for previously remote parties and markets, thus playing a fundamental role in promoting trade and economic development, both domestically and internationally,

Noting that shippers and carriers do not have the benefit of a binding and balanced universal regime to support the operation of contracts of carriage involving various modes of transport,

Recalling that, at its thirty-fourth and thirty-fifth sessions, in 2001 and 2002, the Commission decided to prepare an international legislative instrument governing door-to-door transport operations that involve a sea leg,[1]

Recognizing that all States and interested international organizations were invited to participate in the preparation of the draft Convention on Contracts for the International Carriage of Goods Wholly or Partly by Sea and in the forty-first session of the Commission, either as members or as observers, with a full opportunity to speak and make proposals,

Noting with satisfaction that the text of the draft Convention was circulated for comment to all States Members of the United Nations and intergovernmental organizations invited to attend the meetings of the Commission as observers, and that the comments received were before the Commission at its forty-first session,[2]

Taking note with satisfaction of the decision of the Commission at its forty first session to submit the draft Convention to the General Assembly for its consideration,[3]

Taking note of the draft Convention approved by the Commission,[4]

Expressing its appreciation to the Government of the Netherlands for its offer to host a signing ceremony for the Convention in Rotterdam,

1. *Commends* the United Nations Commission on International Trade Law for preparing the draft Convention on Contracts for the International Carriage of Goods Wholly or Partly by Sea;

2. *Adopts* the United Nations Convention on Contracts for the International Carriage of Goods Wholly or Partly by Sea, contained in the annex to the present resolution;

3. *Authorizes* a ceremony for the opening for signature to be held on 23 September 2009 in Rotterdam, the Netherlands, and recommends that the rules embodied in the Convention be known as the "Rotterdam Rules";

4. *Calls upon* all Governments to consider becoming party to the Convention.

67th plenary meeting
11 December 2008

---

[1] *Official Records of the General Assembly, Fifty-sixth Session, Supplement No. 17* and corrigendum (A/56/17 and Corr.3), paras. 319–345; and ibid., *Fifty-seventh Session, Supplement No. 17* (A/57/17), paras. 210–224.
[2] A/CN.9/658 and Add.1–14 and Add.14/Corr.1.
[3] *Official Records of the General Assembly, Sixty-third Session, Supplement No. 17* and corrigendum (A/63/17 and Corr.1), para. 298.
[4] Ibid., annex I.

Annex

United Nations Convention on Contracts for the International Carriage of Goods Wholly or Partly by Sea

The States Parties to this Convention,

Reaffirming their belief that international trade on the basis of equality and mutual benefit is an important element in promoting friendly relations among States,

Convinced that the progressive harmonization and unification of international trade law, in reducing or removing legal obstacles to the flow of international trade, significantly contributes to universal economic cooperation among all States on a basis of equality, equity and common interest, and to the well-being of all peoples,

Recognizing the significant contribution of the International Convention for the Unification of Certain Rules of Law relating to Bills of Lading, signed in Brussels on 25 August 1924, and its Protocols, and of the United Nations Convention on the Carriage of Goods by Sea, signed in Hamburg on 31 March 1978, to the harmonization of the law governing the carriage of goods by sea,

Mindful of the technological and commercial developments that have taken place since the adoption of those conventions and of the need to consolidate and modernize them,

Noting that shippers and carriers do not have the benefit of a binding universal regime to support the operation of contracts of maritime carriage involving other modes of transport,

Believing that the adoption of uniform rules to govern international contracts of carriage wholly or partly by sea will promote legal certainty, improve the efficiency of international carriage of goods and facilitate new access opportunities for previously remote parties and markets, thus playing a fundamental role in promoting trade and economic development, both domestically and internationally,

Have agreed as follows:

Chapter 1
General provisions

Article 1
Definitions

For the purposes of this Convention:

1.   "Contract of carriage" means a contract in which a carrier, against the payment of freight, undertakes to carry goods from one place to another. The contract shall provide for carriage by sea and may provide for carriage by other modes of transport in addition to the sea carriage.

2.   "Volume contract" means a contract of carriage that provides for the carriage of a specified quantity of goods in a series of shipments during an agreed period of time. The specification of the quantity may include a minimum, a maximum or a certain range.

3.   "Liner transportation" means a transportation service that is offered to the public through publication or similar means and includes transportation by ships operating on a regular schedule between specified ports in accordance with publicly available timetables of sailing dates.

4.   "Non-liner transportation" means any transportation that is not liner transportation.

5.   "Carrier" means a person that enters into a contract of carriage with a shipper.

6.   (*a*)   "Performing party" means a person other than the carrier that performs or undertakes to perform any of the carrier's obligations under a contract of carriage with respect to the receipt, loading, handling, stowage, carriage, care, unloading or delivery of the goods, to the extent that such person acts, either directly or indirectly, at the carrier's request or under the carrier's supervision or control.

    (*b*)   "Performing party" does not include any person that is retained, directly or indirectly, by a shipper, by a documentary shipper, by the controlling party or by the consignee instead of by the carrier.

7.   "Maritime performing party" means a performing party to the extent that it performs or undertakes to perform any of the carrier's obligations during the period between the arrival of the goods at the port of loading of a ship and their departure from the port of discharge of a ship. An inland carrier is a maritime performing party only if it performs or undertakes to perform its services exclusively within a port area.

8.   "Shipper" means a person that enters into a contract of carriage with a carrier.

9.   "Documentary shipper" means a person, other than the shipper, that accepts to be named as "shipper" in the transport document or electronic transport record.

10.   "Holder" means:

    (*a*)   A person that is in possession of a negotiable transport document; and (i) if the document is an order document, is identified in it as the shipper or the consignee, or is the person to which the document is duly endorsed; or (ii) if the document is a blank endorsed order document or bearer document, is the bearer thereof; or

    (*b*)   The person to which a negotiable electronic transport record has been issued or transferred in accordance with the procedures referred to in article 9, paragraph 1.

11.   "Consignee" means a person entitled to delivery of the goods under a contract of carriage or a transport document or electronic transport record.

12.   "Right of control" of the goods means the right under the contract of carriage to give the carrier instructions in respect of the goods in accordance with chapter 10.

13.   "Controlling party" means the person that pursuant to article 51 is entitled to exercise the right of control.

14.   "Transport document" means a document issued under a contract of carriage by the carrier that:

    (*a*)   Evidences the carrier's or a performing party's receipt of goods under a contract of carriage; and

    (*b*)   Evidences or contains a contract of carriage.

15. "Negotiable transport document" means a transport document that indicates, by wording such as "to order" or "negotiable" or other appropriate wording recognized as having the same effect by the law applicable to the document, that the goods have been consigned to the order of the shipper, to the order of the consignee, or to bearer, and is not explicitly stated as being "non-negotiable" or "not negotiable".

16. "Non-negotiable transport document" means a transport document that is not a negotiable transport document.

17. "Electronic communication" means information generated, sent, received or stored by electronic, optical, digital or similar means with the result that the information communicated is accessible so as to be usable for subsequent reference.

18. "Electronic transport record" means information in one or more messages issued by electronic communication under a contract of carriage by a carrier, including information logically associated with the electronic transport record by attachments or otherwise linked to the electronic transport record contemporaneously with or subsequent to its issue by the carrier, so as to become part of the electronic transport record, that:

(a) Evidences the carrier's or a performing party's receipt of goods under a contract of carriage; and

(b) Evidences or contains a contract of carriage.

19. "Negotiable electronic transport record" means an electronic transport record:

(a) That indicates, by wording such as "to order", or "negotiable", or other appropriate wording recognized as having the same effect by the law applicable to the record, that the goods have been consigned to the order of the shipper or to the order of the consignee, and is not explicitly stated as being "non-negotiable" or "not negotiable"; and

(b) The use of which meets the requirements of article 9, paragraph 1.

20. "Non-negotiable electronic transport record" means an electronic transport record that is not a negotiable electronic transport record.

21. The "issuance" of a negotiable electronic transport record means the issuance of the record in accordance with procedures that ensure that the record is subject to exclusive control from its creation until it ceases to have any effect or validity.

22. The "transfer" of a negotiable electronic transport record means the transfer of exclusive control over the record.

23. "Contract particulars" means any information relating to the contract of carriage or to the goods (including terms, notations, signatures and endorsements) that is in a transport document or an electronic transport record.

24. "Goods" means the wares, merchandise, and articles of every kind whatsoever that a carrier undertakes to carry under a contract of carriage and includes the packing and any equipment and container not supplied by or on behalf of the carrier.

25. "Ship" means any vessel used to carry goods by sea.

26. "Container" means any type of container, transportable tank or flat, swapbody, or any similar unit load used to consolidate goods, and any equipment ancillary to such unit load.

27.   "Vehicle" means a road or railroad cargo vehicle.

28.   "Freight" means the remuneration payable to the carrier for the carriage of goods under a contract of carriage.

29.   "Domicile" means (*a*) a place where a company or other legal person or association of natural or legal persons has its (i) statutory seat or place of incorporation or central registered office, whichever is applicable, (ii) central administration or (iii) principal place of business, and (*b*) the habitual residence of a natural person.

30.   "Competent court" means a court in a Contracting State that, according to the rules on the internal allocation of jurisdiction among the courts of that State, may exercise jurisdiction over the dispute.

Article 2
Interpretation of this Convention

In the interpretation of this Convention, regard is to be had to its international character and to the need to promote uniformity in its application and the observance of good faith in international trade.

Article 3
Form requirements

The notices, confirmation, consent, agreement, declaration and other communications referred to in articles 19, paragraph 2; 23, paragraphs 1 to 4; 36, subparagraphs 1 (*b*), (*c*) and (*d*); 40, subparagraph 4 (*b*); 44; 48, paragraph 3; 51, subparagraph 1 (*b*); 59, paragraph 1; 63; 66; 67, paragraph 2; 75, paragraph 4; and 80, paragraphs 2 and 5, shall be in writing. Electronic communications may be used for these purposes, provided that the use of such means is with the consent of the person by which it is communicated and of the person to which it is communicated.

Article 4
Applicability of defences and limits of liability

1.   Any provision of this Convention that may provide a defence for, or limit the liability of, the carrier applies in any judicial or arbitral proceeding, whether founded in contract, in tort, or otherwise, that is instituted in respect of loss of, damage to, or delay in delivery of goods covered by a contract of carriage or for the breach of any other obligation under this Convention against:

   (*a*)   The carrier or a maritime performing party;

   (*b*)   The master, crew or any other person that performs services on board the ship; or

   (*c*)   Employees of the carrier or a maritime performing party.

2.   Any provision of this Convention that may provide a defence for the shipper or the documentary shipper applies in any judicial or arbitral proceeding, whether founded in contract, in tort, or otherwise, that is instituted against the shipper, the documentary shipper, or their subcontractors, agents or employees.

Chapter 2
Scope of application

Article 5
General scope of application

1.   Subject to article 6, this Convention applies to contracts of carriage in which the place of receipt and the place of delivery are in different States, and the port of loading of a sea carriage and the port of discharge of the same sea carriage are in different States, if, according to the contract of carriage, any one of the following places is located in a Contracting State:

(*a*)   The place of receipt;

(*b*)   The port of loading;

(*c*)   The place of delivery; or

(*d*)   The port of discharge.

2.   This Convention applies without regard to the nationality of the vessel, the carrier, the performing parties, the shipper, the consignee, or any other interested parties.

Article 6
Specific exclusions

1.   This Convention does not apply to the following contracts in liner transportation:

(*a*)   charter parties; and

(*b*)   Other contracts for the use of a ship or of any space thereon.

2.   This Convention does not apply to contracts of carriage in non-liner transportation except when:

(*a*)   There is no charter party or other contract between the parties for the use of a ship or of any space thereon; and

(*b*)   A transport document or an electronic transport record is issued.

Article 7
Application to certain parties

Notwithstanding article 6, this Convention applies as between the carrier and the consignee, controlling party or holder that is not an original party to the charter party or other contract of carriage excluded from the application of this Convention. However, this Convention does not apply as between the original parties to a contract of carriage excluded pursuant to article 6.

Chapter 3
Electronic transport records

Article 8
Use and effect of electronic transport records

Subject to the requirements set out in this Convention:

(*a*)   Anything that is to be in or on a transport document under this Convention may be recorded in an electronic transport record, provided the issuance and subsequent use of an electronic transport record is with the consent of the carrier and the shipper; and

(*b*)   The issuance, exclusive control, or transfer of an electronic transport record has the same effect as the issuance, possession, or transfer of a transport document.

Article 9
Procedures for use of negotiable electronic transport records

1.   The use of a negotiable electronic transport record shall be subject to procedures that provide for:

(*a*)   The method for the issuance and the transfer of that record to an intended holder;

(*b*)   An assurance that the negotiable electronic transport record retains its integrity;

(*c*)   The manner in which the holder is able to demonstrate that it is the holder; and

(*d*)   The manner of providing confirmation that delivery to the holder has been effected, or that, pursuant to articles 10, paragraph 2, or 47, subparagraphs 1 (*a*) (ii) and (*c*), the electronic transport record has ceased to have any effect or validity.

2.   The procedures in paragraph 1 of this article shall be referred to in the contract particulars and be readily ascertainable.

Article 10
Replacement of negotiable transport document or negotiable electronic transport record

1.   If a negotiable transport document has been issued and the carrier and the holder agree to replace that document by a negotiable electronic transport record:

(*a*)   The holder shall surrender the negotiable transport document, or all of them if more than one has been issued, to the carrier;

(*b*)   The carrier shall issue to the holder a negotiable electronic transport record that includes a statement that it replaces the negotiable transport document; and

(*c*)   The negotiable transport document ceases thereafter to have any effect or validity.

2.   If a negotiable electronic transport record has been issued and the carrier and the holder agree to replace that electronic transport record by a negotiable transport document:

(*a*)   The carrier shall issue to the holder, in place of the electronic transport record, a negotiable transport document that includes a statement that it replaces the negotiable electronic transport record; and

(*b*)   The electronic transport record ceases thereafter to have any effect or validity.

Chapter 4
Obligations of the carrier

Article 11
Carriage and delivery of the goods

The carrier shall, subject to this Convention and in accordance with the terms of the contract of carriage, carry the goods to the place of destination and deliver them to the consignee.

Article 12
Period of responsibility of the carrier

1. The period of responsibility of the carrier for the goods under this Convention begins when the carrier or a performing party receives the goods for carriage and ends when the goods are delivered.

2. (*a*) If the law or regulations of the place of receipt require the goods to be handed over to an authority or other third party from which the carrier may collect them, the period of responsibility of the carrier begins when the carrier collects the goods from the authority or other third party.

(*b*) If the law or regulations of the place of delivery require the carrier to hand over the goods to an authority or other third party from which the consignee may collect them, the period of responsibility of the carrier ends when the carrier hands the goods over to the authority or other third party.

3. For the purpose of determining the carrier's period of responsibility, the parties may agree on the time and location of receipt and delivery of the goods, but a provision in a contract of carriage is void to the extent that it provides that:

(*a*) The time of receipt of the goods is subsequent to the beginning of their initial loading under the contract of carriage; or

(*b*) The time of delivery of the goods is prior to the completion of their final unloading under the contract of carriage.

Article 13
Specific obligations

1. The carrier shall during the period of its responsibility as defined in article 12, and subject to article 26, properly and carefully receive, load, handle, stow, carry, keep, care for, unload and deliver the goods.

2. Notwithstanding paragraph 1 of this article, and without prejudice to the other provisions in chapter 4 and to chapters 5 to 7, the carrier and the shipper may agree that the loading, handling, stowing or unloading of the goods is to be performed by the shipper, the documentary shipper or the consignee. Such an agreement shall be referred to in the contract particulars.

Article 14
Specific obligations applicable to the voyage by sea

The carrier is bound before, at the beginning of, and during the voyage by sea to exercise due diligence to:

(*a*) Make and keep the ship seaworthy;

(*b*)   Properly crew, equip and supply the ship and keep the ship so crewed, equipped and supplied throughout the voyage; and

(*c*)   Make and keep the holds and all other parts of the ship in which the goods are carried, and any containers supplied by the carrier in or upon which the goods are carried, fit and safe for their reception, carriage and preservation.

Article 15
Goods that may become a danger

Notwithstanding articles 11 and 13, the carrier or a performing party may decline to receive or to load, and may take such other measures as are reasonable, including unloading, destroying, or rendering goods harmless, if the goods are, or reasonably appear likely to become during the carrier's period of responsibility, an actual danger to persons, property or the environment.

Article 16
Sacrifice of the goods during the voyage by sea

Notwithstanding articles 11, 13, and 14, the carrier or a performing party may sacrifice goods at sea when the sacrifice is reasonably made for the common safety or for the purpose of preserving from peril human life or other property involved in the common adventure.

Chapter 5
Liability of the carrier for loss, damage or delay

Article 17
Basis of liability

1.   The carrier is liable for loss of or damage to the goods, as well as for delay in delivery, if the claimant proves that the loss, damage, or delay, or the event or circumstance that caused or contributed to it took place during the period of the carrier's responsibility as defined in chapter 4.

2.   The carrier is relieved of all or part of its liability pursuant to paragraph 1 of this article if it proves that the cause or one of the causes of the loss, damage, or delay is not attributable to its fault or to the fault of any person referred to in article 18.

3.   The carrier is also relieved of all or part of its liability pursuant to paragraph 1 of this article if, alternatively to proving the absence of fault as provided in paragraph 2 of this article, it proves that one or more of the following events or circumstances caused or contributed to the loss, damage, or delay:

(*a*)   Act of God;

(*b*)   Perils, dangers, and accidents of the sea or other navigable waters;

(*c*)   War, hostilities, armed conflict, piracy, terrorism, riots, and civil commotions;

(*d*)   Quarantine restrictions; interference by or impediments created by governments, public authorities, rulers, or people including detention, arrest, or seizure not attributable to the carrier or any person referred to in article 18;

(*e*)   Strikes, lockouts, stoppages, or restraints of labour;

(*f*)   Fire on the ship;

(*g*)   Latent defects not discoverable by due diligence;

(*h*)   Act or omission of the shipper, the documentary shipper, the controlling party, or any other person for whose acts the shipper or the documentary shipper is liable pursuant to article 33 or 34;

(*i*)   Loading, handling, stowing, or unloading of the goods performed pursuant to an agreement in accordance with article 13, paragraph 2, unless the carrier or a performing party performs such activity on behalf of the shipper, the documentary shipper or the consignee;

(*j*)   Wastage in bulk or weight or any other loss or damage arising from inherent defect, quality, or vice of the goods;

(*k*)   Insufficiency or defective condition of packing or marking not performed by or on behalf of the carrier;

(*l*)   Saving or attempting to save life at sea;

(*m*)   Reasonable measures to save or attempt to save property at sea;

(*n*)   Reasonable measures to avoid or attempt to avoid damage to the environment; or

(*o*)   Acts of the carrier in pursuance of the powers conferred by articles 15 and 16.

4.   Notwithstanding paragraph 3 of this article, the carrier is liable for all or part of the loss, damage, or delay:

(*a*)   If the claimant proves that the fault of the carrier or of a person referred to in article 18 caused or contributed to the event or circumstance on which the carrier relies; or

(*b*)   If the claimant proves that an event or circumstance not listed in paragraph 3 of this article contributed to the loss, damage, or delay, and the carrier cannot prove that this event or circumstance is not attributable to its fault or to the fault of any person referred to in article 18.

5.   The carrier is also liable, notwithstanding paragraph 3 of this article, for all or part of the loss, damage, or delay if:

(*a*)   The claimant proves that the loss, damage, or delay was or was probably caused by or contributed to by (i) the unseaworthiness of the ship; (ii) the improper crewing, equipping, and supplying of the ship; or (iii) the fact that the holds or other parts of the ship in which the goods are carried, or any containers supplied by the carrier in or upon which the goods are carried, were not fit and safe for reception, carriage, and preservation of the goods; and

(*b*)   The carrier is unable to prove either that: (i) none of the events or circumstances referred to in subparagraph 5 (*a*) of this article caused the loss, damage, or delay; or (ii) it complied with its obligation to exercise due diligence pursuant to article 14.

6.   When the carrier is relieved of part of its liability pursuant to this article, the carrier is liable only for that part of the loss, damage or delay that is attributable to the event or circumstance for which it is liable pursuant to this article.

Article 18
Liability of the carrier for other persons

The carrier is liable for the breach of its obligations under this Convention caused by the acts or omissions of:

(*a*)   Any performing party;

(*b*)   The master or crew of the ship;

(*c*)   Employees of the carrier or a performing party; or

(*d*)   Any other person that performs or undertakes to perform any of the carrier's obligations under the contract of carriage, to the extent that the person acts, either directly or indirectly, at the carrier's request or under the carrier's supervision or control.

Article 19
Liability of maritime performing parties

1.   A maritime performing party is subject to the obligations and liabilities imposed on the carrier under this Convention and is entitled to the carrier's defences and limits of liability as provided for in this Convention if:

(*a*)   The maritime performing party received the goods for carriage in a Contracting State, or delivered them in a Contracting State, or performed its activities with respect to the goods in a port in a Contracting State; and

(*b*)   The occurrence that caused the loss, damage or delay took place: (i) during the period between the arrival of the goods at the port of loading of the ship and their departure from the port of discharge from the ship; (ii) while the maritime performing party had custody of the goods; or (iii) at any other time to the extent that it was participating in the performance of any of the activities contemplated by the contract of carriage.

2.   If the carrier agrees to assume obligations other than those imposed on the carrier under this Convention, or agrees that the limits of its liability are higher than the limits specified under this Convention, a maritime performing party is not bound by this agreement unless it expressly agrees to accept such obligations or such higher limits.

3.   A maritime performing party is liable for the breach of its obligations under this Convention caused by the acts or omissions of any person to which it has entrusted the performance of any of the carrier's obligations under the contract of carriage under the conditions set out in paragraph 1 of this article.

4.   Nothing in this Convention imposes liability on the master or crew of the ship or on an employee of the carrier or of a maritime performing party.

Article 20
Joint and several liability

1.   If the carrier and one or more maritime performing parties are liable for the loss of, damage to, or delay in delivery of the goods, their liability is joint and several but only up to the limits provided for under this Convention.

2.   Without prejudice to article 61, the aggregate liability of all such persons shall not exceed the overall limits of liability under this Convention.

Article 21
Delay

Delay in delivery occurs when the goods are not delivered at the place of destination provided for in the contract of carriage within the time agreed.

Article 22
Calculation of compensation

1.   Subject to article 59, the compensation payable by the carrier for loss of or damage to the goods is calculated by reference to the value of such goods at the place and time of delivery established in accordance with article 43.

2.   The value of the goods is fixed according to the commodity exchange price or, if there is no such price, according to their market price or, if there is no commodity exchange price or market price, by reference to the normal value of the goods of the same kind and quality at the place of delivery.

3.   In case of loss of or damage to the goods, the carrier is not liable for payment of any compensation beyond what is provided for in paragraphs 1 and 2 of this article except when the carrier and the shipper have agreed to calculate compensation in a different manner within the limits of chapter 16.

Article 23
Notice in case of loss, damage or delay

1.   The carrier is presumed, in absence of proof to the contrary, to have delivered the goods according to their description in the contract particulars unless notice of loss of or damage to the goods, indicating the general nature of such loss or damage, was given to the carrier or the performing party that delivered the goods before or at the time of the delivery, or, if the loss or damage is not apparent, within seven working days at the place of delivery after the delivery of the goods.

2.   Failure to provide the notice referred to in this article to the carrier or the performing party shall not affect the right to claim compensation for loss of or damage to the goods under this Convention, nor shall it affect the allocation of the burden of proof set out in article 17.

3.   The notice referred to in this article is not required in respect of loss or damage that is ascertained in a joint inspection of the goods by the person to which they have been delivered and the carrier or the maritime performing party against which liability is being asserted.

4.   No compensation in respect of delay is payable unless notice of loss due to delay was given to the carrier within twenty-one consecutive days of delivery of the goods.

5.   When the notice referred to in this article is given to the performing party that delivered the goods, it has the same effect as if that notice was given to the carrier, and notice given to the carrier has the same effect as a notice given to a maritime performing party.

6.   In the case of any actual or apprehended loss or damage, the parties to the dispute shall give all reasonable facilities to each other for inspecting and tallying the goods and shall provide access to records and documents relevant to the carriage of the goods.

Chapter 6
Additional provisions relating to particular stages of carriage

Article 24
Deviation

When pursuant to applicable law a deviation constitutes a breach of the carrier's obligations, such deviation of itself shall not deprive the carrier or a maritime performing party of any defence or limitation of this Convention, except to the extent provided in article 61.

Article 25
Deck cargo on ships

1. Goods may be carried on the deck of a ship only if:

    (*a*) Such carriage is required by law;

    (*b*) They are carried in or on containers or vehicles that are fit for deck carriage, and the decks are specially fitted to carry such containers or vehicles; or

    (*c*) The carriage on deck is in accordance with the contract of carriage, or the customs, usages or practices of the trade in question.

2. The provisions of this Convention relating to the liability of the carrier apply to the loss of, damage to or delay in the delivery of goods carried on deck pursuant to paragraph 1 of this article, but the carrier is not liable for loss of or damage to such goods, or delay in their delivery, caused by the special risks involved in their carriage on deck when the goods are carried in accordance with subparagraphs 1 (*a*) or (*c*) of this article.

3. If the goods have been carried on deck in cases other than those permitted pursuant to paragraph 1 of this article, the carrier is liable for loss of or damage to the goods or delay in their delivery that is exclusively caused by their carriage on deck, and is not entitled to the defences provided for in article 17.

4. The carrier is not entitled to invoke subparagraph 1 (*c*) of this article against a third party that has acquired a negotiable transport document or a negotiable electronic transport record in good faith, unless the contract particulars state that the goods may be carried on deck.

5. If the carrier and shipper expressly agreed that the goods would be carried under deck, the carrier is not entitled to the benefit of the limitation of liability for any loss of, damage to or delay in the delivery of the goods to the extent that such loss, damage, or delay resulted from their carriage on deck.

Article 26
Carriage preceding or subsequent to sea carriage

When loss of or damage to goods, or an event or circumstance causing a delay in their delivery, occurs during the carrier's period of responsibility but solely before their loading onto the ship or solely after their discharge from the ship, the provisions of this Convention do not prevail over those provisions of another international instrument that, at the time of such loss, damage or event or circumstance causing delay:

(*a*) Pursuant to the provisions of such international instrument would have applied to all or any of the carrier's activities if the shipper had made a separate and direct contract with the carrier in respect of the particular stage of carriage where the loss of, or damage to goods, or an event or circumstance causing delay in their delivery occurred;

(*b*)   Specifically provide for the carrier's liability, limitation of liability, or time for suit; and

(*c*)   Cannot be departed from by contract either at all or to the detriment of the shipper under that instrument.

Chapter 7
Obligations of the shipper to the carrier

Article 27
Delivery for carriage

1.   Unless otherwise agreed in the contract of carriage, the shipper shall deliver the goods ready for carriage. In any event, the shipper shall deliver the goods in such condition that they will withstand the intended carriage, including their loading, handling, stowing, lashing and securing, and unloading, and that they will not cause harm to persons or property.

2.   The shipper shall properly and carefully perform any obligation assumed under an agreement made pursuant to article 13, paragraph 2.

3.   When a container is packed or a vehicle is loaded by the shipper, the shipper shall properly and carefully stow, lash and secure the contents in or on the container or vehicle, and in such a way that they will not cause harm to persons or property.

Article 28
Cooperation of the shipper and the carrier in providing information and instructions

The carrier and the shipper shall respond to requests from each other to provide information and instructions required for the proper handling and carriage of the goods if the information is in the requested party's possession or the instructions are within the requested party's reasonable ability to provide and they are not otherwise reasonably available to the requesting party.

Article 29
Shipper's obligation to provide information, instructions and documents

1.   The shipper shall provide to the carrier in a timely manner such information, instructions and documents relating to the goods that are not otherwise reasonably available to the carrier, and that are reasonably necessary:

(*a*)   For the proper handling and carriage of the goods, including precautions to be taken by the carrier or a performing party; and

(*b*)   For the carrier to comply with law, regulations or other requirements of public authorities in connection with the intended carriage, provided that the carrier notifies the shipper in a timely manner of the information, instructions and documents it requires.

2.   Nothing in this article affects any specific obligation to provide certain information, instructions and documents related to the goods pursuant to law,

regulations or other requirements of public authorities in connection with the intended carriage.

Article 30
Basis of shipper's liability to the carrier

1.   The shipper is liable for loss or damage sustained by the carrier if the carrier proves that such loss or damage was caused by a breach of the shipper's obligations under this Convention.

2.   Except in respect of loss or damage caused by a breach by the shipper of its obligations pursuant to articles 31, paragraph 2, and 32, the shipper is relieved of all or part of its liability if the cause or one of the causes of the loss or damage is not attributable to its fault or to the fault of any person referred to in article 34.

3.   When the shipper is relieved of part of its liability pursuant to this article, the shipper is liable only for that part of the loss or damage that is attributable to its fault or to the fault of any person referred to in article 34.

Article 31
Information for compilation of contract particulars

1.   The shipper shall provide to the carrier, in a timely manner, accurate information required for the compilation of the contract particulars and the issuance of the transport documents or electronic transport records, including the particulars referred to in article 36, paragraph 1; the name of the party to be identified as the shipper in the contract particulars; the name of the consignee, if any; and the name of the person to whose order the transport document or electronic transport record is to be issued, if any.

2.   The shipper is deemed to have guaranteed the accuracy at the time of receipt by the carrier of the information that is provided according to paragraph 1 of this article. The shipper shall indemnify the carrier against loss or damage resulting from the inaccuracy of such information.

Article 32
Special rules on dangerous goods

When goods by their nature or character are, or reasonably appear likely to become, a danger to persons, property or the environment:

(*a*)   The shipper shall inform the carrier of the dangerous nature or character of the goods in a timely manner before they are delivered to the carrier or a performing party. If the shipper fails to do so and the carrier or performing party does not otherwise have knowledge of their dangerous nature or character, the shipper is liable to the carrier for loss or damage resulting from such failure to inform; and

(*b*)   The shipper shall mark or label dangerous goods in accordance with any law, regulations or other requirements of public authorities that apply during any stage of the intended carriage of the goods. If the shipper fails to do so, it is liable to the carrier for loss or damage resulting from such failure.

Article 33
Assumption of shipper's rights and obligations by the documentary shipper

1.   A documentary shipper is subject to the obligations and liabilities imposed on the shipper pursuant to this chapter and pursuant to article 55, and is entitled to the shipper's rights and defences provided by this chapter and by chapter 13.

2.   Paragraph 1 of this article does not affect the obligations, liabilities, rights or defences of the shipper.

Article 34
Liability of the shipper for other persons

The shipper is liable for the breach of its obligations under this Convention caused by the acts or omissions of any person, including employees, agents and subcontractors, to which it has entrusted the performance of any of its obligations, but the shipper is not liable for acts or omissions of the carrier or a performing party acting on behalf of the carrier, to which the shipper has entrusted the performance of its obligations.

Chapter 8
Transport documents and electronic transport records

Article 35
Issuance of the transport document or the electronic transport record

Unless the shipper and the carrier have agreed not to use a transport document or an electronic transport record, or it is the custom, usage or practice of the trade not to use one, upon delivery of the goods for carriage to the carrier or performing party, the shipper or, if the shipper consents, the documentary shipper, is entitled to obtain from the carrier, at the shipper's option:

(*a*)   A non-negotiable transport document or, subject to article 8, subparagraph (*a*), a non-negotiable electronic transport record; or

(*b*)   An appropriate negotiable transport document or, subject to article 8, subparagraph (*a*), a negotiable electronic transport record, unless the shipper and the carrier have agreed not to use a negotiable transport document or negotiable electronic transport record, or it is the custom, usage or practice of the trade not to use one.

Article 36
Contract particulars

1.   The contract particulars in the transport document or electronic transport record referred to in article 35 shall include the following information, as furnished by the shipper:

(*a*)   A description of the goods as appropriate for the transport;

(*b*)   The leading marks necessary for identification of the goods;

(*c*)   The number of packages or pieces, or the quantity of goods; and

(*d*)   The weight of the goods, if furnished by the shipper.

2.   The contract particulars in the transport document or electronic transport record referred to in article 35 shall also include:

(*a*)   A statement of the apparent order and condition of the goods at the time the carrier or a performing party receives them for carriage;

(*b*)   The name and address of the carrier;

(*c*)   The date on which the carrier or a performing party received the goods, or on which the goods were loaded on board the ship, or on which the transport document or electronic transport record was issued; and

(*d*)   If the transport document is negotiable, the number of originals of the negotiable transport document, when more than one original is issued.

3.   The contract particulars in the transport document or electronic transport record referred to in article 35 shall further include:

(*a*)   The name and address of the consignee, if named by the shipper;

(*b*)   The name of a ship, if specified in the contract of carriage;

(*c*)   The place of receipt and, if known to the carrier, the place of delivery; and

(*d*)   The port of loading and the port of discharge, if specified in the contract of carriage.

4.   For the purposes of this article, the phrase "apparent order and condition of the goods" in subparagraph 2 (*a*) of this article refers to the order and condition of the goods based on:

(*a*)   A reasonable external inspection of the goods as packaged at the time the shipper delivers them to the carrier or a performing party; and

(*b*)   Any additional inspection that the carrier or a performing party actually performs before issuing the transport document or electronic transport record.

Article 37
Identity of the carrier

1.   If a carrier is identified by name in the contract particulars, any other information in the transport document or electronic transport record relating to the identity of the carrier shall have no effect to the extent that it is inconsistent with that identification.

2.   If no person is identified in the contract particulars as the carrier as required pursuant to article 36, subparagraph 2 (*b*), but the contract particulars indicate that the goods have been loaded on board a named ship, the registered owner of that ship is presumed to be the carrier, unless it proves that the ship was under a bareboat charter at the time of the carriage and it identifies this bareboat charterer and indicates its address, in which case this bareboat charterer is presumed to be the carrier. Alternatively, the registered owner may rebut the presumption of being the carrier by identifying the carrier and indicating its address. The bareboat charterer may rebut any presumption of being the carrier in the same manner.

3.   Nothing in this article prevents the claimant from proving that any person other than a person identified in the contract particulars or pursuant to paragraph 2 of this article is the carrier.

Article 38
Signature

1.   A transport document shall be signed by the carrier or a person acting on its behalf.

2.   An electronic transport record shall include the electronic signature of the carrier or a person acting on its behalf. Such electronic signature shall identify the signatory in relation to the electronic transport record and indicate the carrier's authorization of the electronic transport record.

Article 39
Deficiencies in the contract particulars

1.   The absence or inaccuracy of one or more of the contract particulars referred to in article 36, paragraphs 1, 2 or 3, does not of itself affect the legal character or validity of the transport document or of the electronic transport record.

2.   If the contract particulars include the date but fail to indicate its significance, the date is deemed to be:

(*a*)   The date on which all of the goods indicated in the transport document or electronic transport record were loaded on board the ship, if the contract particulars indicate that the goods have been loaded on board a ship; or

(*b*)   The date on which the carrier or a performing party received the goods, if the contract particulars do not indicate that the goods have been loaded on board a ship.

3.   If the contract particulars fail to state the apparent order and condition of the goods at the time the carrier or a performing party receives them, the contract particulars are deemed to have stated that the goods were in apparent good order and condition at the time the carrier or a performing party received them.

Article 40
Qualifying the information relating to the goods in the contract particulars

1.   The carrier shall qualify the information referred to in article 36, paragraph 1, to indicate that the carrier does not assume responsibility for the accuracy of the information furnished by the shipper if:

(*a*)   The carrier has actual knowledge that any material statement in the transport document or electronic transport record is false or misleading; or

(*b*)   The carrier has reasonable grounds to believe that a material statement in the transport document or electronic transport record is false or misleading.

2.   Without prejudice to paragraph 1 of this article, the carrier may qualify the information referred to in article 36, paragraph 1, in the circumstances and in the manner set out in paragraphs 3 and 4 of this article to indicate that the carrier does not assume responsibility for the accuracy of the information furnished by the shipper.

3.   When the goods are not delivered for carriage to the carrier or a performing party in a closed container or vehicle, or when they are delivered in a closed container or vehicle and the carrier or a performing party actually inspects them, the carrier may qualify the information referred to in article 36, paragraph 1, if:

(*a*)   The carrier had no physically practicable or commercially reasonable means of checking the information furnished by the shipper, in which case it may indicate which information it was unable to check; or

(*b*)   The carrier has reasonable grounds to believe the information furnished by the shipper to be inaccurate, in which case it may include a clause providing what it reasonably considers accurate information.

4.   When the goods are delivered for carriage to the carrier or a performing party in a closed container or vehicle, the carrier may qualify the information referred to in:

(*a*)   Article 36, subparagraphs 1 (*a*), (*b*), or (*c*), if:

(i)   The goods inside the container or vehicle have not actually been inspected by the carrier or a performing party; and

(ii)   Neither the carrier nor a performing party otherwise has actual knowledge of its contents before issuing the transport document or the electronic transport record; and

(*b*)   Article 36, subparagraph 1 (*d*), if:

(i)   Neither the carrier nor a performing party weighed the container or vehicle, and the shipper and the carrier had not agreed prior to the shipment that the container or vehicle would be weighed and the weight would be included in the contract particulars; or

(ii)   There was no physically practicable or commercially reasonable means of checking the weight of the container or vehicle.

Article 41
Evidentiary effect of the contract particulars

Except to the extent that the contract particulars have been qualified in the circumstances and in the manner set out in article 40:

(*a*)   A transport document or an electronic transport record is prima facie evidence of the carrier's receipt of the goods as stated in the contract particulars;

(*b*)   Proof to the contrary by the carrier in respect of any contract particulars shall not be admissible, when such contract particulars are included in:

(i)   A negotiable transport document or a negotiable electronic transport record that is transferred to a third party acting in good faith; or

(ii)   A non-negotiable transport document that indicates that it must be surrendered in order to obtain delivery of the goods and is transferred to the consignee acting in good faith;

(*c*)   Proof to the contrary by the carrier shall not be admissible against a consignee that in good faith has acted in reliance on any of the following contract particulars included in a non-negotiable transport document or a non-negotiable electronic transport record:

(i)   The contract particulars referred to in article 36, paragraph 1, when such contract particulars are furnished by the carrier;

(ii)   The number, type and identifying numbers of the containers, but not the identifying numbers of the container seals; and

(iii)   The contract particulars referred to in article 36, paragraph 2.

Article 42
"Freight prepaid"

If the contract particulars contain the statement "freight prepaid" or a statement of a similar nature, the carrier cannot assert against the holder or the consignee the fact that the freight has not been paid. This article does not apply if the holder or the consignee is also the shipper.

Chapter 9
Delivery of the goods

Article 43
Obligation to accept delivery

When the goods have arrived at their destination, the consignee that demands delivery of the goods under the contract of carriage shall accept delivery of the goods at the time or within the time period and at the location agreed in the contract of carriage or, failing such agreement, at the time and location at which, having regard to the terms of the contract, the customs, usages or practices of the trade and the circumstances of the carriage, delivery could reasonably be expected.

Article 44
Obligation to acknowledge receipt

On request of the carrier or the performing party that delivers the goods, the consignee shall acknowledge receipt of the goods from the carrier or the performing party in the manner that is customary at the place of delivery. The carrier may refuse delivery if the consignee refuses to acknowledge such receipt.

Article 45
Delivery when no negotiable transport document or negotiable electronic transport record is issued

When neither a negotiable transport document nor a negotiable electronic transport record has been issued:

(a) The carrier shall deliver the goods to the consignee at the time and location referred to in article 43. The carrier may refuse delivery if the person claiming to be the consignee does not properly identify itself as the consignee on the request of the carrier;

(b) If the name and address of the consignee are not referred to in the contract particulars, the controlling party shall prior to or upon the arrival of the goods at the place of destination advise the carrier of such name and address;

(c) Without prejudice to article 48, paragraph 1, if the goods are not deliverable because (i) the consignee, after having received a notice of arrival, does not, at the time or within the time period referred to in article 43, claim delivery of the goods from the carrier after their arrival at the place of destination, (ii) the carrier refuses delivery because the person claiming to be the consignee does not properly identify itself as the consignee, or (iii) the carrier is, after reasonable effort, unable to locate the consignee in order to request delivery instructions, the carrier may so advise the controlling party and request instructions in respect of the delivery of the goods. If, after reasonable effort, the carrier is unable to locate the controlling party, the carrier may so advise the shipper and request instructions in respect of the delivery of the goods. If, after reasonable effort, the carrier is unable to locate the shipper, the carrier may so advise the documentary shipper and request instructions in respect of the delivery of the goods;

(d) The carrier that delivers the goods upon instruction of the controlling party, the shipper or the documentary shipper pursuant to subparagraph *(c)* of this article is discharged from its obligations to deliver the goods under the contract of carriage.

Article 46
Delivery when a non-negotiable transport document that requires surrender is issued

When a non-negotiable transport document has been issued that indicates that it shall be surrendered in order to obtain delivery of the goods:

(a) The carrier shall deliver the goods at the time and location referred to in article 43 to the consignee upon the consignee properly identifying itself on the request of the carrier and surrender of the non-negotiable document. The carrier may refuse delivery if the person claiming to be the consignee fails to properly identify itself on the request of the carrier, and shall refuse delivery if the non-negotiable document is not surrendered. If more than one original of the non-negotiable document has been issued, the surrender of one original will suffice and the other originals cease to have any effect or validity;

(b) Without prejudice to article 48, paragraph 1, if the goods are not deliverable because (i) the consignee, after having received a notice of arrival, does not, at the time

or within the time period referred to in article 43, claim delivery of the goods from the carrier after their arrival at the place of destination, (ii) the carrier refuses delivery because the person claiming to be the consignee does not properly identify itself as the consignee or does not surrender the document, or (iii) the carrier is, after reasonable effort, unable to locate the consignee in order to request delivery instructions, the carrier may so advise the shipper and request instructions in respect of the delivery of the goods. If, after reasonable effort, the carrier is unable to locate the shipper, the carrier may so advise the documentary shipper and request instructions in respect of the delivery of the goods;

(c) The carrier that delivers the goods upon instruction of the shipper or the documentary shipper pursuant to subparagraph (b) of this article is discharged from its obligation to deliver the goods under the contract of carriage, irrespective of whether the non-negotiable transport document has been surrendered to it.

Article 47
Delivery when a negotiable transport document or negotiable electronic transport record is issued

1. When a negotiable transport document or a negotiable electronic transport record has been issued:

(a) The holder of the negotiable transport document or negotiable electronic transport record is entitled to claim delivery of the goods from the carrier after they have arrived at the place of destination, in which event the carrier shall deliver the goods at the time and location referred to in article 43 to the holder:

(i) Upon surrender of the negotiable transport document and, if the holder is one of the persons referred to in article 1, subparagraph 10 (a) (i), upon the holder properly identifying itself; or

(ii) Upon demonstration by the holder, in accordance with the procedures referred to in article 9, paragraph 1, that it is the holder of the negotiable electronic transport record;

(b) The carrier shall refuse delivery if the requirements of subparagraph (a) (i) or (a) (ii) of this paragraph are not met;

(c) If more than one original of the negotiable transport document has been issued, and the number of originals is stated in that document, the surrender of one original will suffice and the other originals cease to have any effect or validity. When a negotiable electronic transport record has been used, such electronic transport record ceases to have any effect or validity upon delivery to the holder in accordance with the procedures required by article 9, paragraph 1.

2. Without prejudice to article 48, paragraph 1, if the negotiable transport document or the negotiable electronic transport record expressly states that the goods may be delivered without the surrender of the transport document or the electronic transport record, the following rules apply:

(a) If the goods are not deliverable because (i) the holder, after having received a notice of arrival, does not, at the time or within the time period referred to in article 43, claim delivery of the goods from the carrier after their arrival at the place of destination, (ii) the carrier refuses delivery because the person claiming to be a holder does not properly identify itself as one of the persons referred to in article 1, subparagraph 10 (a) (i), or (iii) the carrier is, after reasonable effort, unable to locate the holder in order to request delivery instructions, the carrier may so advise the shipper and request instructions in respect of the delivery of the goods. If, after reasonable effort, the carrier is unable to locate the shipper, the carrier may so advise

the documentary shipper and request instructions in respect of the delivery of the goods;

(b)   The carrier that delivers the goods upon instruction of the shipper or the documentary shipper in accordance with subparagraph 2 (*a*) of this article is discharged from its obligation to deliver the goods under the contract of carriage to the holder, irrespective of whether the negotiable transport document has been surrendered to it, or the person claiming delivery under a negotiable electronic transport record has demonstrated, in accordance with the procedures referred to in article 9, paragraph 1, that it is the holder;

(c)   The person giving instructions under subparagraph 2 (*a*) of this article shall indemnify the carrier against loss arising from its being held liable to the holder under subparagraph 2 (*e*) of this article. The carrier may refuse to follow those instructions if the person fails to provide adequate security as the carrier may reasonably request;

(d)   A person that becomes a holder of the negotiable transport document or the negotiable electronic transport record after the carrier has delivered the goods pursuant to subparagraph 2 (*b*) of this article, but pursuant to contractual or other arrangements made before such delivery acquires rights against the carrier under the contract of carriage, other than the right to claim delivery of the goods;

(e)   Notwithstanding subparagraphs 2 (*b*) and 2 (*d*) of this article, a holder that becomes a holder after such delivery, and that did not have and could not reasonably have had knowledge of such delivery at the time it became a holder, acquires the rights incorporated in the negotiable transport document or negotiable electronic transport record. When the contract particulars state the expected time of arrival of the goods, or indicate how to obtain information as to whether the goods have been delivered, it is presumed that the holder at the time that it became a holder had or could reasonably have had knowledge of the delivery of the goods.

Article 48
Goods remaining undelivered

1.   For the purposes of this article, goods shall be deemed to have remained undelivered only if, after their arrival at the place of destination:

(a)   The consignee does not accept delivery of the goods pursuant to this chapter at the time and location referred to in article 43;

(b)   The controlling party, the holder, the shipper or the documentary shipper cannot be found or does not give the carrier adequate instructions pursuant to articles 45, 46 and 47;

(c)   The carrier is entitled or required to refuse delivery pursuant to articles 44, 45, 46 and 47;

(d)   The carrier is not allowed to deliver the goods to the consignee pursuant to the law or regulations of the place at which delivery is requested; or

(e)   The goods are otherwise undeliverable by the carrier.

2.   Without prejudice to any other rights that the carrier may have against the shipper, controlling party or consignee, if the goods have remained undelivered, the carrier may, at the risk and expense of the person entitled to the goods, take such action in respect of the goods as circumstances may reasonably require, including:

(a)   To store the goods at any suitable place;

(b)   To unpack the goods if they are packed in containers or vehicles, or to act otherwise in respect of the goods, including by moving them; and *(c)* To cause the goods to be sold or destroyed in accordance with the practices or pursuant to the law or regulations of the place where the goods are located at the time.

3. The carrier may exercise the rights under paragraph 2 of this article only after it has given reasonable notice of the intended action under paragraph 2 of this article to the person stated in the contract particulars as the person, if any, to be notified of the arrival of the goods at the place of destination, and to one of the following persons in the order indicated, if known to the carrier: the consignee, the controlling party or the shipper.

4. If the goods are sold pursuant to subparagraph 2 *(c)* of this article, the carrier shall hold the proceeds of the sale for the benefit of the person entitled to the goods, subject to the deduction of any costs incurred by the carrier and any other amounts that are due to the carrier in connection with the carriage of those goods.

5. The carrier shall not be liable for loss of or damage to goods that occurs during the time that they remain undelivered pursuant to this article unless the claimant proves that such loss or damage resulted from the failure by the carrier to take steps that would have been reasonable in the circumstances to preserve the goods and that the carrier knew or ought to have known that the loss or damage to the goods would result from its failure to take such steps.

Article 49
Retention of goods

Nothing in this Convention affects a right of the carrier or a performing party that may exist pursuant to the contract of carriage or the applicable law to retain the goods to secure the payment of sums due.

Chapter 10
Rights of the controlling party

Article 50
Exercise and extent of right of control

1. The right of control may be exercised only by the controlling party and is limited to:

(a) The right to give or modify instructions in respect of the goods that do not constitute a variation of the contract of carriage;

(b) The right to obtain delivery of the goods at a scheduled port of call or, in respect of inland carriage, any place en route; and

(c) The right to replace the consignee by any other person including the controlling party.

2. The right of control exists during the entire period of responsibility of the carrier, as provided in article 12, and ceases when that period expires.

Article 51
Identity of the controlling party and transfer of the right of control

1. Except in the cases referred to in paragraphs 2, 3 and 4 of this article:

(a) The shipper is the controlling party unless the shipper, when the contract of carriage is concluded, designates the consignee, the documentary shipper or another person as the controlling party;

(b) The controlling party is entitled to transfer the right of control to another person. The transfer becomes effective with respect to the carrier upon its notification of the transfer by the transferor, and the transferee becomes the controlling party; and

(c) The controlling party shall properly identify itself when it exercises the right of control.

2. When a non-negotiable transport document has been issued that indicates that it shall be surrendered in order to obtain delivery of the goods:

(a) The shipper is the controlling party and may transfer the right of control to the consignee named in the transport document by transferring the document to that person without endorsement. If more than one original of the document was issued, all originals shall be transferred in order to effect a transfer of the right of control; and

(b) In order to exercise its right of control, the controlling party shall produce the document and properly identify itself. If more than one original of the document was issued, all originals shall be produced, failing which the right of control cannot be exercised.

3. When a negotiable transport document is issued:

(a) The holder or, if more than one original of the negotiable transport document is issued, the holder of all originals is the controlling party;

(b) The holder may transfer the right of control by transferring the negotiable transport document to another person in accordance with article 57. If more than one original of that document was issued, all originals shall be transferred to that person in order to effect a transfer of the right of control; and

(c) In order to exercise the right of control, the holder shall produce the negotiable transport document to the carrier, and if the holder is one of the persons referred to in article 1, subparagraph 10 *(a)* (i), the holder shall properly identify itself. If more than one original of the document was issued, all originals shall be produced, failing which the right of control cannot be exercised.

4. When a negotiable electronic transport record is issued:
    (a) The holder is the controlling party;

(b) The holder may transfer the right of control to another person by transferring the negotiable electronic transport record in accordance with the procedures referred to in article 9, paragraph 1; and

(c) In order to exercise the right of control, the holder shall demonstrate, in accordance with the procedures referred to in article 9, paragraph 1, that it is the holder.

Article 52
Carrier's execution of instructions

1. Subject to paragraphs 2 and 3 of this article, the carrier shall execute the instructions referred to in article 50 if:

(a) The person giving such instructions is entitled to exercise the right of control;

(b) The instructions can reasonably be executed according to their terms at the moment that they reach the carrier; and

(c) The instructions will not interfere with the normal operations of the carrier, including its delivery practices.

2.   In any event, the controlling party shall reimburse the carrier for any reasonable additional expense that the carrier may incur and shall indemnify the carrier against loss or damage that the carrier may suffer as a result of diligently executing any instruction pursuant to this article, including compensation that the carrier may become liable to pay for loss of or damage to other goods being carried.

3.   The carrier is entitled to obtain security from the controlling party for the amount of additional expense, loss or damage that the carrier reasonably expects will arise in connection with the execution of an instruction pursuant to this article. The carrier may refuse to carry out the instructions if no such security is provided.

4.   The carrier's liability for loss of or damage to the goods or for delay in delivery resulting from its failure to comply with the instructions of the controlling party in breach of its obligation pursuant to paragraph 1 of this article shall be subject to articles 17 to 23, and the amount of the compensation payable by the carrier shall be subject to articles 59 to 61.

Article 53
Deemed delivery

Goods that are delivered pursuant to an instruction in accordance with article 52, paragraph 1, are deemed to be delivered at the place of destination, and the provisions of chapter 9 relating to such delivery apply to such goods.

Article 54
Variations to the contract of carriage

1.   The controlling party is the only person that may agree with the carrier to variations to the contract of carriage other than those referred to in article 50, subparagraphs 1 (*b*) and (*c*).

2.   Variations to the contract of carriage, including those referred to in article 50, subparagraphs 1 (*b*) and (*c*), shall be stated in a negotiable transport document or in a non-negotiable transport document that requires surrender, or incorporated in a negotiable electronic transport record, or, upon the request of the controlling party, shall be stated in a non-negotiable transport document or incorporated in a non-negotiable electronic transport record. If so stated or incorporated, such variations shall be signed in accordance with article 38.

Article 55
Providing additional information, instructions or documents to carrier

1.   The controlling party, on request of the carrier or a performing party, shall provide in a timely manner information, instructions or documents relating to the goods not yet provided by the shipper and not otherwise reasonably available to the carrier that the carrier may reasonably need to perform its obligations under the contract of carriage.

2.   If the carrier, after reasonable effort, is unable to locate the controlling party or the controlling party is unable to provide adequate information, instructions or documents to the carrier, the shipper shall provide them. If the carrier, after reasonable effort, is unable to locate the shipper, the documentary shipper shall provide such information, instructions or documents.

Article 56
Variation by agreement

The parties to the contract of carriage may vary the effect of articles 50, subparagraphs 1 (*b*) and (*c*), 50, paragraph 2, and 52. The parties may also restrict or exclude the transferability of the right of control referred to in article 51, subparagraph 1 (*b*).

Chapter 11
Transfer of rights

Article 57
When a negotiable transport document or negotiable electronic transport record is issued

1.   When a negotiable transport document is issued, the holder may transfer the rights incorporated in the document by transferring it to another person:

(a)   Duly endorsed either to such other person or in blank, if an order document; or

(b)   Without endorsement, if: (i) a bearer document or a blank endorsed document; or (ii) a document made out to the order of a named person and the transfer is between the first holder and the named person.

2.   When a negotiable electronic transport record is issued, its holder may transfer the rights incorporated in it, whether it be made out to order or to the order of a named person, by transferring the electronic transport record in accordance with the procedures referred to in article 9, paragraph 1.

Article 58
Liability of holder

1.   Without prejudice to article 55, a holder that is not the shipper and that does not exercise any right under the contract of carriage does not assume any liability under the contract of carriage solely by reason of being a holder.

2.   A holder that is not the shipper and that exercises any right under the contract of carriage assumes any liabilities imposed on it under the contract of carriage to the extent that such liabilities are incorporated in or ascertainable from the negotiable transport document or the negotiable electronic transport record.

3.   For the purposes of paragraphs 1 and 2 of this article, a holder that is not the shipper does not exercise any right under the contract of carriage solely because:

(a)   It agrees with the carrier, pursuant to article 10, to replace a negotiable transport document by a negotiable electronic transport record or to replace a negotiable electronic transport record by a negotiable transport document; or

(b)   It transfers its rights pursuant to article 57.

Chapter 12
Limits of liability

Article 59
Limits of liability

1.   Subject to articles 60 and 61, paragraph 1, the carrier's liability for breaches of its obligations under this Convention is limited to 875 units of account per package or other shipping unit, or 3 units of account per kilogram of the gross weight of the goods that are the subject of the claim or dispute, whichever amount is the higher, except when the value of the goods has been declared by the shipper and included in the contract particulars, or when a higher amount than the amount of limitation of liability set out in this article has been agreed upon between the carrier and the shipper.

2.   When goods are carried in or on a container, pallet or similar article of transport used to consolidate goods, or in or on a vehicle, the packages or shipping units enumerated in the contract particulars as packed in or on such article of transport or vehicle are deemed packages or shipping units. If not so enumerated, the goods in or on such article of transport or vehicle are deemed one shipping unit.

3.   The unit of account referred to in this article is the Special Drawing Right as defined by the International Monetary Fund. The amounts referred to in this article are to be converted into the national currency of a State according to the value of such currency at the date of judgement or award or the date agreed upon by the parties. The value of a national currency, in terms of the Special Drawing Right, of a Contracting State that is a member of the International Monetary Fund is to be calculated in accordance with the method of valuation applied by the International Monetary Fund in effect at the date in question for its operations and transactions. The value of a national currency, in terms of the Special Drawing Right, of a Contracting State that is not a member of the International Monetary Fund is to be calculated in a manner to be determined by that State.

Article 60
Limits of liability for loss caused by delay

Subject to article 61, paragraph 2, compensation for loss of or damage to the goods due to delay shall be calculated in accordance with article 22 and liability for economic loss due to delay is limited to an amount equivalent to two and one-half times the freight payable on the goods delayed. The total amount payable pursuant to this article and article 59, paragraph 1, may not exceed the limit that would be established pursuant to article 59, paragraph 1, in respect of the total loss of the goods concerned.

Article 61
Loss of the benefit of limitation of liability

1.   Neither the carrier nor any of the persons referred to in article 18 is entitled to the benefit of the limitation of liability as provided in article 59, or as provided in the contract of carriage, if the claimant proves that the loss resulting from the breach of the carrier's obligation under this Convention was attributable to a personal act or omission of the person claiming a right to limit done with the intent to cause such loss or recklessly and with knowledge that such loss would probably result.

2.   Neither the carrier nor any of the persons mentioned in article 18 is entitled to the benefit of the limitation of liability as provided in article 60 if the claimant proves that

the delay in delivery resulted from a personal act or omission of the person claiming a right to limit done with the intent to cause the loss due to delay or recklessly and with knowledge that such loss would probably result.

Chapter 13
Time for suit

Article 62
Period of time for suit

1.   No judicial or arbitral proceedings in respect of claims or disputes arising from a breach of an obligation under this Convention may be instituted after the expiration of a period of two years.

2.   The period referred to in paragraph 1 of this article commences on the day on which the carrier has delivered the goods or, in cases in which no goods have been delivered or only part of the goods have been delivered, on the last day on which the goods should have been delivered. The day on which the period commences is not included in the period.

3.   Notwithstanding the expiration of the period set out in paragraph 1 of this article, one party may rely on its claim as a defence or for the purpose of set-off against a claim asserted by the other party.

Article 63
Extension of time for suit

The period provided in article 62 shall not be subject to suspension or interruption, but the person against which a claim is made may at any time during the running of the period extend that period by a declaration to the claimant. This period may be further extended by another declaration or declarations.

Article 64
Action for indemnity

An action for indemnity by a person held liable may be instituted after the expiration of the period provided in article 62 if the indemnity action is instituted within the later of:

(a)   The time allowed by the applicable law in the jurisdiction where proceedings are instituted; or

(b)   Ninety days commencing from the day when the person instituting the action for indemnity has either settled the claim or been served with process in the action against itself, whichever is earlier.

Article 65
Actions against the person identified as the carrier

An action against the bareboat charterer or the person identified as the carrier pursuant to article 37, paragraph 2, may be instituted after the expiration of the period provided in article 62 if the action is instituted within the later of:

(a)   The time allowed by the applicable law in the jurisdiction where proceedings are instituted; or

(b) Ninety days commencing from the day when the carrier has been identified, or the registered owner or bareboat charterer has rebutted the presumption that it is the carrier, pursuant to article 37, paragraph 2.

Chapter 14
Jurisdiction

Article 66
Actions against the carrier

Unless the contract of carriage contains an exclusive choice of court agreement that complies with article 67 or 72, the plaintiff has the right to institute judicial proceedings under this Convention against the carrier:

(a) In a competent court within the jurisdiction of which is situated one of the following places:

    (i) The domicile of the carrier;

    (ii) The place of receipt agreed in the contract of carriage;

    (iii) The place of delivery agreed in the contract of carriage; or

    (iv) The port where the goods are initially loaded on a ship or the port where the goods are finally discharged from a ship; or

(b) In a competent court or courts designated by an agreement between the shipper and the carrier for the purpose of deciding claims against the carrier that may arise under this Convention.

Article 67
Choice of court agreements

1. The jurisdiction of a court chosen in accordance with article 66, subparagraph *b*), is exclusive for disputes between the parties to the contract only if the parties so agree and the agreement conferring jurisdiction:

(a) Is contained in a volume contract that clearly states the names and addresses of the parties and either (i) is individually negotiated or (ii) contains a prominent statement that there is an exclusive choice of court agreement and specifies the sections of the volume contract containing that agreement; and

(b) Clearly designates the courts of one Contracting State or one or more specific courts of one Contracting State.

2. A person that is not a party to the volume contract is bound by an exclusive choice of court agreement concluded in accordance with paragraph 1 of this article only if:

(a) The court is in one of the places designated in article 66, subparagraph *(a)*;

(b) That agreement is contained in the transport document or electronic transport record;

(c) That person is given timely and adequate notice of the court where the action shall be brought and that the jurisdiction of that court is exclusive; and

(d) The law of the court seized recognizes that that person may be bound by the exclusive choice of court agreement.

Article 68
Actions against the maritime performing party

The plaintiff has the right to institute judicial proceedings under this Convention against the maritime performing party in a competent court within the jurisdiction of which is situated one of the following places:

(a) The domicile of the maritime performing party; or

(b) The port where the goods are received by the maritime performing party, the port where the goods are delivered by the maritime performing party or the port in which the maritime performing party performs its activities with respect to the goods.

Article 69
No additional bases of jurisdiction

Subject to articles 71 and 72, no judicial proceedings under this Convention against the carrier or a maritime performing party may be instituted in a court not designated pursuant to article 66 or 68.

Article 70
Arrest and provisional or protective measures

Nothing in this Convention affects jurisdiction with regard to provisional or protective measures, including arrest. A court in a State in which a provisional or protective measure was taken does not have jurisdiction to determine the case upon its merits unless:

(a) The requirements of this chapter are fulfilled; or

(b) An international convention that applies in that State so provides.

Article 71
Consolidation and removal of actions

1.	Except when there is an exclusive choice of court agreement that is binding pursuant to article 67 or 72, if a single action is brought against both the carrier and the maritime performing party arising out of a single occurrence, the action may be instituted only in a court designated pursuant to both article 66 and article 68. If there is no such court, such action may be instituted in a court designated pursuant to article 68, subparagraph (*b*), if there is such a court.

2.	Except when there is an exclusive choice of court agreement that is binding pursuant to article 67 or 72, a carrier or a maritime performing party that institutes an action seeking a declaration of non-liability or any other action that would deprive a person of its right to select the forum pursuant to article 66 or 68 shall, at the request of the defendant, withdraw that action once the defendant has chosen a court designated pursuant to article 66 or 68, whichever is applicable, where the action may be recommenced.

Article 72
Agreement after a dispute has arisen and jurisdiction when the defendant has entered an appearance

1.	After a dispute has arisen, the parties to the dispute may agree to resolve it in any competent court.

2.   A competent court before which a defendant appears, without contesting jurisdiction in accordance with the rules of that court, has jurisdiction.

Article 73
Recognition and enforcement

1.   A decision made in one Contracting State by a court having jurisdiction under this Convention shall be recognized and enforced in another Contracting State in accordance with the law of such latter Contracting State when both States have made a declaration in accordance with article 74.

2.   A court may refuse recognition and enforcement based on the grounds for the refusal of recognition and enforcement available pursuant to its law.

3.   This chapter shall not affect the application of the rules of a regional economic integration organization that is a party to this Convention, as concerns the recognition or enforcement of judgements as between member States of the regional economic integration organization, whether adopted before or after this Convention.

Article 74
Application of chapter 14

The provisions of this chapter shall bind only Contracting States that declare in accordance with article 91 that they will be bound by them.

Chapter 15
Arbitration

Article 75
Arbitration agreements

1.   Subject to this chapter, parties may agree that any dispute that may arise relating to the carriage of goods under this Convention shall be referred to arbitration.

2.   The arbitration proceedings shall, at the option of the person asserting a claim against the carrier, take place at:

   (*a*)   Any place designated for that purpose in the arbitration agreement; or

   (*b*)   Any other place situated in a State where any of the following places is located:

      (i)   The domicile of the carrier;

      (ii)   The place of receipt agreed in the contract of carriage;

      (iii)   The place of delivery agreed in the contract of carriage; or

      (iv)   The port where the goods are initially loaded on a ship or the port where the goods are finally discharged from a ship.

3.   The designation of the place of arbitration in the agreement is binding for disputes between the parties to the agreement if the agreement is contained in a volume contract that clearly states the names and addresses of the parties and either:

   (a)   Is individually negotiated; or

   (b)   Contains a prominent statement that there is an arbitration agreement

and specifies the sections of the volume contract containing the arbitration agreement.

4.   When an arbitration agreement has been concluded in accordance with paragraph 3 of this article, a person that is not a party to the volume contract is bound by the designation of the place of arbitration in that agreement only if:

(a)   The place of arbitration designated in the agreement is situated in one of the places referred to in subparagraph 2 (*b*) of this article;

(b)   The agreement is contained in the transport document or electronic transport record;

(c)   The person to be bound is given timely and adequate notice of the place of arbitration; and

(d)   Applicable law permits that person to be bound by the arbitration agreement.

5.   The provisions of paragraphs 1, 2, 3 and 4 of this article are deemed to be part of every arbitration clause or agreement, and any term of such clause or agreement to the extent that it is inconsistent therewith is void.

Article 76
Arbitration agreement in non-liner transportation

1.   Nothing in this Convention affects the enforceability of an arbitration agreement in a contract of carriage in non-liner transportation to which this Convention or the provisions of this Convention apply by reason of:

(a)   The application of article 7; or

(b)   The parties' voluntary incorporation of this Convention in a contract of carriage that would not otherwise be subject to this Convention.

2.   Notwithstanding paragraph 1 of this article, an arbitration agreement in a transport document or electronic transport record to which this Convention applies by reason of the application of article 7 is subject to this chapter unless such a transport document or electronic transport record:

(a)   Identifies the parties to and the date of the charter party or other contract excluded from the application of this Convention by reason of the application of article 6; and

(b)   Incorporates by specific reference the clause in the charter party or other contract that contains the terms of the arbitration agreement.

Article 77
Agreement to arbitrate after a dispute has arisen

Notwithstanding the provisions of this chapter and chapter 14, after a dispute has arisen the parties to the dispute may agree to resolve it by arbitration in any place.

Article 78
Application of chapter 15

The provisions of this chapter shall bind only Contracting States that declare in accordance with article 91 that they will be bound by them.

Chapter 16
Validity of contractual terms

Article 79
General provisions

1.   Unless otherwise provided in this Convention, any term in a contract of carriage is void to the extent that it:

(a)   Directly or indirectly excludes or limits the obligations of the carrier or a maritime performing party under this Convention;

(b)   Directly or indirectly excludes or limits the liability of the carrier or a maritime performing party for breach of an obligation under this Convention; or

(c)   Assigns a benefit of insurance of the goods in favour of the carrier or a person referred to in article 18.

2.   Unless otherwise provided in this Convention, any term in a contract of carriage is void to the extent that it:

(a)   Directly or indirectly excludes, limits or increases the obligations under this Convention of the shipper, consignee, controlling party, holder or documentary shipper; or

(b)   Directly or indirectly excludes, limits or increases the liability of the shipper, consignee, controlling party, holder or documentary shipper for breach of any of its obligations under this Convention.

Article 80
Special rules for volume contracts

1.   Notwithstanding article 79, as between the carrier and the shipper, a volume contract to which this Convention applies may provide for greater or lesser rights, obligations and liabilities than those imposed by this Convention.

2.   A derogation pursuant to paragraph 1 of this article is binding only when:

(a)   The volume contract contains a prominent statement that it derogates from this Convention;

(b)   The volume contract is (i) individually negotiated or (ii) prominently specifies the sections of the volume contract containing the derogations;

(c)   The shipper is given an opportunity and notice of the opportunity to conclude a contract of carriage on terms and conditions that comply with this Convention without any derogation under this article; and

(d)   The derogation is neither (i) incorporated by reference from another document nor (ii) included in a contract of adhesion that is not subject to negotiation.

3.   A carrier's public schedule of prices and services, transport document, electronic transport record or similar document is not a volume contract pursuant to paragraph 1 of this article, but a volume contract may incorporate such documents by reference as terms of the contract.

4.   Paragraph 1 of this article does not apply to rights and obligations provided in articles 14, subparagraphs (*a*) and (*b*), 29 and 32 or to liability arising from the breach thereof, nor does it apply to any liability arising from an act or omission referred to in article 61.

5.   The terms of the volume contract that derogate from this Convention, if the volume contract satisfies the requirements of paragraph 2 of this article, apply between the carrier and any person other than the shipper provided that:

(a)   Such person received information that prominently states that the volume contract derogates from this Convention and gave its express consent to be bound by such derogations; and

(b)   Such consent is not solely set forth in a carrier's public schedule of prices and services, transport document or electronic transport record.

6.   The party claiming the benefit of the derogation bears the burden of proof that the conditions for derogation have been fulfilled.

Article 81
Special rules for live animals and certain other goods

Notwithstanding article 79 and without prejudice to article 80, the contract of carriage may exclude or limit the obligations or the liability of both the carrier and a maritime performing party if:

(a)   The goods are live animals, but any such exclusion or limitation will not be effective if the claimant proves that the loss of or damage to the goods, or delay in delivery, resulted from an act or omission of the carrier or of a person referred to in article 18, done with the intent to cause such loss of or damage to the goods or such loss due to delay or done recklessly and with knowledge that such loss or damage or such loss due to delay would probably result; or

(b)   The character or condition of the goods or the circumstances and terms and conditions under which the carriage is to be performed are such as reasonably to justify a special agreement, provided that such contract of carriage is not related to ordinary commercial shipments made in the ordinary course of trade and that no negotiable transport document or negotiable electronic transport record is issued for the carriage of the goods.

Chapter 17
Matters not governed by this convention

Article 82
International conventions governing the carriage of goods by other modes of
transport

Nothing in this Convention affects the application of any of the following international conventions in force at the time this Convention enters into force, including any future amendment to such conventions, that regulate the liability of the carrier for loss of or damage to the goods:

(a)   Any convention governing the carriage of goods by air to the extent that such convention according to its provisions applies to any part of the contract of carriage;

(b)   Any convention governing the carriage of goods by road to the extent that such convention according to its provisions applies to the carriage of goods that remain loaded on a road cargo vehicle carried on board a ship;

(c)   Any convention governing the carriage of goods by rail to the extent that such convention according to its provisions applies to carriage of goods by sea as a supplement to the carriage by rail; or (*d*)   Any convention governing the carriage of goods by inland waterways to the extent that such convention according to its provisions applies to a carriage of goods without trans-shipment both by inland waterways and sea.

Article 83
Global limitation of liability

Nothing in this Convention affects the application of any international convention or national law regulating the global limitation of liability of vessel owners.

Article 84
General average

Nothing in this Convention affects the application of terms in the contract of carriage or provisions of national law regarding the adjustment of general average.

Article 85
Passengers and luggage

This Convention does not apply to a contract of carriage for passengers and their luggage.

Article 86
Damage caused by nuclear incident

No liability arises under this Convention for damage caused by a nuclear incident if the operator of a nuclear installation is liable for such damage:

(*a*)   Under the Paris Convention on Third Party Liability in the Field of Nuclear Energy of 29 July 1960 as amended by the Additional Protocol of 28 January 1964 and by the Protocols of 16 November 1982 and 12 February 2004, the Vienna Convention on Civil Liability for Nuclear Damage of 21 May 1963 as amended by the Joint Protocol Relating to the Application of the Vienna Convention and the Paris Convention of 21 September 1988 and as amended by the Protocol to Amend the 1963 Vienna Convention on Civil Liability for Nuclear Damage of 12 September 1997, or the Convention on Supplementary Compensation for Nuclear Damage of 12 September 1997, including any amendment to these conventions and any future convention in respect of the liability of the operator of a nuclear installation for damage caused by a nuclear incident; or

(*b*)   Under national law applicable to the liability for such damage, provided that such law is in all respects as favourable to persons that may suffer damage as either the Paris or Vienna Conventions or the Convention on Supplementary Compensation for Nuclear Damage.

Chapter 18
Final clauses

Article 87
Depositary

The Secretary-General of the United Nations is hereby designated as the depositary of this Convention.

Article 88
Signature, ratification, acceptance, approval or accession

1.   This Convention is open for signature by all States at Rotterdam, the Netherlands, on 23 September 2009, and thereafter at the Headquarters of the United Nations in New York.

2.   This Convention is subject to ratification, acceptance or approval by the signatory States.

3.   This Convention is open for accession by all States that are not signatory States as from the date it is open for signature.

4.   Instruments of ratification, acceptance, approval and accession are to be deposited with the Secretary-General of the United Nations.

Article 89
Denunciation of other conventions

1.   A State that ratifies, accepts, approves or accedes to this Convention and is a party to the International Convention for the Unification of certain Rules of Law relating to Bills of Lading signed at Brussels on 25 August 1924, to the Protocol to amend the International Convention for the Unification of certain Rules of Law relating to Bills of Lading, signed at Brussels on 23 February 1968, or to the Protocol to amend the International Convention for the Unification of certain Rules of Law relating to Bills of Lading as Modified by the Amending Protocol of 23 February 1968, signed at Brussels on 21 December 1979, shall at the same time denounce that Convention and the protocol or protocols thereto to which it is a party by notifying the Government of Belgium to that effect, with a declaration that the denunciation is to take effect as from the date when this Convention enters into force in respect of that State.

2.   A State that ratifies, accepts, approves or accedes to this Convention and is a party to the United Nations Convention on the Carriage of Goods by Sea concluded at Hamburg on 31 March 1978 shall at the same time denounce that Convention by notifying the Secretary-General of the United Nations to that effect, with a declaration that the denunciation is to take effect as from the date when this Convention enters into force in respect of that State.

3.   For the purposes of this article, ratifications, acceptances, approvals and accessions in respect of this Convention by States parties to the instruments listed in paragraphs 1 and 2 of this article that are notified to the depositary after this Convention has entered into force are not effective until such denunciations as may be required on the part of those States in respect of these instruments have become effective. The depositary of this Convention shall consult with the Government of Belgium, as the depositary of the instruments referred to in paragraph 1 of this article, so as to ensure necessary coordination in this respect.

Article 90
Reservations

No reservation is permitted to this Convention.

Article 91
Procedure and effect of declarations

1.   The declarations permitted by articles 74 and 78 may be made at any time. The initial declarations permitted by article 92, paragraph 1, and article 93, paragraph 2, shall be made at the time of signature, ratification, acceptance, approval or accession. No other declaration is permitted under this Convention.

2.   Declarations made at the time of signature are subject to confirmation upon ratification, acceptance or approval.

3.   Declarations and their confirmations are to be in writing and to be formally notified to the depositary.

4.   A declaration takes effect simultaneously with the entry into force of this Convention in respect of the State concerned. However, a declaration of which the depositary receives formal notification after such entry into force takes effect on the first day of the month following the expiration of six months after the date of its receipt by the depositary.

5.   Any State that makes a declaration under this Convention may withdraw it at any time by a formal notification in writing addressed to the depositary. The withdrawal of a declaration, or its modification where permitted by this Convention, takes effect on the first day of the month following the expiration of six months after the date of the receipt of the notification by the depositary.

Article 92
Effect in domestic territorial units

1.   If a Contracting State has two or more territorial units in which different systems of law are applicable in relation to the matters dealt with in this Convention, it may, at the time of signature, ratification, acceptance, approval or accession, declare that this Convention is to extend to all its territorial units or only to one or more of them, and may amend its declaration by submitting another declaration at any time.

2.   These declarations are to be notified to the depositary and are to state expressly the territorial units to which the Convention extends.

3.   When a Contracting State has declared pursuant to this article that this Convention extends to one or more but not all of its territorial units, a place located in a territorial unit to which this Convention does not extend is not considered to be in a Contracting State for the purposes of this Convention.

4.   If a Contracting State makes no declaration pursuant to paragraph 1 of this article, the Convention is to extend to all territorial units of that State.

Article 93
Participation by regional economic integration organizations

1.   A regional economic integration organization that is constituted by sovereign States and has competence over certain matters governed by this Convention may similarly sign, ratify, accept, approve or accede to this Convention. The regional economic integration organization shall in that case have the rights and obligations of a Contracting State, to the extent that that organization has competence over

matters governed by this Convention. When the number of Contracting States is relevant in this Convention, the regional economic integration organization does not count as a Contracting State in addition to its member States which are Contracting States.

2.   The regional economic integration organization shall, at the time of signature, ratification, acceptance, approval or accession, make a declaration to the depositary specifying the matters governed by this Convention in respect of which competence has been transferred to that organization by its member States. The regional economic integration organization shall promptly notify the depositary of any changes to the distribution of competence, including new transfers of competence, specified in the declaration pursuant to this paragraph.

3. Any reference to a "Contracting State" or "Contracting States" in this Convention applies equally to a regional economic integration organization when the context so requires.

Article 94
Entry into force

1.   This Convention enters into force on the first day of the month following the expiration of one year after the date of deposit of the twentieth instrument of ratification, acceptance, approval or accession.

2.   For each State that becomes a Contracting State to this Convention after the date of the deposit of the twentieth instrument of ratification, acceptance, approval or accession, this Convention enters into force on the first day of the month following the expiration of one year after the deposit of the appropriate instrument on behalf of that State.

3.   Each Contracting State shall apply this Convention to contracts of carriage concluded on or after the date of the entry into force of this Convention in respect of that State.

Article 95
Revision and amendment

1.   At the request of not less than one third of the Contracting States to this Convention, the Secretary-General of the United Nations shall convene a conference of the Contracting States for revising or amending it.

2.   Any instrument of ratification, acceptance, approval or accession deposited after the entry into force of an amendment to this Convention is deemed to apply to the Convention as amended.

Article 96
Denunciation of this Convention

1.   A Contracting State may denounce this Convention at any time by means of a notification in writing addressed to the depositary.

2.   The denunciation takes effect on the first day of the month following the expiration of one year after the notification is received by the depositary. If a longer period is specified in the notification, the denunciation takes effect upon the expiration of such longer period after the notification is received by the depositary.

DONE at New York, this eleventh day of December two thousand and eight, in a single original, of which the Arabic, Chinese, English, French, Russian and Spanish texts are equally authentic.

IN WITNESS WHEREOF the undersigned plenipotentiaries, being duly authorized by their respective Governments, have signed this Convention.

MOCK EXAMINATION

Do not turn to the next page until you have followed the suggestions below.

Overleaf is a sample examination paper. In your own interest do not look at it yet but instead, do the same revision of the course as you would do for any examination.

On completing your revision, put away your notes, have pen and paper ready and set aside three hours when you will not be interrupted. In other words create as near as possible examination room conditions.

It is recommended that you hand write this mock examination. You will have to write the actual examination and many students find that it is difficult to write legibly for three hours without practice. If your writing is illegible you will lose marks. Examiners cannot mark what they cannot read.

Carry out the instructions on the question paper and send your answers to your course tutor for marking (Note your start and finish times on the front of your answer paper)

THE INSTITUTE OF CHARTERED SHIPBROKERS

INTRODUCTION TO SHIPPING

Time allowed –Three hours

Answer any FIVE questions – All questions carry equal marks

1. A 'Liner' service and a 'Tramp' ship carry cargoes by sea. Describe both types and comment upon their suitability for different types of goods.

2. The People's Republic of China is one of the world's major consumers of iron ore. Which type and size ships carry this mineral? Sketch a map of the world and upon it enter sources and voyage patterns.

3. You are a mixed fleet owner with several dry bulk carriers approaching 'Special Survey'. There is uncertainty about the immediate market future. From which parties would you seek guidance and what are the likely options?

4. Discuss what would influence a charterer's decision when considering whether to fix on a voyage charter or a time charter basis.

5. Book-keeping is probably one of the most basic sectors of accounting with the Book-keeper carefully recording sales and the cost of servicing those sales. How is this data summarised and how would this information affect company policy?

6. Demand fuelled by advancing technology, is the principal reason for growth in cargo capacity size of all ship types; however, other factors limit this growth. Discuss these factors with examples taken from all trades.

7. A Bill of Lading is said to be a 'Document of title'. Discuss how this role is utilised.

8. Stevedores and Dry Cargo brokers, when describing ships' carrying capacity and cargoes, frequently use the terms 'Measurement', 'Deadweight', Bale space' and 'Grain Cubic'. Explain the meaning of these expressions.